Virtual Reality and Augmented Reality

Series Editor
Jean-Charles Pomerol

Virtual Reality and Augmented Reality

Myths and Realities

Edited by

Bruno Arnaldi
Pascal Guitton
Guillaume Moreau

WILEY

First published 2018 in Great Britain and the United States by ISTE Ltd and John Wiley & Sons, Inc.

ISTE Ltd
27-37 St George's Road
London SW19 4EU
UK

www.iste.co.uk

John Wiley & Sons, Inc.
111 River Street
Hoboken, NJ 07030
USA

www.wiley.com

© ISTE Ltd 2018
The rights of Bruno Arnaldi, Pascal Guitton and Guillaume Moreau to be identified as the authors of this work have been asserted by them in accordance with the Copyright, Designs and Patents Act 1988.

Library of Congress Control Number: 2018930832

British Library Cataloguing-in-Publication Data
A CIP record for this book is available from the British Library
ISBN 978-1-78630-105-5

Contents

Chapter 5. Scientific and Technical Prospects 247

Caroline BAILLARD, Philippe GUILLOTEL, Anatole LÉCUYER, Fabien
LOTTE, Nicolas MOLLET, Jean-Marie NORMAND and Gaël SEYDOUX

Preface

"Virtual reality", a strange oxymoron, is back in common use in the media, like in the early 1990s, a quarter of a century ago! A period that today's young innovators are not very familiar with. Yes, at the risk of shocking some people, we must reveal that this science and the associated techniques are no invention of the 21st Century but date back well into the previous century!

Today, we are witnessing the renaissance and democratization of virtual reality, with its share of relevant and effective applications, as well as a host of technological difficulties that no developer can afford to ignore. Some enthusiasts wish to create new applications and believe that skills in innovation are all that is required. However, this approach is doomed to failure unless it is preceded by a detailed study of the state of the art of virtual reality techniques and a knowledge of the fundamentals and existing uses. Many young entrepreneurs have contacted me, thinking they have a novel virtual reality application when they don't even have a basic understanding of this science or its techniques. I have had to tell others, "but this already exists in the industry, it is already being marked by companies that are over twenty years old". The latest innovation, the "low-cost" visioheadset or immersive headset, may have sparked off a mad buzz in the media, but the field of virtual reality has existed long before this! 2016 was not 1 V.R. (the first year of our science, Virtual Reality)! However, the considerable decrease in the price of visioheadsets has made it possible to open this technology up to large-scale use. The media and websites dedicated to virtual reality are most often run by non-specialists and are abound with indiscriminately proposed applications: some of these have existed for several years now, and others, while useful, would be inappropriate or even crazy. Virtual reality is not a magic wand. Let us remember that it is not sufficient to use an innovative technology for its own sake. This innovation must be made functional for the user, using new technological devices, whether a visioheadset or any other equipment.

Research and development in virtual reality has been undertaken for more than a quarter of a century by the VR community in France and in other parts of the world. It would be a great misfortune to be unaware of this work. However, if you are reading this now, then you have made the right choice! The fruit of all the research and professional developments in the field over the past decade is now presented in this volume. And who better than Bruno Arnaldi, Pascal Guitton and Guillaume Moreau to guide you through this arduous journey through the past 10 years in R&D in virtual development, as well as to give a glimpse of what the future may hold?

The three editors of this book are major actors in the field of virtual reality and augmented reality. All of them have participated in developing research in France, via the Groupe de Travail GT-RV (GT-VR Work Group) at CNRS (1994) and then through the Association Française de Réalité Virtuelle (The French Virtual Reality Association), which they established in 2005 as co-founders and in which they are very active members: President, Vice-President or members of the administrative council. This association has made it possible to efficiently structure the entire community (teachers, researchers, industrialists and solution providers). In parallel to this, thanks to their enthusiastic and indispensable support, I was able to organize and edit a collective work with contributions from more than a hundred authors, over five volumes: the *Virtual Reality Treatise*. There were three coordinators in this project. However, the third edition of this book is now 10 years old, and we needed a more recent publication to step into the breach.

It is essential to have a strong basic knowledge of virtual reality before plunging into the field, whether you are a student or an entrepreneur. The contents of this book, to which 30 authors have contributed, cover all the current problems and research questions, as well as the commercially available solutions: the immersion of a user, the user's interfacing with the artificial space and the creation of this artificial space. All the technology and software available today are discussed here. The human factor is also taken into account, and there is a detailed description of methods of evaluation.

There is also a section devoted to the risks associated with the use of visioheadsets.

A recent community that has come up in France, under the Think Tank UNI-VR, is bringing together professionals from the world of movies and audiovisual material. Using new 360° cameras, which enable the creation of artificial worlds made out of 360 images and not synthetic images, this group aims to create a new art, with two complementary approaches: one that produces "360 videos", where the user remains a spectator, but with a bodily and proprioceptive immersion in the 360° video; the other designs "VR videos", where the user becomes a "spect-actor", as if they are able to interact with the story that unfolds the characters and the artificial environment, this being the authentic field of virtual reality. This artistic goal is close to that of "interactive digital arts", even though these two communities do not know much about each other. Towards the end of the 1980s, French and international artists in the digital arts appropriated virtual reality to create interactive artistic creations, ("les pissenlits" (The Dandelions) by E. Couchot, M. Bret and M-H. Tramus, 1988; "L'autre" (The Other) by Catherine Ikam, 1991). A journalist from "Les Cahiers du Cinéma" once interviewed me, stating that "virtual reality is the future of the movies!" A strange remark, when we know of the antagonism between the movies (where the spectator is passive) and virtual reality (where the user is active, interacting with the artificial environment)! Another journalist was carried away by an innovation without bothering to learn about the fundamentals of this innovation and its impact on the individual! However, like all specialists, I did not imagine that 20 years later 360° would also enable the creation of an artificial world, where a user could be immersed in the heart of a film. By allowing the user to interact here, we enter into the field of virtual reality or augmented reality, by blending the real world and the artificial space. Unlike cinema, here there is no longer "a story to be told" but "a story to be lived". With this book, readers have a source of detailed information that will allow them to successfully develop their own "VR videos".

However, the digital modeling of an artificial world and its visual representation through synthetic images will remain the chief avenue for the development of the uses of virtual reality. For at least 15 years now, professional applications (e.g. industrial and architectural designs, training and learning, health) have made use of this. Different communities must collaborate more closely on theorizing this discipline and its techniques, which are exhaustively presented in this book by Bruno Arnaldi, Pascal Guitton and Guillaume Moreau. The merits of this book cannot be overstated – they must be bought!

Philippe FUCHS
January 2018

Introduction

It can have escaped no one that 2016 and 2017 often features in the media as "The Time" for virtual reality and augmented reality. It is no less obvious that in the field of technology, many and regular breakthroughs are announced, each more impressive than the last. In the face of this media clamor, it is useful to step back and take a pragmatic look at some historical facts and information:

– The first of these is the fact (however difficult to accept) that virtual reality and augmented reality date back several decades and that there is a large international community working on these subjects. This work is being carried out both at the scientific level (research teams, discoveries, conferences, publication) and at the industrial level (companies, products, large-scale production). It is also useful to remember that many companies, technological or not, have been successfully using virtual reality and augmented reality technologies for many years now.

– Many of these technological announcements talk about the design of "new" virtual reality headsets (e.g. HTC Vive, Oculus Rift) and augmented reality headsets (e.g. HoloLens). But the fact is that the invention of the first "visioheadset"[1] dates back to almost 50 years, to Ivan Sutherland's seminal work [SUT 68].

– Let us also note that these "visioheadsets" only represent a small part of the equipment used in virtual reality, whether for display (with projection systems, for example), motion-capture or interaction.

Introduction written by Bruno ARNALDI, Pascal GUITTON and Guillaume MOREAU.
1 This is what we will call these gadgets in this book. The reason for this will be made clear later.

– The concept and applications of virtual reality are described in the series *Le traité de la réalité virtuelle* (The Virtual Reality Treatise), an encyclopedic volume produced collectively by many French authors (both academics and voices from the industry), the breadth and scope of which remains unmatched even today. The different editions of this are:

- the first edition in 2001 (Presses de l'Ecole des Mines), written by Philippe Fuchs, Guillaume Moreau and Jean-Paul Papin with 530 pages;

- the second edition in 2003 (Presses de l'Ecole des Mines), edited by Philippe Fuchs and Guillaume Moreau with help from 18 contributors, running to 930 pages in 2 volumes;

- the third edition in 2005 (Presses de l'Ecole des Mines), edited by Philippe Fuchs and Guillaume Moreau, with over 100 contributors, running to 2,200 pages in 5 volumes;

- an English version "Virtual Reality: Concepts and Technologies", in 2011 (CRC Press), edited by Philippe Fuchs, Guillaume Moreau and Pascal Guitton with 432 pages.

– Finally, we must mention the creation of the "Association Française de Réalité Virtuelle" (AFRV) or the French Virtual Reality Association, established in 2005. The association has made it possible to structure the community better by bringing together teachers and researchers from universities and research institutions as well as engineers working within companies. From 2005 onward, the AFRV has been organizing an annual conference that sees presentations, activities and exchanges among participants.

As can be seen from this overview, there are already several communities at the international level as well as a wealth of literature on the subject and anyone who wishes to establish a scientific and/or technological culture will benefit from referring to publications such as [FUC 16] (in French) or [LAV 17, SCH 16], to mention a few.

I.1. The origins of virtual reality

When we talk about historic references relating to virtual reality, we may commence by discussing Plato's Allegory of the Cave [PLA 07]. In Book VII of Plato's Republic, there is a detailed description of the experiences of several men chained in a cave, who can only perceive shadows (thrown against the walls of the cave) of what happens in the outside world. The notion of reality and perception through what is and what is perceived becomes the subject of analysis, in particular concerning the passage from one world to another.

A few centuries later, in 1420, the Italian engineer Giovani Fontana wrote a book, *Bellicorum instrumentorum liber* [FON 20], in which he describes a magic lantern capable of projecting images onto the walls of a room (see Figure I.1(a)). He proposed that this could be used to project the images of fantastic creatures. This mechanism brings to mind the large immersion system (CAVE) developed a few centuries later by Carolina Cruz-Neira *et al.* [CRU 92] at the University of Illinois.

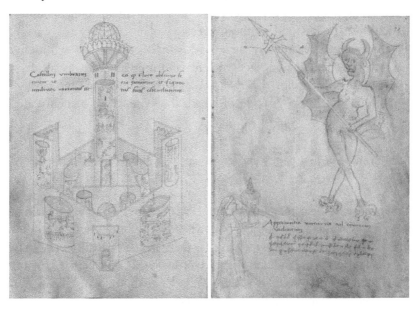

Figure I.1. *a) Diagram of Giovani Fontana's magic lantern, b) using the magic lantern. For a color version of this figure, see www.iste.co.uk/arnaldi/virtual.zip*

In books that recount the history of VR, we often come across the (legitimate) controversy around the first appearance of the term "virtual reality". Some authors attribute it to Jaron Lanier, during a press conference in 1985, while others attribute it to Antonin Artaud, in his 1983 essay, *Le théâtre et son double* (published in English as "The Theatre and its Double") [ART 09].

Artaud was unarguably the inventor of this term, which he used in his collection of essays on Theatre and, more specifically, in the chapter titled *Le théâtre alchimique* ("The Alchemical Theatre"). It must be noted that in this volume, Artaud talks at length about reality and virtuality (these words being frequently used in the text). The precise citation where the term "virtual reality" appears is on page 75 of the 1985 edition, collection Folio/essais de Gallimard:

"All true alchemists know that the alchemical symbol is a mirage as the theater is a mirage. And this perpetual allusion to the materials and the principle of the theater found in almost all alchemical books should be understood as the expression of an identity (of which alchemists are extremely aware) existing between the world in which the characters, objects, images and in a general way all that constitutes the *virtual reality* of the theater develop and the purely fictitious and illusory world in which the symbols of alchemy are evolved".

Furthermore, a few pages earlier, he speaks about Plato's Allegory of the Cave.

However, it is clear that Jaron Lanier was the first person to use this term in the sense that it is used in this book, when he used the English term *virtual reality*. It is also useful to remember that there is a subtle difference between the English term *virtual* and the French word *virtuel* (see Chapter 1, Volume 1 of the *Virtual Reality Treatise*, edition 3). In English, the word means "acting as" or "almost a particular thing or quality". However, in French, the word indicates "potential", what is "possible" and what "does not come to pass". Linguistically speaking, the more appropriate French term would have been "réalité vicariante" – a reality that substitutes or replaces another.

Science-fiction writers, especially those writing in the "speculative fiction" genre (a genre which, as its name indicates, consists of imagining what our world could be like in the future) have also written books that integrate and/or imagine the VR-AR technologies we will discuss in this volume. The list of such books is quite long, and the four books presented here have been chosen simply for the impact they had. In chronological order, these are:

– Vernor Vinge, in his 1981 novella *True Names*, introduced a cyberspace (without explicitly naming it thus), where a group of computer pirates use virtual reality immersion technology to fight against the government. He is also the creator of the concept of "singularity": that point in time when machines will be more intelligent than human beings;

– William Gibson, in his 1984 novel *Neuromancer*, described a world of networks where virtual reality consoles allow a user to live out experiences in virtual worlds. Gibson "invented" the term cyberspace, which he described as "a consensual hallucination experienced daily by billions of legitimate operators". This concept of cyperspace spans different worlds: the digital world, the cybernetic world and the space in which we evolve;

– Neal Stephenson, in his 1992 novel *Snow Crash*, introduced the concept of the metaverse (a virtual, thus fictional, world in which a community, represented by avatars, is evolving); a universe like the one in the online virtual world *Second Life*;

– Ernest Cline, in his 2011 novel *Ready Player One*, offferred us a world where humanity lives in an enormous virtual social network to escape the slums in real life. This network also contains the key to riches, leading to a new kind of quest for the holy grail.

Literature is not the only field in which early references to virtual reality set up links between the real and the virtual. For example, we must mention the pioneering work of Morton Leonard Heilig in the world of cinema. Following a project he had worked on since the 1950s, he patented the *Sensorama* system in 1962. This system allowed users to virtually navigate an urban setting on a motorbike, in an immersive experience based on stereoscopic visualization, the sounds of the motorbike and by reproducing the vibration of the engine and the sensation of wind against rider's face.

Cinema has made use of the emergence of new technologies quite naturally. In 1992, Brett Leonard directed *The Lawnmower Man*, starring Pierce Brosnan as a man who is the subject of scientific experiments based on virtual reality (see Figure I.2). Unsurprisingly, the story revolves around some of the undesirable effects. An interesting point about this film is that during shooting, actors used real equipment from the VPL Research company, set up by Jaron Lanier (who had already filed for bankruptcy by this time). Of course, no one can forget the 1999 film *The Matrix*, the first film in the Matrix trilogy, directed by Les Wachowski, starring Keanu Reeves and Laurence Fishburne. The plot is centered on frequent journeys between the real and the virtual worlds, the hero's duty being to liberate humans from the rule of the machines by taking control of the matrix. The technology in this film is much more evolved as there is total immersion, and it is so credible that the user has a few clues to tell whether he is in the real or the virtual world. Another cult film, oriented more towards human–machine interaction (HMI) than VR itself, was Steven Spielberg's 2002 film *Minority Report*, starring Tom Cruise (see Figure I.3). This film describes an innovative technology that allows a person to interact naturally with data (which would serve as inspiration for many future research projects in real labs). These three films are certainly not the only ones that talk about VR – a great many others could be named here; however, these three are iconic in this field.

Figure I.2. *A still from the movie* The Lawnmower Man

Figure I.3. *A still from the movie* Minority Report

After having discussed the mention of VR-AR in different fields of art, it is also interesting to analyze how this technology is used in these contexts. Cinema will become an intensive user of VR through the use of 360° cinema, for instance (and on the condition that the spectator finally becomes the spect-actor). In the artistic world, we have to work on the codes and rules for cinematographic writing that these new operational modes will bring about. In particular, in traditional cinema, the narration is constructed on the principle that the director, through their frames, will almost "lead the spectator by hand" to the point from which they want the spectator to view a particular scenic element. In a context where the spectator can freely create their own point of view, artistic construction does not remain the same. If we add to this the fact that the user has the ability to interact with their environment and therefore modify elements in the scene, the narrative complexity deepens and begins to approach the narrative mechanisms used in video games. Combining real and digital images (mixed reality) is another path for development and study, which will emerge soon.

The world of comic books/graphic novels is also influenced either through the development of immersion projects (e.g. *Magnétique*, by Studio Oniride in 2016; http://www.oniride.com/magnetique/) or through using VR in the world of a comic series as is the case with *S.E.N.S*, a project co-produced by Arte

France and Red Corner studio in 2016, inspired by the work of Marc-Antoine Mathieu (see Figure I.4). Indeed, as the universe in VR experiences is not necessarily a reproduction of a real world, it could also be the fruit of pure fantasy and a comic book world lends itself readily to such experimentation.

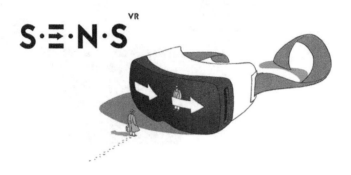

Figure I.4. *Projet* S.E.N.S

I.2. Introduction to the basic concepts

This section aims to briefly describe the fields of VR and AR. We will review the principal concepts for each and provide some definitions[2] in order to clearly define the scope of this book. Readers who seek more information on this are invited to consult the *Virtual Reality Treatise* [FUC 05].

I.2.1. *Virtual reality*

We will first and foremost remind ourselves that the objective of VR is to allow the user to virtually execute a task while believing that they are executing it in the real world. To generate this sensation, the technology must "deceive the brain" by providing it with information identical to the information the brain would perceive in the real environment.

Let us take an example that we will use for the rest of this section: you have always dreamed of flying a private aircraft without ever having acted on this

2 Several different definitions can be found in other books; those that we have chosen here are brief and correspond to a general consensus.

desire. Well then, a VR system could help you to (virtually) realize this dream, by simulating the experience of flying the plane. To start with, it is essential that you are given synthetic images that reproduce the view from a cockpit, the runway first and then an aerial view of the territory you will fly over. In order to give you the impression of "being in the plane", these images must be large and of good quality, so that the perception of your real environment is pushed to the background or even completely replaced by that of the virtual environment (VE). This phenomenon of modifying perception, called *immersion*, is the first fundamental principle of VR. VR headsets, which will be called *visioheadsets* in this book, offer a good immersion experience as the only visual information perceived is delivered through this device.

If the system also generates the sound of the aircraft engine, your immersion will be greater as your brain will perceive this information rather than the real sounds in your environment, which then reinforces the impression of being in an aircraft. In a manner similar to that of the visioheadset, an audio headset is used, as it can insulate against ambient noise.

A real pilot acts in the real environment by using a joystick and dials to steer the plane. It is absolutely indispensable that these actions be reproduced in the VR experience if we wish to simulate reality. Thus, the system must provide several buttons to control the behavior of the aircraft and a joystick to steer it. This *interaction* mechanism between the user and the system is the second fundamental principle of VR. It also serves to differentiate VR from applications that offer good immersion but no real interaction. For example, movie theaters can offer visual and auditory sensations of very high quality, but the spectator is offered absolutely no interaction with the story unfolding on the screen. The same observation can be made for "VR-videos", which have recently become quite popular, but the only interaction offered is a change in point of view (360°). While this family of applications cannot be challenged, they do not qualify as VR experiences as the user is only a spectator and not an actor in the experience.

Let us return to our earlier example: in order to reproduce reality as closely as possible, we must be able to steer the aircraft using a force-feedback joystick, which will generate forces in order to simulate the resistance experienced when using a real joystick, which can be due to air resistance, for example. This haptic information significantly reinforces the user's immersion in the VE. Moving further towards faithfully reproducing reality, let us imagine that we can provide a real aircraft cockpit fitted with real seats and control apparatus and that we can perfectly adapt the external screens so as to ensure that the synthetic images appear naturally in the windows and the windscreen of the aircraft. The impression is then even better as we give our brain additional visual impressions (the components of the cockpit), auditory information (the sound of the buttons being clicked or pressed) and haptic feedback (the feeling of being seated in the airplane seat). This type of a device will, undoubtedly, convince any brain that it is really seated in a cockpit, piloting an aircraft. And of course, these devices *do* exist in reality: these are the aircraft simulators that have been in use for many years, used first to train military pilots and then commercial pilots, and available today as entertainment devices for non-pilots who want to feel like they are flying a plane.

On the basis of this example, we can define VR as the capacity given to one (or more) user(s) to carry out a set of real tasks in a virtual environment, this simulation being based on the immersion of a user in this virtual environment through the use of interactive feedback from and interaction with the system.

Some remarks on this definition:

– "Real tasks": in effect, even though the task is carried out in a VE, it is real. For example, you could start learning to fly a plane in a simulator (as real pilots actually do) because you are developing the skills that will then be used in a real aeroplane.

– "Feedback": this is sensory information (e.g. visual, auditory, haptic) that the computer synthesizes using digital models, that is, descriptions of the form and appearance of an object, the intensity of a sound or of a force.

– "Interactive feedback": these synthetic operations result from relatively complex software processing, and this therefore takes a certain amount of time. If this duration is too long, then our brain perceives the display of a fixed image, then another, destroying any sense of visual continuity and therefore of movement. It is consequently imperative that the feedback is interactive – imperceptible – to obtain a good immersion experience.

– "Interaction": this term designates the functionalities offered to the user to act on the behavior of the system, by moving round, manipulating and/or displacing objects in VE; and in a symmetric manner, the information that is then delivered by the VE to the user, whether visual, auditory or haptic. Let us note that if there is no interaction, then we cannot refer to the experience as VR.

Generally speaking, why do we use VR? This technology was developed to achieve several objectives:

– *Design*: engineers have used VR for a long time, in order to improve the construction of a building or a vehicle, either for moving around within or around these objects or using them virtually in order to detect any design flaws there may be. These tests, which were once carried out using models of increasing complexity, up to a scale 1, were progressively replaced by VR experiences, which are less expensive and can be produced more quickly. It must be noted that these virtual design operations have been extended to contexts beyond tangible objects, for example, for movements (surgical, industrial, sports) or complex protocols.

– *Learning*: as we have seen in our example above, it is possible, today, to learn to pilot any kind of vehicle: plane, car (including F1 cars), ship, space shuttle or spaceship, etc. VR offers many advantages, the first and foremost being that of safety while learning. There is also an ease of replication and the possibility of intervening in the pedagogic scenario (simulating the breakdown of a vehicle or a weather event). Let us note that these learning operations have extended beyond steering vehicles to more complex processes such as the management of a factory or a nuclear center from a control room, or even learning to overcome phobias (of animals, empty spaces, crowds, etc.) using behavioral therapy that is based on VR.

– *Comprehension*: VR can offer learning supports through the interactive feedback it provides (especially visual), in order to better understand certain complex phenomena. This complexity can result from a difficulty or even an impossibility in accessing information on the subject as this information may no longer exist, may be difficult to access (underground or underwater, for oil prospecting; or it may be the surface of a planet that we wish to study), may be too voluminous for our brain to take in (big data) or may be imperceptible to the human senses (temperature, radioactivity). In many contexts, we seek this deeper understanding in order to enable better decision-making: where do we drill for oil? What financial action must we carry out? And so on.

To conclude, it is important to note that very precise and formal definitions for VR exist. For example, in Chapter 1 of Volume 1 (which presents the fundamental principles of the domain) of the *Virtual Reality Treatise* [FUC 05], we find this definition: "virtual reality is a scientific and technical field that uses computer science and behavioral interfaces in order to simulate, in a virtual world, the behavior of 3D entities that interact with each other in real time and with one or more users immersed in a pseudo-natural manner through sensorimotor channels".

I.2.2. *Augmented reality*

The goal of AR is to enrich the perception and knowledge of a real environment by adding digital information relating to this environment. This information is most often visual, sometimes auditory and is rarely haptic. In most AR applications, the user visualizes synthetic images through glasses, headsets, video projectors or even through mobile phones/tablets. The distinction between these devices is based on the superimposition of information onto natural vision that the first three types of devices offer, while the fourth only offers remote viewing, which leads certain authors to exclude it from the field of AR.

To illustrate this, let us use the example of a user who wishes to build a house. While they will only have blueprints, initially, AR will allow them to move around the plot, visualize the future building (by overlaying synthetic images onto their natural vision of the real environment) and perceive general volumes and the implantation in the landscape. As they move on to the process of construction, the user can compare several design and/or furnishing possibilities by visualizing painted walls or furniture arranged in different layouts in a structure that is still under construction. Going beyond interior design and furnishing, it is also possible for an electrician to visualize the placement of insulation and for a plumber to visualize the placement of pipes, even though these are to be hidden behind concrete screeds or concealed in a wall. In addition to placement, the electrician can also see the diameters used and thus the strength of the current being transported, and the plumber can visualize the color and thus the temperature of the water being supplied.

Why develop AR applications? There are several important reasons:

– *Driving assistance*: originally intended to help fighter jet pilots by displaying crucial information on the cockpit screen so that they would not need to look away from the sky to look at dials or displays (which can/could have been be crucial in combat), AR gradually opened up the option of assisted driving to other vehicles (civil aircraft, cars, bikes) including navigation information such as GPS.

– *Tourism*: by enhancing the capabilities of the audio-guides available to visitors of monuments and museums[3], certain sites offer applications that combine images and sound.

– *Professional gesture assistance*: in order to guide certain professional users in their activities, AR can allow additional information to be overlaid onto their vision of the real environment. This information may not be visible in the real environment, as it is often "buried". Thus, a surgeon may operate with greater certainty, by visualizing the blood vessels or anatomical structures that are invisible to them, or a worker participating in constructing an aeroplane may visually superimpose a drilling diagram directly onto the fuselage, without having to take measurements themselves, which leads them to gain speed, precision and reliability.

– *Games*: while it was popularized by *Pokémon Go* in 2016, AR made inroads into this field a long time ago, through the use of augmented versions of games such as *Morpion*, *PacMan* or *Quake*. It is clear that this sector will see a lot more development based on this technology, which will make it possible to combine the real environment and fictional adventures.

Even though they share algorithms and technologies, VR and AR can be clearly distinguished from each other. The main difference is that in VR the tasks executed remain virtual, whereas in AR they are real. For example, the virtual aircraft that you piloted never really took off and thus never produced CO_2 in the real world, but the electrician using AR may cut through a gypsum board partition to install a real switch that can turn on or off a real light.

---

3 These can be considered to belong to the field of AR, as they offer visitors auditory information that enhances their knowledge of the real environment.

As regards AR, compact definitions have been proposed by many scientists. For example, in 1997, Ronald T. Azuma defined AR as a collection of applications that verify the following three properties [AZU 97]:

1) a combination of the real and the virtual;

2) real-time interaction;

3) integration of the real and the virtual (e.g. recalibration, obstruction, brightness).

I.3. The emergence of virtual reality

I.3.1. *A brief history*

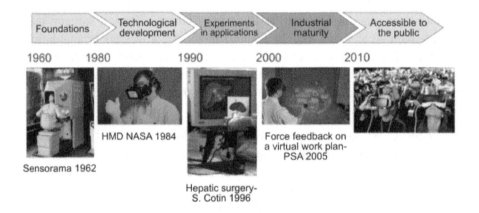

Figure I.5. *Evolution of the field of virtual reality. For a color version of this figure, see www.iste.co.uk/arnaldi/virtual.zip*

Another analysis of the state of virtual reality today allows us to draw a timeline for the stages in the evolution of this field (see Figure I.5). The broad stages of evolution are:

– *before 1960 – the foundations*: numerous approaches and methods (used even today in virtual reality) were perfected well before the birth of "virtual reality" as a field. We have the first representations of reality through paintings (pre-historic), perspectives (Renaissance), panoramic displays (18th Century), stereoscopic vision and cinema (19th Century) and the British pilot training flight-simulators from World War II. Finally, we have the very notion of immersion, the heart of virtual reality, which was used by Morton Heilig from 1956 onwards in his *Sensorama*, with its multimodal feedback, and in 1969 with his *Experience Theater*, the precursor to all large-screen dynamic movie theaters.

– *1960–1980 – the first steps*: the emergence of computer sciences enabled the development of all the elementary components that would then lead to the advent of virtual reality. Components used in the synthetic images that, even today, represent virtual environments are the modeling and manipulation of 3D objects, rendering algorithms (above all, the Z-buffer algorithm [CAT 74]) and the treatment of light and lighting models [GOU 71, PHO 75]. Components for interaction between the user and the system, were Sketchpad [SUT 63], the first visioheadset (or head-mounted display, abbreviated to HMD) [SUT 68] or the GROPE system, the first work carried out on force feedback (initiated in 1971 at the University of North Carolina by Frederick Brooks), which formed the basis for haptic feedback. On the application front, developments around flight simulators progressed rapidly, for instance, within the VITAL and VCASS projects carried out by the United States Air Force.

– *1980–1990 – technological development*: this stage was characterized by the development of technology specific to 3D interaction, in particular. In 1985, Michael McGreevy and Scott Fish (NASA Ames Research) rediscovered the virtual reality display system and gave it the name by which it was known forevermore – HMD: head-mounted display [FIS 87]. In 1986, Scott Fisher proposed spatialized sound restitution. Jaron Lanier (an American) and Jean-Jacques Grimaud (a Frenchman) established the company VPL Research, which sold the first virtual reality applications, using their Data Glove coupled with a visioheadset that it had designed. Incidentally, in 1987, Jaron Lanier "invented" the term *virtual reality*. Thanks to the progress in computer equipment, Frederick Brooks' GROPE system became operational with the manipulation of molecules close to 1,500 atoms ([BRO 90].

– *1990–2000 – experiments in application*: this is the decade in which the integration of material and software solutions made it possible to implement experimental applications that were credible and operational. Let us begin with the video game industry, which was one of the first to foresee the potential benefits of virtual reality and to offer innovative solutions using equipment that was specifically developed for this use: Virtuality (1991), Sega VR (1993), Virtual Boy (1995) and VFXA Headgear, a range of products that, 20 years later, still influence present-day solutions. Industries related to transport (automobile, aeronautic, aerospace, maritime) first used virtual reality to design vehicles and then to learn how to drive them. The medical sector also saw some experimentation using VR in this period. For example, Hunter Hoffman and his colleagues used virtual reality to reduce pain perception among patients who had suffered severe burns at the University of Washington Harborview Burn Center, and Stéphane Cotin *et al.* proposed a complete simulation system for hepatic surgery with force feedback [COT 96]. The field of energy and especially the oil industry also had an early understanding of the value of and return on investment possible using these new technologies.

– *2000–2010 – industrial maturity*: after having focused on product-design and learning how to drive vehicles, the applications of VR evolved towards maintenance and training, using simulation to control industrial processes (monitoring a factory from a command room, for example).

We can also see the increase in the number of applications that use VR to better understand an environmental phenomenon, especially to better decide how to proceed. Let us take the case of the petroleum industry, which studies subsoils in order to optimize the placement of drilling wells, or even the world of finance, where spaces composed of share revenues and growth curves are visually studied in order to better decide what actions to take (buying, selling). The goal of better understanding for better decision-making can also be seen in product-design, during project reviews, which reduces or even eliminates the need for physical models.

As regards equipment, the dawn of this decade saw significant progress in the installation of immersive rooms (CAVE and, above all, the SGI Reality Center) in both the academic world and (large) companies. Users can also easily find capture, localization and orientation equipment, such as the force-feedback arm (haptic feedback).

Last, but certainly not least, this period saw a very noticeable evolution in the development of VR applications: alongside the techno-centric approach adopted by the pioneers in the field, there arose an anthropocentric approach. This change was due to two factors playing out simultaneously:

- the increasing diffusion of VR led researchers in the social sciences, mainly in the cognitive sciences, to study this new paradigm. This opened up fields of reflection that were unknown until then;

- application developers, noticing the rejection of some uses as well as the discomfort that certain users experienced, began looking for solutions that were not just purely technological.

A new fashion of thinking about applications, which would take into account the human factor, emerged from the convergence between the knowledge and results obtained by researchers and the needs of the developers, and this approach continues to be used today.

– *2010 onward* – *deployment towards the larger public*: this last period was marked by the arrival of new equipment at costs that were much lower than those of earlier devices, while also offering a high level of performance. This rebound is largely due to the development of smart phones as well as that of video games. Even though visioheadsets have been publicized the most in the media (e.g. Oculus Rift, HTC Vive), new motion-capture systems have also emerged. This explosion has resulted in numerous articles being published in the general media, bringing information about these technologies to a wider public: first addressing professionals in companies that were smaller than the large groups that worked on designing new uses for VR-AR, and then relaying information directly to the general public, which was entranced by the announcements (even those that were completely unrealistic) and grew interested in the possibilities offered by various sectors.

In parallel to this new equipment, which was just the tip of the iceberg, new software environments established themselves, often arising from the world of video games (such as Unity 3D). This made it possible for "new" developers, from the above-mentioned SMEs, to independently develop their solutions.

It is clear that this is just the beginning of VR-AR becoming accessible to the general public; after a phase of media uproar, the true benefits will emerge and there is no doubt that the coming years will witness an explosion in the mass use of these technologies.

Given these facts, which by no means constitute an exhaustive history of the field, our book aims to answer the following question: *what has happened over the last 10 years?* (this period corresponds to the time since the publication of the last edition of the *Virtual Reality Treatise*). Before providing an extensive description of notable events in the evolution of the field over the last decade, and in order to understand *what* has truly changed, it will be useful to study the evolution of the socio-economic context.

Indeed, 10 years ago, the landscape consisted of:

– research laboratories that develop fundamental methods and technologies;

– large industrial entities, often manufacturing industries or industries depending on large infrastructure that make use of technologies (e.g. in France: PSA, Renault, Airbus, SNCF, etc.);

– a few technological startups that proposed software tools and (often experimental) equipment, for example Haption, Virtools and Laster.

The manufacture of products was often realized thanks to collaboration between these three categories of actors in ambitious projects. Professional integrated software solutions were quite a heavy burden, both for the application developer and for the end-user.

I.3.2. *A revolution among actors*

In the last decade, there have been several profound transformations in this landscape.

– First of all, there have been some startups that have had real commercial success with their innovations:

- Oculus Rift (2013[4]), which was bought by Facebook, resulting in a massive diffusion of the products;

- Leap Motion and its lightweight position sensors (2013).

– And then there are large organizations with considerable resources in terms of capital and development teams that have now stepped in and taken an interest in these technologies, whether in designing them or buying them from existing actors. For example:

– These companies offer the following products:

- the Microsoft Kinect sensor (2010);

---

4 The dates mentioned here correspond to their diffusion in France; they may thus differ from the start dates for the projects or the announcement dates.

- Google Glass (2013) (even though this was not a commercial success, it saw significant distribution);

- Samsung Gear VR headset (2015);

- Microsoft HoloLens headset (2016);

- Sony PS-VR headset (2016);

- HTC Valve Vive headset (2016);

- development kit for the Apple smart phone range. Apple acquired Metaio, a well-established actor in the field of Augmented Reality (2017).

I.3.3. *Technological revolution*

Both on the material and software plane, this decade has been rich in breakthrough new products:

– In the field of software, we must note the availability of professional integrated software solutions that are available for free, allowing anyone with the know-how to develop their own solutions:

- the release of the first free version of Unity 3D in October 2009;

- the release of Apple's ARKit in 2017.

– Another point that became a determining factor in the democratization of technology and its uses was the evolution of terminals. In effect, in June 2007, Apple sold its first iPhone, and everyone knows the impact that this had on the mobile telephone market, as well as on the general field of mobile applications. This evolution rapidly led to users having access to a terminal equipped with a high-quality screen, coupled with a camera and several sensors (e.g. accelerometers, tactile screen). It was a short step from here to giving the average user access to mobile VR or AR applications, which had, hitherto, been unknown or too expensive. Nonetheless, we must note that, of the number of mobile applications claiming to be VR or AR applications, very few actually bring either AR or VR into play and most are rather counterproductive to the development of these technologies. The advent of tablets also led to the development of VR and AR by removing an important limiting factor in the mobile phones: screen size.

– Finally, video games have been majorly pushed as well as recent progress in the field of visioheadsets (virtual reality and augmented reality headsets), which have allowed for a massive democratization of these technologies, mainly as a result of very low acquisition costs as compared to earlier equipment, with a quality that is perfectly satisfactory.

– Another technological revolution that had a significant impact was the large-scale introduction of specialized architectures such as the GPUs (Graphics Processing Unit) as co-processors in high-performance computing. Indeed, each computer now has a graphics card that gives it a considerably higher computing speed than the computers of a decade ago; processing power (CPU) has also increased. This increase in performance must be placed in the context of a growing demand for calculations by AR or VR applications. This is, of course, because of the increasing quality of computer-generated images required, as well as interaction with a user, which requires very short cycle times (high calculation frequency, low lag). For example, let us note that in the *Virtual Reality Treatise*, we count on the fingers of one hand the number of times the term GPU is used in the first four books, and this is the same for video processing or the processing of sound signals.

I.3.4. *A revolution in use and users*

The other profound change in the landscape relates to the fact that applications that were initially intended for a few professional fields (often specialized fields, such as design offices and professional experts) were extended to all of society, even entering our homes (e.g. games, services, home automation systems). Over the past 10 years, the augmented reality user has shifted from being an expert working in an office to every Joe and Jane at home or on the move. This also holds for VR-AR equipment, which, up to a decade ago, was only sold by a few distributors known only to insiders. Today, any mainstream vendor selling electronic systems will carry, on their shelves and in catalogues, a complete range of equipment (visioheadsets, sensors) that we can also see sold in large retail stores. It is no longer uncommon for "conventional" stores to offer clients the opportunity to try applications or equipment. This evolution in the use of VR-AR will undoubtedly continue in the years to come.

I.4. The contents of this book

The editorial choices that led to this book resulted mainly from one simple principle: to describe the most notable facts of the last decade and imagine those that may occur over the next decade. Along with the authors of the different chapters, we have therefore prioritized pertinence rather than exhaustivity. Indeed, an exhaustive account of the evolution of such an active field over the last 10 years would require a few thousand pages! Finally, the reader will see, in the bibliographical references listed at the end of each chapter, that some references date back to 10 years or, in some cases, even further back! We have tried to specify original sources in order to honor the history associated with a technology or a scientific contribution, while also showcasing important recent results.

This book is thus organized as follows:

1) Chapter 1: the discussion here is centered on the social impact of virtual reality and augmented reality. What do they bring in and how can they be used in broad fields of applications?

2) Chapter 2: this chapter analyzes the technological revolution in detail, from the viewpoints of both equipment and software, and discusses the impacts of this evolution.

3) Chapter 3: this chapter reviews essential concepts in both technological sciences (computer sciences, electronics) and human sciences (cognitive sciences, ergonomics) and describes the main challenges related to each field.

4) Chapter 4: based on the questions that remain, what are the paths that allow us to offer more satisfactory solutions and allow, among others, for richer user experiences?

5) Chapter 5: in this chapter, we discuss the main evolutions we foresee, while acknowledging the difficulties of this exercise given the strong splits possible in this field. A brief recap of the analysis of evolutions over the past 10 years is sufficient to persuade ourselves of this difficulty.

6) Chapter 6: we will analyze the potential for development related to a mass distribution of VR and AR, while also touching on the potential risks associated with this, with respect to both user safety and unrestrained use of technology.

7) Conclusion: this chapter reviews the different elements discussed in the book and opens up a debate on the concept of virtual reality, as it has been fantasized about in movies or in the literature. We have also attempted to sketch out a few broad paths for the future, inspired, notably, by a debate carried out in the AFRV general assembly[5].

This book approaches a complex and relatively unknown field. The "target audience" is therefore quite wide: students, developers of software solutions, decision-makers, those curious about technology, etc. We thus thought it was important to try and make this book readable across audiences rather than offering a linear reference from the first page to the last. We thought it should be a bit like navigating a website, allowing each reader to click on whatever interests them. Thus, while our structure is based on a certain logic, these chapters may be read more or less independent of each other, depending on the competence and needs of each reader. As a result of this, however, some concepts or notions may be repeated across chapters. This is not to belabor the point, but simply to help each chapter remain "self-sufficient".

For your assistance, we propose, based on your profile, a nonlinear navigation that allows you to directly arrive at the information you consider to be most important:

– VR or AR student: what can we say except that we recommend that students read it all the way through?

– Software solution developer: we suggest that developers, who may not have the time to read everything, review concepts and recent evolutions (Chapter 1), recall the scientific challenges related to VR-AR and then approach current and future solutions (Chapters 4–6). Here again, we can only recommend that it would be ideal to read the book in its entirety!

– Decision-makers in organizations: apart from this short introduction, it would be important to get an idea of the current and emerging applications (Chapter 2) and then to familiarize yourself with current evolutions in equipment and software (Chapter 3). Having done this, a decision-maker is likely to be very interested in the new developments discussed in Chapter 7.

---

5 http://www.af-rv.fr

– A curious reader, a technology enthusiast: here again, we would recommend the basics in this introduction, before suggesting you to go through Chapters 2 and 3, which offer a panoramic view of current applications and the technologies used. Chapter 4 will help you understand why implementation is not so simple and why the technologies we see in movies do not yet exist. The conclusion (Chapter 8) will also provide more details on this last point.

– SHS (Social and Human Sciences) experimenters: while reading Chapters 1 and 3 is, of course, recommended so as to understand advances in the field, the human factor is discussed chiefly in Chapter 4 (challenges) and Chapter 5 (current solutions). A brief review of applications (Chapter 2) would not be irrelevant, in light of the earlier chapters. Finally, Chapters 7 and 8 discuss some future prospects that raise important questions for researchers in human sciences.

– A professional in an applicative field: Chapter 2 is obviously essential; Chapter 3 may enlighten the reader as to technologies required for the realization of these applications. Finally, the reader would probably need to go over the solutions in use today to address various problems faced by developers.

I.4.1. *Authors/contributors*

To help integrate this book, we called upon experts from French laboratories, who are very active in the fields of VR-AR, as well as experts from the industrial world, both for offering material and/or software solutions, and for discussing the usage and the integration of these technologies. These experts were brought in with the aim of covering a wide range of competencies inherent to the fields of VR-AR (e.g. computer sciences, signal processing, automation human sciences). We have had long-standing professional relationships with many of them (especially within the AFRV). The list of contributors to each chapter is specified on the first page of the chapter, and a complete and detailed list of all contributors is provided at the end of the book.

I.5. Bibliography

[ART 09] ARTAUD A., *Le théâtre et son double; suivi de, Le théâtre de Seraphin*, Gallimard, France, 2009.

[AZU 97] AZUMA R.T., "A survey of augmented reality", *Presence: Teleoperators and Virtual Environments*, vol. 6, no. 4, pp. 355–385, August 1997.

[BRO 90] BROOKS JR. F.P., OUH-YOUNG M., BATTER J.J. *et al.*, "Project GROPE – Haptic displays for scientific visualization", *SIGGRAPH Computer Graphic*, vol. 24, no. 4, pp. 177–185, September 1990.

[CAT 74] CATMULL E.E., A Subdivision Algorithm for Computer Display of Curved Surfaces, PhD thesis, The University of Utah, 1974.

[COT 96] COTIN S., DELINGETTE H., CLEMENT J.-M. *et al.*, "Geometric and Physical Representations for a Simulator of Hepatic Surgery", *Medicine Meets Virtual Reality IV*, IOS Press, 1996.

[CRU 92] CRUZ-NEIRA C., SANDIN D.J., DEFANTI T.A. *et al.*, "The CAVE: Audio Visual Experience Automatic Virtual Environment", *Communication ACM*, vol. 35, no. 6, pp. 64–72, June 1992.

[FIS 87] FISHER S.S., MCGREEVY M., HUMPHRIES J.*et al.*, "Virtual Environment Display System", *Proceedings of the 1986 Workshop on Interactive 3D Graphics*, I3D '86, New York, USA, pp. 77–87, 1987.

[FON 20] FONTANA G., *Bellicorum instrumentorum liber*, 1420.

[FRE 14] FREY J., GERVAIS R., FLECK S. *et al.*, "Teegi: Tangible EEG Interface", *Proceedings of the 27th Annual ACM Symposium on User Interface Software and Technology*, UIST'14, New York, USA, pp. 301–308, 2014.

[FUC 05] FUCHS P., MOREAU G. (eds), *Le Traité de la Réalité Virtuelle*, 3rd edition, Les Presses de l'Ecole des Mines, Paris, 2005.

[FUC 09] FUCHS P., MOREAU G., DONIKIAN S., *Le traité de la réalité virtuelle Volume 5 - Les humains virtuels*, Mathématique et informatique, 3rd edition, Les Presses de l'Ecole des Mines, Paris, 2009.

[FUC 16] FUCHS P., *Les casques de réalité virtuelle et de jeux vidéo*, Les Presses de l'Ecole des Mines, Paris, 2016.

[GOU 71] GOURAUD H., "Continuous shading of curved surfaces", *IEEE Transactions on Computers*, vol. C-20, no. 6, pp. 623–629, June 1971.

[JON 13] JONES B.R., BENKO H., OFEK E. *et al.*, "IllumiRoom: peripheral projected illusions for interactive experiences", *Proceedings of the SIGCHI Conference on Human Factors in Computing Systems*, CHI'13, New York, USA, pp. 869–878, 2013.

[JON 14] JONES B., SODHI R., MURDOCK M. *et al.*, "RoomAlive: magical experiences enabled by scalable, adaptive projector-camera units", *Proceedings of the 27th Annual ACM Symposium on User Interface Software and Technology*, UIST'14, New York, USA, pp. 637–644, 2014.

[LAV 17] LAVIOLA J.J., KRUIJFF E., MCMAHAN R. *et al.*, *3D User Interfaces: Theory and Practice*, 2nd Edition, Addison Wesley, 2017.

[PHO 75] PHONG B.T., "Illumination for computer generated pictures", *Communication ACM*, vol. 18, no. 6, pp. 311–317, June 1975.

[PLA 07] PLATO, *The Republic*, Penguin Classics, London, 2007.

[SCH 16] SCHMALSTIEG D., HÖLLERER T., *Augmented Reality: Principles and Practice (Usability)*, Addison-Wesley Professional, Boston, 2016.

[SUT 63] SUTHERLAND I.E., "Sketchpad: a man-machine graphical communication system", *Proceedings of the May 21–23, 1963, Spring Joint Computer Conference*, AFIPS'63 (Spring), New York, USA, pp. 329–346, 1963.

[SUT 68] SUTHERLAND I.E., "A head-mounted three dimensional display", *Proceedings of the December 9–11, 1968, Fall Joint Computer Conference, Part I*, AFIPS '68 (Fall, part I), New York, USA, pp. 757–764, 1968.

1

New Applications

This chapter aims to give an overview of the new families of applications that have emerged or that have undergone massive development in this last decade. The first section (section 1.1) will analyze the manufacturing industry, exploring the development of virtual reality (VR), the emergence of augmented reality (AR) and the question of return on investment. This is mainly illustrated by real industrial examples, shared by the concerned actors themselves. The second section (section 1.2) explores the field of health and analyzes the impact VR and AR have had on training, on preparation for intervention and on uses in the world of surgery. Section 1.3 will examine applications related to city life, architecture and urbanism and will focus especially on developing mobility. Finally, we will end the chapter by looking at recent results in the field of training and in the field of heritage (section 1.4).

1.1. New industrial applications

1.1.1. *Virtual reality in industry*

Until recently, it was impossible to think of virtual reality without imagining using heavy and complex machinery that needed a dedicated team to operate it. These characteristics have certainly put the brakes on this technology being integrated into companies for whom ROI (return on

Chapter written by Bruno ARNALDI, Stéphane COTIN, Nadine COUTURE, Jean-Louis DAUTIN, Valérie GOURANTON, François GRUSON and Domitile LOURDEAUX.

investment) is a near-essential criterion for any decision related to making investments.

The broad periods across which companies were involved in AR can be described as follows.

1.1.1.1. *The age of pioneers: researchers*

Until 2005, only a few large industrial groups were interested in virtual reality. Their participation was strongly linked to the group's research activities (fundamental and industrial research) and its interconnections with the higher education and research community. In France, the companies that were involved in research all possessed in-house Research and Development departments that were made up of researchers, doctors, engineers and research engineers working within national and Europe-wide projects, in close collaboration with researchers in large public sector research laboratories (e.g. Inria centers, CNRS units, university laboratories). PSA, RENAULT and AIRBUS are the companies that established this process with the CRV at PSA, RENAULT's Technocentre and EADS IW (renamed the AIRBUS Innovation Group) for Airbus.

1.1.1.2. *The experimenter's age: innovative engineers*

From 2005 to 2010 or so, many large companies learned of the emergence of this technology for virtual 3D prototyping and level 1 immersion. They wished to carry out experiments in order to analyze the potential of virtual reality in different professions (especially research department and organization and methods departments). The approach they adopted was quite different from that of the "pioneers": they did not wish to set up an internal research center, but developed "innovation departments" that were associated with certain platforms for technological resources such as CLARTE at Laval or ENSAM at Chalon-sur-Saône. We can also give the example of DCNS, Plastic Omnium and many more.

1.1.1.3. *The age of shared platforms*

From 2010 to 2014, the widely used model was that of a shared platform available to companies in the region. In effect, as technology matured and its application for various purposes became more robust, many companies requested an institutional environment that allowed sharing of equipment (CAVE, Cadwall) on which the ROI was not realistically high enough for each company to invest in it. This model was initiated at LAVAL in 2000 by CLARTE and its technical platform for companies paved the way for platforms such as CIRV at St Nazaire, Industrilab in Picardie and Holo3 in Strasbourg.

1.1.1.4. *The age of VR headsets and applications distributed on a very large scale: major players on the offensive*

From late 2014, we have witnessed a techno-economic revolution in the field of VR. The field was fundamentally transformed by the appearance of the first Oculus headset, followed by its eponymous successors, as well as other headsets from other companies (each outperforming the other), such as the HTC Vive, all of which were also available at very low costs. Obviously, a headset cannot and may never be able to do the same things a high-end visiocube can. However, the "user-usability-immersion" cost equation for an HMD is such that actors within companies cannot help exploring them and factoring them into their deliberations. At best, they are considered complementary to the visiocube and, in the worst case scenario, they can replace them. It must be noted that the economic model of the HMD has nothing in common with the visiocube. In fact, the HMD is considered, in accounting terms, to be a consumable. Investment related to virtual reality is currently completely related to software and not to equipment, which significantly modifies the decision-making center.

1.1.2. *Augmented reality and industrial applications*

Augmented reality is a technology that has sparked off a lot of fantasies but delivered very little. In effect, many communicators rode on the message "add the virtual onto the real", creating sensational videos that led the viewer to believe that we would completely naturally be able to watch a car that did not exist; visualize the sofa we would buy in our living room; get up close to people who were far away or even people who had died. In brief, that real life would be exactly like a TV series!

However, these promises far outstripped the possibilities that technology can offer today. The consequent backlash resulted in a strong rejection of AR by the public and general users today content themselves with "pseudo-AR" games, like *Pokémon Go*. Unlike with VR, here we cannot trace the stages through which companies appropriated this technology. This is because the needs expressed and the predicted uses resulted in a "pseudo-offering", which claimed to respond to their demands by using tricks and artifice that did not long stand up to scrutiny. The Gartner Hype curve for 2017 (Figure 1.1) offers an interesting illustration: it quite brutally plots AR in the "trough of disillusionment".

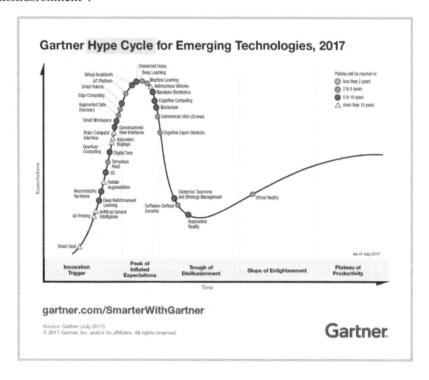

Figure 1.1. *Courbe de Hype 2017. For a color version of this figure, see www.iste.co.uk/arnaldi/virtual.zip*

A careful analysis, however, shows us that *where industrial applications (and these alone) are concerned,* augmented reality has already entered the next phase, the "Slope of Enlightenment", with market stability expected in the next two-to-five years.

1.1.3. *VR-AR for industrial renewal*

Before we get into a detailed examination of the impact VR-AR technologies have had on the world of business, let us listen to a voice from the industry – Stéphane Klein, Deputy Director of STX (Chantiers de l'Atlantique) and head of the RetD. He offers a succinct summary of the pragmatic steps taken by several leading industrialists and the impact that they have observed:

> *"Innovation is in the DNA of the STX France shipyard in Saint-Nazaire. This is probably why it is the last remaining large maritime construction company and why it is seeing, today, an unprecedented resurgence in activity, with the order-book completely full for the next five years! Keen to offer its clients ever more innovative products, at the cutting edge of technology, STX has constantly upgraded its production system in order to remain on the offensive in a highly competitive global market. The use of virtual reality in association with a new 3D CAD has certainly been among the most significant changes in the STX research department over the last five years. Just a few years ago, Virtual Reality was nothing but a simple "Work Package" in a R&D project – but it has rapidly become an integral and indispensable part of STX study processes and marketing. Today it is mature and systematically used. STX is now looking to use Augmented Reality. This may find applications in the building and operation of ships; in the field of navigation or maintenance of equipment, and also in the construction process. With respect to this last point, STX is currently evaluating the use of augmented reality to assist linesmen/women working with electrical power systems and fluid networks. The initial results from this experimentation are very promising and the gains in productivity and quality have been noted. The industrial use of augmented reality to fit-out ships is quite imminent. What remains is to fortify the solutions studied within this R&D project".*

1.1.3.1. *The fundamentals: research and communication-marketing*

From the early 2000s, leading industrialists have focused on two main subjects, namely:

– virtual reality within the research office (extending 3D CAD) for immersive project review, for verification of assembly–disassembly activities and for interactive design in an immersive experience. VR here is a tool that aids decision-making (Figures 1.2 and 1.3);

– virtual reality within communication-marketing departments, used as a marketing tool to aid sales and adding value to the company's products and services.

Figure 1.2. *The layout for the command post of a ship at DCNS (© CLARTE – NAVAL Group (ex DCNS))*

Figure 1.3. *Project review at NEXTER (© Nexter)*

These two areas of development have made it possible for the concerned companies to generate a great deal of enthusiasm within their internal services (see PSA and its CRV) and have allowed France's leading industrial companies to project an image of innovation and to come together and anticipate a new industrial revolution based on collaborative practices (e.g. co-designing with sub-contractors and clients, remote collaboration within entities of the same group). While it is still too early to talk of an industrial revolution, it is clear that VR has contributed to a change in behaviors within research departments and has certainly contributed to the development of new user-centered design approaches, as well as AGILE methods.

Over the years, hardware and software platforms have become professional and, from adopting a rather exploratory approach (the early 2000s), have today become reliable, high-performance and intuitive tools which can be used even by the uninitiated. A few examples of the platforms on the market are: ICIDO from EsiGroup, HIM from Optis, RHEA from Airbus (for Airbus' own requirements), IMPROOV from MiddleVr and TECHVIZ's eponymous platform.

Jean Leynaud (Director of Systems Engineering at NEXTER) gives a detailed account of the impact VR has had on the company's approach to the factories of the future:

"Ever since the creation of the GIAT industries in 1971, from design boards to 3D digital models, the weapons manufacturer Nexter Systems has ceaselessly evolved practices and tools to boost performance and innovation. It was in this context that in 2013 Nexter System equipped itself with a virtual reality system (four-sided system working with CLARTE's IMPROOV software).

"Virtual reality now makes it possible to involve the end-user more than ever before in the preliminary design phases, as the approach used up to now – reading and understanding CAD views – is not something that everyone can do. This immersion in a 3D environment has sparked off discussions that are much more pragmatic and directly related to operational use. Thanks to VR, the end-user can enter into the environment much more easily and feel as if they are already in their vehicle. It is thus easier for them to describe what they feel and what they need. This collaborative design is a significant advance for Nexter and their clients. This

new manner of direct design also makes it possible to concentrate on the architecture and to go further with the innovation of future products in the NS range. For about three years now, VR has been an important part of the Nexter development process. Each project uses 3D immersion for reviewing concepts. This makes it possible for all actors, especially those who cannot access CAD routinely, to share in the global vision of the product at key points in the development and to better understand the different choices in architecture. VR has become an indispensable resource in developing new products in order to choose an architecture and to "de-risk" the launch of a physical mock-up (without replacing it). For example, reworking a physical model will require several months for the retrofit and a large financial investment, while modifications carried out on the virtual model will require only as much time as it takes to manipulate it on the computer. This allows a great deal of flexibility and speed of iteration for the model, which is significant especially in an industrial context where development time is restricted."

Another representative example is that of La Redoute. After their research department had worked on the layout of their new warehouse and the ergonomics of different production posts, the company used virtual reality as a social mediation tool by putting into place a large-scale internal communication operation. A presentation of the virtual model for this future warehouse was presented to all the collaborators via HMDs within the company over the period of a week. The impact was tremendous, as Marc Grosclaude recounts in an article published in La Voix du Nord: *"In a year and a half, La Martinoire will have been completely transformed: farewell to the [old] warehouse, which was considered "ultramodern" when its foundation stone was laid in 1968. To comprehend the scope of the transformation, the employees of La Redoute were able to explore the order-processing site in 3D. We were given the same virtual tour...."*

Thanks to VR, we can talk about industrial and social renewal in very concrete terms. Let us note, however, that SMEs, and even larger businesses, were quite nervous about using VR until quite recently. This was because of the large cost of acquiring and then using the equipment, and also because the ROI is hard to calculate. If some companies did manage to understand, quite early on, the benefits of using this technology (direct ROI vs. the less-quantifiable indirect ROI), it was because clients with large orders led to their entering the world of collaborative projects.

1.1.3.2. *Ergonomics and training: perfect illustrations for value added by VR*

1.1.3.2.1. Ergonomics – objective: reducing musculoskeletal disorders

While the decade from 2000 to 2010 saw large-scale development in applications in the vertical sectors of the industry (terrestrial, petrochemical, naval and aeronautical vehicles), recent years have seen many transversal uses emerge, such as ergonomics and collaborative work on virtual prototyping and training. The economic stakes for all three fields are huge and the ROI is relatively easy to calculate.

As concerns ergonomics, two different areas are involved: ergonomics of usage (pilot's seat or command and control posts) that make it possible to concretely improve the usability and intuitiveness of various equipment, and postural ergonomics (ergo-design of production posts and lines), which makes it possible to drastically reduce musculoskeletal problems by carrying out a downstream study of workposts (Figure 1.4).

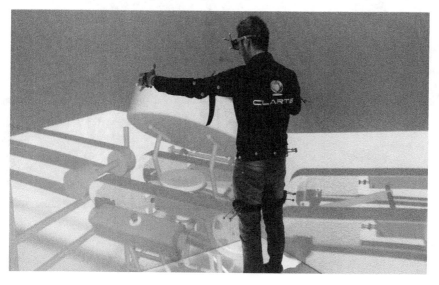

Figure 1.4. *Ergonomic study on a Lactalis production post (© CLARTE). For a color version of this figure, see www.iste.co.uk/arnaldi/virtual.zip*

One of the most interesting examples of this approach is that of the company INERGY (Plastic Omnium group), which was one of the first companies to experiment with an Ergo-designing application for production posts, developed by CLARTE. Very quickly after a few tests were carried out on some new production lines (Figure 1.5), the company decided to systematize this process: since 2011, any new production post (in any INERGY site around the world) has been designed via an ergonomics study carried out using VR and the RULA (Rapid Upper Limb Assessment) method. The impact this application had was so significant that Plastic Omnium decided to create its own virtual reality center within its technical center (Compiègne) and to use it for its businesses. INERGY estimates that it has managed to shave off about 20% of the time spent on its design-creation phase and has seen its "reworking due to design error" rates plummet for new posts, as the downstream participation of workers in the company has been particularly beneficial.

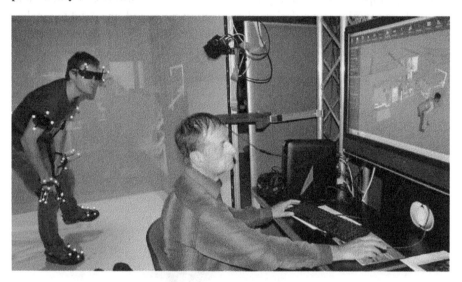

Figure 1.5. *Ergonomic study of an Inergy production post (© AFERGO)*

The typology of companies using this approach is interesting. There are, of course, large groups, as well as a good number of their sub-contractors, generally placed between medium- and large-scale businesses, as well as several medium-scale businesses that today use "virtual design" in their sales arguments.

1.1.3.2.2. Training: a revolution in engineering pedagogy

Training is certainly one of the sectors where VR has had the greatest impact (Figure 1.6). The four main reasons for this are:

1) the simulation of work situations using 1:1 scale immersion and multisensory interactions that make it possible to put in place a new pedagogy for engineering that is perfectly in line with training objectives;

2) total "de-risking": the learner can be placed in all kinds of work situations, including those that are dangerous, in order to teach them the actions and procedures to adopt and to help them acquire the correct reflexes in case of danger;

3) savings on consumables (e.g. training in industrial painting without spoiling any raw material) and heavy equipment (e.g. production equipment need not be set aside for training, resulting in improved productivity overall);

4) the attraction of using 3D images and immersion can help offset the more boring aspects of traditional training.

Figure 1.6. *Training to land and take-off on a helicopter carrier (in choppy conditions) (© CLARTE - NAVAL Group (ex DCNS))*

Let us note that beyond the innovative training process, many companies use VR applications to sensitize future employees (e.g. youngsters, job applicants) to the work and the available posts. Virtual reality here becomes an extremely efficient communication tool used by HR services to add value, to help build understanding and to recruit. The associated business model is still simple, as the ROI is calculated using the following equation: (savings on raw material + savings due to production equipment not being blocked for training) – (cost of acquiring and using the VR training platform).

The recent emergence of low-cost and very high-performance HMDs makes this a highly positive equation, resulting in the current boom in teaching and training applications.

1.1.4. *And what about augmented reality?*

While AR is simpler for the general public to understand as they have used smartphone and tablet applications, we have seen that they lost interest in it. However, AR continues to progress in the professional, especially industrial, world.

There has also been a remarkable evolution of equipment. Microsoft's HoloLens glasses mark a significant progress in this field.

Even in 2017, it is still difficult to talk of industrial renewal being ushered in by AR, as the applications that are most mature and used concretely within companies are focused on communication, marketing and improving sales.

Having said that, there are many ongoing research projects, and it is quite probable that mature applications will be available in the coming years, initially using tablets and other intermediate screens and later using semi-transparent glasses. Moreover, some applications have already attained a degree of maturity that will allow them to participate in the industrial renewal we are currently living through.

Let us take the example of MIRA (Figure 1.7) developed by AGI (Airbus Group Innovation) *"This solution was first used so the aviator could verify the integrity of the correct placement of thousands of parts installed in airplanes, such as the fixed supports that hold up electric cabling, hydraulic pipes or air-conditioning pipes"* (an Airbus source).

Figure 1.7. *The MIRA application from the Airbus Innovation Group*
(© Airbus Group). For a color version of this figure, see
www.iste.co.uk/arnaldi/virtual.zip

Let us also give the example of ARPI (Figure 1.8), an experimental device to control the assembly of equipment in a "panel factory" within STX (the ship-building yard at St Nazaire), which made it possible to save a significant amount of time.

Unlike virtual reality, which largely concerns research departments and Organization and Methods departments, augmented reality is used in the field, even within production units and in the construction of the industrial world. The equipment used (tablets, PCs, AR glasses) is thus quite strenuously tested, and it is imperative that it be robust, reliable and intuitive when implemented. If this is the case (a real challenge!), the value added by these AR applications is very large and is much easier to measure by ROI and productivity specialists than for VR.

Offering assistance to an operator in a control room, helping a metallurgical worker in guiding and positioning, offering local or remote technical assistance to a technical maintenance officer – all of these uses will lead to measurable gains in the productivity of several dozen percentage points.

Figure 1.8. *The ARPI application to control panels (25 m*25 m) STX (© CLARTE - STX)*

1.2. Computer-assisted surgery

Software for the simulation, planning and training to carry out operations: navigational help; AR devices; remote interventions; robotics... computer-assisted surgery is a growing field and one that has already entered several operation theaters. This section gives a description of the current situation in the field and the main challenges and prospective paths in this revolutionary sector, by focusing on the contributions of VR-AR to the past decade and to the coming decade.

1.2.1. *Introduction*

Ever since the first radiograph and the first use of X-rays in 1895, medical imaging has only improved and diversified. It saw significant progress from the 1970s onwards with the development of the CT scan, and from the emergence of nuclear medicine and magnetic resonance imaging, which appeared in the early 1980s. This major evolution in the medical field was, however, only possible due to the joint development of computer sciences and digital image processing methods, which made it possible to interpret and process increasingly larger and more complex images with greater precision and efficiency.

Today, we see a new revolution taking place in the medical field, thanks to techniques such as digital simulation, 3D modeling, biomechanical characterization, and virtual and augmented reality. These developments have also set up links with medical imaging and robotics by widening their scope of application. There are already many uses for VR in medicine, if only to interactively visualize 3D patient data reconstructed from a CT or MRI scanner. It is, however, possible to go much further, combining results achieved in different scientific fields.

In this section, we will examine the field of computer-assisted surgery, which is at the heart of this revolution but also poses several challenges. The three main challenges are: 1) the use of VR to train surgeons in an appropriate training course, where there is no risk to a patient; 2) upstream planning of complex interventions, in order to reduce surgical time and risks; and 3) the use of AR in the operation theater in order to bring together, *in situ*, the essential information needed for the intervention to be carried out smoothly. In different applications, several physiological, biomechanical and geometric parameters are brought into an equation and calculated: for example, deformation on the liver, electrophysiological activity in the heart or even physical interactions between surgical instruments and an organ (see Figure 1.9).

There are strong associations between these different objectives that make it possible to share scientific results. In most cases, therapeutic targets are soft tissue[1]. Organs such as the liver, heart, brain and blood vessels represent a large part of anatomical structures on which surgical interventions are carried out. Modeling these structures, not only from an anatomical point of view but also from a biomechanical point of view, is an initial challenge that is common to all three objectives. The simulations used for learning and for assistance during surgical operations also share another common point,

---

1 Soft tissue is any tissue in the body other than bone, such as muscle, fat, fibrous tissues, blood vessels or any other supporting tissue.

related to computing time. In order to allow interactions or instant display of information, these applications require the result in real time. This is difficult given the complexity of the biomechanical models discussed earlier, which require several parameters (and thus computations) to be taken into account. Finally, pre-operation planning and intraoperative[2] assistance require a high level of precision in predicting the results supplied by the calculations. This precision is achieved by using increasingly powerful digital calculation methods, and also by specific modeling, adapted to the patient, and not the generic modeling that is usually used in learning software. We use the term "personalized medicine".

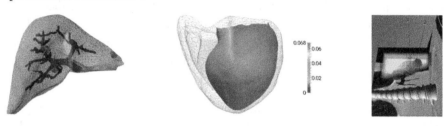

Figure 1.9. *Left: digital model of the liver and its vascular network, created using a patient's CT scan and adapted to real-time simulations. Center: simulation of electrophysiological activity of the heart, parametrized using patient data. Right: simulation of the cryoablation of a renal tumor and its calculation grid (in yellow and red). For a color version of this figure, see www.iste.co.uk/arnaldi/virtual.zip*

In this chapter, we will first discuss the AR techniques that can potentially visually enrich information through a fusion of intraoperative images and preoperative data (e.g. images, virtual 3D models), which help guide the surgeon during the operation. However, in order to progressively introduce the different concepts brought into play by this domain, we will begin with results from the use of VR in the learning context (section 1.2.2) and in the planning of operations (section 1.2.3).

1.2.2. *Virtual reality and simulation for learning*

In this section, we will briefly present a few examples of VR being used in the context of learning in the field of surgery. Rather than providing an

---

2 Anything that is done during the surgical intervention is called an intraoperative procedure.

extensive report on existing projects and products in the field, we wish to introduce a set of concepts that will be helpful in understanding the rest of section 1.2. Generally speaking, interactive digital simulations developed in this context are mainly meant for minimally invasive surgeries[3]. These new approaches offer multiple advantages to the patient such as lowering the risk of infection and hemorrhage as well as shortening the duration of hospitalization and rehabilitation. However, given the reduced field for the surgery (because it is viewed through an endoscopic camera) as well as the absence of any tactile information during these interventions, specialized training is absolutely necessary. Fortunately, this surgical technique presents characteristics that made it easy to develop VR tools and simulations. As there is no direct manipulation of the organs, nor a direct visualization of the surgical site (see Figure 1.10), it is possible to develop devices that faithfully reproduce what the surgeon perceives in reality.

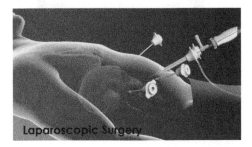 

Figure 1.10. *General principle of laparoscopic surgery: miniaturized instruments and a camera are introduced into the abdomen through small incisions. The surgeon then operates using a monitor that displays what the camera captures. For a color version of this figure, see www.iste.co.uk/arnaldi/virtual.zip*

These concepts also cover the fields of micro-surgery or vascular surgery. In the first case, the surgical site is most often visualized through a stereoscopic microscope and the instruments are sometimes similar to those used in laparoscopic surgery[4], but in a miniaturized form (see Figure 1.11).

3 Minimally invasive surgery consists of operating using miniaturized instruments, inserted through small incisions and manipulated with the help of imaging techniques.

4 Laparoscopic surgery is an example of minimally invasive surgery, used for abdominal surgery. The imaging device is a miniaturized camera (the laparoscope), which allows a visualization of the abdominal cavity.

As concerns vascular surgery, also called interventional radiology, the visualization of the anatomy is carried out through a system of X-ray images and the therapeutic action is carried out via flexible instruments (catheters and guides), navigating up to the concerned region through the arterial or venous system (see Figure 1.12). This technique allows vascular surgeons to carry out interventions on arteries (e.g. aorta, carotid, coronary) or to treat pathologies that can be directly accessed through the vascular network (e.g. cardiac valves, local chemotherapy for hepatic tumors).

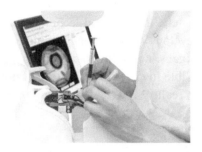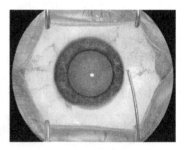

Figure 1.11. *Micro-surgery is also a field of application where simulations can be developed for learning. Here, we have the simulation of a cataract operation and its force-feedback system (© HelpMeSee)*

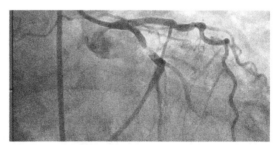

Figure 1.12. *Vascular surgery uses microsurgery which navigates the vascular network, until it reaches the pathology. The visualization of the intervention is carried out through a real-time X-ray imaging system called fluoroscopy*

Regardless of the field of application, a preliminary step consists of generating a 3D anatomical model. The interventions are most often specific to an organ and thus this model is limited to a few anatomical structures (e.g. liver, heart, eye), but may, sometimes, be wider, such as a model of the vascular system. This model may be constructed directly, using volumetric medical imaging (CT, MRI or other methods) or using 3D modeling tools. Current approaches tend to combine both these methods, first creating a model based on real data and then editing this to match the simulation constraints or to add anatomical or pathological variations.

Creating a precise 3D representation of anatomy, even only locally, still poses a challenge today. There are several reasons for this. First of all, surgery is essentially based on visual perception and surgeons are trained to interpret visual inconsistencies as indicators of possible problems or a pathology. Thus, in order to make the virtual representations as realistic as possible, each geometric detail or texture must be integrated and cannot be deleted to make the representation lighter, as is done in other fields (e.g. industrial design, architecture). Furthermore, this anatomical model, unlike other VR applications, cannot remain a simple geometric representation. It will be used as the basis for a physical model (e.g. mechanical, electrical), which also brings in its own set of constraints. We will return to this further down. Figure 1.13 illustrates one of these representations of anatomy, in this context being used for training in local anesthesia.

Figure 1.13. *Modeling anatomy, as well as creating geometric models adapted to different calculations, is the first key step in simulation for learning. It can provide different levels of detail. For a color version of this figure, see www.iste.co.uk/arnaldi/virtual.zip*

This technique consists of injecting the anesthetic directly into the nerves, thereby avoiding the need for general anesthesia. This model therefore needs to include different levels of representation, going from the skin and muscles up to nerves and arteries. A CT scan and an MRI were the basic images used to obtain these multiple levels. After processing the image and then carrying out 3D reconstruction, the different meshes were reworked so as to guarantee certain properties.

The characteristics that we wish to obtain in these meshes are related to the geometry and topology of the mesh. For example, it is important that the meshes be "smooth", as most anatomical structures have this property. It is also important to guarantee that the surfaces are closed when they define volumes. This will make it possible to manage contact between virtual objects (if there is a hole in the mesh, we can go through the object without detecting any collision) and we can also create volumetric meshes that can be used as supports in computing strains (see Figure 1.14).

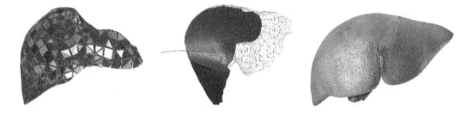

Figure 1.14. *Left: finite element mesh of the liver, made up of tetrahedra and hexahedra. Center: simulation of the interaction between a radiofrequency electrode and the liver, which requires computing strains and calculating the contacts between the instrument and the organ. Right: visual model of the liver, with realistic rendering using textures and different lighting models (shaders). For a color version of this figure, see www.iste.co.uk/arnaldi/virtual.zip*

Apart from a few specialized surgical fields, such as orthopedics, the anatomical structures that we are examining are considered deformable. To accurately integrate them in the context of learning, planning or surgical assistance involves modeling their biomechanical behavior. This modeling is most often based on the laws of physics, but with different degrees of approximation with respect to real behavior. Thanks to the development of new digital approaches, it is now possible to use behavioral models that are quite evolved while remaining compatible with real-time computation [COT 99, COM 08]. Many researchers prefer using the finite element method (FEM) to achieve this, given its numerical precision. This method requires the creation of a volumetric mesh (see Figure 1.14), composed of simple geometric elements on which the computations are carried out. As Figure 1.15 illustrates, the precision and rapidity of the computations are influenced by the type and number of these elements.

Figure 1.15. *Left: finite element mesh of the liver, composed of 1500 tetrahedra, with a computation time of 8 ms (i.e. 125 images/second). Center: finite element mesh of the liver composed of 4700 tetrahedra, with a computation time of 25 ms (i.e. 40 images/second). Right: finite element mesh of the liver composed of 21,600 tetrahedra, with a computation time of 140 ms (i.e. 7 images/second)*

Regardless of the chosen approach, what sets the field of surgery apart from all the other fields where VR is used is the deformable nature of the structures. This also explains why the term *simulation* is often substituted for "VR", as the real-time digital simulation of strains and the interactions with virtual instruments remain the predominant source of complexity. These interactions may be of widely varying natures depending on the organ, the pathology and the surgical technique. In the case of a "traditional" surgery, the instruments are mostly rigid and used to cut, cauterize and suture the organ. In other cases, such as vascular surgery, the instruments are flexible and will interact with the blood vessels, which are more rigid than the instrument. This results in different modeling techniques where the computation time will essentially be given to compute the strain on the instrument and not on the organ (see Figure 1.16).

1.2.3. *Augmented reality and intervention planning*

In some cases, surgical planning is absolutely essential to the success of the surgery. In the case of a hepatectomy[5], for example, this planning will

---

5 Hepatectomy is a surgical process whereby a part of the liver is removed as a treatment for hepatic tumors.

make it possible to maximize the volume of the liver remaining after the surgery, in order to increase the patient's chances of survival. In other cases, this planning will lead to a decrease in the duration of the intervention, thereby also reducing the period of hospitalization. In general, the patient first undergoes medical imaging exams (e.g. scan, MRI, X-ray) in order to obtain images of the anatomical region to be operated on. Today, these images are the basic information used to plan the intervention.

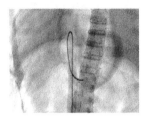  

Figure 1.16. *Examples of interactions between the virtual models of organs and the instruments. Left: simulation of the navigation of a catheter in vascular surgery. Center: simulation of an incision in laparoscopic surgery. Right: simulation of a suture in laparoscopic surgery. The interactions are complex in all three cases and in the first and the last examples, the interactions involve other deformable structures apart from the organ itself (© Mentice (left), 3D systems (LAP Mentor) (right))*

They are first studied by radiologists in order to establish a diagnosis and are then examined by a surgeon. However, in certain cases, it is difficult to judge the best strategy to use based solely on these images, or at least based on only viewing them in native form (see Figure 1.17). Hence, these images are most often processed using different software, allowing for an optimal visualization and better manipulation in 3D.

The most widely used method of visualizing these 3D medical images consists of using volumetric rendering techniques. This technique is widely available on workstations in radiology departments and is sufficient to yield a good 3D visualization of anatomical and pathological structures. However, some computations and manipulations are not possible using this technique. In many cases, we need to calculate the volume of tumors; or, using the example of the planning required for a hepatectomy, we need to calculate the liver volume remaining after the surgery as this is a critical factor in determining the success of the intervention. This is done by recognizing and marking out each anatomical and pathological structure in the medical image.

The 3D models obtained (e.g. arteries, veins, nerves, tumors) may then be visualized and manipulated individually, offering a solution that is better adapted to surgical use and planning. Today, a large number of software allow the surgeon to carry out these manipulations: Myrian (Intrasense, Montpellier France), MeVisLab (MeVis Medical Solution, Germany), ScoutLiver (Pathfinder Therapeutics, USA) or even VP Planning (Visible Patient, France). The virtual patient obtained using the software can then be used to facilitate or optimize the diagnosis or planning of the surgery.

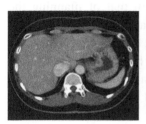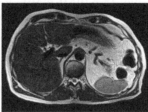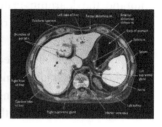

Figure 1.17. *Examples of medical images used for diagnosis or planning. Left: image taken from a CT scan. Center: image from an MRI scan. Right: labeled image indicating the different anatomical structures visible in the image*

Figure 1.18. *Planning of a hepatic surgery in virtual reality, using 3D reconstructions of the patient's anatomy. Here, the regions of the liver containing the tumor are clearly marked in order to estimate the liver volume, which will remain an essential criterion for post-operation survival (© IRCAD & Visible Patient). For a color version of this figure, see www.iste.co.uk/arnaldi/virtual.zip*

By visualizing and manipulating this virtual copy from all angles, the surgeon can refine the diagnosis and, above all, plan the surgical gestures to perform with a high degree of precision. At this point, we can define three levels of assistance that VR can offer surgeons. The first consists of providing software that makes it possible to simulate the operation in 3D, but without seeking to have a real-time interaction with or manipulation of the realistic virtual model. This is primarily a desktop tool that enables certain calculations or geometric and topological operations to be carried out on the virtual model(s). The second scenario goes further along the path of "virtualizing" the operation, as it can provide an opportunity to rehearse the key part of the operation, after having planned it, in real conditions. Here, we combine the learning principle described above with that of planning the surgery. This service is offered by different companies that specialize in simulation for learning purposes (e.g. Mentice, Simbionix or CAE Healthcare) and is also used by research teams [CHE 13, REI 06]. Finally, the last level of assistance consists of transposing the result of this planning into the operation theater, using complex algorithms that allow the *preoperative* planning to be adapted to the *intraoperative* context.

In all of the above scenarios, scientists focused mainly on improving the quality of simulation and planning, the objective being to make these processes capable of using more data. With the development of new modalities of imaging and sensor systems, it is possible to measure an ever-increasing quantity of information. This diversity allows the surgeon to take more informed decisions and carry out planning that is better adapted to the patient. However, in order to do this, it is essential that these different sources of information and different kinds of data be combined, so that the user can make better sense of them.

For example, by combining the mechanical characteristics of the patient's heart (such as its elasticity) with its electrical activity, the doctor is able to determine the strategy that is best adapted to that patient [TAL 13]. The concept of personalized medicine is thus strongly linked to intervention planning (see Figure 1.19). This evolution takes place through the fusion of data from diverse sources (e.g. MRI, scan, ultrasound), through the development of new sensor systems, and through the creation of more powerful algorithms. For example, a personalized model of the heart, which combined biomechanical and electrophysiological aspects, was developed within the European project, euHeart [TAL 16]. Similarly, in neurosurgery, the combination of preoperative images, 3D modeling and simulation techniques made it possible to offer enhanced tools for the planning of an intervention to carry out deep brain stimulation [BIL 14, BIL 11]. In this surgical procedure, an electrode must be inserted into a zone measuring $8 \times 2 \times 2$ mm^3, located in the center of the brain. Without precise planning, and if the movements of the brain during the operation are not taken into account, locating this structure becomes very complicated and highly time-consuming, not to mention the impact this may have on the patient.

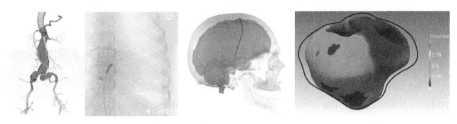

Figure 1.19. *Examples of the simulations associated with surgical planning. Left: patient-specific simulation of a vascular surgery. Center: simulating the insertion of an electrode in a deformable model of the brain to plan a deep brain stimulation. Right: combining a biomechanical model and an electrophysiological model of the heart, configured using data recorded from a patient. For a color version of this figure, see www.iste.co.uk/arnaldi/virtual.zip*

Finally, the specifications and constraints associated with the use of VR in planning surgeries are very different from those defined earlier for learning. Interactivity and real-time processing are no longer mandatory, unless we wish to combine the planning and interactive simulation. However, the precision of the digital simulation remains an essential factor. While a generic and plausible deformable model is sufficient when learning, when the tool is being used for planning, we must go much further with the modeling. As the constraint related to computing time is less demanding, it is possible to use finer meshes for finite element calculation, thereby making it possible to gain in precision. We must also ensure that the physical model that describes the phenomenon is able to correctly represent this phenomenon. We expect the simulation to be predictive. A large body of experimental work is first required to model the phenomenon (e.g. strain, physiology, diffusion of heat) correctly and then to use new data to confirm whether the simulation's predictions are as close to reality as possible [CHA 15]. Obtaining this data is a delicate task and requires the definition of complex experimental protocols and access to specialized equipment. This work, however, remains essential in order to provide surgeons with a tool they can rely on.

The final step, after planning, is the actual surgical intervention. Here, VR gives way to AR in order to combine the information collected during the operation with models developed in the planning stage. Many challenges must be resolved before arriving at this stage in order to guarantee precision, interactivity and robustness in an environment that is less controlled than that of a research laboratory.

1.2.4. *Augmented reality in surgery*

The striking developments in medical imaging over the past 20 years have, today, resulted in the emergence of hybrid surgeries. These are surgeries where imaging systems, usually restricted only to diagnosis, are also used in the operation theater. Surgeons are thus faced with the task of mentally integrating this information (2D or 3D images) into the surgical field. In addition, apart from the rare cases, where the surgeon has access to a hybrid operation theater (see Figure 1.20), interventional imaging resources remain limited (in availability and technical capabilities). The images acquired in an operation theater are thus less precise and less usable than those taken before the intervention using a CT or MRI scan, for example. However, most often, the only device accessible in operation theaters remains the surgeon's laparoscopic camera which only allows them to view the surface of the organs.

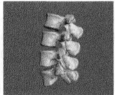

Figure 1.20. *Augmented reality in the operation theater. Left: hybrid operation theatre integrating different imaging systems that allow the visualization of the patient's internal anatomy during an operation. Center: 3D reconstruction of the vertebra before a vertebral column surgery. Right: view in AR facilitating the positioning of a vertebral screw (© Philips)*

To help the surgeon overcome these difficulties, AR aims to display the 3D model of the patient's anatomy by overlaying the real video-operative images. The surgeon's real view is enriched and informed by the virtual information.

The patient thus becomes virtually transparent to the surgeon's view, allowing them to visualize structures within the organs (e.g. vessels, tumors), which they would otherwise be able to perceive only through the sense of touch. An example of AR application in rigid structures is a surgery of the vertebral column. This surgery is a difficult and high-risk procedure as vital parts of the anatomy of the vertebral column and the neurovascular structures are not visible to the surgeon. In order to overcome this, a hospital in Stockholm, in collaboration with Philips, developed an AR technique that combined an external high-resolution view of the patient's surface with a 3D internal view of their anatomy (see Figure 1.20). While, in this case, the complexity of the system is limited, as there are no deformable structures to take into account, this real-time 3D view enables the surgeon to improve the planning of the procedure, the precision of placement of the implant and the treatment time [ELM 16].

Although commercial AR applications for medicine are still very limited, much research is being carried out in this field [FIS 07, HAO 13, LEI 14]. However, they often hypothesize advanced imaging techniques or dedicated markers, in order to facilitate tracking the movement of an organ or instruments. In addition, in order to simplify the algorithmic problems and computation times, it is also often assumed that the anatomy is not deformed (or this deformation is negligible) between the preoperative acquisition and the time of the surgery. Though this hypothesis is acceptable for certain anatomical structures, such as bones, this is not the case for the majority of organs, which are made up of soft tissue. One of the first studies on the use of AR in laparoscopy was proposed by Fuchs et al. [FUC 98]. This project focused on the extraction of information on depth from the laparoscopic images, in order to improve AR visualization during the surgery. In the context of visualization again, Suthau et al. [SUT 02] described the general principles that still prevail in applications for augmented surgery. In 2004, Wesarg et al. [WES 04] described an AR system for minimally invasive interventions in which only rigid transformations, between pre- and intra-operative images are considered. In the same year, Marescaux et al. [MAR 04] reported the first AR-assisted laparoscopic adrenalectomy, based on a manual alignment of the virtual model and the surgery images (alignment carried out from a control room located outside the operation theater). Similar results have been obtained from other surgical fields, such as vascular surgery [ANX 13]. However, just as with the earlier results, deformations in anatomy have been ignored or assumed to be negligible. The earliest AR approaches on deformable organs were carried out using markers or navigation systems placed at proximity to the operating field [TEB 09]. These methods have demonstrated that automatic AR systems in surgery are feasible, but generally impose some restrictions on the equipment in the operating room or require manual interaction. (see Figure 1.21).

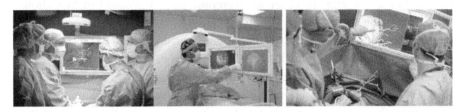

Figure 1.21. *Example for the use of a navigation system in surgery. We can see the cameras used to track the movement of the instruments and the markers situated on the instruments and/or on the organ to facilitate the repositioning of the virtual view, depending on the surgical view. This approach does not manage deformations in the organ nor the visual overlapping of the virtual model and the real image (© CAScination)*

Two terms co-exist in the field of surgical assistance when we examine the fusion of pre- and intra-operative data: if the image is in 2D, whether this is acquisition through X-rays or an image from a laparoscopic camera, the positioning of the virtual object on the real object is often called *pose estimation*. The pose estimation aims to determine the characteristics of the imaging equipment (typically a camera), so as to define a virtual camera having the same characteristics, thereby guaranteeing the optimal overlay of real and virtual images. This alignment is called *calibration* when the interventional image is volumetric, or sometimes just through a misuse of language. This process consists of finding similarities between images, or between an image and a model, so as to define a set of common points between the data. When the calibration is rigid, only a few points are needed. When the calibration is deformable, a much larger number of points must be determined, which is usually more complex to compute. In this case, the deformable model plays a determinant role because, if it describes the physical properties of the organ well, it offers the possibility of precisely extrapolating movement beyond these points, even though they are small in number. As the stereoscopic camera in surgery becomes more widely accessible, Haouchine *et al.* [HAO 15] use them via a method that uses a pre-calibrated stereo-endoscope. Points of interest are marked on the surface of the liver on the pair of stereo images, and these points are then temporally tracked using an optical flux method. This makes it possible to define a characteristic set of points based on their "signature" in the image, which can be identified in each pair of stereoscopic images. By matching the closest neighbor between the points of interest, we can then reconstruct a 3D point cloud by triangulation, which is then smoothed out using the Moving Least Squares method, so as to obtain the least noisy reconstruction of the organ surface (see Figure 1.22).

Figure 1.22. *3D reconstruction of the surface of the liver, using a stereo-endoscopic image. Left: left image with extraction of points of interest (in green). Center: partial 3D reconstruction of the liver based on these points of interest. Right: right image with extraction of points of interest (in green). For a color version of this figure, see www.iste.co.uk/arnaldi/virtual.zip*

It is, of course, possible to use other methods to identify the characteristic points in intraoperative data, with each approach often being linked to a specific imaging modality. Thus, when the interventional images are X-ray images, we can use very small radio-opaque markers so as to obtain visible points both in the pre-operative image and in the intra-operative image. These markers are percutaneously inserted (using a needle) into the organ before the pre-operative scan. By matching the markers visible at the time of the intervention with those extracted from the preoperative image, it is possible to define a transformation between the two sets of points. When we examine a deformable anatomical region, such as the brain or the liver, this transformation is complex but may be assumed to be locally rigid, in a zone around a tumor, for example (see Figure 1.23). The CyberKnife® system makes use of this hypothesis to locate the position of a tumor in 3D using the position of a set of markers placed on the periphery. These markers are captured by two X-ray cameras installed in the wall of the operating room and the 3D position of the tumor is then used to guide a robotic arm onto which a compact linear accelerator is installed. Thanks to the estimate of the position of the tumor, this accelerator focuses a beam of gamma rays onto the tumor, with great precision, minimizing the impact on the healthy tissue around it [KIL 10].

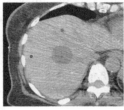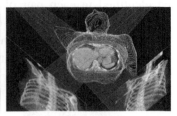

Figure 1.23. *Use of radio-opaque markers to match the pre-operative and intra-operative data. Left: CyberKnife system for radiotherapy. Center: pre-operative image showing the tumor and the markers placed on the periphery. Right: double X-ray beam to identify the 3D position of the markers during the intervention (© Accuray Incorporated)*

In the majority of situations, however, it is difficult to place markers or extract points of interest in an image in immediate proximity to the tumor. As the organs are deformable, in these cases, it is essential that the *calibration* method takes into account the nature of these deformations. Biomechanical models have proven the most appropriate choice for this, as they make it possible to define the organ's elastic properties and, using this, deduce the movements of structures deep within [SUW 11]. The calibration is carried out either by resolving mechanical equations, considering the tracked points as external constraints [SUW 11], or by making use of the concept of active model. The latter is done by minimizing an energy that takes into account the internal behavior of the model and external constraints that measure the degree of the match between the model and the image indices [SHE 11]. A method using a heterogeneous biomechanical model was proposed in Plantefeve *et al.* [PLA 15], the aim of which was to enhance the quality of the AR while also guaranteeing real-time performances. The virtual liver is described by a model composed of parenchyma and vascular network, so as to best represent the anatomical reality while modeling the heterogeneity and anisotropy of the deformations. This model is computed using the finite elements method and can take into account nonlinear, real-time elastic deformations. Peterlik *et al.* [PET 12] demonstrated the precision and high computing speed of this model. This volumetric model is therefore capable of propagating within the volume the 3D deformations observed on the surface using a stereo-endoscopic camera; virtual models of tumors or blood vessels may then be re-projected, in real-time, onto the image of the organ (see Figure 1.24). This solution is intuitive, as it does not require any specific equipment, nor any large modification of the operating procedure. The research results were validated using a silicone liver, and then using real data from patients. They showed that the margin of error between the estimated and real positions of the tumor were lower than current margins of error in surgery. There is, nonetheless, a long way to go before these techniques are entirely validated for routine use in the operation theater.

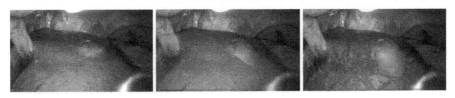

Figure 1.24. *Different steps in a hepatic surgery, clearly showing the amplitude of deformations of the liver. We can see that despite the significant deformation, the virtual model remains correctly positioned on the laparoscopic image. The images from top to bottom show the different anatomical structures that are easy to visualize or hide, depending on the surgeon's requirements. For a color version of this figure, see www.iste.co.uk/arnaldi/virtual.zip*

1.2.5. *Current conditions and future prospects*

AR has made significant progress in the field of surgery over the last five years, and AR applications are slowly emerging from experimental protocols to be integrated into real-life uses. With reduced surgical risk and shorter hospitalization periods, these new surgical techniques that use VR, digital simulation and interventional imagining, promise to be the future of surgical procedures. However, in order to achieve this, research and development must be pursued, especially with respect to the robustness of algorithms and also the predictive capacity of simulations. There are still only a few practitioners who are working on this topic in France. In spite of this, over 150 operations using AR were carried out there between 2014 and 2017, making France one of the leading actors in this field. Nonetheless, this remains an emerging technology, which still requires more validation and experimentation, as well as true complementarity of competencies from the development of the algorithms up to the surgery itself.

This (r)evolution in surgery and interventional medicine, in the broad sense, resembles the transformation wrought 20 years ago by the arrival of computer programs dedicated to the processing of medical images. Through information processing, numerical computations, visualization and easy manipulation of complex concepts, AR and VR have widened the field of possibilities, which in turn has led to the development of connected technologies or made it easier to use these technologies. While it is still difficult to state precisely what direction these evolutions will take, we see two fields emerging today: robotics and 3D printing. A central element in robotics is the control loop, which consists of a set of algorithms that process data in real-time in order to give the right commands to the robot. This control is often based on the analysis of images from one or more cameras. We then speak of a visual Master–Slave setup. This becomes very complex when the robot has to interact with soft tissue, for instance, during the insertion of a needle in a tumor. A direct link is then established between the AR and robotics systems, with the surgeon being able to define the optimal positioning for the needle via a planning phase. Thanks to a real-time simulation, the surgeon can then control the robotized needle through the AR. Hence, 3D printing has sparked off much interest among surgeons – it allows them to create objects that can easily be manipulated in 3D and are faithful to the patient's anatomy. The projection of the virtual model onto the physical model of the organ will soon offer surgeons new possibilities of tangible interfaces. [FRE 14].

Regardless of the case, as its name indicates, the purpose of assisted surgery is to help the surgeon carry out the operation and make decisions, but it can never replace them. The surgeon must remain the main decision-maker and actor.

1.3. Sustainable cities

What are the VR-AR applications that have made an impact in the last decade on the urban landscape, and what applications are likely to emerge over the coming years?

The objective of this section is to provide some answers to this (vast) question. We have chosen to do this by focusing on three main axes:

– traveling and, more specifically, mobility aids in an urban setting;

– buildings and, more broadly, architecture;

– the city and, more broadly, urbanism.

1.3.1. *Mobility aids in an urban environment*

The omnipresence of outdoor navigation tools, associated with an increasingly precise map of the world is, by now, well established. We can also see that precise urban cartography is no longer exclusively the domain of the technical services of a city's administration; the considerable developments in this field over the past 10 years are the result of work by industrial giants (e.g. Google, Apple, Microsoft, Tom Tom, Mappy, Here; see Figures 1.25, 1.26 and 1.27).

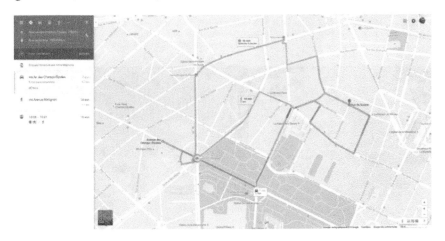

Figure 1.25. *Google Maps: 2D map (© Google Maps)*

2D and 3D visualizations are present in more and more applications meant for general use (e.g. Google Maps), which can guide the user to a location by marking a route that the user may not have known about before. These applications often offer us additional information, for example, pointing out the geographical location of points of interest (e.g. food, culture, business) along the route or close to our destination. The user may not always be interested in these points of interest, but they often show up because the advertising can finance part of the development of these tools.

Figure 1.26. *Google Maps: 3D view (© Google Maps)*

Figure 1.27. *Google Maps: Streetview (© Google Maps)*

Given the difficulty of reading maps that are too often abstract (many people have difficulty reading a 2D map), AR was soon seen as a good answer to this issue of facilitating mobility [KIM 06, KRE 10]. It enables the user to visualize a path that is superimposed onto an image of their real, observed environment on a smartphone or a tablet (see Figure 1.28).

Figure 1.28. *AR application from Here indicating the route to follow (© Here)*

Moreover, AR has made it possible to overcome the main constraints of a good navigation assistance tool, namely making it easy to read the map and identify locations without endangering the user (pedestrian, cyclist or motorist) by giving them too many difficult cognitive tasks such that they pay less attention to possible risks in their environment.

Thus, maps on a mobile terminal have rapidly developed over the past 10 years [SCH 07]. The increasingly realistic 3D visualization of information, coupled with GPS capabilities of locating the user and orienting the view of the map based on their direction of travel, were key factors in this strong growth.

While we wait for the advent of driverless cars, there is an alternative to using these mobile terminals in vehicles: visualizing these images overlaid on the windscreen, so that our eyes are always on the road. Indeed, looking away from the road to focus on the navigation device distracts the user and consequently increases the reaction time if we need to react unexpectedly. We thus talk about "Head-Up Display" (HUD). These have long been in use in aviation (first military and now civil aviation) to visualize information in the cockpit. These systems were developed many years ago by automobile manufacturers and outfitters; the only reason they are currently restricted to a few vehicles, usually high-end vehicles, is because of the marketing strategies used. It is clear that these devices will become more generalized in the coming years [YOO 15].

However, one challenge remains to be addressed before these AR applications can be widely adopted: that of anticipation while driving. In effect, in GPS tools for cars, changes along the route (turning at an intersection, for example) are announced and visualized in advance. This allows the driver to prepare themselves, by replacing their current point of view with what they will see a few dozen meters ahead. In AR applications, where visualization is centered on the user's current position, it is not possible, at the moment, to anticipate this change in point of view. This situation is not problematic for pedestrians as they are travelling at low speeds that enable them to react in real time, unlike users in automobiles, travelling at much higher speeds and where anticipation is absolutely essential. Another illustration of this vision centered on the user's position: is it more effective to view nearby shops in AR (see Figure 1.29), or on a map, in order to correctly gauge the relative spatial distribution?

This problem can be addressed using existing 3D databases to alternate between user-centered vision and a more general perspective (aerial?), which facilitates anticipation and the viewing of nearby information.

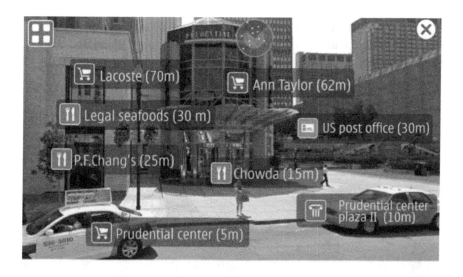

Figure 1.29. *An AR view showing Points of Interest (© Nokia Live)*

Another challenge is the management of masking, due to the unique two-dimensional character of the images, which are displayed with no depth information whatsoever. Consequently, it is sometimes very difficult to determine whether an element is situated in front of or behind a building, for example. In an urban context, where there is a high density of buildings, this difficulty in accurately perceiving the environment hampers the greater development of AR applications. As depth-capture tools are available, the question then arises as to which method must be used to visualize this information in a way that will be optimal for the user.

1.3.2. *Building and architecture*

When it comes to sustainable urban systems, we are more specifically interested in devices that make it possible to study, present and co-construct the city. As the city is composed of buildings, among other structures, there is an obvious link between the city and architecture.

Synthetic images used in architecture have evolved considerably over the last decade (see Figures 1.30 and 1.31), most notably due to the progress made in visualization algorithms, as well as modeling software, both professional and for general use. However, it is the insertion of elements from daily life which have seen the most spectacular progress over the last five years. Given the number of characters and decorative elements, even the image of the building tends to disappear behind the narrative of the life around it.

Figure 1.30. *Old synthetic image (© Archivideo)*

Figure 1.31. *Modern-day synthetic image (© Kreaction)*

Figure 1.32. *Virtual reality outdoors (© Rennes Métropole)*

Figure 1.33. *Augmented reality associated
with a ground-plan (© Artikel)*

The use of AR for architecture still remains rather anecdotal today and is often limited to overlaying a 3D representation of a building onto a ground plan. Beyond the initial excitement experienced, we may legitimately wonder what real benefits this type of representation can offer with respect to the "classic" visualization of a 3D model of the building, which offers internal navigation. Moreover, the use of AR outdoors [ART 12] poses the same problems as the use of mobile navigation tools, but even more acutely, as concerns geo-positioning and mask management.

VR, on the other hand, has offered architecture a host of tools to play around with almost from its first appearance on the scene. Many architects dream of "Walking around" in a future building [CHI 13], which in reality may still only be at the blueprint stage. Already sensitive to multisensory perception (sight, sound, touch), professionals in the field of architecture are an ideal audience for VR. It must be noted, however, that even though there are frequent references to the use of this type of application, they are often only anecdotal. Other than the financial barrier, which may be removed by reducing the large cost of the VR equipment (headsets and large-screen immersive systems), the main obstacle to development is more cultural than anything else! The fact is many architects believe that it is difficult for a client to understand an object that is yet to be completely finalized; they thus use VR only for the final presentation of the project, focusing on a high degree of realism. This restricts the use of VR to a communication tool reserved for large projects. At the same time, some architects or "high-end" promoters are reluctant to use this as the headset cuts off visual contact with the client, which is essential in a sales pitch. One solution to this may be to introduce the architect in the VR application in the form of an avatar.

This situation is now evolving, thanks to the increased use of collaborative work at different stages of construction design, as well as in the creation of models that are more and more refined and easily updatable. These innovations, jointly called BIM (Building Information Modeling) [SUC 09], are key elements in the use of VR in architecture. More specifically, BIM was presented by Eastman *et al.* [EAS 08] as a new approach to design, construction and the management of installations, in which a digital representation of the construction process is used to facilitate the exchange and interoperability of information.

It is interesting to analyze the use of 3D, and potentially VR, among interior design vendors (e.g. bathrooms, kitchens; see Figure 1.34). This profession has quite rapidly progressed from 2D diagrams to interactive 3D representations. The reason for this is quite simple: a sale is facilitated when all of the members of the family that will invest in this equipment commit to the idea. The limitations in the use of the 2D plan were quickly revealed. However, the immersive visualization makes it possible to heighten the client's acquisitive impulse. It is therefore not surprising that these professions are among the leading users of VR, thanks especially to the new low cost equipment which has recently appeared.

Figure 1.34. *Ixina Kitchen (© Ixina - Dassault Systèmes)*

1.3.3. *Cities and urbanism*

Contrary to the widespread idea, nurtured even by certain professionals, the technological approaches adopted for urbanism are not the same as those used in architecture. While a city is made up of buildings, their digital models (and thus, the modeling methods used to construct them) are very different. Today, it is easy for someone who has one of these software on a standard computer to create a realistic model of a building and to obtain an interactive visualization; they may therefore imagine that they can do this with many buildings, to construct an island, then a neighborhood and then a city. Unfortunately, this is a false belief. First of all, there is the question of complexity: the difference in scale is not a "reasonable" one for an urban environment made up of dozens, hundreds or even thousands of buildings. Second, the impact of the increase in the size of the digital data is not linear -

there are thresholds (especially those related to the volume of available and effectively usable memory on a computer) that limit the use of certain software solutions. Finally, and most importantly, a city is not made up only of buildings but also has other objects of different and complex natures and may even be invisible (e.g. roadways, signage, networks that may be underground). Furthermore, the scale of reading the city may vary a lot: from a macroscopic view to analyze road traffic problems or study urban strategies (city planning), to a view centered on a single building, similar to that used in architecture (urban design).

All of these factors explain why complete modeling (see Figure 1.35) is not yet widespread and why we often restrict ourselves to taking into account only the neighborhood around a specific project.

Figure 1.35. *Image in an immersive room (© IRISA)*

Even though the digital urban data sometimes has a third dimension (height), the old-fashioned software used to model and visualize the city are constructed using a planar approach (2D), which limits their use to approaches that can more appropriately be called 2.5D. This is due not only to technical simplifications (e.g. optimization of the display on the ground, the use of planar projection), but also to the established culture of using a 2D map.

Despite the fact that this technique has existed for a long time, orthophotography has only really become popular in the last few years thanks to applications such as GéoPortail, Google Maps and Google Earth. These applications are based on the display of aerial photographs whose geometry has been modified so that they can be associated with geo-referenced earth tiles that pave the surface of the region. For a 3D representation of the city, this visualization (called "oblique aerial imagery") is by far the most widely used, as it allows the user to easily perceive the environment, or the program in the case of a project [KAA 05] (see Figure 1.36). This perception makes use of a decoding process that is based largely on the imagination: we have all seen (in the cinema or on television) similar visual sequences, even though we have never been in an aeroplane.

Figure 1.36. *Data base from aerial data (© Rennes Métropole)*

If we want to have a truly immersive view of an urban environment, we have to adopt a different modeling method. In effect, all users have had experience as pedestrians, where vertical elements (buildings, sidewalks, signposts, vegetation) play quite an important role in the processes of perception and positioning of oneself.

The reconstruction of a city in this way, for an immersive visual experience (see Figure 1.37), is still far from being completely automatic. In fact, the people who build these virtual cities dedicate a great deal of time to ensuring that there is coherence between elements that cannot be automatically processed using existing data, generally taken from Geographic Information Systems (GIS) and used mainly by local administration (e.g. land registration, networks). Obtaining flat roads, integrating bridges, or even worse, interchanges, erasing traces such as the impression of trees along the routes or on the buildings (resulting from the orthophotography or from images taken by a mobile scanner): all these and more pose so many obstacles that they cannot all be processed without eventual human intervention, which is quite demanding and not at all easy. The result of this processing is that the production of cities for visual immersive experiences is still quite financially heavy and the return on investment is hard to estimate.

Figure 1.37. *A virtual Paris, Archivideo (© Archivideo)*

This latter observation may seem inconsistent with recent evolutions in the urban databases produced by Google or Apple using massive correlation algorithms (see Figure 1.38). We must remember that these applications, which produce visual results with an excellent degree of realism, use orthophotography primarily and not 3D databases. If the user exits the aerial view and wishes to "come down", visual aberrations soon start appearing. Hence, these applications forbid trajectories that are "too low". In order to remove these restrictions on navigation, Google Streetview uses a database of photos that are not taken from an aerial view, but from the ground in specific photographic missions (using vehicles equipped with cameras and GPS systems) to offer an exhaustive coverage of all the streets in a city. This application then proposes a 360° view, from a specific point in a street, of all the surrounding buildings. The view is captured so as to be at eye-level for an average pedestrian on that spot.

Figure 1.38. *Google Maps (© Google Maps)*

We must, however, specify that these views do not really qualify as VR. They are, in fact, based on photographs taken from precise points and thus cannot respond to a user's desire to move around freely (to go into a garden, for example). Thus, they cannot be re-oriented or extend to suit a user's desire to move freely. The difference can be explained quite simply by recalling that VR is based on the real-time computation of synthetic images from any point of view and in any direction, thanks to a 3D model which gives the user total liberty, as opposed to applications based on photos.

Finally, let us specify that this distinction is by no means a value judgment: each approach has its own advantages and disadvantages. These are often complementary, depending on the desired objectives and available means.

1.3.4. *Towards sustainable urban systems*

Let us return to the heart of the question we posed at the beginning of this chapter. Going beyond purely technical considerations and the barriers that must be removed, what are the functions that we would wish to develop for VR-AR in the coming decade in the case of what are called sustainable cities? We can state three distinct uses:

– The first use is directly related to the communication tools used for the project. Even though this observation is not very old, it is now commonly admitted that 3D visualizations are more effective than a map and, above all, that they are more useful in a presentation. Urban specialists today often wish to communicate their projects to a population that has little or no technical expertise, such as elected officials or citizens. The challenge here is to put across the project clearly and avoid errors in interpreting the information. VR-AR can then be brought in from the user's point of view. Given its limited aspect, the representation can easily shift from the user's point of view (what they perceive) to the project details (how the project works).

– The second use is a consequence of the opening up of technical services within communities. This is done to avoid the effects of working "in silos", where each expert addresses their own problem without engaging with the collateral effects on other projects. Collaborative work around a common and enriched model of the city is starting to take shape for designing, realizing and maintaining the city more efficiently. The pooling of technical knowledge can be made easier by the use of shared immersive viewing in VR during a project review (as we have already seen happening in other sectors – e.g. manufacturing industries, sciences). As for AR, it is likely to see considerable evolution for use in the maintenance of public spaces.

– The third use is related to the first and arises from the fact that some municipal administrations wish to co-construct the city with their citizens by giving them the option of participating in the definition and development of projects. They are asked, "What kind of city would you like to see, in terms of renovation, layout and transport?". Successfully adopting this procedure requires that certain questions be addressed. Those in the "upstream" phase are how to present the problem, and the possible scenarios. In the "downstream" phase they are how to list and summarize citizen suggestions. It is clear that VR provides part of the answer, as it allows a heterogeneous group to visualize an urban environment at the same time and in the same place; it then allows the visual simulation of the object in question (e.g. adding a new building, modifying a transport line) so as to facilitate a collective debate on the issue.

We hope that the arrival of low-cost VR technology, in association with generalized applications that allow the handling of urban data, will usher in a new era of dialogue between the city and its citizens. The example of experiments such as RennesCraft (see Figures 1.39 and 1.40) or the layout of the eco-friendly neighborhood, Niel, in Bordeaux can be viewed as being emblematic of this process.

Figure 1.39. *RennesCraft (© Rennes Métropole - Hit Combo)*

Figure 1.40. *RennesCraft (© Rennes Métropole - Hit Combo)*

1.4. Innovative, integrative and adaptive societies

It must be stated that the impact that VR-AR have had on society is far from negligible. Section 1.3 focused on sustainable cities: by definition, these include a social component. The rest of this chapter is dedicated to two specific fields of application where VR-AR can participate in evolution in our societies: first of all, through education and then through arts and culture. These domains have already been discussed in [FUC 05], but uses have developed considerably since then and we think it is important to revisit these topics.

1.4.1. *Education*

1.4.1.1. *Context and history*

There are many advantages to using VR in a teaching (professional and academic) or training context, which are described in detail in [BUR 06, LOU 12]. To name a few: the removal of risk to humans; the use of material that is rare or difficult to access, as well as cumbersome and/or costly; an ability to recreate situations that may be complex; a reduction in costs; availability of equipment; and, finally, being able to control the learning environment/situation. Group learning using VR can make it possible to overcome the problem of having collaborators available, thanks to virtual humans. It is also possible to bring in remote participants or moderate the behavior of fictional coworkers. VR also makes it possible to very realistically reproduce elements of real life [BUR 06, LOU 12]. The simulated system is assumed to react like the real system it represents, so as to give the learner an understanding of certain aspects of the experience, which they will then be able to draw on in real-life situations. At the same time, these situations are much more flexible than real situations (e.g. the ability to modify the situation, the simulation of rare conditions, controlling specific parameters, the reusability and adaptability of scenarios, reversibility of actions, ability to monitor learners).

Often used for training in situations that are very close to the real situation, virtual environments do not always offer pedagogic control. When functionalities for control and monitoring are available, it is possible to personalize the content for each learner by offering them the most relevant situation (progression along the learning path, remediation of errors, reflexive approach, etc.). In order to control and adapt situations according to the learner's needs, the following points can be considered:

– Diagnosing erroneous concepts and dynamic learner profiling: the general idea is to be able to detect erroneous behavior and then to try and associate this behavior with errors in knowledge or the wrong application of this knowledge. This type of approach is often implemented by smart trainers [BUC 10]. Two types of approaches can be used to diagnose errors: the generative approach and the evaluative approach. The generative approach consists of generating the solution to the given problem as well as certain typical errors and then comparing this with the solution given by the student. These steps are not always sufficient to determine the type of intervention to be carried out, and their ability to explain behavior remains rather limited. The evaluative approach is based on what is called the "constraint-oriented" approach, where the trainer verifies how far the learner respects certain conditions. This type of approach is well adapted to diagnostic tasks but is less useful for procedural tasks where respecting an order is primordial. [LUE 09] proposes alternative methods of diagnosis, based on an epistemological model of knowledge of the subject, which examines actions and the reasons behind these actions (in themselves, and not relative to an expected solution). The error is considered a symptom of the knowledge.

– Assistance: assistance or feedback may be offered to allow the learner to adopt reflexive learning (i.e. allow them to reflect on the task and their learning). We can make use of certain functionalities that VR offers (slowing down the scene, speeding it up, changing the point of view, looking through obstacles, visualizing processes that are not accessible to our senses, asking for sensory reinforcement or substitution, concretizing abstract concepts). We can define two kinds of assistance based on whether they occur within or externally to the situation: intra-diegetic and extra-diegetic [CAR 15].

– Controlling the scenarios: this has to do with deciding on and orchestrating the situations and narrative that will allow the student to learn better (verification of acquired skills, reinforcement of skills and development of new skills). Controlling the learning process often means that there is no adaptability. Freedom of action is not compatible with control and trying to marry control and adaptability can risk bringing in incoherence, and so on [BAR 14]. We talk of the narrative paradox when discussing the fundamental opposition between interactivity and narration: giving the player a greater capacity for action will interfere with the script prepared by the author.

Variability in scenarios is sometimes achieved only at the cost of a great deal of design work, where all possible deviations must be explicitly, manually described. The effort needed to bring in coherent and precisely controlled scenarios is called an authoring bottleneck [SPI 09]. This highlights the necessity of putting in place scriptwriting systems that make it possible to create easily adaptable environments. However, it is quite frequently the case that systems stop applying an overlayer of control on a simulation composed of independent entities, and that interventions by these systems will disrupt the coherence of the environment by modifying the simulation states on the fly. There are two ways of overcoming this problem: scenario-oriented approaches (which steer the virtual environment at the global level) and independent virtual-character-oriented approaches, which bring in scenarios based on the behavior of the user and the virtual characters. The scenario-oriented approaches emphasize the overall quality of the scenario (a complete overview of this is given in [CAR 15]). The complete description of all possible scenarios in the simulation must be defined. There is thus complete and centralized control over the simulation. The level of guidance may, however, vary from completely guided, to total freedom for the user. These narrative models are mainly based on specific representations of the 3D environment which make it possible to enrich the geometry of objects through higher level information: informed environments (smart-objects or objects-relations models). In the other, character-oriented approaches, the narrative is built out of the interactions between the user and the virtual characters that populate the environment. Control is distributed and each character is responsible for their own decision-making. These approaches are focused on the creation of cognitive virtual characters (a comprehensive introduction to this can be found in [BAR 14]).

In reality, a very fine line exists between these two approaches, and several parameters must be taken into account, such as the production of scenarios in a static manner (scripted approach), or a dynamic manner (generative approach), or even whether the control is centralized or distributed. Finally, most approaches use a hybrid of these two orientations to address the above-mentioned problems. Examples of these are Thespian [SI 10] and Crystal Island [ROW 09].

1.4.1.2. *Scenario models: two examples*

In this section, we describe two platforms that use a hybrid approach to control scenarios: the character-oriented HUMANS and the collaborative, virtual-environment-oriented #(FIVE,SEVEN) with a pre-defined scenario model.

Figure 1.41. *HUMANS: character-centered approach (© EMISSIVE)*

1) The HUMANS (Human models based artificial environments software platform) approach, a character-centered approach, is a system used to create varied situations; it is highly dynamic, subject to random and sometimes critical errors, whereby there are situations with no ideal solutions. HUMANS has set of objectives that often seem contradictory: freedom of action for the learner, allowing them to learn through errors; a dynamic nature and effective control over the scenario to guarantee learning; consistency in the behaviors presented in order to make the system self-explanatory; and, finally, the adaptability of the system in order ensure the variability of the scenarios. The virtual characters are independent in order to allow the system to be adaptable. They have emotions, diverse personalities and social relationships. They have "human" behaviors and can compromise, transgress safety regulations, commit errors, disrupt or facilitate teamwork, etc. [HUG 16, CAL 16]. In order to control the learning situations and preserve the coherence of the world, a scenario-generating system must indirectly orient the unfolding of events by occasionally modifying conditions governing the virtual world or the virtual characters, without giving them orders [BAR 14].

A scenario-generator uses the learner's activity traces to diagnose their dynamic profile [CAR 15]. This profile operationalizes the zone of proximal development (ZPD), described by [VYG 78]. A vector space of the class of situations is associated with the values of belief in the ability of the learner to manage the situations that they describe. The engine selects the objectives of each scenario in the form of scenario spaces in the ZPD. Based on the learner's results, the engine selects situations in the proximal zone or extends this zone. Moreover, it determines the objectives in the form of desirability values in specific situations and general restrictions on the properties of the scenario (e.g. complexity, criticality). By using the models underlying the simulation, the scenario-generator predicts the evolution of the simulation using a planning engine [BAR 14]. It calculates a scenario based on these predictions and a set of possible modifications. Three types of changes can be used to ensure coherence: triggering exogenous events that have no relation to the coherence of the system, late commitments (this principle makes it possible to progressively specify, during the simulation, states that were left uncertain at the initialization) and co-occurrence constraints (forcing stochastic behaviors). If the actual scenario deviates from the planned scenario, the engine plans a new scenario. HUMANS has been deployed in a variety of training applications: risk-prevention, aeronautics, rescuing injured persons, etc.

2) The #(FIVE,SEVEN) approach proposes a reactive, collaborative environment with a pre-defined scenario model (Figure 1.42). A VR application is defined with the help of several components, among which is a model of an informed environment and a model of scenarios. STORM [MOL 07], a generic objects-relations type model, was proposed. Later on, a new generation of a reactive, collaborative informed environment, #FIVE (Framework for Interactive Virtual Environments) [BOU 15], was proposed. This model makes it possible to describe and rationalize objects, which may participate in an action (and actions may use objects) using requests. In parallel to this, LORA [MOL 06], a single-user, scenario specification language, based on parallel hierarchical finite state machines, has been proposed. In this, actions are represented via the STORM model. This was extended to collaborative scenarios using LORA++ [GER 07]. However, the interaction with the environment beyond the action of the actors is not immediate and the environmental model is fixed.

Figure 1.42. *#(FIVE,SEVEN): Approach centered on using predefined scenarios (© IRISA)*

The scenario model #SEVEN (Scenarios Engine for Virtual Environment) [CLA 14a, CLA 15b] was developed to address these limitations. It represents the complex temporal layouts possible for the technical and procedural events of the simulation. It is based on the Petri network and is enriched by sensor-effectors that connect it to the environment. It is compact, expressive, independent of the field of application, collaborative with multi-user management (real or virtual users) and implements a model that uses dynamic roles [CLA 15a]. #SEVEN was also designed for use by industry experts who are not software engineers and has an offline editor and online events generator. Productivity is essential for designing a VR application. #FIVE makes it possible to independently define objects and interactions in the informed environment, which may be done in the form of activities. #SEVEN describes the set of possible solutions in a compact manner with an author tool for editing and is independent of informed environment models. We have, however, proposed a coupling between these two models.

When we want users to be interchangeable (i.e. the users may be virtual humans or real humans) [GER 08], these models must abstract and trivialize the collaborative interaction with the objects for the actors (virtual and real). The Shell concept [LOP 13] was introduced: an abstract entity connecting an actor (real or virtual) to the virtual world, in order to allow the actors to exchange roles via a protocol [LOP 14], while also guaranteeing the continuity of actions and the gathering of knowledge.

These models and concepts are used in varied domains: industrial, medical and cinema. [BOU 16]. They are under study for use in the area of cultural heritage.

1.4.2. *Arts and cultural heritage*

Art and cultural heritage are particularly apt areas for the development of innovative methodologies related to interaction and immersion. VR and AR make it possible to combine advanced technologies based on images, sound and multimodal interactions to plunge the user into artistic or cultural experiences that enhance user experience (UX). 3D printing further opens up the field of possibilities by offering supports for visualization and interaction that were hitherto unknown. The user can thus become an active part of a work of art or experience learning through an immersive scientific mediation. The user can also be a historian or archaeologist interacting with a physical and/or virtual representation of the object they are studying, which can allow them to collect new information from it.

1.4.2.1. *Performing arts: dance*

For computer engineers, it is possible to "use" dance and dancers in case studies and for experimental environments. The artists' creativity leads them to formulate needs, which then orient research in VR and AR and help advance these technologies. Where the dancers are concerned, this science is in itself a world to be explored through their art. The questions the computer scientists ask, so as to model the context of the interaction, lead the dancer-choreographer to revisit the fundamentals of dance. Finally, developing these technologies offers the dancers new artistic tools with which they can explore virtual worlds.

AR provides an ideal framework with which to negotiate this joint research, as can be seen in the brief discussion below, starting with the work that laid the foundations of this domain.

One of the precursors to this, which began in 1998, is Hand-Drawn Spaces, a performance created by the famous innovator and choreographer Merce Cunningham, in collaboration with Paul Kaiser and Shelley Eshkar from the company Unreal Pictures. This performance, presented during the international conference SIGGRAPH' 98 [KAI 98], was a landmark moment in dance and motion capture: there is a virtual landscape with three screens and hand-drawn figures; dancers appear in the form of full-scale designs. 2002 saw the première of the Jew of Malta at the Munich Opera Festival in Germany [SAU 02]. This performance, which was located within the AR paradigm, was a co-production between Büro Staubach of the Opera Biennale

Munich and the ART+COM studio: it combined architecture and costumes generated in real time, depending on the music and the singer's position on the stage.

Experiments of this kind were seen in France from 2006 onwards, starting with the Lyon contemporary arts Biennale, which associated dance and technology. 2013 saw "M. et Mme Rêve", a performance that was emblematic of the marriage of engineering and the Arts, produced by "le Théâtre du corps Pietragalla-Derouault" in association with the company Dassault Systèmes. This was a performance where dance and 3D technology met on stage to transport the spectator into a unique, 3D virtual reality experiment. In 2009, the concept of an "augmented dance show" was demonstrated for the first time, combining ballet and AR. Then there was the "festival les Ethiopiques" in Bayonne, which in 2009 and 2010 offered enhanced improvised performances that combined dance, music, readings and a virtual world [DOM 09, CLA 10a]. In 2010 again, there was the festival "Le Temps d'aimer la Danse" (A Time to Love Dance), which laid an emphasis on performances that allied digital art and dance, like Gaël Domenger's creation "Un coup de dés jamais n'abolira le hasard" (Dice Thrown will Never Annul Chance), a tribute to Mallarmé and his typographic poem.

In these creations, the objective is to allow the artist to create a virtual world on the stage, a world in which they can evolve and create their art, making their process of creation and its result visible to the audience. In effect, earlier performances were limited to the projection of virtual content onto the stage. What was needed was being able to generate and animate 3D images using the hands and the body, within a vast space, while also allowing other people (here, the audience) to participate in these transformations. One of the major challenges that has been addressed in these performances is allowing the creation and animation of virtual objects projected in real time [COU 10, CLA 10b, CLA 12] (Figure 1.43). The dancer controls the virtual world by not only manipulating pre-defined virtual elements, but also creating them by using their hands to generate the visual material. The dancer thus becomes a sculptor and their gestures and movements become frozen in time; the sculpture creates a work of art, but the movements that lead to that creation are sublimated into a choreography [CLA 14c, CLA 14b].

From 2016 onwards, the Kinect position sensor from Microsoft has been widely used in the creation of dance performances, as it allows a basic visualization (pixelated), which is very well adapted to artistic rendering (see [KEN 16, FIS 16]). The living performance is enriched by VR: for example, "TREEHUGGER, a virtual reality experience" [MAR 16] or even "l'Arbre Intégral" [GAE 16] (Figure 1.44), and many other artistic experiments created using "augmented performances" [SIT 17].

Figure 1.43. *3D-augmented Ballet, Biarritz, 2010 [CLA 12] (© Frédéric Nery)*

Figure 1.44. *L'arbre Intégral (The Integral Tree) (2016) [GAE 16]*

In conclusion, as demonstrated by the works mentioned above, art and engineering are no long separate; the division between them has become porous, and they mutually enrich each other. This is a trend that is most certainly going to continue, both in France and other countries. In the United States, for example, this will be through the school of thought called "from

STEM to STEAM" (STEM for Science, Technology, Engineering and Math; STEAM for STEM + Art). This combination is also a reality in the case of the worlds of computer science and cultural heritage.

1.4.2.2. *Cultural heritage: archeology*

Both VR and AR offer new perspectives in the field of cultural heritage and, more specifically, in the field of archeology.

1.4.2.2.1. Cultural heritage and virtual reality

VR can quite naturally be used as a support with which to implement tools and working methods for archeologists [FUC 06] (pp. 229–233). Introduced a long time ago, notably by Robert Vergnieux, interactive simulation makes it possible to reproduce and validate gestures and to establish the physical coherence and technical feasibility of reconstructions [VER 11]. Since then, Pujol Tost *et al.* [PUJ 07] have argued that archeology must take into account interaction and perception as well as VR simulation, rather than focusing only on the visualization of 3D models. The importance of perception is notably illustrated by Le Cloirec [LEC 11] through the use of 3D reconstitutions in immersive structures in order to evaluate the functional or symbolic roles of the architectural elements and spaces being studied. A scale-1 functional and interactive reconstitution of an environment, such as a ship (Figure 1.45), allows the historian or archeologist to become the actor in the simulation [BAR 15].

Figure 1.45. *An interactive reconstitution of The Boullongne, a 17th-Century ship (© Inria)*

The unique features of archeology often pose particular problems for VR. First of all, we must recall that the reconstitutions of sites are based on the observations of fragments and on hypotheses proposed by experts. If we wish to ensure that these models are credible in any way, it is absolutely essential to take into account this uncertainty surrounding the hypothesis, both for the reconstitution process and for the final restitution, working closely with the archeological expert [APO 16]. This consideration is often ignored in the 3D reconstitution of antique monuments that have been destroyed (temples, habitations). These reconstitutions are widely diffused (over television or the web) and offer highly realistic renderings, close to those in video games, for example. As human perception is highly sensitive to visual details, it is nearly impossible for a non-expert user to distinguish between reality and details imagined up by the authors of these images. In other words, there is an ethical responsibility involved that is often forgotten in these applications.

Furthermore, archeological sites, by definition, are ancient and therefore have evolved over time (sometimes significantly). Here again, a dynamic and interactive representation of the changes is required. This is so that they can be better studied by the archeologists, on the one hand [LAY 08], and non-expert users can understand them, on the other hand.

Both these characteristics (uncertainty and change) are unique to archeology and are not found in other fields where VR is used, such as an industrial setup, where the objects studied are "stable". Hence, researchers must invent specific modes of representations that are adapted to this particular context.

The interaction with archeological objects also poses certain unique problems when compared with the objects that are usually encountered in other domains where VR is applied. The artifacts that archeologists study are often closer to nature than manufactured objects encountered in industry, for example, which implies a greater complexity in the geometries to be manipulated [BRU 10, PAC 07]. Additionally, these artifacts may be inaccessible without a destructive analysis. The 3D printing of reproductions enables a tangible interaction with the object (Figure 1.46), while preserving the actual archeological artifacts [NIC 15].

Let us also specify that the proprioception and motor skills of a user in VR allow them to reproduce and better understand certain technical gestures from the past that have disappeared today [DUN 13]. Finally, archeologists are also able to preserve a visual trace of their reflections by adding annotations to the digital model [KLE 08].

Figure 1.46. *Interaction with a tangible object: the gallic weight (© IRISA)*

1.4.2.2.2. Cultural heritage, augmented virtuality and spatial augmented reality

Augmented virtuality (AV) consists of including real physical information in a virtual world. By construction, VA is the paradigm of Tangible Interfaces. In effect, the task is situated in the virtual world and the user acts on digital information by manipulating physical objects that represent either the digital information or a control on the digital information or both. An interactor is the abstraction of an entity that is capable of both input and output in an interactive system. Consequently, the interactor is a mixed object that possesses both physical and digital properties and the computer system connects these properties. An example of AV in archeology is ArcheoTUI [REU 10], which is based on the concept of bi-manual interaction and allows efficient interaction for the manipulation and assembly of archeological fragments, which have been digitized into 3D beforehand (a bit like a 3D puzzle). Automatic matching techniques are also possible [HUA 06], but their performances are still limited. It would therefore be interesting to be able to offer archeologists a system that makes it possible to combine purely manual assembling with automatic assembling, as in the work carried out by [MEL 10] as part of the ANR SeARCH project, motivated by a clearly defined archeological project: the partial reconstruction of the lighthouse at Alexandria and the statues around it.

Spatial Augmented Reality (SAR) is based on projective displays. It uses projectors that make it possible to directly display virtual elements onto real objects. They offer a strong potential for introducing new techniques for interaction. This is because the co-localization of the space of perception and the space of interaction in the real world make it possible not to upset our spontaneous habits of interaction. For example, direct interaction using our hands. An example of SAR in archeology is the development of a "magic" virtual torch, a revealing flashlight [RID 14]: this is an interactor with six degrees of freedom, meant to enhance the visual analysis of a real object by the overlaying of digital information using projection. This interactor, a tangible surface as per Fisckin's classification [FIS 04], refers to a flashlight with three metaphors: the zone to be inspected is determined by the position/orientation, the angle of inspection (characterized by the direction) and the intensity of the visualization (determined by the distance). Thanks to the object being digitized in 3D form beforehand and a multi-level geometric analysis of the surface, the real object is augmented with expressive visualization that reveals details on the object that are sometimes invisible to the naked eye, such as curves of different scales, and along different angles. This interactor has notably been used on an Egyptian stele (headstone), the inscription on which was almost completely lost, and the interactor made it possible to improve the legibility without losing the link between the real object and abstract information.

1.4.3. Conclusion

By shedding light on these technologies, which are often ignored, a larger field of application for training is likely to emerge in VR-AR, as these allow the learner to actively participate in the learning (changing their point of view through gesture interaction, etc.), adding significantly to the learning process.

The research in the field of interactive storytelling and in ITS (Intelligent Tutoring System) today overlap with the work carried out in VR and, in the coming year, it will enrich content and models. Taking into account certain psychological characteristics, such as emotion or interest, and motivation of the learners, will enable personalized adaptations of the most relevant content.

There are also multi-disciplinary research projects, which must be carried out to demonstrate the pedagogic effectiveness and ecological acceptability (in the situation) of these virtual environments for human learning [LOU 16b].

For Spatial AR in large spaces (e.g. augmented ballets), we must also take into account the question of the spectator's point of view. How do we construct a virtual image, so that it is equally meaningful from different points of view? Does this not imply that we must construct different images depending on these points of view? One path forward is to work on the differences in perception and use this to orient the procedure to follow, combining art and science to respond to this problem.

Finally, VR also offers a real opportunity to create new practices and tools for professions related to cultural heritage and to thus promote access to new knowledge. It can also be used as a first-order support to help in the conservation of heritage; as a vector for adding value and sharing reconstitutions and 3D digitization of sites in danger (whether due to natural wear and tear, urbanization or their geographical location exposing them to seismic risks, wars or the consequences of global warming). As concerns AR, creating a better targeted learning experience is a real challenge and one that many promising research projects are working on. [LOU 16a, CIE 11, LEC 16].

1.5. Bibliography

[ANX 13] ANXIONNAT R., BERGER M.-O., KERRIEN E., "Time to go augmented in vascular interventional neuroradiology?", in LINTE C., CHEN E., BERGER M.-O. *et al.* (eds), *Augmented Environments for Computer-Assisted Interventions*, vol. 7815, Lecture Notes in Computer Sciences, pp. 3–8, Springer, 2013.

[APO 16] APOLLONIO F.I., *Classification Schemes for Visualization of Uncertainty in Digital Hypothetical Reconstruction, in 3D Research Challenges in Cultural Heritage II*, vol. 10025, Lecture Notes in Computer Science, 2016.

[ARN 03] ARNALDI B., FUCHS P., JACQUES T., *Le Traité de la Réalité Virtuelle*, Les Presses de l'Ecole des mines, 2nd edition, 2003.

[ART 12] ARTH C., MULLONI A., SCHMALSTIEG D., "Exploiting sensors on mobile phones to improve wide-area localization", *Proceedings of the 21st International Conference on Pattern Recognition (ICPR2012)*, pp. 2152–2156, November 2012.

[ART 15] ARTH C., PIRCHHEIM C., VENTURA J. *et al.*, "Instant outdoor localization and SLAM initialization from 2.5D Maps", *IEEE Transactions on Visualization and Computer Graphics*, vol. 21, no. 11, 2015.

[BAR 14] BAROT C., Scénarisation d'environnement virtuel. Vers un équilibre entre contrôle, cohérence et adaptabilité, PhD thesis, University of Technology of Compiègne, Compiègne, 2014.

[BAR 15] BARREAU J.-B., NOUVIALE F., GAUGNE R. *et al.*, "An Immersive Virtual Sailing on the 18th-Century Ship Le Boullongne", *Presence: Teleoperators and Virtual Environments*, vol. 24, no. 3, Massachusetts Institute of Technology Press (MIT Press), 2015.

[BEN 12] BENKO H., JOTA R., WILSON A., "Miragetable: freehand interaction on a projected augmented reality tabletop", *Proceedings of the SIGCHI Conference on Human Factors in Computing Systems*, pp. 199–208, ACM, New York, 2012.

[BER 66] BERGER P., LUCKMANN T., *The social construction of reality: a treatise in the sociology of knowledge*, Anchor Books, 1966.

[BIL 11] BILGER A., DEQUIDT J., DURIEZ C. *et al.*, "Biomechanical simulation of electrode migration for deep brain stimulation", in FICHTINGER G., MARTEL A., PETERS T. (eds), *14th International Conference on Medical Image Computing and Computer-Assisted Intervention - MICCAI 2011*, vol. 6891/2011, pp. 339–346, Toronto, Springer, September 2011.

[BIL 14] BILGER A., BARDINET E., FERNÁNDEZ-VIDAL S. *et al.*, "Intra-operative registration for deep brain stimulation procedures based on a full physics head model", *MICCAI 2014 Workshop on Deep Brain Stimulation Methodological Challenges - 2nd edition*, Boston, September 2014.

[BOU 15] BOUVILLE R., GOURANTON V., BOGGINI T. *et al.*, "#FIVE: high-level components for developing collaborative and interactive virtual environments", *Proceedings of Eighth Workshop on Software Engineering and Architectures for Realtime Interactive Systems (SEARIS 2015), conjunction with IEEE Virtual Reality (VR)*, Arles, March 2015.

[BOU 16] BOUVILLE R., GOURANTON V., ARNALDI B., "Virtual reality rehearsals for acting with visual effects", *International Conference on Computer Graphics & Interactive Techniques*, pp. 1–8, GI, Victoria, 2016.

[BRU 10] BRUNO F., BRUNO S., SENSI G.D. *et al.*, "From 3D reconstruction to virtual reality: A complete methodology for digital archaeological exhibition", *Journal of Cultural Heritage*, vol. 1, no. 11, pp. 42–49, 2010.

[BUC 10] BUCHE C., BOSSARD C., QUERREC R. *et al.*, "PEGASE: A generic and adaptable intelligent system for virtual reality learning environments", *International Journal of Virtual Reality*, vol. 9, no. 2, pp. 73–85, IPI Press, September 2010.

[BUR 06] BURKHARDT J.-M., LOURDEAUX D., MELLET-D'HUART D., "La réalité virtuelle pour l'apprentissage humain", in MOREAU G., ARNALDI B., GUITTON P. (eds), *Le Traité de la réalité virtuelle*, vol. 4, 2006.

[CAL 16] CALLEBERT L., LOURDEAUX D., BARTHÈS J.A., "A trust-based decision-making approach applied to agents in collaborative environments", *Proceedings of the 8th International Conference on Agents and Artificial Intelligence (ICAART 2016)*, vol. 1, pp. 287–295, Rome, February 24–26, 2016.

[CAR 15] CARPENTIER K., Scénarisation personnalisée dynamique dans les environnements virtuels pour la formation, PhD thesis, University of Technology of Compiègne, Compiègne, 2015.

[CHA 15] CHANTEREAU P., Biomechanical and histological characterization and modeling of the ageing and damaging mechanism of the pelvic floor, Thesis, Lille 2 University of Health and Law, 2015.

[CHE 13] CHEN Y.W., KAIBORI M., SHINDO T. et al., "Computer-aided liver surgical planning system using CT volumes", *35th Annual International Conference of the IEEE Engineering in Medicine and Biology Society (EMBC)*, pp. 2360–2363, July 2013.

[CHI 13] CHI H.-L., KANG S.-C., WANG X., "Research trends and opportunities of augmented reality applications in architecture, engineering, and construction", *Automation in Construction*, vol. 33, pp. 116–122, 2013.

[CIE 11] CIEUTAT J.-M., HUGUES O., GHOUAIEL N. et al., "Une pédagogie active basée sur l'utilisation de la Réalité Augmentée Observations et expérimentations scientifiques et technologiques, Apprentissages technologiques", *Journées de l'Association Française de Réalité Virtuelle, Augmentée et Mixte et d'Interaction 3D*, 2011.

[CLA 10a] CLAY A., DOMENGER G., DELORD E. et al., Improvisation dansée augmentée: capture d'émotions, Les Ethiopiques' 10, Bayonne, 2010.

[CLA 10b] CLAY A., DELORD E., COUTURE N. et al., "Augmenting a ballet dance show using the dancer's emotion: conducting Joint research in dance and computer science", *Arts and Technology*, vol. 30, Lecture Notes of the Institute for Computer Sciences, Social Informatics and Telecommunications Engineering, pp. 148–156, Springer Berlin Heidelberg, 2010.

[CLA 12] CLAY A., COUTURE N., NIGAY L. et al., "Interactions and systems for augmenting a live dance performance", *Proceedings of the 11th IEEE International Symposium on Mixes and Augmented Reality (ISMAR)*, pp. 29–38, IEEE Computer Society, Atlanta, November 2012.

[CLA 14a] CLAUDE G., GOURANTON V., BOUVILLE BERTHELOT R. et al., "Short paper: #SEVEN, a sensor effector based scenarios model for driving collaborative virtual environment", in NOJIMA T., REINERS D., STAADT O. (eds), *ICAT-EGVE, International Conference on Artificial Reality and Telexistence, Eurographics Symposium on Virtual Environments*, Bremen, Germany, December 2014.

[CLA 14b] CLAY A., DOMENGER G., CONAN J. et al., "Integrating augmented reality to enhance expression, interaction & collaboration in live performances: a ballet dance case study", *IEEE International Symposium on Mixed and Augmented Reality (ISMAR-2014)*, pp. 21–29, Munich, Germany, September 2014.

[CLA 14c] CLAY A., LOMBARDO J.-C., COUTURE N. et al., "Bi-manual 3D painting: an interaction paradigm for augmented reality live performance", in CIPOLLA-FICARRA F. (ed.), *Advanced Research and Trends in New Technologies, Software, Human-Computer Interaction, and Communicability*, Hershey, Information Science Reference, 2014.

[CLA 15a] CLAUDE G., GOURANTON V., ARNALDI B., "Roles in collaborative virtual environments for training", in IMURA M., FIGUEROA P., MOHLER B. (eds), *Proceedings of International Conference on Artificial Reality and Telexistence Eurographics Symposium on Virtual Environments*, Kyoto, Japan, 2015.

[CLA 15b] CLAUDE G., GOURANTON V., ARNALDI B., "Versatile scenario guidance for collaborative virtual environments", *Proceedings of 10th International Conference on Computer Graphics Theory and Applications (GRAPP'15)*, Berlin, Germany, March 2015.

[COM 08] COMAS O., TAYLOR Z.A., ALLARD J. *et al.*, "Efficient nonlinear FEM for soft tissue modelling and its GPU implementation within the open source framework SOFA", *Procceding of the International Symposium on Biomedical Simulation*, pp. 28–39, Springer Berlin Heidelberg, 2008.

[COT 99] COTIN S., DELINGETTE H., AYACHE N., "Real-time elastic deformations of soft tissues for surgery simulation", *IEEE Transactions on Visualization and Computer Graphics*, vol. 5, no. 1, pp. 62–73, 1999.

[COU 10] COUTURE N., Interaction Tangible, de l'incarnation physique des données vers l'interaction avec tout le corps., HDR, University of Bordeaux, 2010.

[CRU 92] CRUZ-NEIRA C., SANDIN D.J., DEFANTI T.A. *et al.*, "The CAVE: audio visual experience automatic virtual environment", *Communication ACM*, vol. 35, no. 6, pp. 64–72, June 1992.

[DOM 09] DOMENGER G., REUMAUX A., CLAY A. *et al.*, Un Compte Numérique, Les Ethiopiques'09, Bayonne, 2009.

[DUN 13] DUNN S., WOOLFORD K., "*Reconfiguring experimental archaeology using 3D movement reconstruction*", pp. 277–291, Springer, London, 2013.

[EAS 08] EASTMAN C., TEICHOLZ P., SACKS R. *et al.*, *BIM Handbook: A Guide to Building Information Modeling for Owners, Managers, Designers, Engineers and Contractors*, Wiley Publishing, 2008.

[ELM 16] ELMI-TERANDER A., SKULASON H., SODERMAN M. *et al.*, "Surgical navigation technology based on augmented reality and integrated 3D intraoperative imaging: a spine cadaveric feasibility and accuracy study", *Spine*, vol. 41, no. 21, pp. 1303–1311, 2016.

[ENG 14] ENGEL J., SCHÖPS T., CREMERS D., "LSD-SLAM: Large-Scale Direct Monocular SLAM", *European Conference on Computer Vision*, 2014.

[FIS 04] FISHKIN K., "A taxonomy for and analysis of tangible interfaces", *Personal and Ubiquitous Computing*, vol. 8, no. 5, pp. 347–358, 2004.

[FIS 07] FISCHER J., EICHLERA M., BARTZA D. *et al.*, "A hybrid tracking method for surgical augmented reality", *Computer and Graphics*, vol. 31, no. 1, pp. 39–52, 2007.

[FIS 16] FISCHER A., GRIMM S., BERNASCONI V. *et al.*, "Nautilus: real-time interaction between dancers and augmented reality with pixel-cloud avatars", *28ième conférence francophone sur l'Interaction Homme-Machine*, pp. 50–57, alt.IHM, Fribourg, Switzerland, October 2016.

[FLE 15] FLECK S., HACHET M., BASTIEN J.M.C., "Marker-based augmented reality: instructional-design to improve children interactions with astronomical concepts", *Proceedings of the 14th International Conference on Interaction Design and Children*, pp. 21–28, ACM, New York, USA, 2015.

[FOL 13] FOLLMER S., LEITHINGER D., OLWAL A. *et al.*, "inFORM: dynamic physical affordances and constraints through shape and object actuation", *Proceedings of the 26th Annual ACM Symposium on User Interface Software and Technology*, pp. 417–426, ACM, New York, USA, 2013.

[FRE 14] FREY J., GERVAIS R., FLECK S. *et al.*, "Teegi: tangible EEG interface", *Proceedings of the 27th Annual ACM Symposium on User Interface Software and Technology*, pp. 301–308, ACM, New York, USA, 2014.

[FUC 98] FUCHS H., LIVINGSTON M.A., RASKAR R. *et al.*, "Augmented reality visualization for laparoscopic surgery", *Proceedings of the First International Conference on Medical Image Computing and Computer-Assisted Intervention*, pp. 934–943, 1998.

[FUC 05] FUCHS P., MOREAU G. (eds), *Le Traité de la Réalité Virtuelle*, Les Presses de l'Ecole des mines, Paris, 3rd edition, March 2005.

[FUC 06] FUCHS P., MOREAU G., ARNALDI B., *Le traité de la réalité virtuelle Volume 4 - Les applications de la réalité virtuelle*, Mathématique et informatique, Les Presses de l'Ecole des Mines, March 2006.

[FUC 09] FUCHS P., MOREAU G., DONIKIAN S., *Le traité de la réalité virtuelle Volume 5 - Les humains virtuels*, 3rd edition, Mathématique et informatique, Les Presses de l'Ecole des Mines, 2009.

[GAE 16] GAEL D., L'Arbre intégral, http://malandainballet.com/actualites/article/larbre-integral, 2016.

[GER 07] GERBAUD S., MOLLET N., ARNALDI B., "Virtual environments for training: from individual learning to collaboration with humanoids", Edutainment, Hong Kong SAR China, June 2007.

[GER 08] GERBAUD S., MOLLET N., GANIER F. *et al.*, "GVT: a platform to create virtual environments for procedural training", *IEEE Virtual Reality*, pp. 225–232, Reno, USA, March 2008.

[GER 16] GERVAIS R., ROO J.S., HACHET M., "Tangible viewports: getting out of flatland in desktop environments", *Proceedings of the TEI'16: Tenth International Conference on Tangible, Embedded, and Embodied Interaction*, pp. 176-184, ACM, New York, USA, 2016.

[HAO 13] HAOUCHINE N., DEQUIDT J., PETERLIK I. *et al.*, "Image-guided simulation of heterogeneous tissue deformation for augmented reality during hepatic surgery", *2013 IEEE International Symposium on Mixed and Augmented Reality (ISMAR)*, pp. 199–208, October 2013.

[HAO 15] HAOUCHINE N., COTIN S., PETERLIK I. *et al.*, "Impact of soft tissue heterogeneity on augmented reality for liver surgery", *IEEE Transactions on Visualization and Computer Graphics*, vol. 21, no. 5, pp. 584–597, 2015.

[HAR 11] HARRISON C., BENKO H., WILSON A.D., "OmniTouch: wearable multitouch interaction everywhere", *Proceedings of the 24th Annual ACM Symposium on User Interface Software and Technology*, pp. 441–450, ACM, New York, USA, 2011.

[HEE 92] HEETER C., "Being there: the subjective experience of presence", *Presence: Teleoperators and Virtual Environments*, vol. 1, no. 2, pp. 262–271, 1992.

[HEN 08] HENDERSON S.J., FEINER S., "Opportunistic controls: leveraging natural affordances as tangible user interfaces for augmented reality", *Proceedings of the 2008 ACM Symposium on Virtual Reality Software and Technology*, pp. 211–218, ACM, New York, USA, 2008.

[HIL 12] HILLIGES O., KIM D., IZADI S. *et al.*, "HoloDesk: direct 3D interactions with a situated see-through display", *Proceedings of the SIGCHI Conference on Human Factors in Computing Systems*, pp. 2421–2430, ACM, New York, USA, 2012.

[HUA 06] HUANG Q.-X., FLÖRY S., GELFAND N. *et al.*, "Reassembling fractured objects by geometric matching", *ACM Transaction Graphic*, vol. 25, no. 3, pp. 569–578, ACM, 2006.

[HUG 16] HUGUET L., SABOURET N., LOURDEAUX D., "Simuler des erreurs de communication au sein d'une équipe d'agents virtuels en situation de crise", *Rencontres des Jeunes Chercheurs en Intelligence Artificielle (RFIA 2016)*, Clermont-Ferrand, France, June 2016.

[INA 03] INAMI M., KAWAKAMI N., TACHI S., "Optical camouflage using retro-reflective projection technology", *Proceedings of 2003 IEEE / ACM International Symposium on Mixed and Augmented Reality (ISMAR)*, pp. 348–349, 2003.

[ISH 12] ISHII H., LAKATOS D., BONANNI L. *et al.*, "Radical atoms: beyond tangible bits, toward transformable materials", *Interactions*, vol. 19, no. 1, pp. 38–51, ACM, January 2012.

[JAN 15] JANKOWSKI J., HACHET M., "Advances in interaction with 3D environments", *Computer Graphics Forum*, vol. 34, pp. 152–190, Wiley, 2015.

[JON 13] JONES B.R., BENKO H., OFEK E. *et al.*, "IllumiRoom: peripheral projected illusions for interactive experiences", *Proceedings of the SIGCHI Conference on Human Factors in Computing Systems*, pp. 869–878, ACM, New York, USA, 2013.

[JON 14] JONES B., SODHI R., MURDOCK M. *et al.*, "RoomAlive: magical experiences enabled by scalable, adaptive projector-camera units", *Proceedings of the 27th Annual ACM Symposium on User Interface Software and Technology*, pp. 637–644, ACM, New York, USA, 2014.

[KAA 05] KAARTINEN H., GÜLCH E., VOSSELMAN G. *et al.*, "Accuracy of the 3D city model: EuroSDR comparison", in *The International Archives of the Photogrammetry, Remote Sensing and Spatial Information Sciences*, pp. 227–232, 2005.

[KAI 98] KAISER P., "Hand-Drawn Spaces", *SIGGRAPH'98*, ACM, p. 134, 1998.

[KAN 87] KANT E., *Kritik der reinen Vernunft*, J. F. Hartknoch, 1787.

[KEN 16] KEN JYUN WU, https://vimeo.com/189359517, 2016.

[KIL 10] KILBY W., DOOLEY J.R., KUDUVALLI G. *et al.*, "The cyberKnife robotic radiosurgery system in 2010", *SAGE Technology in Cancer Research & Treatment*, vol. 9, no. 5, pp. 433–452, 2010.

[KIM 06] KIM S., KIM H., EOM S. *et al.*, "A reliable new 2-stage distributed interactive TGS system based on GIS database and augmented reality", *IEICE Transactions*, vol. 89-D, no. 1, pp. 98–105, 2006.

[KLE 08] KLEINERMANN F., DE TROYER O., CREELLE C. *et al.*, "Adding semantic annotations, navigation paths and tour guides to existing virtual environments", *Proceedings of the 13th International Conference on Virtual Systems and Multimedia*, Springer-Verlag, pp. 100–111, 2008.

[KRE 10] VAN KREVELEN D.W.F., POELMAN R., "A survey of augmented reality technologies, applications and limitations", *International Journal of Virtual Reality*, vol. 9, no. 2, pp. 1–20, June 2010.

[LAV 17] LAVIOLA J.J., KRUIJFF E., MCMAHAN R. *et al.*, *3D user interfaces: theory and practice*, 2nd edition, Addison Wesley, 2017.

[LAY 08] LAYCOCK R.G., DRINKWATER D., DAY A.M., "Exploring cultural heritage sites through space and time", *Journal Computer Culturage Heritage*, vol. 1, no. 2, November 2008.

[LEC 11] LE CLOIREC G., "Bais, Le bourg St Père, proposition de restitution des volumes", in POUILLE D., La villa gallo-romaine du bourg St Père Bais (35), DFS de fouille archéologique préventive, Inrap, Rennes, 2011.

[LEC 16] LE CHENECHAL M., Awareness Model for Asymmetric Remote Collaboration in Mixed Reality, Thesis, INSA de Rennes, 2016.

[LEI 14] LEIZEA I., ALVAREZ H., AGUINAGA I. *et al.*, "Real-time deformation, registration and tracking of solids based on physical simulation", *2014 IEEE International Symposium on Mixed and Augmented Reality (ISMAR)*, 2014.

[LOM 97] LOMBARD M., DITTON T., "At the heart of It all: the concept of presence", *Journal of Computer-Mediated Communication*, vol. 3, no. 2, Blackwell Publishing Ltd, 1997.

[LOP 13] LOPEZ T., NOUVIALE F., GOURANTON V. *et al.*, "The ghost in the shell paradigm for virtual agents and users in collaborative virtual environments for training", *VRIC 2013*, p. 29, Laval, France, March 2013.

[LOP 14] LOPEZ T., BOUVILLE BERTHELOT R., LOUP-ESCANDE E. *et al.*, "Exchange of avatars: toward a better perception and understanding", *IEEE Transactions on Visualization and Computer Graphics*, pp. 1–10, March 2014.

[LOU 12] LOURDEAUX D., "Réalité virtuelle et formation", *Techniques de l'ingénieur*, 2012.

[LOU 16a] LOUP G., SERNA A., IKSAL S. *et al.*, "Immersion and persistence: improving learners' engagement in authentic learning situations", *European Conference on Technology Enhanced Learning*, pp. 410–415, Springer, 2016.

[LOU 16b] LOUP-ESCANDE E., JAMET E., RAGOT M. *et al.*, "Effects of stereoscopic display on learning and user experience in an educational virtual environment", *International Journal of Human–Computer Interaction*, pp. 1–8, Taylor & Francis, 2016.

[LUE 09] LUENGO V., Les rétroactions épistémiques dans les Environnements Informatiques pour l'Apprentissage Humain, HDR, Université Joseph Fourier - Grenoble I, 2009.

[MAR 03] MARSH T., *Staying there: an activity-based approach to narrative design and evaluation as an antidote to virtual corpsing*, Ios Press, Amsterdam, 2003.

[MAR 04] MARESCAUX J., "Augmented reality assisted laparoscopic adrenalectomy", *Journal of American Medical Association*, vol. 292, no. 18, pp. 2214–2215, 2004.

[MAR 14a] MARNER M.R., SMITH R.T., WALSH J.A. *et al.*, "Spatial user interfaces for large-scale projector-based augmented reality", *IEEE Computer Graphics and Applications*, vol. 34, no. 6, pp. 74–82, 2014.

[MAR 14b] MARZO A., BOSSAVIT B., HACHET M., "Combining multi-touch input and device movement for 3D manipulations in mobile augmented reality environments", *ACM Symposium on Spatial User Interaction*, Honolulu, United States, October 2014.

[MAR 16] MARSHMALLOW LASER FEAST, http://www.treehuggervr.com, 2016.

[MEL 10] MELLADO N., REUTER P., SCHLICK C., "Semi-automatic geometry-driven reassembly of fractured archeological objects", *Proceedings of the 11th International Conference on Virtual Reality, Archaeology and Cultural Heritage*, pp. 33–38, Eurographics Association, Aire-la-Ville, Switzerland, 2010.

[MER 45] MERLEAU-PONTY M., *Phénoménologie de la perception*, Gallimard, 1945.

[MIL 94] MILGRAM P., KISHINO F., "A taxonomy of mixed reality visual displays", *IEICE Transactions on Information Systems*, vol. E77-D, no. 12, pp. 1–15, 1994.

[MOL 06] MOLLET N., ARNALDI B., "Storytelling in virtual reality for training", *Edutainment*, pp. 334–347, Hangzhou, April 2006.

[MOL 07] MOLLET N., GERBAUD S., ARNALDI B., "STORM: a generic interaction and behavioral model for 3D objects and humanoids in a virtual environment", *IPT-EGVE the 13th Eurographics Symposium on Virtual Environments*, pp. 95–100, Weimar, Germany, July 2007.

[MUR 15] MUR-ARTAL R., MONTIEL J.M.M., TARDÛS J.D., "ORB-SLAM: A versatile and accurate monocular SLAM system", *IEEE Transactions on Robotics*, vol. 31, no. 5, pp. 1147–1163, 2015.

[MUR 16] MURATORE I., NANNIPIERI O., "L'expérience immersive d'un jeu promotionnel en réalité augmentée destiné aux enfants", *Décisions Marketing*, vol. 81, pp. 27–40, 2016.

[NAN 15a] NANNIPIERI O., MURATORE I., DUMAS P. *et al.*, "Immersion, subjectivité et communication", in *Technologies, communication et société*, L'Harmattan, 2015.

[NAN 15b] NANNIPIERI O., MURATORE I., MESTRE D. *et al.*, "Au-delà des frontières : vers une sémiotique de la présence dans la réalité virtuelle", in *Frontières Numériques* L'Harmattan, 2015.

[NEW 11] NEWCOMBE R., IZADI S., HILLIGES O. *et al.*, "KinectFusion: real-time dense surface mapping and tracking", *International Symposium on Mixed and Augmented Reality*, 2011.

[NIC 15] NICOLAS T., GAUGNE R., TAVERNIER C. *et al.*, "Touching and interacting with inaccessible cultural heritage", *Presence: Teleoperators and Virtual Environments*, vol. 24, no. 3, Massachusetts Institute of Technology Press (MIT Press), 2015.

[PAC 07] PACANOWSKI R., GRANIER X., SCHLICK C., "Managing geometry complexity for illumination computation of cultural heritage scenes", in VERGNIEUX R. (ed.), *Virtual Retrospect, Collection Archéovision*, pp. 109–113, 2007.

[PET 12] PETERLÍK I., DURIEZ C., COTIN S., "Modeling and real-time simulation of a vascularized liver tissue", *Proceeding Medical Image Computing and Computer-Assisted Intervention*, pp. 50–57, 2012.

[PIU 13] PIUMSOMBOON T., CLARK A.J., BILLINGHURST M. *et al.*, "User-defined gestures for augmented reality", *Human-Computer Interaction - INTERACT 2013 - 14th IFIP TC 13 International Conference, Part II*, pp. 282–299, Cape Town, South Africa, September 2–6, 2013.

[PLA 15] PLANTEFÈVE R., PETERLIK I., HAOUCHINE N. *et al.*, "Patient-specific biomechanical modeling for guidance during minimally-invasive hepatic surgery", *Annals of Biomedical Engineering*, Springer-Verlag, August 2015.

[PUJ 07] PUJOL TOST L., SUREDA JUBRANY M., "Vers une Réalité Virtuelle véritablement interactive", *Virtual Retrospect*, pp. 77–81, 2007.

[REI 06] REITINGER B., BORNIK A., BEICHEL R. *et al.*, "Liver surgery planning using virtual reality", *IEEE Computer Graphics and Applications*, vol. 26, no. 6, pp. 36–47, November 2006.

[REU 10] REUTER P., RIVIERE G., COUTURE N. *et al.*, "ArcheoTUI—driving virtual reassemblies with tangible 3D interaction", *J. Comput. Cult. Herit.*, vol. 3, no. 2, pp. 1–13, ACM, 2010.

[RID 14] RIDEL B., REUTER P., LAVIOLE J. *et al.*, "The revealing flashlight: interactive spatial augmented reality for detail exploration of cultural heritage artifacts", *Journal on Computing and Cultural Heritage*, vol. 7, no. 2, pp. 1–18, Association for Computing Machinery, May 2014.

[ROW 09] ROWE J., MOTT B., MCQUIGGAN S. *et al.*, "Crystal island: a narrative-centered learning environment for eighth grade microbiology", *Workshop on Intelligent Educational Games at the 14th International Conference on Artificial Intelligence in Education*, pp. 11–20, Brighton, UK, 2009.

[RUB 15] RUBENS C., BRALEY S., GOMES A. *et al.*, "BitDrones: towards levitating programmable matter using interactive 3D quadcopter displays", *Adjunct Proceedings of the 28th Annual ACM Symposium on User Interface Software & Technology*, pp. 57–58, ACM, New York, USA, 2015.

[SAU 02] SAUTER J., http://www.joachimsauter.com/en/work/thejewofmalta.html, 2002.

[SCH 99] SCHUBERT T., FRIEDMANN F., REGENBRECHT H., *"Embodied Presence in Virtual Environments"*, pp. 269–278, Springer, London, 1999.

[SCH 01] SCHUBERT T., FRIEDMANN F., REGENBRECHT H., "The experience of presence: factor analytic insights", *Presence: Teleoperators and Virtual Environments*, vol. 10, no. 3, pp. 266–281, MIT Press, June 2001.

[SCH 07] SCHMALSTIEG D., REITMAYR G., *"Augmented Reality as a Medium for Cartography"*, Springer Berlin Heidelberg, pp. 267–281, 2007.

[SHE 11] SHEN T., LI H., HUANG X., "Active volume models for medical image segmentation", *IEEE Transaction Medeam Imaging*, vol. 30, no. 3, pp. 774–791, 2011.

[SI 10] SI M., Thespian: a decision-theoretic framework for interactive narratives, PhD thesis, University of Southern California, 2010.

[SIT 17] http://www.augmentedperformance.com/, 2017.

[SPI 09] SPIERLING U., SZILAS N., "Authoring issues beyond tools", *Interactive Storytelling*, pp. 50–61, Springer, 2009.

[SUC 09] SUCCAR B., "Building information modelling framework: A research and delivery foundation for industry stakeholders", *Automation in Construction*, vol. 18, no. 3, pp. 357–375, 2009.

[SUT 02] SUTHAU T., VETTER M., HASSENPFLUG P. *et al.*, "A concept work for Augmented Reality visualisation based on a medical application in liver surgery", *The International Archives of Photogrammetry, Remote Sensing and Spatial Information Sciences*, vol. 34, no. 5, pp. 274–280, 2002.

[SUW 11] SUWELACK S., TALBOT H., RÖHL S. *et al.*, "A biomechanical liver model for intraoperative soft tissue registration", vol. 7964, pp. 79642I–79642I-6, 2011.

[TAC 14] TACHI S., INAMI M., UEMA Y., "The transparent cockpit", *IEEE Spectrum*, vol. 51, no. 11, pp. 52–56, November 2014.

[TAL 13] TALBOT H., MARCHESSEAU S., DURIEZ C. *et al.*, "Towards an interactive electromechanical model of the heart", *Interface Focus*, vol. 3, no. 2, p. 4, Royal Society publishing, April 2013.

[TAL 16] TALBOT H., SPADONI F., DURIEZ C. *et al.*, "Interactive training system for interventional electrocardiology procedures", *Lecture Notes in Computer Science*, vol. 8789, pp. 11–19, Springer, 2016.

[TAN 04] TANG A., BIOCCA F., LIM L., "Comparing differences in presence during social interaction in augmented reality versus virtual reality environments: an exploratory study", in RAYA M., SOLAZ B. (eds), *7th Annual International Workshop on Presence*, Valence, Spain, 2004.

[TEB 09] TEBER D., GUVEN S., SIMPFENDORFER T. *et al.*, "Augmented reality: a new tool to improve surgical accuracy during laparoscopic partial nephrectomy? preliminary *in vitro* and *in vivo* results", *European Urology*, vol. 56, no. 2, pp. 332–338, 2009.

[VER 11] VERGNIEUX R., "Archaeological research and 3D models (Restitution, validation and simulation)", *Virtual Archeology Review*, vol. 2, no. 4, pp. 39–43, May 2011.

[VER 15] VERDIE Y., YI K.M., FUA P. *et al.*, "TILDE: A Temporally Invariant Learned DEtector", *Conference on Computer Vision and Pattern Recognition*, 2015.

[VYG 78] VYGOTSKY L.S., *Mind in Society*, Harvard University Press, Cambridge, 1978.

[WES 04] WESARG S., SCHWALD B., SEIBERT H. *et al.*, "An augmented reality system for supporting minimally invasive interventions", *Workshop Augmented Environments for Medical Imaging*, pp. 41–48, 2004.

[WUE 07] WUEST H., WIENTAPPER F., STRICKER D., "Adaptable model-based tracking using analysis-by-synthesis techniques", *International Conference on Computer Analysis of Images and Patterns*, 2007.

[YOO 15] YOON C., KIM K.H., "Augmented reality information registration for head-up display", *2015 International Conference on Information and Communication Technology Convergence (ICTC)*, pp. 1135–1137, October 2015.

[ZEI 15] ZEISL B., SATTLER T., POLLEFEYS M., "Camera pose voting for large-scale image-based localization", *International Conference on Computer Vision*, 2015.

The Democratization of VR-AR

The objective of this chapter is to examine the key advances (both software and material) over the past 10 years.

2.1. New equipment

2.1.1. *Introduction*

Virtual reality and augmented reality are built on interactive feedback (e.g. visual, audio, haptic). As a result, developments in this field, from its very inception, have been based on position and orientation sensors as well as restitution devices. The first part of this chapter will therefore provide a detailed discussion on the technology used today, both in a professional context and in those used by the general public. Indeed, equipment, which has been restricted to professional applications until recently, is now available at low prices and this has revolutionized the industry. It is thus important that we step back and appraise existing solutions.

In most of the following sections, we will give examples of commercial equipment or software. Naturally, this is not a ranking of the best solutions nor is this an exhaustive list; we have, instead, chosen to mention products that, between them, make up the *de facto* market standards.

Chapter written by Sébastien KUNTZ, Richard KULPA and Jérôme ROYAN.

2.1.2. *Positioning and orientation devices*

To compute the image that corresponds to the position of an observer, we must first know their position and the orientation of their point of view (explained in detail in section 3.2). The first VR headset, developed in 1968 by I. Sutherland and R. Sproull, adopted a very simple solution using rotary encoders to detect movements of the head. Some years later, these became sensors that were based on electromagnetic technology (notably with the Polhemum company), which would become the prevailing technology used for several years. Today, optical technologies are increasingly seen in the VR world. The specific problem of location and positioning in AR will be discussed in the last part of this section. In section 4.1, we will look more closely at algorithms, especially vision-based location positioning.

We will now look at the existing professional solutions, which pose technological challenges that VR and AR must resolve.

2.1.2.1. *Professional solutions*

High-speed infrared cameras (up to 250 Hz) can be used for tracking. They identify a set of markers in space which reflect infrared rays (in practice, we use small spheres, less than a centimeter in diameter). These markers (also called targets or constellations) form rigid groups of markers (or "rigid bodies") and are placed on a part of the human body (most often the hand, but it could also be the elbow, the shoulder, the pelvis, etc.) as well as on the objects whose position and spatial orientation we wish to follow, for example, stereo glasses or any accessory involved in virtual simulation. Figure 2.1 gives an example of this.

Among the leading groups of companies that sell positioning and orientation devices, the major actors are A.R.T[1] and Vicon[2], both of which offer solutions based on optical technology. These high-end systems offer high-precision (millimetric) tracking, high robustness and low latency. The surface to be captured can be very large (over 100 m^2), which would require a sufficient number of cameras. However, the installation for this takes longer: all cameras must be positioned in a very stable manner and connected to a

---

1 http://www.ar-tracking.com/
2 https://www.vicon.com/

computer; they require a simplified but pain-staking calibration procedure. Moreover, we must ensure that each rigid body is visible to several cameras.

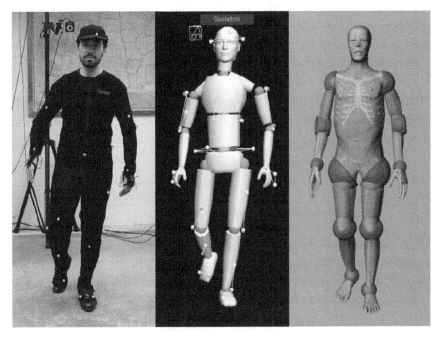

Figure 2.1. *Example of rigid bodies (© Wikimedia Commons - Vasquez88).*

Let us also mention the company Natural Point[3], which offers a mid-range set of cameras called Optitrak that carries out the same functions as the systems described above.

The companies 4D Views[4] and Organic Motion[5] offer basic solutions based on "traditional" video cameras, without any targets positioned on the user. Their approach consists of extracting silhouettes from the images taken by the cameras and then combining them to construct, in real-time, a 3D model of the human body, either in minimalist form (a simplified skeleton) or

---

3 https://www.naturalpoint.com/
4 https://www.4dviews.com/
5 http://www.organicmotion.com/

in a complete form. We can thus follow the movements of a human body without the user having to wear any equipment. On the other hand, we must carry out the tracking in a dedicated space with a solid background (which is most often green) in order to obtain the best extraction of the silhouette. The precision and latency are of inferior quality to solutions that use markers but the performance gap between them is shrinking steadily.

Finally, let us recall that there are other technologies that make it possible to follow a position and orientation in space using electro-magnetic fields, ultrasound fields, etc.

2.1.2.2. *Solutions for mass distribution*

2.1.2.2.1. Accessories for gaming consoles

The emergence of games that required tracking the gamer's position and orientation led to the emergence of specific devices for consoles. It must be noted that, today, some of these devices have also been adopted for professional applications because of their high performance and low cost.

– *Depth sensor – Microsoft Kinect*[6]: the Microsoft Kinect is the mass-produced version of a relatively recent kind of camera: 3D or depth cameras. A classic camera only allows you to capture information in 2D: an image or a video in the form of pixels. A 3D camera, however, uses different techniques to add information on depth for each pixel of the image. It is thus possible to find out how far an object in the 3D scene is from the center of the camera. This information is very important for a relatively precise positioning in space of all elements that are visible to a 3D camera without fitting them with markers. This kind of camera does, however, suffer from problems with precision, with managing inter-object occultation as well as having quite a large latency in comparison to professional sensors. As a result they cannot yet be used for VR systems that require information to be processed very rapidly.

– *Stereoscopic cameras – Leap Motion*[7]: the Leap Motion system makes it possible to capture the user's hands very precisely, allowing for more natural interactions.

---

6 http://www.xbox.com/fr-FR/xbox-one/accessories/kinect
7 https://www.leapmotion.com/

This system uses two infrared cameras to rapidly extract and specify the position and orientation of the fingers. The cameras may be placed on a table, for example, and the interaction space will then be located above the cameras. We can also mount this system into a VR headset, which will make it possible to follow the hands using line of vision and the tracking will not suffer if the hands move out of the camera's field of vision.

Interestingly, the system still suffers *a priori* from a limited field of vision and, above all, from occlusion problems: in fact, Leap Motion can only extract data when the fingers are completely visible.

– *Electro-magnetic sensors – Hydra/STEM*[8]: a few years ago, the company Sixense, in collaboration with the company Razer, proposed the Razer Hydra system, which is made up of two controllers localized in space. These descendants of the famous Nintendo Wiimote not only have the classic joystick or gamepad buttons, but also offer a solution to measure position and orientation in space, which makes it possible to have 3D interactions. This system is based on an electromagnetic field emitted by a base placed on a table and detected by the sensors present in the joystick. Having almost no other competitor in the market when it came out, Hydra was used above all by the few passionate VR users who existed before Oculus Rift arrived. Rapid, precise and easy to use, the system had the same problem as any electro-magnetic base sensor: interference (from proximity to a power source, to a metallic mass, etc.) that may distort the field and therefore skew the measurements. Moreover, the tracking reliability did not exceed 50 cm.

Sixense is working on an updated system, named STEM, which is not yet out on the market at the time of publication of this book.

– *Inertial sensors – Perception Neuron*[9]: the Chinese company Noitom is a newcomer to the field of sensors dedicated to capturing all or part of the user's body. Their product, Perception Neuron, combines motion capture and highly aggressive pricing and yields good results.

The system is based only on inertial units. Thanks to algorithms that use biomechanical models of the human body, they are able to precisely determine the spatial positioning of most body parts.

_____

8 http://sixense.com/razerhydra-3
9 https://neuronmocap.com

2.1.2.3. *Systems integrated into VR headsets*

Modern HMDs have inbuilt positioning systems and we offer below some examples of these:

– *Inertial unit – Samsung GearVR*: the Samsung GearVR headset[10] (Figure 2.2) offers tracking based only on inertial units and made up of an accelerometer, a gyroscope and a magnetometer. This device yields very rapid and quite reliable rotational information. High-performance fusion algorithms make it possible to use the three sensors optimally in order to rapidly provide reliable information. However, these sensors only allow us to obtain rotational information and are not precise enough to measure translational information.

– *Coupling of optical and inertial units – Oculus Rift*: Oculus Rift[11] (Figure 2.3) offers a tracking solution that is very close to the above-mentioned professional solutions. In effect, one or more cameras capture infrared LEDs located in the headset (behind a shell), which make it possible to calculate the position and orientation of the headset in space.

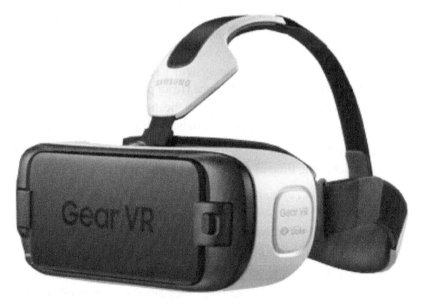

Figure 2.2. *Samsung Gear VR (© Samsung)*

10 http://www.samsung.com/global/galaxy/gear-vr/
11 https://www.oculus.com/rift/

Figure 2.3. *Oculus Rift V1 (© Oculus)*

An inertial unit makes it possible to further reduce latency and increase tracking precision. However, while the cameras are indeed rapid, they require image processing, which is slower than the fusion computation used by accelerometers, gyroscopes and magnetometers.

– Laser beam and inertial unit – HTC Vive: the HTC Vive headset[12] (Figure 2.4) makes use of a different principle from those mentioned above. We could call it a symmetrical principle. While Oculus Rift requires an external sensor (a camera) that observes passive targets in the headset (the infrared LED), the Lighthouse system adopted by HTC places the sensors on the headset and the targets are external.

We see what look like cameras, but are actually the Lighthouses, which sweep through space using two laser beams – one sweeping horizontally and the other vertically. The helmet is equipped with a set of sensors that detect at what point the laser beam reaches them. By combining the information yielded by multiple sensors, we are able to obtain a position and orientation in space for the headset. As with the Oculus Rift, an inertial unit is added to minimize the system's latency and enhance precision.

---

12 https://www.vive.com/fr/

– *SLAM* – *HoloLens*: all the sensors we have described so far require an external referential, a base, to determine the positioning and orientation of an object. We now look at a new trend where external referentials are no longer used. For example, the HoloLens headset developed by Microsoft (Figure 2.5) uses only in-built sensors to situate itself in space. This is a mini-revolution in the industry.

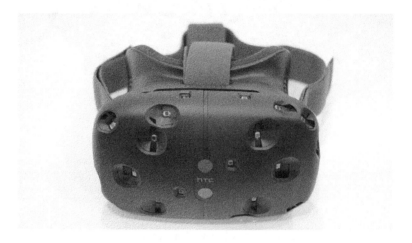

Figure 2.4. *HTC Vive (© HTC)*

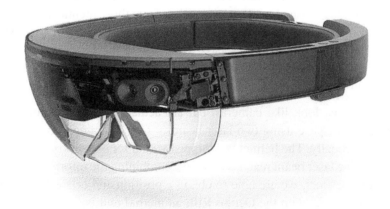

Figure 2.5. *Microsoft HoloLens (© Microsoft)*

Grouped under the title SLAM (Simultaneous Location And Mapping, [REI 10], see [WAG 10] for a smartphone VR application), the algorithms used are the result of research initiated in the late 1980s. These have been widely used, especially in the field of robotics, to allow an independent robot to situate itself in a workspace. The system is based, first of all, on recognizing the environment: a 3D map of space is created based on information received from the cameras capturing depth. Analyses of images mixed with the information from the inertial unit make it possible to then find the position and orientation of the headset in this space.

2.1.2.4. *Positioning solutions in VR*

VR depends on the superposition of a synthetic visual information (image, symbol, text) onto the user's natural vision. In order to be relevant, this superposition requires spatial recalibration with the user's real environment. An Augmented Reality device thus requires a positioning solution to determine its position and orientation with respect to a geodesic system or with respect to some reference in the real environment (e.g. marker, image, object, building). The solutions used for the VR systems presented above could potentially meet the needs of AR systems as long as the user remains within the zone covered by the sensors. This, however, means that they are not very useful if we want to move beyond immersive rooms. Thus, in order to offer a low-cost positioning system that would cover a large area, AR systems use technologies available on smartphones, namely GPS for external use, an inertial unit (magnetometer, accelerometer and gyroscope), one or more color cameras, and even one or more depth sensors. The data captured by these different sensors will be fused together in order to precisely locate the AR system.

Thus, GPS gives us the position of the device with a precision that ranges from within a few meters to within ten meters or so, depending on the environment (e.g. open, urban, interior) and depending on the usage (e.g. mass distribution, military). Coupled with a magnetometer (or compass), a smartphone can easily supply its approximative location in a real environment. However, an imprecision of about ten meters may generate some dysfunctions. For example, if the desired contextual information is displayed behind the user when it is supposed to be located in front of him - or simply if the address used to display an advertisement or notice of some sort is not the right address.

Hence, in order to refine the precision of the positioning and orientation, an AR system generally depends on its vision sensors (cameras, depth sensors) coupled with computer vision algorithms. This precision does away with ambiguities, and thus, an AR system can indicate to a maintenance operator exactly which bolt must be loosened or which connector must be disconnected.

AR mainly uses two families of computer vision algorithms. The first is a group of relocalization algorithms that use a knowledge of the real environment (e.g. a QRCode or fiducial-type marker, an image, a 3D model, a mapping of points of interest) to estimate the position and orientation of an AR system. The second covers tracking algorithms that may estimate the displacement of the AR device in space. The SLAM methods (mentioned in the previous section) can be seen here, and they iteratively calculate the position based on a 3D reconstruction of the real environment, which, in itself, is computed using the earlier position estimates. While this solution is capable of estimating the movement of the sensor without any knowledge of the environment, these kinds of methods are subject to temporal deviations. The vision-based algorithms will be presented in greater detail in section 4.1.

2.1.3. *Restitution devices*

Visual restitution devices used in VR have evolved a lot since the first headset developed by I. Sutherland and R. Sproull. However, we must not forget that a gap of close to 50 years separates the latest generation of VR devices from that first headset and that much other equipment has been widely used in the world of VR. Most of these were based on the display or projection of images on large screens in order to allow for a collective immersive experience. Let us take, for example, devices such as the visiocube, starting with the Cave developed by C. Cruz-Neira in 1992 [CRU 93], or even the Reality Centre commercialized two years later by the Silicon Graphics company, which also manufactured the majority of computers used in VR in this period. These solutions are still used as the building blocks on which today's professional immersive rooms are built.

We bet that the mass-distribution market, where these HMDs have appeared, will go through the same evolution as the professional world has, with collective solutions based on "mini" video-projectors that offer a large display surface (e.g. the wall of a room).

Moreover, we must not forget haptic and audio restitution devices that compete to reinforce the user's immersion by offering them rich and coherent sensory information.

As concerns AR, here again the equipment used has seen great technological advances that have multiplied over the past few years, especially with the explosion of smartphones and tablets.

2.1.3.1. *VR HMDs*

We decided to begin by discussing equipment that does not, strictly speaking, meet the quality standards for VR but which is, nonetheless, always associated with this technology in the press. Indeed, these devices are based on the use of a smartphone screen, which drastically limits the complexity and quality of the virtual environments that are created. Moreover, the quality of the optical systems placed between the eyes and the screen is not high enough to allow comfortable, sustained usage of a long period of time. Rather than ignoring these devices, we will briefly present them in order to give you, the reader, a complete overview of the field.

2.1.3.1.1. Systems that use smartphones

This category includes HMDs available at very low prices, as they do not include the price of the smartphone that is required to use them.

– *Google Cardboard*: Google's ambition is to make VR available to the masses by reducing costs to a minimum. They thus designed a cardboard box, equipped with two plastic lenses, into which a cellphone can be inserted. The screen of this phone is "cut" into two parts, each displaying an image meant for each eye, following the principle used by the first stereoscopes that were developed in the mid-19th century. Today's smartphones include inertial units and are capable of capturing rotations of this headset. They are thus able to react by modifying the stereoscopic image displayed in order to change the user's point of view.

Of course, given that cellphones have a limited computing power, only 360° videos or light, real-time 3D applications are really usable. In effect, the latency between the user's movement and the result being displayed is too large to provide a true immersive experience and this may soon produce nausea and headaches. As per the latest news from Google regarding their Daydream platform, they do not seem to have solved these fundamental problems yet.

Other manufacturers hastened to copy this concept, offering plastic boxes rather than cardboard, ensuring better ergonomics, better lenses and greater compatibility with a wider range of telephones. However, the basic problem remains: current smartphones do not have sensors that perform at the required level (speed and precision).

– *Samsung Gear VR*: Samsung, in partnership with Oculus, has managed to create a cellphone-based helmet, which may be classified as VR. To achieve this objective, they had to:

- include high-quality optical systems and additional sensors that performed better than those included in standard cellphones;

- develop specific, very high-performance algorithms in order to reduce the total latency of the system;

- use only the most evolved smartphones from the manufacturer, which have a sufficient computing power.

Despite these innovations, the system presents limitations when compared with headsets connected to a computer or video game console, especially as there are no controllers (no joysticks, for example) and only the user's rotations are taken into consideration. However, the headset is easily transportable and easy to use and, if used within its limitations, offers a good immersive experience.

2.1.3.1.2. HMDs connected to a computer

As a result of the limitations in quality discussed above, new low-cost headsets have appeared which still, however, use some smartphone technologies (especially the screens):

– *Oculus Rift*: born out of a project that saw a much greater success than its creators had hoped on the crowdfunding site Kickstarter in 2012, the diffusion of the Oculus Rift headset paved the way for a series of announcements regarding new VR headsets that offered high performance at lower costs than existing equipment.

While initially "reserved" for developers in 2013, and having only low resolution and a single rotation captor, the first version (called "developer kit" or DK1) was the first headset that offered both low latency and a large vision field – which had been the main obstacle to a good immersive experience.

By 2014, Oculus Rift had been bought over by Facebook. Its first commercial version (CV1), released in 2016, offered a much better resolution, large field of vision as well as position tracking of the head and the two controllers (Oculus Touch, optional additions) thanks to one or more external cameras, which must all be connected to the same computer. This headset is also, at present, the lightest headset and has the lowest latency of all mid-range headsets.

Having been designed first and foremost for use while being seated, it can also be used while standing in a room ("spatial" or "roomscale" mode).

– *HTC Valve Vive*: the HTC Vive is one of Oculus Rift's biggest competitors. Based on technology developed by the company Valve, which had initially collaborated with Oculus, its standard version comes with two controllers, which allows app developers the chance to create simulations that use both hands, without worrying whether the user has bought the additional set of controllers, as is the case with Oculus Rift.

Its innovative tracking system, the Lighthouse, which has been described above, makes it possible to implement tracking in an easier manner than using the "spatial mode". To the best of our knowledge, this is the most widely used headset among professionals today.

– *PSVR*: Sony's has a long history with VR as the company had started selling VR headsets such as the Glasstron as far back as 1996. A few years ago, before Oculus Rift arrived on the scene, Sony had also proposed selling a stereoscopic headset, for mass distribution, to watch 3D films. Hence, nobody was surprised by the announcement of a headset dedicated to the Playstation 4.

On the technology end, tracking is carried out by an inertial unit as well as through the standard camera on the Playstation. This camera also makes it possible to capture the Playstation Move controllers

The main limitation concerns the tracking volume, which is limited by the camera's field of vision, as well as situations where occlusions occur: if we turn around, our body comes between the controllers and the cameras, thereby stopping the tracking process, and the controllers no longer relay information on position.

The low latency of the system, coupled with its ease of installation and high graphical capacity, makes this a good VR device. Having recently become available to the general public, this headset seems to be enjoying some success, especially as the catalog of games available is the largest across all platforms.

– *Other VR headsets*: there are, of course, many other headsets on the market (e.g. Microsoft, Vrvana Totem, FOVE) as well as those being developed for commercialization. However, given limited space and editorial concerns, especially as regards continuity of information, it is impossible to discuss all of them at length.

2.1.3.2. Large screens

Invented with headsets that offered individual experiences, VR then opened up to other display modes when it was adopted by sectors where teamwork was indispensable. An aircraft or car, for instance, is not designed just by individually immersing experts in a virtual environment. On the contrary, there are follow-up meetings for the project that involves multi-disciplinary teams who wish to collectively visualize the state of development of their product. This is the main reason why innovations designed by researchers in this field have rapidly met with great success - so much so that they provided the basic principles used for most immersive rooms today.

The first idea leading to this development was that of replacing the headset with a large-size screen that would make it possible to provide the Scale 1 visualization of models that are so highly prized in the industrial world due to their large field of vision. For technological reasons, this visualization first took place via video projectors that made it possible to move far beyond the maximum size of existing monitors.

The second idea that was used to improve the immersive experience of the user was placing the user within parallelepipeds where all or part of the faces (between 3 and 6, whose sizes varied between 3 m and approximately 10 m) were screens: thus, we have the visiocube invented by C. Cruz-Neira in 1992 with the first CAVE system, which is still in use 25 years later (see Figure 2.6). The concept for the Reality Center was based on the same idea but required an environment (notably, a building) that was lighter and would therefore cost less. The Reality Center proposed a display on a third of a cylinder (about 10 m × 3 m), and this was marketed by the Silicon Graphics company two years later (see Figure 2.7). It was a huge success and is still in use in many companies and research centers.

Figure 2.6. *Example of a visiocube with five faces: the SAS[3] (© CLARTE)*

Figure 2.7. *Reality Center marketed by Barco (© Barco)*

The characteristics that are common to these different families of equipment are as follows:

– high-quality, or even very high-quality immersion: the user does not suffer from limitations related to a restricted field of vision as with a helmet;

– the user can see their body as well as their interlocutors, which is conducive for dialogue and exchange;

– resolution, contrast and brightness can be adjusted based on the needs of the user. In fact, the projected pixel size and its brightness can be reduced simply by increasing the number of projectors. However, this does add to the cost;

– the image computation is carried out based on the position of the user's head, which is tracked using one of the systems we described at the beginning of the chapter;

– the same systems also allow the tracking of other parts of the user's body (hands, for example) as well as objects handled by the user.

These systems have two main limitations: first of all, due to costs involved (setting up the room, buying equipment and, of course, maintenance), these systems are mainly restricted to professional applications, either within companies or in research laboratories. Second, in the case of collective use by a group, the image perception is ideal for a user who is tracked by the system, but the perception is impaired depending on the distance at which the user is positioned as the images are then deformed. There are, however, several multi-user solutions that preserve perception (perspective and stereoscopy) at the cost of additional equipment or lower performance.

Over the years, these systems have undergone several changes with respect to the geometry of the screens (e.g. planar, parallelepiped, cylinder, sphere) and with respect to the technology used in the video projectors (e.g. tubes, LCD, DLP).

The main trends over the coming years will be the move towards laser-based video-projectors and the large-scale appearance of monitor walls. In fact, technological progress has made it possible to refine the existing "border" between the displayed surface and the edge of a monitor to such an extent that it almost disappears. It is thus possible to construct monitor walls that offer a near-perfect image and thus obtain a good immersive experience. While preserving existing geometries (planes, parallelepipeds), these systems will undoubtedly develop significantly, thanks to the quality of the display, their reduced consumption of electricity (and thus, reduced heat), the reduced size and the costs involved, which are substantially lower than those of the video projectors.

2.1.3.3. *Augmented reality equipment*

It is possible to divide the restitution devices used in AR into different categories based on their physical support:

– carried in front of the user's eyes: depending on the complexity of the device, we will either use the term "Augmented Reality Headset" or "Augmented Reality Glasses". We differentiate between "optical see-through" systems, which allow direct natural vision, and "video see-through" systems, where the environment is perceived indirectly, through a camera;

– hand-held devices: these are smartphones and tablets. The massive distribution of these devices on the market has allowed the general public to discover and explore AR;

– fixed or mobile devices: video-projectors that project an image directly onto objects in the real environment, thereby bringing about a natural superimposition. This modality (called Spatial Augmented Reality or SAR) has been widely developed within industrial applications such as repairing or maintaining equipment where the information from technical manuals makes it possible to see the texts, assembly diagrams or even videos *in-situ*, without the user having any equipment themselves;

– contact-lens-based systems have been developed recently but are yet to see definite progress. At the moment, these systems display only highly simplified symbols and images. The main technological challenge is improving the resolution and energy consumption and taking into account the human factor: acceptance and ease of use.

In the following sections, we will focus primarily on the first category of equipment: headsets and glasses.

2.1.3.3.1. Google Glass

Announced in 2012, Google Glass has long been the center of attention, especially in the media, and was representative of "all" AR technology in the eyes of non-specialists. The earliest versions, available in limited numbers at 1500 USD, offered the possibility of visualizing images on a screen with a dimension of 1.3 cm, which was fitted onto a very light pair of glasses (let us also recall their highly limited field of vision and the offset axis of the screen, with respect to the gaze axis). Interaction with the system took place in a vocal and tactile manner (a touchpad located on the side of the glasses). The initial versions offered the use of "in-house" apps such as Google Maps or Gmail and also allowed the user to take photos or videos. Seeing the enormous potential of this device, many solution developers rushed into the breach and the range of applications widened and diversified rapidly: sports, health, media and, of course, military.

The sudden passion aroused by this new equipment was tempered by various kinds of problems. First among them were legal problems, brought about when a driver wearing Google Glass caused a road accident and several American states banned the use of these glasses while driving. Next were ethical problems – users could identify and record people without their consent. Finally, initial users gave up wearing the glasses as they ended up being seen as too visible and even stigmatizing. These problems led to Google announcing, at the end of 2014, that they were stopping sales of the device.

However, the company discreetly continued working on the product with several partner companies and announced, in mid-2017, that they would resume sales for professionals after some improvements to the glasses.

2.1.3.3.2. Google Tango

Announced in 2014, Tango is a project for a Google AR platform which would be available on smartphones and tablets. It makes it possible to measure the position and orientation of the device. The software uses vision (tracking) algorithms, a fusion of data with other classic sensors (accelerometer, gyroscope) as well as a depth camera. This is the first "light" system to carry such a camera, even though the earliest versions used an infrared depth camera, which meant that it could not be used outdoors. It must be noted that Tango is a platform that can be deployed on various devices: Google offers developers the prototypes for Peanut (smartphone) and Yellowstone (tablets); Lenovo manufactures the tablet Phab2 and Asus makes the cellphone Zenphone AR.

2.1.3.3.3. HoloLens

Developed by Microsoft, HoloLens is an AR headset that was unveiled in 2015. It is equipped with a waveguide that has a diagonal field of vision that extends up to approximately 35° (30° × 17.5°) with a very high resolution for each eye (1280 × 720) and an accommodation of 2 m. The HoloLens is loaded with sensors: 4 cameras used for location and positioning, a time-of-flight depth sensor with low energy consumption, a frontal camera with large field of vision (120° × 120°) and an inertial unit. The power of the HoloLens resides primarily in its computing architecture: not only thanks to its CPU and its GPU but, above all, in the part that Microsoft misleadingly calls its HPU (Holographic Processing Unit), which has nothing to do with holographs and which is more commonly called a VPU (Vision Processing Unit). This processor allows us to obtain pose computations that perform 200 times better than a classic software implementation, while also consuming very little energy (only 10 watts). This architecture results in very good autonomy and a pose estimate that is much more robust and rapid compared with state-of-the-art methods.

The HoloLens' speed of pose computations in its environment is an essential factor that greatly enhances the user's experience. In effect, the above-mentioned optical see-through AR systems do not integrate material solutions to optimize pose estimation. As a result, the computation may take between 200 ms and 1 s depending on the software solution and equipment used. This results in a perceptible lag between a rapid movement by the user and the display of the resulting image. This latency results in the displayed content "floating" and generates discomfort that could result in a form of rejection when the user moves their head too rapidly.

It must be noted that this flotation effect is not perceptible when we use a tablet or a smartphone as the video is displayed with a latency that is similar to the pose computation time of the system. Thus, the video and augmentation are delayed in a similar manner, offering a perceived recalibration that seems precise (as long as the pose estimation is correct).

The HoloLens is also equipped with a calibration system for the user that is essential for obtaining a precise recalibration. This calibration must be carried out each time that the headset moves around the user's head. Fortunately, the headset attachment system is well designed and prevents the device from moving unexpectedly when the user makes such a movement.

2.1.3.3.4. Magic Leap

The start-up Magic Leap was created in 2010 by Rony Abovitz. This was not his first venture - in 2004 he had already founded MAKO Surgical Corp. (manufacturing robotic arms for the medical field). Magic Leap today holds the record for the most amount raised (about 1.4 billion dollars) without any public demonstration of the product. It is shrouded in mystery because apart from a few prospective videos, there is no technical information communicated as yet, other than to the rare test-users who sign non-disclosure agreements stipulating that they cannot even reveal having met with Magic Leap. As a result, we can only hypothesize about this solution, announced as a highly innovative device. The company has stated that their solution will offer far superior ocular comfort than any of its competitors by addressing the convergence-accommodation problem (described in 3.4.2). The patents submitted by Magic Leap, which have been published these past few years, give little information as to the technical solution. They do not describe an implementation, but rather a host of solutions that are more or less inspired by state-of-the-art science. It does, however, look like the chosen technology is based on the use of light fields, which will simulate luminous wavefronts that are naturally captured by the visual system using spatial light modulators. This will make the product far more comfortable to use when compared with the existing solutions. At the time of writing, Magic Leap is the biggest open question in the world of AR restitution devices: revolution or damp squib?

2.1.3.3.5. Other AR glasses

Apart from these three companies, which can mobilize considerably large investments in the development of AR glasses, there are dozens of other actors that propose devices based on optical see-through systems. In order to compare them easily, we propose the following set of criteria:

– *The optical system*: in most cases, optical see-through systems are based on optical waveguides that propagate the image emitted by a micro-screen towards the user's eye. These optical waveguides make it possible to position the physical screen onto the sides or the upper edge of the glasses, while offering a transparent display that gives the user a direct perception of the real environment. There are several waveguide technologies that can be used: diffractive, reflective, polarized or holographic [SAR 13]. Another solution consists of using a semi-transparent mirror (generally curved) that directly or indirectly reflects a screen positioned in the glasses. In the latter case, the difficulty is in finding an accommodation distance that is large enough and gives the user the impression that this screen is located several meters away from them. Finally, CastAR proposes an original solution: this is based on a projection system integrated into the glasses, which emit an image that reflects off a specific surface positioned in the real environment. This surface is made up of catadioptric microscopes (similar to the reflective surfaces on high-visibility vests) that make it possible to reflect the projected images towards the source alone (the glasses). Thus, one system does not interfere with another, which opens up the possibility for a multi-user solution. Furthermore, this device is equipped with a pico-projector for each eye that is synchronized with an active stereoscopic vision system integrated into the glasses, thereby offering a stereoscopic visual experience of the virtual content.

– *The positioning of the display*: the display can be located either in the user's peripheral vision, as with Google Glass (thereby making it possible to display data that is non-recalibrated into the real environment and disengaged from the field of vision), or it can be located in the central portion of the user's visual field (making it possible to display information that is perfectly positioned in the real environment). It must be noted that some devices, such as the Optinvent ORA glasses, can switch from one configuration to the other.

– *Monocular versus binocular*: we differentiate between systems that offer an optical see-through system for only one eye or those that offer binocular vision, with an optical see-through system for each eye. Monocular systems are simpler to configure, but can provoke a phenomenon called "binocular rivalry" (discomfort related to the fact that information is visible only to one eye). Binocular systems offer a greater ease of use, as long as the system is perfectly configured. This remains a complicated process and is dependent on the user.

– *Visual field*: the relatively small visual field of AR glasses remains, and will remain for some years to come, a strong limitation. The values are generally angular and given by the diagonal of the screen. This value is only indicative, as it depends on the distance between the virtual screen and the user's eye. At present, the best optical see-through systems offer a visual field of 40°, or even up to 60° for some prototypes that are not yet on the market. However, given the wavelength of visible light and the waveguide principle, it will be difficult to exceed 60° of the visual field [MAI 14].

– *Light intensity*: in AR glasses, the lower the brightness of the pixels, the more transparent they are and vice versa. It is thus impossible to display black, or even dark objects in these glasses, and it is always preferable to display virtual content with light colors in order to improve their perception by the user. Moreover, whenever there is greater ambient brightness, the display from the wave guides becomes harder to see and thus less perceptible. Optical see-through systems must therefore offer displays even at high brightness in order to be usable in all conditions. Hence, many AR glasses have the option of a solar filter: this improves the display quality in conditions of high brightness. The GaN micro-screen technology developed by CEA-LETI is able reach a brightness of a million candelas per m^2, and this will, in the future, enable the sale of AR glasses that adapt to ambient light in the real environment.

– *Sensors*: as mentioned earlier, AR glasses must be precisely located in the real environment. In order to do this, they are generally equipped with a GPS, an inertial unit (made up of accelerometers, a gyroscope and a magnetometer) and vision captors with one or more color cameras or even a depth sensor. The robustness and precision of the superimposing of the virtual content onto the real environment depends on these sensors. The various difficulties inherent to this problem of integrating real and virtual worlds are discussed in detail in section 3.2 and the proposed solutions to these problems are discussed in section 4.1. Let us note that, from a purely material point of view, accelerometers may be disturbed by the earth's gravitational field, resulting in noisy signals. Similarly, magnetometers may be disturbed by the surrounding magnetic field and provide a wrong orientation from the sensor. The majority of RGB cameras are equipped with a rolling shutter that generates a deformed image when the sensor or the scene is in motion (the image acquisition is done line by line). As a result, it is preferable to use global shutter cameras that capture the environment instantaneously without any deformation of the image. While a fish-eye lens makes it possible to capture a much larger area in the real environment, and thus detect several points of interest that would help improve recalibration, the vision algorithms used must be heavily modified. Thus, the best available solutions at present, such as the Microsoft HoloLens or Google Tango, use multiple vision sensors.

– *Integrated computing capacity*: not all AR devices are equipped with integrated computing capacity. Some devices only offer a display feature and must be connected to an external terminal to process information such as pose estimation or feedback on virtual elements. Other devices integrate all the electronic components required for the various computations (e.g. memory, chipsets) either remotely (a box worn on the belt) or directly into the glasses.

However, the complexity of the computations, the increase in the number of sensors and the need to compute the pose of the device in a few milliseconds make it necessary to use dedicated processors. Thus, the latest devices integrate not only a CPU but also a Graphic Processing Unit (GPU) and, more recently, a Vision Processing Unit (VPU) or Digital Signal Processor (DSP). Apart from their performance in carrying out signal processing and optimization computations, the advantage of using these processors is that they have low energy consumption, which greatly enhances the independence of the mobile devices.

– *Ergonomics*: the ergonomics of an AR device is a key factor in its success. The device may potentially be carried for several hours either for professional use or by a general user, and thus, comfort and impeccable ease-of-use are essential. The difficulty is in designing a device that is usually worn on the head, and thus, thought to be light, when it comes loaded with micro-screens, optical see-through systems, sensors, computation capacity as well as batteries. It is, hence, essential to obtain a balanced distribution of weight and good stability with respect to the user's eyes. Moreover, the heat emitted by the device must be controlled, which poses a considerable challenge given that the number of active components keeps increasing and since the direct contact with the user's skin makes even a slight increase in temperature perceptible.

– *Interaction*: the use of AR is not limited to tasks requiring observations – interaction interfaces must also be integrated. Several devices have a tactile surface on the sides of the glasses, while others have started integrating systems to track the user's hands in 3D space and systems for gesture recognition, which can be coupled with gaze tracking systems or vocal recognition systems. Nonetheless, just as techniques had to be adapted to smartphones and other tactile tablets, the ergonomics of the human–machine interfaces specific to AR glasses must be completely rethought and adapted to the capacity for interaction and restitution of each device. Finally, in many cases where these devices are used, for reasons of safety, the user must have an undistorted perception of the real environment, involving optical systems that are as see-through as possible and which do not deform the visual perception of the real environment.

This constitutes a real challenge both in scientific terms (designing these modalities of interaction) and in technological terms (manufacturing the devices while respecting the constraints on robustness, compactness, consumption and costs).

– *Mobility*: AR generally makes sense if the user can move around freely in their environment. Even though some AR glasses are connected to an external terminal using one or more cables in the development stage, in the model that is sold on the market, all the computation processors and batteries are usually integrated into the glasses to make them usable as independent, mobile devices.

Given the growing number of optical see-through AR headsets or glasses, and the rapid technological obsolescence associated with continued technological progress, it would be futile to describe all the different systems available on the market. However, Table 2.1 provides a non-exhaustive overview of several AR glasses and headsets available in early 2017.

Thanks to its very low latency recalibration quality, due to its multiple sensors and large processing capacity, the Microsoft HoloLens was the most advanced solution to offer AR services in early 2017. However, as can be seen in Table 2.1, there are several solutions that could represent an alternative to the HoloLens by outdoing it in some aspects. Certain glasses with many sensors, such as Meta 2, the Atheer Air Glasses or the ODG R-7, could offer a performance similar to that of the HoloLens and, in certain cases, offer a form factor that is more apt for general use. As the range of the visual field is a key characteristic, the waveguide technology developed by Lumus is high performing thanks to its relatively large visual field and high brightness, when compared with its competitors. Lumus defines itself not as a manufacturer of AR glasses, but rather as a developer of integrated optical systems. Optinvent, which offers a waveguide system that is less efficient but substantially less expensive, is also an expert in developing optical systems that are more compact but offer many advantages, such as a variable accommodation distance, as well as good tolerance of poor alignment between the user's gaze axis and the optical axis of the glasses (this tolerance zone is called the *eye box*). Several products are also dedicated to professional use, generally hardy, such as the Epson Moverio pro BT-2000 and especially the Daqri headset. This headset is a helmet that is equipped with a large number of sensors, allowing it to respond to the many needs of the industry. Finally, we have the castAR solution, which stands apart thanks to the technology used (projective) and the target market (the video game market).

Brand	Model	Optical system	Display location	Mono- or binocular vision	Visual field	Resolution per eye	Light intensity	Sensors	Computation capacity	Ergonomics	Mobility	OS	Version	Price
Microsoft	HoloLens	Waveguide	Visual field	Binocular	~35°	1268 × 720	?	IMU 9 axes, 4 cameras, 1 fish-eye camera, 3D sensor	CPU, GPU, VPU (HPU)	579g, gesture interaction	All integrated	Windows	Dev kit and commercial	3299€
Magic Leap	?	?	Visual field	Binocular	?	?	?	?	?	?	?	?	?	? €
Epson	Moverio bt-200	Waveguide	Visual field	Binocular	~23°	960 × 540	?	IMU 9-axes, GPS, VGA camera	ARM Cortex A9 Dual Core 1.2 GHz	88g, remote touchpad	Remote box	Android 4.0.4	Commercial	699€
	Moverio bt-300	Waveguide	Visual field	Binocular	~23°	1280 × 720	Si-OLED high intensity	GPS, IMU 9 axes, 5 MP camera	Intel Cherry Trail Atom × 5 1.44 GHz	69g, remote touchpad	Remote box	Android 5.1	Commercial	799€
	Moverio pro bt-2000	Waveguide	Visual field	Binocular	~23°	960 × 540	?	GPS, IMU 9 axes, 2 5 MP stereo cameras	ARM Cortex A9 Dual Core 1.2 GHz	290g, remote touchpad	Remote box	Android 4.0.4	Commercial	3120€
Meta	Meta 2	Mirrors (focus at 0.5 m)	Diagonal visual field	Binocular	~90°	1280 × 1440	?	720p camera, IMU 6 axes, sensors array	None	420g, gesture interaction	Cable	NA	Dev kit	949$
Vuzix	Blade 3000	Waveguide	Visual field	Binocular	?	?	?	GPS, IMU 9 axes, 1080p camera	?	?	?	Android 6.0	Commercial (2017)	?
Atheer	Air Glasses	Waveguide	Visual field	Binocular	~50°	1280 × 720	?	GPS, IMU 9 axes, 2 720p stereo cameras, depth camera	NVidia Tegra K1 (quad-core CPU and Kepler GPU)	Gesture interaction	Remote box	Android	Commercial (2017)	3950$

		Optics	Display	Type / FOV	Resolution	Brightness	Sensors	CPU	Weight / Interaction	Connectivity	OS	Status	Price
ODG	R-7	Waveguide	Visual field	Binocular ~30° (proto at ~50°)	1280 × 720 (proto at 1920 ×1280)	?	IMU 9 axes, altimeter, 1080p camera	Qualcomm Snapdragon 805 2.7 GHz Quad-core	125g, touchpad on side of glasses	All integrated	Android 4.4	Commercial	2750$
Lumus	DK-50	Waveguide	Visual field	Binocular ~40° (proto at ~60°)	1280 × 720	3500 cd/m^2	IMU 9 axes, 4MP stereo camera	Qualcomm Snapdragon	Smartphone interface for interaction	All integrated	Android	Dev Kit	3000$
Optinvent	ORA 2	Waveguide	Visual field or remote	Monocular ~24°	640 × 480	> 3000 cd/m^2	GPS, IMU 9 axes, 5 MP camera	CPU Dual core with GPU	90g, touchpad on the side of the glasses	All integrated	Android 4.4.2	Commercial	699€
Laster	Lumina	Mirrors	Visual field	Binocular ~25° (proto at ~50°)	800 × 600	220cd/m^2	GPS, IMU 9 axes, 720p camera	MTK 6595 Octacore	165g, touchpad on the side	All integrated	Android 4.4	Prototype	?
Daqri	Smart Helmet	Waveguide	Visual field	Binocular ~80° ?	?	?	IMU 9 axes, 5 cameras (360), Depth, temperature and pressure sensor	Intel Core	1000g	All integrated	Android	Prototype	5000-15000
Technical illusions	CastAR	Stereo projection with active glasses	Visual field	Binocular ~90°	1280 × 720	?	IMU, head tracking	None	100g, Joypad	Cable	NA	Commercial (2017)	~400$

Table 2.1. Description of optical see-through AR systems

In early 2017, we were only at the fledgeling stages of the technological development of transparent AR devices. However, for a true democratization of AR, first in a professional context and later for general use, considerable effort is required for development related to miniaturization and the performance of electronic components, batteries and optical systems. Are AR glasses the next revolution after the smartphone? Given the large investments in the field, it would seem that several actors think so!

2.1.3.4. *Audio restitution*

The sound dimension is essential to the immersive experience that is desired from VR applications and which is also important for AR. In both cases, high-quality audio restitution can significantly enhance user experience. However, this experience may also be impaired if the audio feedback does not respect certain constraints.

In the VR-AR context, audio restitution is generally carried out using earphones, which are most often integrated into the visualization headset. The user may situate a virtual sound source in 3D thanks to *Binauralization*, which reproduces the characteristics of sound propagation into the listener's ear canal. These characteristics include, for each ear, an attenuation and modifications of the frequency spectrum, which are dependent on the position of the source of the sound. In practice, binaturalization is carried out using digital filters derived from acoustic measurements.

In a VR-AR application, the user regularly changes their point of view, especially through movements where they rotate their head. An immersive audio feedback therefore requires consequent movement (inverse rotation) of the virtual audio sources relative to the user. This rotation must be carried out in real time, and the latency must be within a few dozen milliseconds so that the user does not perceive any lag that can disrupt the immersion experience. Let us mention that the presentation of the sound scene is in the *ambisonics* format, which makes it possible to carry out rotations with a low computation cost. Incidentally, this is one of the reasons why YouTube and Facebook chose the ambisonics format for their $360°$ contents.

The quality of the equipment used (e.g. earphones, sound card) plays a definitive role in the quality of audio restitution. It is especially important to ensure the absence of any cross-talk (mix-up of the channels for the left and right ears), which could ruin the binaural feedback. The fidelity of earphones and the absence of distortion must also be taken into account.

There are a certain number of sound restitution engines on the market for VR and AR. Notable among these are: Wwise (Audiokinetic), Rapture3d (Blue Ripple Sound), the Audio Spatializer SDK for Unity, Facebook's Spatial Audio Workstation and RealSpace3d (VisiSonics).

2.1.4. *Technological challenges and perspectives*

2.1.4.1. *Visual field*

A VR or AR display device must ideally aim for the production of a visual signal that is free of any artifact that can be detected by the human visual system. It is therefore necessary to understand the capacity of the human visual system before defining the optimal characteristics of a VR or AR display system.

First of all, the human visual field, without turning the head, is considered on average to be 180 degrees horizontally (which can go up to 220 degrees for some individuals) and 130 degrees vertically. However, a human does not clearly perceive their environment over the whole of this region: optimal visual acuity, called foveal acuity, covers only approximately 3° to 5° of the total visual field. Thus, when you read this text, only 20° of your visual field is used, and 40° to allow you to perceive symbols. Colors are perceived in 60° of the central visual field and binocular vision covers 120°. However, these values are only valid for eyes in fixed position. However, eyes generally sweep across the scene and are thus capable of clearly perceiving an area that is much larger than the foveal acuity.

The earliest professional VR headsets that were sold covered a view angle between 100° and 110°, which is slightly smaller than the visual field coverage of binocular human vision. Moreover, extreme peripheral vision can detect movements that can warn you, for example, of an incoming danger from the side, or that can help a juggler catch his clubs while looking straight ahead. Thus, the VR headsets whose view angle is smaller than 110° generate a tunnel effect, that is, an unnatural perception of one's environment that reduces the field of peripheral vision.

Let us recall that the earliest solutions to largely overcome this limitation were the PiSight headsets developed by the company Sensics in 2006, which offered a field of vision that could extend up to 180°. This technology was based on a surface tiled with "small" LCD screens (up to 12 per eye) coupled with an optical system of excellent quality. The main drawbacks of this equipment, which hampered its success, were its very high cost and the complexity of producing 24 synchronized signals. Today, there are initial prototypes for VR headsets that use Fresnel lenses to preserve a reduced form factor. These can reach a field of vision of up to 210° (StarVR developed by Starbreeze, which acquired the French startup InfinitEye who had designed the technology). It is thus possible to cover the entire field of human vision using a VR headset, as long as the resolution of the screens is increased so that the image definition is not lost.

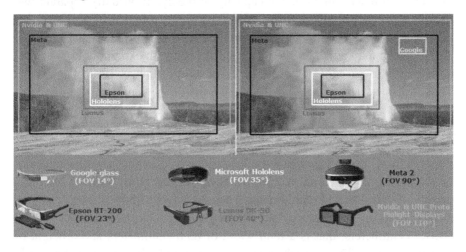

Figure 2.8. *Comparison of the field of vision for different optical see-through vision systems (© Wikimedia Commons - Mark Wagner). For a color version of this figure, see www.iste.co.uk/arnaldi/virtual.zip*

As concerns AR, the field of vision is markedly smaller. Glasses such as the Epson BT-200 have a field of vision of 20°, while Microsoft's HoloLens offers close to 30° (based on the proximity of the screens relative to the user's eyes). Figure 2.8 makes it possible to compare the field of vision of a few AR glasses. This limitation of optical see-through systems remains, even today, far-removed from the human field of vision. It is a large obstacle and one that is difficult to surmount. In effect, the widely used waveguide technology has a physical limitation related to its angle of total reflection (the critical angle where a ray of light passing from one medium to another is completely reflected), which theoretically restricts the field of vision of AR glasses to 60° [MAI 14]. At present, only the prototype for the optical system developed by NVidia, in collaboration with the University of North Carolina, makes it possible to reach a field of vision of 110° [MAI 14]. However, this technology, based on a micro-perforated screen, currently offers a very low-resolution display.

2.1.4.2. *Display resolution*

Another capacity of the visual system that must be taken into consideration when designing display devices for VR or AR is visual acuity, in the form of the power of discrimination: the capacity of the eye to visually separate two distinct objects. In France, visual acuity is often expressed in *tenths*, rather than as a minimum angle of separation. Nonetheless, normal visual acuity of 10/10 (which may go up to 20/10, for individuals with extremely high acuity) corresponds to an angle of one minute of an arc, that is 1/60 of a degree. Thus, a display device that aims to attain a field of vision of 210°, in which a user with 10/10 visual acuity does not perceive pixels must have a resolution greater than 8K per eye (ideally 9000 × 7800 pixels, if we consider that the horizontal field of vision for each eye is 150° and that the perceived size of the pixels is fixed, which is not exactly the case given the radial distortion caused by the lenses). By the end of 2016, the best screens on the market offered a density of 210 pixels per centimeter. Thus, to achieve 9000 × 7800 pixels in the VR headset, we must provide for two screens with a dimension of 42.8 × 37.1 centimeters, that is a total width of 85.6 centimeters and a height of 37.1 centimeters. These numbers are, of course, only theoretical and are only used to provide indications and the order of magnitude needed to adapt to each individual's capacity for perception.

However, several generations have been able to enjoy a wide variety of audiovisual content on television sets with a standard resolution of 720 × 576 pixels without being particularly bothered by the low image quality. The arrival of 720p (1280 × 720 pixels), and then high definition or full HD (1920 × 1080 pixels), followed by ultra-high definition (3840 × 2160 pixels) and the imminent 8K resolution (7680 × 4320 pixels), has made it possible to improve the image quality. However, what impact has this increase in screen resolutions really had on the attention and immersion level of the viewer vis-à-vis audiovisual content? We can thus consider the resolution of current

VR headsets as being a standard resolution (2160 × 1200 pixels). Moreover, in the coming years, these resolutions will increase, as they did for TV screens, resulting in ever-improving image quality until it reaches the optimal resolution that is coherent with the human visual system.

2.1.4.3. *Display frequency*

It is commonly acknowledged that there is no use displaying a video at a rate faster than 24 images per second because of one of the characteristics of the human visual system: persistence of vision, or "retinal persistence". Consequently, the frame rate for cinematographic content has been standardized at 24 images per second, and for television content, it is 25 images per second in Europe and 30 images per second in the United States and in Japan. Retinal persistence is based on the property of projected images being retained on the retina, allowing the human visual system to fuse together a series of isolated images into a fluid, animated image. In the 19th Century, when our understanding of vision was limited to optical and mechanical properties of the human eye, retinal persistence was the only explanation given to explain the human ability to merge a series of images. Today, however, neuropsychologists consider this explanation to be incomplete or even wrong. These neuropsychologists attribute a key role in the merging of images to the visual cortex in the brain. This is mainly thanks to the beta effect that makes it possible to interpolate missing images between two successive images from a dynamic scene, thereby ensuring there is continuity of movement. The beta effect is often confused with the phi effect, which allows us to ignore the flickering of black screens between the displays of two successive images, related to the shutters on the film projectors that were used earlier in cinemas.

If the beta effect makes it possible to interpolate missing images, why are we looking to increase the frame rate in VR and AR devices? The fact is that the beta effect works perfectly for cinematographic content, as the cameras generate a motion blur. It is sufficient to stop on the image of wheel on a car travelling at full speed, or on the blades of a helicopter in flight, to visualize the blur associated with a film camera that required much greater shutter speeds than current digital sensors. Let us also note that the flickering is perceptible when seen on a television with a frame rate of 25 frames per second of video captured by high-speed cameras, where the motion blur is greatly reduced, or even for synthesis images rendered in real-time, which are perfectly clear and show no motion blur, requiring a high-frequency display (120 Hz) in order to provide a high-quality visual experience. As a result, the most recent generation of rendering engines now have an in-built ability to generate this motion blur to improve the visual quality of television screens operating at a frequency of 25 frames per second. This is the same for digital special effects in films, which require a motion-blur post-processing in order to ensure coherence with the capture of images by a cinematographic camera.

We can thus conclude that a rate of 24 frames per second is quite inadequate. At present, HMDs only display about 90 images per second but, in the coming years, this number should go up to 120 frames per second. In theory, the greater the number of images per second, the better the quality of experience for the user; thus, it is essential that the system be able to calculate 120 images per eye per second, or 240 images per second.

2.1.4.4. *Graphical computing capacity*

Assuming that it is technologically possible to produce two 8K screens displaying 120 images per second, projected onto the range of the human field of vision – is it then possible to carry out a real-time feedback using currently available equipment? The response, of course, depends on the complexity of the 3D scene. Generally speaking however, at this point, mid-2017, it would be best to invest in a bundle of graphics cards if we wish to attain the desired speed of 120 images per second.

The latest generation of Graphical Processor architectures, developed by NVidia, the Pascal architecture, offers several optimizations dedicated to multi-screen displays among which are the various VR-AR display devices. Thus, processing of the vertices that make up the virtual scene is carried out in a single operation for all of the screens. Moreover, the distortion of the rendered image, specific to each lens in the VR headset, which allows the user's eyes to perceive a rectified image, is optimized in the post-processing using a dedicated shader. Finally, as the size of the pixel perceived by each eye varies due to the radial distortion generated by the lenses of the VR headset, optimization consists of locally deteriorating the resolution of the image formed from the rendered graphics. Coupled with a gaze-tracking system, it could be possible to carry out a high-resolution restitution in the zone close to the fovea and to optimize the restitution by reducing resolution around the peripheral vision of the user. At this point (mid-2017), there is as yet no headset with in-built gaze-tracking that is rapid and precise enough.

These optimizations, coupled with an increase in the graphical processing centers and the reduction in finesse of etching, allow us to foresee an extremely powerful graphical capacity that will make it possible for future generations of VR headsets to render ultra-realistic images.

It is, nonetheless, essential to remind ourselves that the increase in graphical processing capacity cannot do away with optimization of the 3D scenes for a real-time display. Let us also recall that the approaches used for 3D modeling of the scene are not similar and are based on their use: whether for a video game, a VR-AR application or even an animation film, with each image requiring a computation time that varies from a few milliseconds to a few minutes or even up to a few hours.

The following rules (non-exhaustive) make it possible to improve the feedback time for a 3D scene while also conserving a high level of realism. First of all, we must reduce the geometric complexity of a virtual screen by limiting the number of objects and associated triangles that must be processed by the graphics card for each feedback. There are several possible solutions: the first consists of displaying only what is essential by either suppressing hidden or occluded parts from a scene from a given perspective (occultation management), or by adapting the complexity of a virtual object based on its distance from its viewpoint (level of detail). The second solution is based on the use of shaders, programming interfaces that allow the optimization of the rendering pipeline of the graphic card. For instance, these shaders can "move" some geometrical details to material textures in order to reduce the processing complexity and therefore the computation time. Bump mapping, for example, makes it possible to bring in relief features onto a plane surface by specifying the normals to the surface in a dedicated texture. During the computation of illumination, these will highlight the roughness of a virtual object. Other techniques such as relief mapping or displacement mapping make it possible to create a fine geometry on the fly on the surface of the objects, while not increasing the number of triangles in the original object. Another optimization consists of grouping the different sub-elements of an object into a single mesh and into a single texture. Indeed, in a large majority of rendering effects it is the allocation of memory and loading of geometries and textures that is resource-intensive, rather than the processing of meshes and textures. Thus, the rendering of a virtual scene containing 50 objects made up of 1000 triangles each will always be longer than the rendering of a scene containing a single object made up of 50,000 triangles. A final optimization consists of pre-computing possibilities: for example, the lighting and shadows of the static elements in a virtual scene. This computation will be carried out once and for all and may be combined in real time with the computation of illumination and shadows of dynamic elements (objects and lighting) during the rendering stage.

2.1.4.5. *Mobility*

Mobility is a functionality that greatly enhances the user's experience in VR and AR. Being able to move around in vast spaces is often essential to many functions and in order to have this ability to move around, we need to remove several barriers. We need energy independence, positioning coverage over a large area and a wireless solution that offers a high computation capacity.

Let us begin with energy independence. A mobile VR or AR device is equipped with many electronic components that consume electric energy. From the screens to the sensors to the in-built processing devices (e.g. CPU, GPU, VPU, memories), these devices are severely tested and require oversized batteries in order to provide independent use for a few hours. However, these batteries also represent a significant percentage of the weight of the device and have the disadvantage of heating up, which means that VR and AR headsets and glasses must be very carefully designed in order to ensure that the user is comfortable. Several solutions are currently possible to increase this independence. First of all, new energy-storage technology like lithium-air could, in the next five years, offer a storage-capacity/weight ratio that is much better than the lithium-ion technology used today. The generalization of smartphones has modified the policies of processor manufacturers who no longer aim for simply increasing computing capacity, but also focus on low energy consumption by the electronic components. While waiting for electronic components with very low energy consumption in association with batteries with high-performance storage, the various uses of the device will also require great independence and must use remote batteries (e.g. batteries worn on a belt and connected to the display device through a wire) or batteries that can be easily changed without stopping the device so as to ensure continuity of service.

As concerns the area within which a user or the VR or AR device must be precisely situated (position and orientation), the falling prices of infrared positioning technology makes it possible to imagine that, at least for professional uses, the range of coverage of immersive devices may be extended over vast areas. Indeed, though the Lighthouse of the HTC/Valve is not designed for professional use and while it is not possible, at present, to extend coverage area by duplicating Lighthouses, this new technology should allow, within a few years, the coverage of very vast zones of localization, without requiring an outlay of thousands of euros (as is currently the case for professional motion-capture systems). The ultimate solution would consist of offering positioning services by simply using sensors built into the device, without equipping the real environment with expensive sensors. This is the approach proposed by AR systems that are based uniquely on vision sensors and internal inertial sensors to locate themselves in space. Moreover, Microsoft's HoloLens has shown considerable technological advances with respect to the state of the art in this domain. Even though infrared positioning systems based on external sensors are, at present, much more robust and precise, we must wait and watch over the next five years to see whether this type of independent positioning system will be generalized in VR headsets. It will also be useful to go beyond systems that use structured light projection, which are not usable indoors.

Finally, if we want mobility, there must be no "ball and chain"! That is, the VR headset and AR glasses cannot be linked to any computing unit by a cable. Integrating all these computing capacities into a portable device (via a smartphone or a fully integrated device) offers this freedom of movement. The only caveat is that VR and AR that digitally simulate a virtual environment will require the appropriate computing capabilities in order to offer the user the best experience (see Chapter 3 to understand the challenges involved here). In addition, while the computing resources gap between a mobile device and a graphic station is reducing every year, an experience of optimal quality can only be offered by equipment that offers high-end performance. Consequently, an initial solution would consist of integrating this computing capacity into a dedicated backpack, rather than around the user's head; this backpack would integrate the equivalent of a laptop computer with high computing capacity. This solution offers several advantages, as it combines freedom of movement with high computing capacity, and this is likely to be seen in several VR arcades and theme parks as the company The Void proposes. Nonetheless, this solution is not yet ideal as the users must carry the backpack weighing between 3 and 5 kg (highly inconvenient given the long lines in some theme parks or even for general use at home), which still does not offer the computing capacity of a farm of graphics servers required for certain professional uses.

Hence, the majority of VR headset manufacturers work with their partners to develop a wireless real-time streaming rendered by a graphic station towards the VR headset. In addition, as will be discussed further (see section 3.4.1), a good quality experience for the user requires extremely low latency for the transmission of images, of the order of one to three milliseconds. The problem thus consists of defining a compromise between latency, display quality (resolution and frame rate) and wireless network flow. We may imagine that improvement in image quality at a constant rate would require the use of better performing mechanisms for video compression. Indeed, video compression techniques that offer the best performances are based on an inter-coding mechanism (using past or even future images to compress a current image in the video) that is adapted to the stream called "live" (~200 ms), but which are far from achieving the desired latency levels for VR (~3 ms).

Thus, the only solution that allows for an increase in display quality for a wireless system lies in increasing the network flow. The maximum theoretical 802.1g WiFi rate that is widely used today is 54Mbps. In these conditions, it is difficult to imagine streaming 2160 × 1200 video streams at a frequency of 90 images per second, characteristics of the Oculus Rift CV1 or the HTC/Valve Vive (the equivalent of 5.21Gbps without compression or approximately 2 Gbps with very low latency compression). Only the new generation WiFi at 60 GHz, also called WiGig (Wireless Gigabit), achieves theoretical rates of 7 Gbps. However, WiGig coverage remains restricted and the 2 Gbps required can be reached only in a room of medium size. Thus, WiGig can respond, in the short term, to the problem of wireless transmission of video flow in current VR headsets, but this technology will rapidly realize its limitations as the characteristics of the headsets evolve. What solutions are thus possible for headsets offering a resolution of 4k or even 8K per eye and 120 images per second? Communication technologies that use visible light, such as LiFi, today reach rates of several dozen Gbps in an extremely controlled environment but commercial solutions offer flow rates of the order of a dozen Mbps. What will be the theoretical rates of future generations of WiFi (90 GHz, 120 GHz) and what will be the coverage these technologies offer? The question of wireless streaming of video feed in VR headsets remains complex and poses a sizeable challenge to the VR headset industry.

2.1.5. *Conclusions on new equipment*

2.1.5.1. *Adoption by the general public*

The generalization of VR headsets has begun with the video game and entertainment markets. Oculus, HTC/Valve Vive, Samsung Gear VR and other headsets started out by offering applications that were essentially video games or 360° videos. Among the earliest demonstrations you had roller-coaster simulations that aroused intense, even unpleasant, sensations for many users. These effects, which could not be controlled, eventually proved beneficial. First of all, they heightened the buzz around these headsets. Second, new entrants into the field soon realized what the professional VR world had known for a long time, namely that immersion is first and foremost a user experience and the human factors must be prioritized over any technological consideration.

This is how the largest video game studios put in place user-centered design approaches, moving towards carefully considered application designs that were completely adapted to the restrictions posed by the headsets. The results of this move by the video game industry have already started feeding into the professional VR world. This is also reflected in an interconnection between the video game world and the VR world, as is proven by the development in equipment (as we just saw) as well as new software (as we will see in the next section of this chapter).

It is undeniably true that, despite colossal financial investments being realized by manufacturers, the hypothesis of widespread general use still remains doubtful for several reasons. First of all, the cost. While vendors of these systems present the cost as a small amount, the buyer requires a minimum of a thousand euros to buy the headset and, to this, we must add at least the same amount for a computer that is powerful enough to truly make use of these immersive capabilities. We are still quite far from "low-cost" budgets that the public keep hearing about! Of course, these costs *will* certainly reduce. Let us take the example of the Sony Playstation VR headset, available for around 500€ and which can be connected with a Playstation 4 console.

The second reason has to do with the technological limitations described earlier: whether in terms of field of vision, resolution or display rate, these reduce the comfort and thus the pleasure the user derives from the experience over a long duration (beyond the "Whoa!" effect, experienced the first time they use it).

The third (and certainly not the least important) reason is related to the richness and diversity of the range of applications available. Indeed, other than video games, which only interest a part of the general population (especially the younger generations), suppliers must design applications where the user derives true benefits from VR. Building, tourism and heritage are fields that are already being explored by developers, but it is evident that unless this challenge is taken up, VR headsets for the general public will join the ranks of other technological innovations that met with no long-term success.

As concerns the AR market, the digital giants (e.g. Google, Microsoft, Apple) have again invested billions of dollars in the acquisition of innovative companies and the development of new products, in the hope of ushering in a new technological era to follow the Smartphone Age. Unfortunately, the low technological maturity of these devices does not allow us to foresee, in the short term, any real massive commercialization for the general public. Increasing the field of vision and independence, improving the recalibration of superposed information and, of course, reducing costs - all of these are essential in order for a true democratization. Moreover, let us not forget a necessary improvement of the form in order to make the devices much more discreet and comfortable: will a user agree to carry a piece of equipment visible to other people around them? This is the fundamental question, which could cause all attempts to fail, even though the technological limitations are removed. While waiting for these changes to take place, we may consider the possibility that the market for professional uses will take over and guarantee financial backing for these developments, as there is a considerable economic challenge.

Even though this exercise is a difficult one, let us try and compare the markets for VR and AR. If limitations related to technology and usage are removed, AR glasses will become markedly more successful with the general public as they can potentially be used in a large number of daily activities, especially if can be used as mobile devices. Some actors thus see these as a "natural" extension of the personal-assistant role that the smartphone currently plays, allowing the user to make better decisions. The challenge is one of magnitude, but if it is met it will open the door to a real technological revolution in our lives.

2.2. New software

2.2.1. *Introduction*

The first part of this chapter revealed the multitude of equipment needed to allow a virtual reality system to give the user the sensation of being in a virtual world and interacting with it. Similarly, augmented reality requires specific equipment to analyze the real world and allow the overlay of virtual objects. The software used to build a VR-AR application must therefore make it possible to optimally use all these devices and make them communicate with the digital simulation that processes the information received and computes the information to be restituted to the user. This device must therefore simultaneously manage a large number of functions, as shown in the interaction cycle. This cycle goes from the user's action until the perception of the result of this action (Figure 2.9).

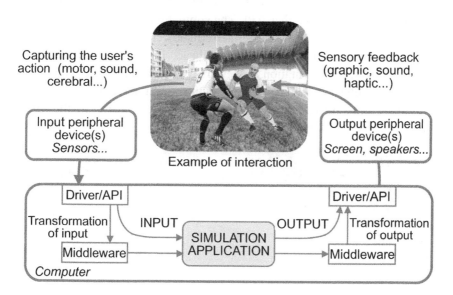

Figure 2.9. *Interaction cycle starting from the user's action until the perception of the result of this action. Developing a VR-AR application requires collecting data from the input devices, processing this information and deducing the sensory feedback to produce, then transmitting this information to the output devices*

Beyond the simulation of the 3D virtual world in which the user is immersed (in the case of VR) or which is superimposed on to the real world (in the case of AR), the application must be able to guarantee interaction between the user and this simulation. That is, it must be able to read the user's motor actions and supply the appropriate sensory information. Let us consider, for example, a VR-based sports training tool, the objective of which is to train a rugby defender to block an attacker who attempts to go around him with or without a body swerve (see Figure 2.10). In order to be successful, the application must provide a virtual adversary who reacts to the defender's real actions and adapts their attack. The first step for such an application consists of collecting the defender's movements using a motion capture device. The motor data is then transmitted to a computer through a driver that the application can consult via an interface called API (Application Programming Interface). The simulation then computes the virtual attacker's reaction, based on the defender's real action. This reaction by the attacker is translated through a modification in his animation, which is then transmitted to the output device via another API. The simulation must also manage other parameters such as change in the immersed subject's (user's) point of view, for example, due to the position of their head, if they are in a CAVE, or through their position/orientation, if they are using a headset (see section 3.2). The sensory feedback is then carried out by the output device or devices, here, for instance, only through a visual feedback in stereovision in the virtual environment that includes the attacker.

Figure 2.10. *Example of the interaction in virtual reality between (a) a real defender, fitted with a VR headset, and (b) a virtual attacker who may or may not use a body swerve to go around him*

Owing to the complexity of developing such VR-AR applications, it is common to use specific software. That is why many companies have specialized in developing solutions for a specific field. Just a few examples are XVR Simulation [XVR 17] for training in the field of safety and security, iris [IRI 17] for architecture, IC.IDO [ESI 17] for industrial prototyping, ParaView [PAR 17] for the analysis and visualization of complex data, FlowVR [FLO 17] for large-scale parallel simulation, and Augment [AUG 17] for managing and visualizing 3D content in AR. It is therefore possible to use this kind of "turnkey" application but, in this chapter, we will be discussing different approaches to creating a specific VR-AR application.

In accordance with the interaction cycle, the development of a VR-AR application can be divided into two parts. The first part, described in section 2.2.2, consists of developing digital simulations that process information obtained by the input devices and that compute the results to be furnished to the output devices. The second part, described in section 2.2.3, concerns the communication between this simulation and the input and output devices.

2.2.2. *Developing 3D applications*

A VR-AR application is based on use in a 3D world in which the user is immersed (in the case of VR) or which has been superimposed on the real world (in the case of AR). There are many ways in which this 3D environment can be managed and visualized, depending on factors such as cost, development time, flexibility or even ease of use. In this section, we will describe these different approaches, beginning with the most "basic" programming, all the way up to specific VR-AR tools.

2.2.2.1. *"Basic" graphic programming*

The most elementary approach consists of creating a 3D application by directly accessing the drivers and programming interfaces of the graphics cards of the equipment used. The drawback of this approach is that each application depends on the device. This difficulty may be overcome using programming interfaces such as OpenGL or DirectX, which make it possible to work outside of a particular type of equipment, rather than restricting oneself to a specific device. The main advantage of this approach is that it offers complete control over the entire creation process from the 3D environment to how it is rendered graphically. It is thus possible to directly control the facets that make up the 3D objects, to create one's own scene graph, the hierarchic structure used to define relations and transformations between objects and notably manage animations or even propose new structures. This also allows us to control the graphic pipeline, the succession of steps required to go from calculating these facets until their final rendering, via the elimination of the hidden parts and application of textures and lighting. It is thus possible to choose during what step of the process this or that action must be carried out to optimize the application's performance.

This option therefore potentially offers the best performance as well as a very high flexibility. However, the work required is much more complex, as it requires the creation of the desired functionalities, the loading of the 3D environment (resulting from a modeler such as 3DS Max or Maya, for instance) and the recovery of data from the motion capture. The main drawback is the inability of such an approach to be portable.

2.2.2.2. *Graphic libraries*

In order to avoid creating all the required functionalities, libraries such as OpenSceneGraph [OPE 17b] offer a slightly greater control of 3D models, thanks mainly to how they manage the loading and saving of these models, animation methods used for the objects and also the control over lighting and shadow, camera placement, etc. These libraries make it possible to significantly speed up the creation of a 3D application. However, they still remain rather restricted to specialists.

In addition, some of these libraries may depend on operating systems such as Windows, Linux or Mac OSX. It is therefore difficult to develop solutions that will also work on mobile telephones or on video game consoles. Finally, in the context of VR-AR applications, one of the major problems is that they focus on the modeling, animation and rendering of 3D objects, but very rarely manage the associated VR-AR devices or the different sensors - all of which are, however, important elements in an interactive application. Apart from the cost of developing these interfaces with these peripheral devices (see section 2.2.3.1), it is, above all, the maintenance and evolution of these applications that pose a problem, given the extremely rapid developments in the field of VR-AR and the constant emergence of new peripheral equipment on the market.

2.2.2.3. *Video game engines*

With the aim of being more productive, the video game industry has, for many years, developed generic environments called "engines", that are central to all their productions. These engines are now associated with highly powerful editors that make it very easy to create 3D applications. These editors (notably, via a graphic interface and without development) make it possible to manage the visual layout of a scene, the sound, the camera, the animation, etc. (see Figure 2.11). In addition, these engines work on different platforms; computers, mobile telephones or video game consoles. Hence, they are widely used to make games, not only on mobile telephones and video game consoles but also for online games.

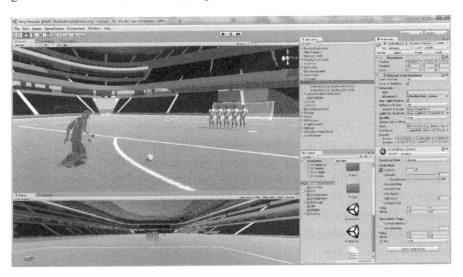

Figure 2.11. *Example of the graphic editor of the game engine Unity, which makes it possible to easily manage the visual layout of a scene, the sound, the camera, placement, etc. For a color version of this figure, see www.iste.co.uk/arnaldi/virtual.zip*

Finally, among the many existing engines, each with its own fame and ease of use, the best-known are: Unity [UNI 17], Unreal [UNR 17], Cry Engine [CRY 17], Ogre3D [OGR 17] and Irrlicht [IRR 17]. Apart from the ability to produce the same content on different platforms in very little time and, above all, using the same application, these engines offer a large number of functionalities that speed up the creation of these applications. These include: managing all the graphic parameters related to the rendering of objects, lighting and camera placement. However, they also additionally permit the management of the physical simulation of objects (taking shocks into account, for example), spatialized sound to diffuse the sound environment by taking into account the sources of the sound, and the animation of complex structures such as virtual humans.

Finally, these tools have resulted in a large community of users who offer many additional resources such as tutorials to make them more accessible, as well as the development of scripts that can widen their functionalities, including within the field of VR-AR, as shown in the following section. Among the engines listed above, Unity has currently emerged as one of the major actors, due to its ease of use. It can thus be used by other communities such as the neurosciences, Sports and Physical Activities, medicine, etc.

2.2.3. *Managing peripheral devices*

After having developed the heart of the application, namely simulation, this must now be made to communicate with the user immersed in the experience, by exploiting the peripheral input devices which acquire motor information from the user and the output peripheral devices, which produce sensory feedback. Just as with the creation of 3D graphic simulations, it is possible to manage the interface with the peripheral devices at different levels, from direct control via a programming interface to the most high-level and most generic tools.

2.2.3.1. *Direct control of peripheral devices*

In order to allow an application to communicate with a peripheral driver, the constructor provides a programming interface that gives access to all the functions, making it possible to control this device or to exchange data with the device. Thus, the developer only needs to call upon these functions to allow an application to manage the peripheral devices. In practice, all equipment differ from one another and the programming interfaces may be very varied, including for peripheral devices that offer exactly the same functionalities. For example, depending on whether the peripheral device is connected through a USB port or through Bluetooth, the interface is likely to be different. Similarly, if you have two rotation sensors developed by two different manufacturers, it is highly unlikely that they will have the same interfaces, at least for the function names.

Fortunately, certain norms have emerged resulting in standardized programming interfaces for classic peripheral devices (keyboards, mouse, joysticks, audio headsets or printers), which make it possible to access any keyboard or mouse without wondering about the manufacturer of the equipment. A change in brand does not prevent the application from working and, above all, requires no modification of its code. Unfortunately, there is no such standard, at present, for VR[13], leading the application developer to update their software for each new device and its associated interface. To avoid having to update these devices for each new equipment, the developer must construct an abstraction of the peripheral devices based on their functionality (a motion capture sensor, for example) and then create a new instance of this abstraction for each new equipment. In addition, the multiplication of the links between the application and the different interfaces increases the problems related to the management of different versions of these interfaces and the auto-detection of each equipment used. With the constant development of a large number of VR-AR tools, directly controlling these peripheral devices poses a large problem to app developers in terms of maintenance.

2.2.3.2. *Libraries for managing peripheral devices*

Libraries to manage peripheral devices were proposed in order to simplify communication with these devices. They offer abstractions that make it possible to address generic equipment offering a standardized interface rather than equipment of one particular brand. For motion sensors, for example, position and/or rotation information may be collected using the same functions, regardless of the technology used by the sensor. These libraries also offer a more or less simple means for the user to specify what peripheral device they are currently using, or even automatically detecting this when the application is launched. Finally, these libraries make it easy to configure peripheral devices by specifying initial data, for example, for display on the screens of a CAVE (see Figure 2.12) or even the initial positions of the joystick or headset.

---

13 In fact, such efforts at bringing in norms have been made in VR as well as AR, but these norms have not been applied.

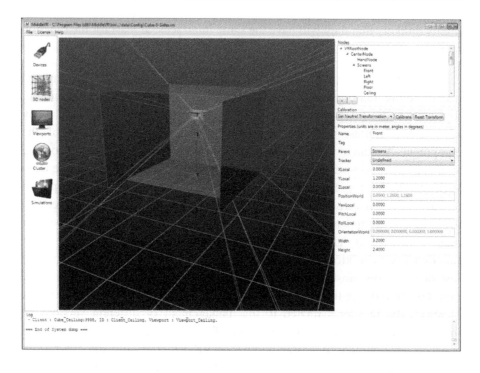

Figure 2.12. *Example for the configuration of a five-face peripheral visualization device, using MiddleVR. For a color version of this figure, see www.iste.co.uk/arnaldi/virtual.zip*

Apart from collecting data from the input peripheral devices, some of these libraries, such as VRPN (Virtual Reality Peripheral Network) [VRP 17] and trackd [TRA 17], are able to take into account the equipment that is connected to one or more computers through the network. This characteristic makes it possible for the developer to distance themselves from the chosen material architecture and communicate with its sensors, whether they are at a distance (through the network) or local (the same machine). Other libraries, such as CAVElib [CAV 17] are focused on the visual restitution of the simulation, with the management of the changes in point of view and stereovision on the varied projection configurations: from a simple screen to multi-screen and multi-machine systems such as the CAVE systems. Finally, some libraries propose managing all these different peripheral devices such as OSVR (Open-Source Virtual Reality for gaming) [OSV 17] or MiddleVR SDK [MID 17] and TechViz [TEC 17], which are libraries that are equipped with a middleware, which is an external software positioned at the interface between the application and the equipment. In this case, its role is to provide a software interface to easily configure the different equipment that is to be used with the same software application.

As concerns AR, several libraries offer specific functionalities such as the evaluation of the position and orientation of the user in interactive time in real space. OpenCV [OPE 17a] makes it possible to acquire and process the images, from the detection of structures ranging from lines to complex motifs. All these functionalities make it possible to superimpose a 3D virtual object onto the real world observed by the user. The largest libraries are ARToolkit [ART 17], Vuforia [VUF 17] and Wikitude [WIK 17], which offer all the functionalities described above, managing mobile platforms and VR-AR headsets, and offer interfaces for the development tools (see section 2.2.4.2). Apple's ARkit will be launched in September 2017, providing the same functionalities to platforms based on iOS.

2.2.4. *Dedicated VR-AR software solutions*

Other higher-level software solutions propose integrating the management of 3D environments and peripheral devices in order to simplify the creation of the VR-AR application.

2.2.4.1. *Dedicated tools for the creation of VR-AR*

Some graphic tools can be used to simplify the process of creating VR-AR applications. For AR, for example, Wikitude offers developers an SDK on which a software solution can be constructed, which allows the recording of images to be recognized and then the content to be associated with these images without programming or even publishing the applications in one's own virtual shop.

The Eon Creator software, distributed by the company Eon Reality [EON 17], offers a similar VR-AR solution, which makes it possible to select 3D models, interact with these models and easily diffuse this content. It also offers a complete development environment to manage functionalities similar to those of video games, such as feedback and physical simulation. In addition to a similar development environment, the WorldViz software [WOR 17] makes it possible to manage peripherals with different projections and/or multiple users, etc. It also offers configurations embedded in the equipment.

These tools dedicated to the creation of VR-AR applications remain small in number, however. Indeed, editors must dedicate a large number of resources to developing them. Restricting them only to VR-AR limits their use to a rather niche market today, which makes it difficult to make these solutions competitive with respect to a generic game engine reinforced with plugins.

2.2.4.2. *VR-AR plugins for video game engines*

Section 2.2.2.3 described the emergence of video game engines for the creation of 3D application content. Even though this software is not originally meant for VR-AR, their ease of use, their multiple functionalities and their openness to developing additional scripts ensure that they are relevant reference tools in these fields. Indeed, to compensate for the absence of management of the peripheral devices, which are one of the main components needed to use an interactive application, the developer community that uses these tools first created specific plugins based on the programming interfaces used by the constructors. With the large rise in numbers in this community, constructors now directly offer plugins to communicate with their new models as soon as these are launched and sometimes engines even integrate them as native tools as is the case with the Oculus and HTC Vive headsets and the Unity software.

Other companies offer more generic plugins used to manage peripheral devices, which are directly integrated into these motors. These plugins also extend existing functionalities with advanced management of stereoscopy, multi-computer synchronization in a cluster, force-feedback peripheral devices and managing multiple users in virtual reality. Some actors have developed generic libraries (see section 2.2.3.2) for output peripheral devices, such as getReal3D, or for all peripheral devices, such as MiddleVR for Unity or Techviz. Similarly, for AR, there are libraries such as Vuforia or Wikitude.

2.2.5. *Conclusion*

VR-AR applications are increasingly being developed with the help of video game engines such as Unity. Indeed, constructors now directly offer plugins that communicate with their new peripheral devices and generic integrated solutions also exist, such as MiddleVR for Unity. This type of development makes it possible to implement solutions much more rapidly and at a lower cost, and to adapt them to the new peripheral devices without even recompiling the application. In addition, and most importantly, they make it possible to easily manage the addition of a new peripheral device, which is essential given the continuous development of new, low-cost VR-AR devices.

2.3. Bibliography

[ART 17] ARTOOLKIT, "ARToolkit", artoolkit.org, 2017.

[AUG 17] AUGMENT, "Augment", www.augment.com, 2017.

[AZU 97] AZUMA R.T., "A survey of augmented reality", *Presence: Teleoperators and Virtual Environments*, vol. 6, no. 4, pp. 355–385, August 1997.

[CAV 17] CAVELIB, "CAVElib", www.mechdyne.com/software.aspx?name=CAVELib, 2017.

[CRU 92] CRUZ-NEIRA C., SANDIN D.J., DEFANTI T.A. *et al.*, "The CAVE: audio visual experience automatic virtual environment", *Communication ACM*, vol. 35, no. 6, pp. 64–72, ACM, June 1992.

[CRU 93] CRUZ-NEIRA C., SANDIN D.J., DEFANTI T.A., "Surround-screen projection-based virtual reality: the design and implementation of the CAVE", *Proceedings of the 20th Annual Conference on Computer Graphics and Interactive Techniques*, ACM, pp. 135–142, 1993.

[CRY 17] CRY ENGINE, "Cry Engine", www.cryengine.com, 2017.

[EON 17] EON REALITY, "EON Reality", www.eonreality.com, 2017.

[ESI 17] ESI GROUP, "IC.IDO", www.esi-group.com, 2017.

[FLO 17] FLOWVR, "FlowVR", flowvr.sourceforge.net, 2017.

[FRE 14] FREY J., GERVAIS R., FLECK S. *et al.*, "Teegi: tangible EEG interface", *Proceedings of the 27th Annual ACM Symposium on User Interface Software and Technology*, UIST'14, New York, USA, ACM, pp. 301–308, 2014.

[FUC 05] FUCHS P., MOREAU G. (eds), *Le Traité de la Réalité Virtuelle*, Les Presses de l'Ecole des Mines, Paris, 2005.

[FUC 09] FUCHS P., MOREAU G., DONIKIAN S., *Le traité de la réalité virtuelle Volume 5 - Les humains virtuels*, Mathématique et informatique, Les Presses de l'Ecole des Mines, Paris, 2009.

[IRI 17] IRIS, "iris", irisvr.com, 2017.

[IRR 17] IRRLICHT, "Irrlicht", irrlicht.sourceforge.net, 2017.

[JON 13] JONES B.R., BENKO H., OFEK E. *et al.*, "IllumiRoom: peripheral projected illusions for interactive experiences", *Proceedings of the SIGCHI Conference on Human Factors in Computing Systems*, CHI'13, New York, USA, ACM, pp. 869–878, 2013.

[JON 14] JONES B., SODHI R., MURDOCK M. *et al.*, "RoomAlive: magical experiences enabled by scalable, adaptive projector-camera units", *Proceedings of the 27th Annual ACM Symposium on User Interface Software and Technology*, UIST'14, New York, USA, ACM, pp. 637–644, 2014.

[LAV 17] LAVIOLA J.J., KRUIJFF E., MCMAHAN R. *et al.*, *3D User Interfaces: Theory and Practice*, Addison Wesley, Boston, 2017.

[MAI 14] MAIMONE A., LANMAN D., RATHINAVEL K. *et al.*, "Pinlight displays: wide field of view augmented reality eyeglasses using defocused point light sources", *ACM Transaction Graphic*, vol. 33, no. 4, pp. 89:1–89:11, ACM, July 2014.

[MID 17] MIDDLEVR, "middleVR", www.middlevr.com, 2017.

[OGR 17] OGRE3D, "Ogre3D", www.ogre3d.org, 2017.

[OPE 17a] OPENCV, "OpenCV", opencv.org, 2017.

[OPE 17b] OPENSCENEGRAPH, "OpenSceneGraph", www.openscenegraph.org, 2017.

[OSV 17] OSVR, "OSVR", www.osvr.org, 2017.

[PAR 17] PARAVIEW, "ParaView", www.paraview.org, 2017.

[REI 10] REITMAYR G., LANGLOTZ T., WAGNER D. *et al.*, "Simultaneous localization and mapping for augmented reality", *2010 International Symposium on Ubiquitous Virtual Reality*, pp. 5–8, July 2010.

[SAR 13] SARAYEDDINE K., MIRZA K., "Key challenges to affordable see-through wearable displays: the missing link for mobile AR mass deployment", *Photonic Applications for Aerospace, Commercial and Harsh Environments IV*, vol. 8720, SPIE, April 2013.

[TEC 17] TECHVIZ, "techviz", www.techviz.net, 2017.

[TRA 17] TRACKD, "trackd", www.mechdyne.com/software.aspx?name=trackd, 2017.

[UNI 17] UNITY3D, "Unity3D", unity3d.com, 2017.

[UNR 17] UNREAL, "Unreal", www.unrealengine.com, 2017.

[VRP 17] VRPN, "VRPN", github.com/vrpn/vrpn/wiki, 2017.

[VUF 17] VUFORIA, "Vuforia", vuforia.com, 2017.

[WAG 10] WAGNER D., REITMAYR G., MULLONI A. *et al.*, "Real-time detection and tracking for augmented reality on mobile phones", *IEEE Transactions on Visualization and Computer Graphics*, vol. 16, no. 3, pp. 355–368, May 2010.

[WIK 17] WIKITUDE, "wikitude", www.wikitude.com, 2017.

[WOR 17] WORLDVIZ, "WorldViz", www.worldviz.com, 2017.

[XVR 17] XVR SIMULATION, "XVR", www.xvrsim.com, 2017.

Complexity and Scientific Challenges

3.1. Introduction: complexity

Simulating a reactive and credible world, in view of 3D interaction with the user, is not an easy task. This is all the more the case if the app designer desires that the virtual environment behave as close to the real environment as possible. Certain industrial VR applications require high fidelity of the environment, its evolution, its reaction to a user interaction and, finally, of an eventual autonomy. The objective of this chapter is to discuss the topics for which solutions exist, but which still pose scientific challenges and elements of complexity which would be helpful to discuss in detail. We will discuss physical models to detect collisions in section 3.1.1. Section 3.1.2 will discuss the problem of the virtual human. We then have section 3.1.3, which examines naturalness of the interaction. Section 3.1.4 proposes an analysis of force feedback.

The scientific challenges discussed here are not the only ones that arise. In AR, for example, given that it establishes a link between the real and virtual world, newer challenges are emerging, which will be discussed in 3.2. To overcome the difficulty of having truly natural interfaces in VR-AR, researchers and app developers have had to work on the creation of user interfaces that are specific to 3D environments. These will be discussed in

Chapter written by Ferran ARGELAGUET SANZ, Bruno ARNALDI, Jean-Marie BURKHARDT, Géry CASIEZ, Stéphane DONIKIAN, Florian GOSSELIN, Xavier GRANIER, Patrick LE CALLET, Vincent LEPETIT, Maud MARCHAL, Guillaume MOREAU, Jérôme PERRET and Toinon VIGIER section 3.3. Finally, this chapter ends with a study of the human factor. Section 3.4 focuses on visual perception, while section 3.5 discusses the more general problem of evaluating virtual environments.

3.1.1. *Physical model and detecting collisions*

In order to simulate real environments in the most credible possible way, it is essential to give a detailed description of the entities (e.g. objects, persons), which make up these environments, as well as of their behavior. To do this, different physical models (e.g. light, displacement, shock) are used, which present varying levels of complexity, among which are:

– models of physical phenomena that make it possible to determine the equations for motion relative to this phenomenon. This step also provides a set of nonlinear differential equations that must be resolved in an approximative manner as there are generally no analytical solutions to resolve them;

– real-time simulation of equations of motion in order to integrate both the action of the user on the system and the phenomenon's own laws of evolution. The question of the "real-time" simulator is a thorny one, as it introduces constraints on performance and/or the simplification of the model, and/or a precision versus response time precision. In effect, the employed iterative methods of resolution (implicit or explicit integration schema) are based on the concept of time steps, which may be fixed or variable, depending on the method. This time step is thus often constrained by restrictions on numerical stability and, in practice, is not generally as large as the application designer would wish. Real time is defined as the fact of requiring that the computation time for the simulation must be lower than the value of the time step. If, for reasons of numerical stability, the time step is very small (e.g. 1/1000th of a second), then as concerns the computing time, the mechanical system will need to resolve computations at least 1000 times per second.

Among the physical phenomena [MAR 14] that can be simulated, we find the following:

– *Solid mechanics*: current simulation techniques allow a real-time interaction with objects, whether these are free rigid bodies, poly-articulated solids [BEN 14a] or even deformable solids [NEA 06, TES 05], as long as these objects remain "reasonable".

– *Fluids and particles*: fluid management [BRI 08] brings in a much higher level of complexity. However, this can still be processed in real-time when the fluid is broken up into particles.

– *Topological changes*: real-time changes in topology, such as objects getting fractured, may be taken into account by associating several models that are particularly effective at producing results in real-time [GLO 12]. The models that are brought into play are based on a modal analysis for the internal vibrational aspect of the object and an algorithm for the propagation of the fracture within the equipment. In Figure 3.1, the simulator reacts to an interaction due to the collision of a virtual hammer.

– *Changing the state of the material*: a unified particle model, such as the SPH (*Smoothed-Particle Hydrodynamics*) [CIR 11b], makes it possible to move in real time in a manner ensuring continuity from a fluid state of the material to a solid state while enabling a bimanual haptic interaction with the objects in the scene (see Figure 3.2).

Figure 3.1. *Interactive fracture in the material*

Figure 3.2. *Interactive fracture in the material*

Another considerable problem is detecting collision between objects in the scene as they move around. Indeed, in the real world, these collisions are "naturally" controlled by the properties of the objects: in general, when two rigid bodies meet, their movement is modified or they stop moving, for example, a ball kicked by a striker in rugby and rebounding off the pole. This problem is expressed as a purely geometric question, the objective of which is to avoid interpenetration between objects in the virtual scene. At each time step of the simulation, the collision detector must be capable of delivering all the interpenetrating objects, in order to provide the physical simulator with the data that will allow it to prevent this interpenetration. The major concern in detecting collisions is the natural combinatorics of the problem. In effect, as any object may come into collision with all the others, an initial naive approach consists of testing the interpenetration of each object relative to all the others, which leads to a natural complexity of $O(n^2)$. This complexity is a very bad property and the objective of all methods using optimization algorithms is to reduce the magnitude of this complexity.

Even though the objective can be expressed in a simple manner, there are still many variants of this problem, depending on the nature of the objects and of the problem posed [KOC 07], leading to different types of solutions:

– discrete detection versus continuous detection: in all discrete methods, the algorithm is applied with a fixed time interval and does not look at what happens between these instants; these methods are quite rapid and may ignore certain interpretations. Contrarily, the continuous methods focus on finding the precise moment of collision, which may intervene between simulation time steps. This strategy is particularly well-adapted when all interpenetrations between objects are to be avoided and when great precision is desired. The price for this, of course, is a higher computing time;

– processing of convex objects versus non-convex objects: a convex object is such that for any pair of points belonging to the object, the segment that connects these points is entirely contained within the object. This property makes it possible to implement simple, and thus rapid, algorithms to ensure the detection of collision. Two strategies are possible for non-convex objects: we either divide the objects into a set of convex objects, which leads us to a simple case, or we make the algorithm more complex in order to take the non-convexity into account;

– a two-body problem versus an N-body problem: in a two-body problem, a single object is mobile and the others are fixed. This greatly simplifies the problem when compared with an N-body problem, where all objects may move [LIN 98].

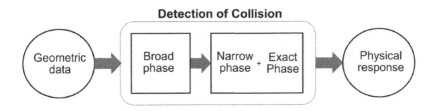

Figure 3.3. *The steps in the detection of collision*

In 1993, Hubbard [HUB 93] proposed breaking down the algorithm to detect collisions in the form of a pipeline. This decomposition is widely used in scientific literature and is given in the form of the diagram in Figure 3.3. The *broad phase* acts like a filter that rapidly eliminates the object-pairs that cannot enter into collision. This filter is very often based on rapid computations of the intersections between encompassing volumes (encompassing the objects). The *narrow phase* executes more precise calculations by locating the parts of the objects that are potentially colliding, while the *exact phase* carries out a very precise geometric calculation of the interpenetration. In recent methods, these last two steps have been grouped into one single step, called the *narrow phase*.

As demonstrated by the scientific references relating to the detection of collision, mentioned in the above paragraphs, the problem is not new and there is a wide range of literature on the subject. What does offer a new point of view on the subject, however, is the appearance of GPUs (*Graphics Processing Units*). While these processors were initially dedicated only to graphic processing, over time they became programmable (GPGPU: *General-Purpose Processing on Graphics Processing Units*) and usable for all sorts of computing, offering a high level of intrinsic parallelism (possibility of breaking down the computations into independent sub-calculations). It was found that the detection of collision is, in essence, highly parallel. Indeed, each elementary calculation (e.g. calculating the intersection between two geometric primitives) is independent of the others. We will thus study the impact of the use of GPUs on the two principal steps in processing:

– *GPU solution for the broad phase*: Avril *et al.* [AVR 12] propose considering the allocation of pairs of objects to be computed as a triangular matricial pathway on the GPU. This was then generalized by Navarro *et al.* [NAV 14]. Le Grand [LEG 07] carried out a filtering of objects based on a spatial subdivision using a regular grid combined with a hashing function. Each object stores the hashing key of the cells that contains the object. The objects storing the same keys are thus potentially in intersection. Founded on *triage*, the implementation on the GPU of the *sweep-and-prune* algorithm [LIU 10] is carried out using a sorting method adapted to the GPU (*radix-sort*), applied on a single separator axis.

– *GPU solution for the narrow phase*: Lauterbach *et al.* [LAU 10] propose a method founded on hierarchies of the surrounding volumes (Bounded Volume Hierarchy or BVH) on the GPU. This method carries out the allocation of geometric primitives over the hierarchic structure (a tree, in practice) in a highly parallel manner; it then calculates the new volumes that bound the hierarchy in a parallel manner. Collision tests are carried out by comparing the two hierarchical structures. In order to maximize the parallelism at the very outset of the calculation, this algorithm makes use of temporal coherence by reusing the results of the calculation to detect collision used in the preceding time step. In this method, the distribution of tasks across the GPU units is based on buffers This distribution has been improved [TAN 11] by representing the writing of the new tasks during the hierarchy pathway in the form of flux. Finally, the use of hashing technology [PAB 10] to use the spatial subdivision, already used for the *broad phase*, has made it possible to obtain high performance in the *narrow phase*. More recently, Le Hericey *et al.* [LEH 15] proposed a new and revised version of the collision detection pipeline, where notably several ray-tracing algorithms may be used in order to optimize the computations (iterative ray-tracing or not); furthermore, specific work has been carried out on relative displacement measures in order to make optimal use of temporal coherence. This algorithmic principle works for both rigid and deformable objects.

Figure 3.4. *Above: 512 non-convex objects fall on a plane floor. Below: 500 objects are progressively inserted. For a color version of this figure, see www.iste.co.uk/arnaldi/virtual.zip*

Figure 3.4 presents two case studies [LEH 16] of building up collision tests: (1) a set of objects fall simultaneously onto a single object; in which case, the number of collisions increases in an abrupt manner, and (2) we progressively add objects to form a pile and the number of collisions increases regularly. In these two cases, the GPU computation makes it possible to obtain performances higher than 60 Hz. Figure 3.5 shows a GPU computation result in a bi-manual interaction with a deformable system [LEG 17] (folding a length of cloth), in which there are many self-collisions.

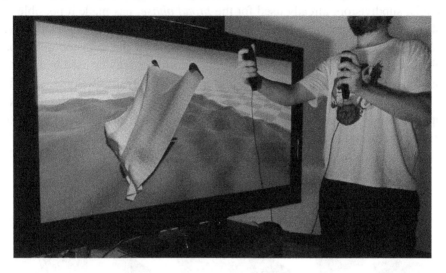

Figure 3.5. *Interaction with a sheet that falls on its side on an irregular surface*

3.1.2. *Populating 3D environments: single virtual human to a surging crowd*

3.1.2.1. *Introduction*

A 3D environment may be populated with virtual humans on different scales and for different needs. Thus, populating the streets of a city may have completely different objectives. For example, a simulation carried out in the context of a study on urban layouts, especially on the intermodality in transport, or populating the background of a scene in a movie (see Figure 3.6). This is the same for populating a factory, whether it is a study on how a future assembly chain for a jumbo jet will function, or for the floor plan in *Monsters Inc.* Similarly, the constraints are also different depending on whether you are populating an interactive virtual world for VR-AR or whether you are populating the background for a big-budget movie. In the first case, the real-life requirement will have a significant influence on the quality of characters and their rendering, while in the second case, the principal criterion will be the budget allocated for the visual special effects.

Figure 3.6. *a) Illustration of a reconstruction project at Roland-Garros by Digital District. b) Populating a scene in a street in the film* Florence Foster Jenkins *by Union VFX. For a color version of this figure, see www.iste.co.uk/arnaldi/virtual.zip*

Brian Thomas Ries [RIE 11] has highlighted in his work that populating an architectural space would reduce the instances of under-estimating distances in a VR exploration. Chu *et al.* [CHU 14] examine how to take into account social behaviors and knowledge of places in an evacuation simulator. Haworth *et al.* [HAW 15] examine how to take into account crowd movements in an architectural space in order to optimize the positioning of the support pillars.

Even though the objectives differ, certain functionalities are common. It is therefore necessary to describe the population through physical characteristics (e.g. morphology, age, comfortable speed, attire, accessories used). Once the bodily envelope of the characters is created, they must be allowed to move and behave in the environment. A certain number of tasks will be carried out to do this and the nature and contents of these tasks will differ, depending on the typology of the simulated behaviors. In [PAR 09], Paris and Donikian present the pyramid of behaviors with different levels of behavior (biomechanical, reactive, cognitive, rational and social) and the related tasks (see Figure 3.7). Depending on the objectives of the populating function, all or a part of this pyramid may be brought into play.

As the objective of this chapter is to give an overview of the recent work carried out on the different blocks required to populate a 3D environment, we propose beginning with a brief account of the field, that provides entry points in addition to a thematic point of view on the simulation of crowds

[BAD 14, DUI 13, ZHO 10]. The fifth volume of the third edition of the *Virtual Reality Treatise* [FUC 09] also serves as a good introduction to the different research topics on virtual humans that we discuss here.

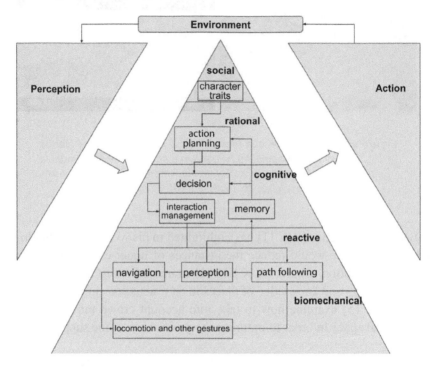

Figure 3.7. *Pyramid of behaviors*

3.1.2.2. *How to populate 3D environments*

Much research has been dedicated to the task called navigation: this consists of managing a person's movement towards a defined point, while avoiding static and dynamic obstacles. We can identify several families of models: particle-based, cellular machines, predictive geometries, agent-oriented, etc. [DON 09]

Some of these models have been confronted with data from the field, from controlled experiments, or video acquisitions. Notably, Wolinski [WOL 16] compared the behavior of several algorithms from the literature to real data, by trying to optimize the parameters of each algorithm vis-à-vis the data sets.

His research does not indicate that any one algorithm is more efficient than the other studied cases. Kok *et al.* [KOK 16] propose an overview that is rich in references to research based on analyses of crowd behaviors, using approaches that draw on physics (particle-based model) and biology (behavior based on rules and heuristics). They also offer a good overview of the analyses of crowd behavior carried out using video observations and vision-based algorithms. Olivier *et al.* [OLI 14] offer a good summary of research that uses VR within experimental protocols in order to better understand human interactions in a crowd. Cassol *et al.* [CAS 16] have used their rule-based model with ground data from the evacuation of a four-storey nightclub. Olivier *et al.* [OLI 13] have shown the non-symmetry of behavior between two people avoiding each other as their paths cross and have highlighted different roles in the interaction. Rio *et al.* [RIO 14] studied the characteristics of the tracking of one pedestrian with respect to the person ahead of them. Gandrud *et al.* [GAN 16] carried out experiments in VR, which tended to show a link between the direction of gaze and the orientation of the head, and the pedestrian's chosen direction. This information could help increase the realism of the animation of characters by automatically managing their head based on the chosen path.

Karamouzas *et al.* [KAR 14] have proposed a law, said to be universal, which governs interactions between pedestrians. This law was constructed based on the analysis of existing data on real trajectories acquired from experimental situations (bottleneck, crossing in a pedestrian zone). This can, in no way, be a universal law, given the small number of cases studied. However, the authors, and others, postulate that such a law must be founded on the use of estimated time to the collision, which is then dependent not only on the distance from the obstacle, but also on the speed. The advantage of speed-based models [PET 12], when compared with position-based models, is that they are able to integrate the concept of anticipation in order to avoid collision; thus, they are able to manage situations with a lower or a non-homogeneous population density in a much more realistic manner.

The initial research carried out focused on taking into account social groups in avoidance strategies [BRU 15, MOU 10]. Other types of group behavior were studied, including movements in formation [HE 16] and emotional contagion in a group [BOS 13]. In order to validate their model, Bosse *et al.* tried to reproduce (using a video) a mass panic situation that occurred in Amsterdam in 2010. They carried out a long and painstaking analysis, focusing on a few individuals in the crowd to extract their movements over time and their behaviors, so they could then model these. They then used a calibration method to determine the optimal values of the parameters for each agent based on the distance between the real and modeled trajectories. The main criticism directed at these models was that they categorized individuals into groups depending on whether they had been contaminants, or susceptible to contamination – but never both at once. This is incompatible with the definition for emotional contagion that is found in psychosociology. In effect, in the case of emotions, each agent is continually the contaminant and contaminated. Further, the complexity of modeling and calibrating these models makes them unusable on the scale of a crowd of thousands of people.

Another task that must be carried out for people to move around in an environment is planning the route. A topological representation of the environment in the form of a Navigation Mesh is required: a representation of the space in the form of a set of convex polygons interconnected by a Roadmap [KAL 14]. It is possible to associate weightings with the cells [JAK 16] in order to indicate the most frequented zones of movement (a pedestrian path, for example). Moreover, the calculation of the path [CUI 12] is carried out using the algorithm A* or with one of its many derivatives that make it possible to carry out hierarchical planning (see, for example, [PEL 16]) or to manage dynamic environments [VAN 15].

If the objective of the population is simply to make the model dynamic as a user virtually navigates it, randomly populating it with trajectories in a loop may be sufficient. K. Jordao proposes [JOR 15a] being able to edit and easily assemble *crowd patches* to populate an urban environment, with characters following a pre-calculated trajectory and thus reducing the computation costs at the time of the navigation.

If, on the other hand, the objective is to study the modeling and simulation of realistic behavior on the scale of an urban space, we then need to either completely script the activity of the characters who populate the space, or to model incarnate and localized activity.

In order to model behavior that is more complex than simply avoiding an obstacle or a random movement, it is necessary to inform the environment so as to offer the virtual humans the capacity for interactions with the environment:

for instance, using an ATM or reading a signpost. We must also model all, or a part of the profile of each of the individuals in the crowd (e.g. goals, knowledge, abilities, emotional model).

Paris *et al.* have thus modeled and simulated the activity of travelers in a station [PAR 09]. Each entity in the population is created at one of the entrances to the station, with a goal to achieve (catch train number X at Y o'clock) and characteristics (ticket already purchased or not). Depending on their knowledge of the spaces (a state that is updated as they move around), a list of realizable actions is updated in order to allow them to advance towards accomplishing the final task. At the start, a traveler must collect a ticket, get it punched, get information on the platform from which their train will depart and, for each activity, identify the place that is best-suited to the accomplishment of that task among all the facilities available (see Figure 3.8).

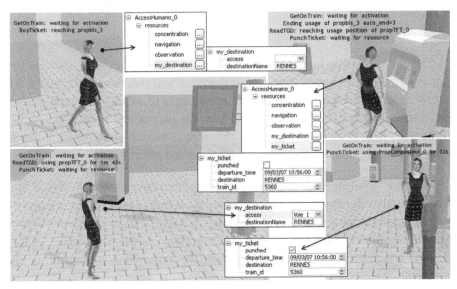

Figure 3.8. *The impact of interaction with the environment on the goals and internal state of a virtual character [PAR 09]. For a color version of this figure, see www.iste.co.uk/arnaldi/virtual.zip*

C.J. Jorgensen has studied the simulation of the activity of residents of a city over a long period [JOR 15b]), which required making connections between the informed environment and the tasks to be carried out, as well as the temporal constraints related to realizing the activities. Trescak *et al.* [TRE 14] propose reducing the modeling of behaviors in a population to a few typical profiles and obtaining the behavior of an entire crowd by genetic crossing. They applied this to the simulation of the behavior of an ancient city (Uruk, 3000 B.C.).

Durupinar *et al.* [DUR 15] have constructed a software architecture on top of the software environment Unity 3D (see section 3.2). This integrates modeling and the simulation of certain psychological characteristics of members in a crowd, such as personality, through the use of the instrument OCEAN (*Openness, Conscientiousness, Extroversion, Agreeableness, Neuroticism*); emotion-management using the OCC mode (*Ortony, Clore, Collins*); and selecting actions using the PAD model (*Pleasure-Arousal-Dominance*). External events will be perceived by certain members of the crowd and will propagate themselves by an emotional contagion mechanism.

3.1.2.3. *Conclusion*

Despite the media buzz surrounding certain research projects, there is no universal model for controlling crowd behavior and movements. It would be useful to work methodically to determine the field of validity for each model so as to avoid a trial-and-error approach on the part of end-users. One of the difficulties here resides in correctly calibrating a model, either to calibrate it with respect to ground data[1], or to obtain a desired effect.

Another challenge is correctly coupling movement models based on kinetics and/or dynamics with commands issued from decision-making layers without generating artifacts, for example, feet slipping on the floor, which constitutes a deviation from the planned trajectory; or the non-respect of the desired speed at a given instant, or even the imposed non-plausibility of acceleration.

Much work remains to be carried out in VR as regards co-presence and the interactions between real and virtual humans. Another area of focus is taking into account other sensory modalities apart from vision, especially integrating localized and spatialized sound. The workshop on "Virtual humans and

---

1 David Wolinski has paved a way for this with his work [WOL 16].

crowds for immersive environments", organized in association with the IEEE VR conference[2] was a good illustration of the diversity and multidisciplinary nature of the research subjects being explored.

As regards the plausibility of the movements and behaviors of virtual humans with whom a real human will interact in a virtual world, here also there are always improvements to put in place so as to emerge from the uncanny valley [TIN 14]. Processing the problem of realistic populations on the scale of a large shopping mall, or a stadium, requires successfully scaling up current algorithms. In the case of a neighborhood in a city, there is a greater necessity for working on coupling these algorithms with those dedicated to the simulation of traffic. All the work done on evaluating and validating models must be prolonged and amplified. The University of North Carolina [CUR 16] is engaged in an interesting initiative: they propose an open-source modular approach, which they call Menge, whose objective is to provide a unique experiment to test and compare unitary components within a software architecture that is dedicated to the simulation of crowds.

3.1.3. *The difficulty of making 3D interaction natural*

3.1.3.1. *Introduction*

A human being moves in a real 3D environment where using their entire body is necessary to accomplish daily tasks: both ordinary tasks (e.g. traveling to the office, handling objects or cooking) as well as more demanding tasks in terms of performance, such as in sports, dance or music. Nonetheless, interaction tasks are, by nature, intrinsically difficult and performance and skill-acquisition take months or even years of practice. Practice and knowledge transform a complex interaction into a natural action such that it becomes intuitive. At present, due to the generalized availability of low-cost solutions for hand and body tracking, gesture-based interfaces are gaining in popularity (see section 3.1). These interfaces, which are sometimes called NUIs (Natural User Interfaces), aim to use our implicit knowledge and, *a priori*, real 3D interactions to generate intuitive user interfaces. These user interfaces may be used with little or no training and are transparent to the user. However, designing natural 3D interaction techniques that are

---

2 http://ieeevr.org/2016/program/workshop-papers/ieee-vr-workshop-on-virtual-humans-and-crowds-for-immersive-environments/

appropriate to virtual environments remain a difficult problem [KUL 09, BOW 04]. When compared with real interactions, with the exception of haptic interactions, the user interacts in a free space with no physical constraints and no multisensory feedback. Indeed, tactile and haptic feedback is rarely available and tridimensional spatial perception may be deformed as a result of limitations due to the display technology. For example, the ocular vergence-accommodation conflict may cause distances to be underestimated or overestimated [BRU 16]. These limitations may increase the physical demands and dexterity required on the part of the user. For example, in an interaction where the perception of distances may be slightly altered, the user will need to continuously correct their movements in order to compensate for the spatial perception error. Any *a priori* knowledge the user may have had can no longer be applied, and this hinders the overall interaction process [ARG 13]. When designing 3D user interfaces, the perception–action cycle as well as the *a priori* knowledge of the user must be taken into account. In addition, this interface will require an additional phase of learning in order to reach the expected efficiency [ARG 13].

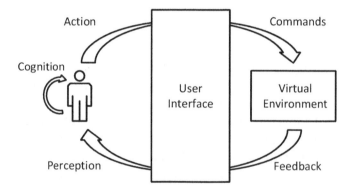

Figure 3.9. *Action-perception cycle*

During the design of a new interaction technique, the *perception–action* cycle must be considered in its entirety. This cycle (Figure 3.9) can be broken down into several phases: (1) the user receives a multisensory feedback from the virtual environment (perception), (2) they decide on and plan the action they wish to carry out (cognition), (3) they execute the planned actions (actions) and (4) the system interprets and executes the user's actions (commands). The execution of these commands generates additional feedback (5), and this completes the cycle.

3.1.3.2. *Perception–action cycle for interaction*

When designing a new technique for interaction, it is essential to consider all the different steps in the interaction cycle to ensure that the interaction technique is well-matched. Returning to the schema in Figure 3.9, the designer of the interaction technique must ensure, first of all, that there is coherence between the action–command coupling and robust and unambiguous laws governing command, and, second, that there is feedback (feedback and perception), which will ensure that the user has a good mental representation of the virtual environment.

The feedback from the virtual environment (e.g. visual, auditory or haptic feedback) must ensure that the user is aware of the present state of the virtual environment and of their own actions (action-perception feedback), and they respect their perception channels. The feedback provided must be precise and complete. The actions carried out by the users are guided by the perceptual construction of the virtual environment; if this construction is erroneous or inexact, it will result in erroneous or inexact actions. Thus, the *fidelity of the perceptual information* is primordial. Indeed, having a precise perception of the spatial layout (sizes, distances) and interrelations in the virtual world are key to any spatial task (e.g. estimating distances, handling objects). While current real-time feedback systems are capable of providing spatial visual cues (e.g. projection in perspective, occlusion, lighting, shadow effects, depth of field effects), distance and perception of size are often skewed in immersive systems [BRU 16].

The nature of the immersive display has an additional impact on the interaction process. Indeed, in non-obstructive display systems (e.g. projection-based systems), the user is constrained by the physical display and no direct interaction is activated for any object presenting a positive parallax [GRO 07]. In addition, the user's own body may hide virtual objects that are virtually closer (Figure 3.10 left). By trying to obtain a virtual object with a negative parallax, the user's hand may mask the projection of this objection, thereby increasing the risk of erroneous selections, especially for small objects. In this case, haptic feedback is rarely provided. When it comes to obtrusive displays (e.g. a visioheadset), we must provide a virtual representation of the user's body. If the user's body is not correctly tracked, the proprioceptive information will be in conflict with the virtual avatar, and this may potentially hinder the process of interaction (Figure 3.10, right). Furthermore, obtrusive screens are more likely to provoke simulator sickness (also known as cybersickness).

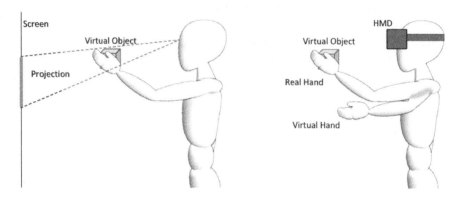

Figure 3.10. *Examples of potential perceptual mismatches. Left, in a projection-based system, objects exhibiting negative parallax can be wrongly occluded by real objects (user's hand) as the projection of the virtual objects in the screen can be occluded. Right, in obtrusive displays, if the user's body is not correctly tracked, proprioceptive and visual channels could differ, which would require motor recalibration*

3.1.3.3. *Interaction and action–command coupling*

To make a 3D interaction more efficient and to provide appropriate feedback, the 3D interface must provide good action–command coupling. When designing interaction techniques, *human control capacity* must be taken into account: interaction in free space is complex, imprecise and can cause greater fatigue. A general design principle consists of minimizing the number of degrees of freedom that are concurrently controlled; the greater the number of degrees of freedom, the more difficult it is for the user to control them efficiently [ARG 13]. Nonetheless, adding degrees of freedom may be beneficial for highly qualified users. In this case, a learning phase may greatly improve the initial performance of the users. An unambiguous correspondence between the interaction techniques and input peripheral device may also facilitate control [HIN 94]. For example, using an input peripheral device with six degrees of freedom to carry out a task that requires fewer degrees of freedom may become a source of confusion if the input peripheral is not restricted [HER 94]. This can be explained by the fact that changes in the degrees of freedom that are unused by the input device are not visible to the user, which leads to imbalance or action-perception incoherence. Finally, additional transfer functions may be used to adjust the gains between command and the movements on display (CD ratio). Well-designed transfer functions may make it possible to go beyond the limitations of human control and thus enhance precision and diminish user fatigue. However, distinct interaction scenarios may require subtly different transfer functions, requiring *ad hoc* adjustments

3.1.3.4. *Conclusion*

We must not, at any rate, forget user characteristics: *individual requirements and limitations*. Indeed, a 3D interaction technique that is natural for one user may not feel natural for another. To begin with, users have individual preferences, differing levels of expertise, and they also carry out actions in different ways. They therefore require selection and/or manipulation techniques that are adapted to their skills or to specific training scenarios. In addition to action–command and feedback–perception coupling, user action must generate additional feedback that allows users to apprehend the impact of their actions on the system. If this feedback is unambiguous, it will enable quicker learning of that interface. The interface designer must take these requirements and limitations into consideration in order to provide the best-suited 3D interface for a given user to use for a given purpose. The quest for a universal 3D interaction experience is still unfulfilled.

3.1.4. *The difficulty of synthesizing haptic feedback*

3.1.4.1. *The problem*

Haptic feedback (from the Greek *haptomai*, "I touch", a term that encompasses all kinesthetic phenomena, that is, force perception and perception of the body in its environment, and tactile phenomena) plays an essential role in a user's immersion in a VR environment. Indeed, if the command devices, proposed as motion capture systems, make it possible to intuitively control the movements of an avatar, the user will be projected in an impalpable virtual world and will be unable to finely control the effort exerted on the manipulated objects. Realistic simulation of touch is, however, a very difficult thing to bring about. This is for various reasons:

– The variety of possible gesture interactions. We can list six exploratory methods used to recognize objects around us (shape, volume, weight, hardness, texture and temperature) [JON 06] and over 30 types of grips used to hold and manipulate them [CUT 89, FEI 09], not to mention certain gestures that are not included in these categories that take place in bodily zones other than the hands.

– The variety and richness of the perceived haptic information. When we touch an object, the skin enters into contact with it, then the contact area increases as the exerted force increases. The pad of the finger may also be locally deformed, depending on the form and texture of the objects touched, or it may be displaced laterally if it is subject to tangential forces. It may further be subject to global or localized vibrations.

– The complexity of the human sensory apparatus. This is made up of a large number of varying physiological receptors [JOH 07] (Meissner corpuscles, Merkel cells, Pacini corpuscles, Ruffini nerve terminals at the cutaneous level, and kinesthetic receptors), whose spatial expanse, sensitivity range in frequency and response types will vary according to the type of receptor. The responses are also processed in a complex manner by the central nervous system (taking into account timing, number and frequency of the nervous activation peaks for each receptor as well as information relating to correlations between the responses of different receptors in the same zone).

– The high sensitivity of a human being, which can differentiate between textures whose amplitudes are between a few dozen nanometers and a few micrometers by running a fingertip over a surface [SKE 13] and detecting a force of a few dozen milli-Newtons [KIN 10], all the way up to frequencies of several hundred Hertz.

– The range of forces to recreate, which can go up to a few dozen kilograms in certain postures and directions [DAA 94], knowing that it should be possible to apply these forces very rapidly to simulate rigid objects (it is essential that the stiffness that the user feels be a minimum of 24200 N/m in order for it to give a convincing impression of rigidity even with closed eyes [TAN 94]).

3.1.4.2. Software aspects

In practice, the synthesis of haptic feedback first requires the simulation of phenomena that come into play during interactions between the user and their environment. In the real world, these interactions are subject to the laws of physics, and thus it is useful to carry out a simulation of these laws in the virtual world. It is, however, difficult to realistically model and compute the set of phenomena involved – for example, the adhesion of surfaces, deformations, fractures and other changes in the state of an object [CIR 13b]. This difficulty is further aggravated by the temporal constraint: in effect, to guarantee correct haptic feedback, the simulation must provide information at a high frequency (typically close to the kilohertz) or else instabilities will appear or the virtual world will appear soft and viscous.

In the field of real-time physical simulations, the last decade has been marked by the rapid development of physical engines for video games. This evolution is a consequence of large investments from private actors, especially manufacturers of the NVIDIA and AMD graphics cards, in partnership with video game editors. It is also linked to the emergence of electronic cards that are adapted for Massive Parallel Processing born out of the GPU (Graphic Processing Unit) technologies, which gave rise to the term PPU (Physics Processing Unit).

Today, we find two principal products. One is PhysX from NVIDIA, which is under a proprietary license but free of cost, and the other is Bullet, initially released through AMD but which has since then been distributed under an Open-Source license [GLO 10]. We must note here that, for both PhysX and Bullet, the simulation of rigid bodies does not benefit from accelerated computations on the GPU which is limited to the simulation of deformable bodies, and the computation of collisions between non-convex objects is problematic. The very recent arrival of FleX by NVIDIA[3], based on a unique approach, could potentially transform the field. However, it is still too early to determine this. Altogether, these physical engines sacrifice exactitude of results to a large extent, in order to improve interactivity. This responds to a requirement that is common to both video games and Virtual Reality; however, it is not sufficient for most professional applications.

Going beyond video games, three physical engines embody the essentials of the progress made in the last few years: Chai3D, SOFA and XDE. Chai3D was initially a project at Stanford University [CON 03], which then became an independent Open-Source[4]. It has profited from several scientific

3 http://developer.nvidia.com/flex
4 http://www.chai3d.org

contributions from a very active society, so much so that today it can be considered a state-of-the art entity in its field. Finally, Chai3D supports most haptic peripheral devices on the market and is simple to use. Unfortunately, this engine is also still unable to process non-convex objects.

Initialized by CEMIT (Boston) and Inria (France) in 2004, SOFA[5] calls itself an Open-Source "Framework" whose goal is to provide real-time simulation tools for medical applications [ALL 07]. The developers have placed a great deal of emphasis on the representativity of the results and combine many simulation techniques in a very well-stocked toolbox: spring–mass systems, finite elements, etc. Some haptic peripherals are supported, but not third-party libraries and only very simple models. In practice, today SOFA is only affordable for digital simulation specialists and has yet to reach maturity in this area.

Finally, the physical engine XDE is being developed by CEA Tech for industrial applications that are characterized by objects with complex geometries and drastic requirements concerning the precision of the results [MER 12]. One of the features that really sets XDE apart is the integration of precise contact models and natively taking into account complex kinematics. For example, the case of simulating a human operator at work.

Furthermore, at this stage, it is useful to remember that the problem of real-time physical simulation has two main components: one is the identification of contact points between the objects, commonly referred to as "collision detection" (see section 4.1), and the other is the integration of solid mechanics and continuous medium mechanics equations, often simply called the "solver". In the field of collision detections, the team headed by Gabriel Zachmann made a significant development with René Weller's work on Inner Sphere Trees and his other research [WEL 11]. Weller proposes Sphere Packing, a method that consists of filling in objects using an arrangement of non-overlapping spheres of varying sizes. As the detection of intersection between two spheres is the same as comparing the distance between their centers with the sum of their radii, the detection of collisions between objects becomes a very rapid process. The crucial problem is filling in objects with spheres. In addition, Weller presents an efficient method to do this, with acceleration using a GPU.

---

5 http://www.sofa-framework.org

A final aspect to be noted is the rapid development of free software platforms that are dedicated to controlling robotics systems, chiefly ROS[6] and OROCOS[7]. These software address the problem of haptic feedback inasmuch as they can promote interoperability between different peripheral devices: after all, a haptic interface is a robot, which needs a control software. Rather than developing specific modules for each product on the market, it is possible to imagine that, in the near future, physical engines will simply propose an interface with ROS and peripheral manufacturers will have to adapt to this.

3.1.4.3. *Material aspects*

The haptic interface must recreate, as accurately as possible, the instructions from the simulation. Over the last few years, many interfaces have been developed to carry this out. They strive to simulate each of the phenomena described above, whether this is the transition between free space and contact with the haptic interfaces and exoskeleton gloves with intermittent contacts [YOS 99, GON 15, NAK 05, FAN 09]; variation of the contact surface area with applied force [AMB 99]; the global form of objects [HOS 94, YOK 05, DOS 05, CIN 05, ARA 10]; vibrations [YAO 10, GIU 10] or the texture of the objects that are touched [BEN 07, WAN 10]. These interfaces are, however, highly specialized and cannot simultaneously simulate all these phenomena. Most of them, moreover, are only at the prototype stage in laboratories. Commercially available devices and those used in the industry are essentially force-feedback interfaces, such as the Virtuose range from Haption (www.haption.com). Consequently, we will focus on this type of interface.

Researchers in this field are in agreement on what criteria to respect in order to effectively stimulate the sense of touch. In particular, the user must have minimum awareness of their presence (we speak of "transparency"). This requires an adequate workspace without singularities; the lightest interface, presenting the least friction possible so that the user can freely move in free space. It also requires effort, stiffness and sufficient bandwidth, so that we clearly feel the presence of obstacles and the transitions between free space and contact [GOS 06]. In order to respect these criteria, regardless

---

6 http://www.ros.org

7 http://www.orocos.org

of the application used, it is essential, in the most general case, that the interface be able to generate forces of several dozen kilograms, have an apparent rigidity of over 24200 N/m and a resolution of at least 1 μm in position and 1mN in force (this is because, as we have seen before, the interface measures the position of the user's entire body in a volume of several cubic meters). Unfortunately, this is not possible using current technology, not to mention the potential danger of such a robot evolving with continued contact with the user.

The result of this is that, in practice, force-feedback interfaces are adapted to the task to be executed. Thus, Phantom Premium devices from Sensable Technologies (recently acquired by Geomagic and then by 3D Systems) were developed towards the end of the 1990s for low-amplitude tasks that required limited force and only along three degrees of freedom. This choice made it possible to obtain remarkably sensitive devices which were widely distributed to laboratories for research into haptic perception. In 2000 and 2010, this range was complemented by interfaces that were mass-produced at low costs (Geomagic Touch X, Geomagic Touch and, more recently, Touch 3D Stylus). This made it possible for this technology to enter design offices, in association with an intuitive 3D modeling software. Other interfaces, such as the Virtuose, range from Haption offered, in the early 2000s, a force feedback at six degrees of freedom and coupling with CAD software such as CATIA or Solidworks, which resulted in their widespread use in engineering offices and design centers. However, these interfaces, as well as their competitors (e.g. products from the company Force Dimension (www.forcedimension.com)) present several limitations.

In the first place, they restrict the user's movements as the user can only interact in a reduced volume, and only via a wristband or pen, thereby severely limiting dexterity. Such interfaces, while they make it possible to effectively interact with a digital mock-up, are no longer sufficient to intervene in the digital factory that appeared in the early 2010s and in which the user wants to simulate not only an assembly-chain but the complete work-environment, including operators, in order to study the ergonomics of workstations or to train virtual operators. Interfaces with a larger workspace and/or allowing for greater dexterity are required for such applications. In order to increase articulations, we can, for example, mount an existing interface on a motorized carrier such as on the Scale1 interface from Haption (see Figure 3.11), use a structure with tensile cables made up of motor blocks attached to a frame (whose dimension may easily be adapted to a CAVE) and connected to the wristband through cables that replace the structure of the robot [HIR 92], or even use an exoskeleton whose movements directly track those of the user [GAR 08]. Another solution to increase the user's freedom of movement is using portable interfaces fixed to the fingertips [TSA 05, MIN 07, CHI 12, TSE 14, GIR 16]. These devices, which act locally on the pad of the finger to give the sense of touch, are compact and light. This makes it possible to preserve the user's dexterity. This is also the case with the wearable exoskeleton gloves that allow a real force feedback to the hands, but at the price of added weight, encumbrance and significantly greater complexity [GOS 12, HAP 16] (see Figure 3.12).

Figure 3.11. *The Scale 1 (left) and Able 7D (right) interfaces from Haption (©PSA Peugeot Citroën and Haption)*

A second recurring fault with most commercially available haptic interfaces towards the end of the 1990s was the relatively low maximum apparent rigidity, which was of the order of 1000 to 3000 N/m. This did not greatly hinder the task of simulating fitting (assembly) tasks, inasmuch as it was possible to play on the visual modality, which predominated with respect to haptic modality, to give a greater impression of rigidity. On the contrary, this is redhibitory for applications used in training in technical actions, which have developed in large measure recently, especially in the medical field. For such applications, it is very important that the gesture be reproduced identically with respect to reality so that the students can reproduce the same sensory-motor schema on the patients as those they learnt in the simulation.

This must be especially precise in dental and osteo-surgery as we are working on very hard objects. Much research has been carried out to increase the rigidity and the bandwidth of the force-feedback interface. The company Moog (www.moog.com) has developed a new haptic interface that is both rigid, thanks to a parallel structure, and very sensitive, thanks to force-sensors. This robot is integrated into a multimodal training platform for training in dentistry – the Simodont Dental Trainer. This is currently being tested by several dentistry schools [BAK 15]. CEA has also developed a new robot for maxillofacial surgery. This has greater rigidity, thanks to a great deal of work done on optimizing the action chain and thanks to a series of parallel hybrid structures. The bandwidth was increased by associating it with high-frequency vibrating wristbands [GOS 13] (see Figure 3.13).

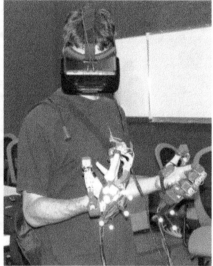

Figure 3.12. *IHS10 Force feedback gloves (left) and MANDARIN (right) from CEA (© CEA)*

A third important limitation for most haptic interfaces is that their prices remain too high for the general public. While a great deal of progress has been made by Sensable Technologies, followed by Geomagic and 3D Systems, with the price of their interfaces progressively reducing from tens of thousands of dollars for the Phantom Premium (end-1990s) to 600 dollars for the Touch 3D Stylus (2015), this is unfortunately at the cost of greatly reduced performance (articulation, force capacity), sensitivity and solidity. Novint's Falcon is also an interesting attempt to democratize this technology, by proposing a force–feedback interface with three degrees of freedom, for only a few hundred euros (www.novint.com). However, despite the fact that it came out in 2008, it has still to find a real market. The only force-feedback interfaces that have had real success with the general public are motorized steering-wheels. We also note that there are some interesting initiatives in the Open-Source community. Several teams thus offer low-cost devices for education, most often in the form of force-feedback interfaces with a single degree of freedom [GOR 12, MAR 16]).

Figure 3.13. *The multimodal technical gesture training platform -SKILLS (© CEA)*

3.1.4.4. *Current situation and future prospects*

For any user, haptic feedback is still often limited to a vibratory tactile feedback, very simple on smartphones, but more complicated on video game controllers that integrate several vibrators whose effects are combined to generate complex haptic effects. This state of things may rapidly change as high-performance Virtual Reality HMDs emerge on the market at a reasonable cost. These already emphasize the lack of peripheral devices adapted for force feedback. Devices such as the MANDARIN glove (see

Figure 3.12), which makes use of a great deal of optimization work that is yet to be completed, or the Dexmo F2 glove from Dexta Robotics (www.dextarobotics.com), are attempting to meet this demand.

3.2. The real–virtual relationship in augmented reality

A virtual environment is one extreme of a continuum (see Figure 3.14), whose other extreme is the real world in which we live. Close to the real environment, AR applications insert virtual information into a real environment. For augmented virtuality (AV), the predominant environment is the virtual environment, for example, a 3D scene where one element is a real objet, such as photos of paintings in a virtual museum. More generally, all applications that combine both environments create "Mixed Reality" (RM).

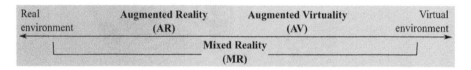

Figure 3.14. *Milgram and Kishini's reality–virtuality continuum [MIL 94]*

Figure 3.15. *Interactions and transfers between the real world and virtual worlds*

AR is therefore characterized by the combination of real and virtual information, especially from a visual point of view. To achieve this mix, at first sight, it is essential that we have data from the real world. Any AR system, as shown in Figure 3.15, requires a system of measurement: this is the acquisition phase. The raw data are not directly usable as they are (e.g. a point cloud from a scan requires a reconstruction step to determine the corresponding surfaces from it). It is thus necessary to process this information. Once the necessary information is extracted, it may be combined with generated data such as illuminated 3D objects. Finally, the result of this combination must be viewed through a display device which is a return to reality.

The real world is governed by the laws of physics for data from the environment, and also those related to the presence of a user. In general, it is therefore essential to provide a coherent combination of reality and virtuality, whether this is from the point of view of the laws of physics or as perceived by the user: this depends on the application, which may also combine these two aspects. If it is desired that the virtual object is naturally integrated, then its movements, illumination and interactions with the real world must be as correct as is possible. When the objective is to create a real-time system, this real→virtual→real loop brings in a latency that we must minimize. This strong constraint influences all parts of the system.

3.2.1. *Acquisition and restitution equipment*

AR is mainly used in the visible domain, with the length of lightwaves going from 380 to 780 nm. Thus, most acquisition and rendering tools function in this field. The current democratization of AR applications is essentially the democratization of tools, important among which are cameras and visualization equipment (screens, visioheadsets, projectors), all of them in a single portable peripheral device: the telephone.

In order to interact with the environment we need to acquire and take into account a lot more data than just images acquired by a camera: what is the surrounding geometry and what are the sources of light here, and the properties of reflection and refraction? What are the movements of the objects and of users? Situating the user in space is one of the crucial points of AR, and it works on the hypothesis that the real and virtual data are *co-localized*; that is, they appear to be part of the same world. The following section focuses in particular on this localization problem. To capture information, we most often use digital tools resulting from computer vision. However, signals beyond the visible spectrum may also be used: optical signals out of the visible range (e.g. infrared, which Kinect uses; see the following section), magnetic waves (highly precise, but require a mapping of the magnetic field – use in controllable environments such as a cockpit), sound waves (especially for the geometry of an environment, for example sonar) and mechanical energy (accelerometers included in mobile phones, tablets, controllers, etc.). We will see that interaction tools are based on all these technologies.

3.2.2. *Pose computation*

As can be seen in Figure 3.16, the rendering of virtual elements requires knowledge of the disposition (transformation A) of these elements from the user's point of view. However, this disposition is mainly defined with respect to a fixed point (transformation B). We then estimate the user's point of view with respect to this same fixed point (transformation C). It is then sufficient to link transformations B and C to arrive again at transformation A.

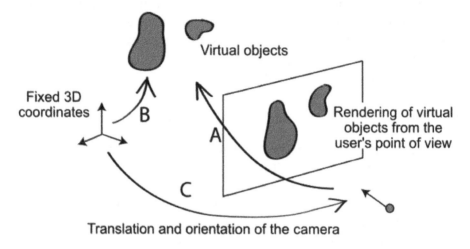

Figure 3.16. *Pose calculation (see the beginning of section 3.2.2)*

This may be formalized by estimating a position and orientation in 3D, often collectively called "pose". In general, six parameters must be estimated: three for position and three for orientation. Sometimes, some simplifying hypotheses are postulated: many smartphone applications do not compute the height of the smartphone and use a reasonable value.

Many different approaches have been proposed for estimating a user's pose, but this problem remains difficult, chiefly because:

– the pose computation must be precise: indeed, an angular deviation of less than a degree will correspond to a deviation of approximately 2 m at a distance of approximately 100 m. This is not acceptable in driving simulations, for example;

– the pose computation must be done very quickly to limit latency. A very low refresh rate will result in both poor geometric integration and the risk of provoking nausea in the user;

– the space in which the user moves around can also pose several problems. For example, GPS is usable only outdoors and offers a precision of only a few dozen meters. Markers, which will be discussed in greater detail a little further on, must take up a large part of the image on a camera, which limits the envisaged workspace. If the workspace is large, we must consider using multi-scale approaches, for example, GPS for initialization and then visual tracking in a smaller space.

We now move on to reviewing these different approaches.

3.2.2.1. *Sensor-based localization (external to the camera)*

An electromagnet triplet, oriented along three perpendicular directions, may determine its position and spatial orientation by measuring the magnetic field applied on it by another triplet. However, this solution is very sensitive to the presence of metallic objects, which disrupt the magnetic fields. Systems that use ultrasound emitters and captors may be very precise; however, they are expensive and require major infrastructure.

Smartphones are now equipped with GPS functions that allow them to locate themselves, and with accelerometers and compasses that allow them to measure their orientation. For example, the highly successful game Pokémon-GO uses this technology to offer AR visualization. This approach, however, does not allow great precision: the GPS can offer, at best, precision up to a few meters and the compass can offer precision of a few dozen degrees. Furthermore, GPS is not accessible indoors, and it has a low update frequency.

3.2.2.2. *Marker-based localization*

A tempting approach is to base ourselves on an image captured from the user's point of view. This approach is, in fact, very natural for AR and the localization of cameras is an important field of research in the domain of computer vision.

A simple solution to using the contents of an image for pose computation is to add markers similar to that shown in Figure 3.17. These markers are designed so as to be easily detectable and recognizable by an automatic image-analysis method. It can thus enable the pose computation of the camera. Nevertheless, it is not always possible to use this approach as the markers must be placed and localized in advance, which is restrictive. They are also often unesthetic and distract vision in the real environment.

Figure 3.17. *Using a marker to locate a camera. Markers facilitate the pose computation of a camera, but cannot be used for all applications (© Daniel Wagner)*

3.2.2.3. *Image-based localization*

Image-based methods make it possible to calculate the camera's pose using the image itself, without the need to manipulate the scene, unlike the approaches discussed above.

Figure 3.18 illustrates how this functions: if the spatial localization of several elements in the real scene is known, and if their 2D positions in the image are also known, it is then possible to calculate the camera's pose. For example, if these elements are points in 3D, they appear as 3D points in the image and the camera's pose may be computed through triangulation [GAO 03].

However, while the geometry of the problem is now well-controlled, the principal difficulty is automatically interpreting images to find the known elements in the image. People who are unfamiliar with computer vision often underestimate this difficulty: although it seems easy to interpret images that we see, our visual cortex mobilizes hundreds of millions of neurons for this interpretation. This analysis by our visual cortex is carried out in an essentially unconscious manner, which explains its apparent ease of interpretation. However, it is very complex and still not well understood.

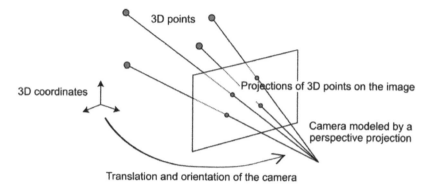

Figure 3.18. *Image-based spatial localization. If the spatial position of several points in the scene is known, as well as their reprojections in the image, it is then possible to localize the camera in the same reference as these points*

A popular approach in computer vision is based on the use of *points of interest*. As Figure 3.19 demonstrates, points of interest are 2D points that correspond to discontinuities in the images. These discontinuities are considered stable when the camera moves or when the lighting conditions are modified: two images in the same scene, taken from two different points of view, or under different lighting conditions, have points of interest that correspond to the same physical points in the scene.

If we can measure the 3D position of these points of interest and identify them in the images captured from the user's point of view, it is then possible to compute the user's pose. This is, in fact, the starting point for many methods in the scientific literature in this field. However, this approach may fail for several reasons: for instance, a scene may offer very few points of interest. This is often the case indoors; the appearance of the points of interest may also vary considerably, making it difficult to identify them – this may happen outdoors, where light can change quite drastically between morning and evening, summer and winter, or even due to weather conditions. It is thus useful to use pose computation methods that can remedy the over- or under-detection of points of interest, as well as poor matches between the 2D and 3D points.

Figure 3.19. *"Points of interest" detected automatically in two images of the same scene. These points correspond to prominent sites in the images and most of them correspond to the same physical points in both images. They may be used, for example, to localize the camera if their positions in 3D are known. Many points are detected on certain objects and very few on others, for instance, here, on the tablecloth and mug, respectively. Objects such as the mug are thus more difficult to use to localize the camera. For a color version of this figure, see www.iste.co.uk/arnaldi/virtual.zip*

Rather than using a classic camera, which does not perceive colors, localization methods may use cameras that perceive information on depth. The Kinect camera, distributed with Microsoft gaming consoles, is one of the best known examples of this. Different technologies exist: some cameras use "structured light", which consists of projecting a known motif in infrared. This enables a reliable, stereographic reconstruction. Others use the "time-of-flight" of a laser beam. The depth charts given by the cameras are a huge help in localization, and they are used by different methods. However, these cameras also have significant limitations: they are active sensors and can only function in an indoor medium with restricted space; metallic environments cause imprecisions; they also consume more energy and rapidly deplete the battery of a mobile device.

3.2.3. *Realistic rendering*

Rendering virtual objects in AR is also important for convincing rendering. Certain applications require realistic rendering. As shown in Figure 3.20, the geometry and light in the real scene must be taken into account so that a virtual object appears similar to the real object with the same geometry and is made up of the same materials:

– first of all, the real objects must occlude those parts of the virtual objects that are situated behind them. This requires estimating the geometry of these real objects and the point of view with great precision;

– the virtual object must appear to be illuminated by the real light sources, which requires knowing the properties of these sources, for example, their spatial position, their geometry or their power;

– the virtual object must cast a shadow onto the real scene. This requires information on the geometry of the real scene, in addition to the real sources of light;

– more generally, light exchanges between real and virtual parts must be simulated. This can become very complex. For example, a virtual object must diffuse the real light that falls onto it towards a real object, thereby changing their appearance.

(a)   (b)   (c)

Figure 3.20. *Realistic rendering. Once the point of view is known (a), the parts of the virtual objects situated behind the real objects must be identified and deleted from the final rendering (b). The light interactions between the real and virtual must also be rendered. Here, removing hidden sections and throwing a shadow onto the car helps the user perceive it in the desired position. For a color version of this figure, see www.iste.co.uk/arnaldi/virtual.zip*

This is not simply a question of esthetic effects: each of these aspects helps in the visual interpretation of the scene. However, they are not all equally important. For example, the position of the light sources need not be very precisely known. This is because the visual cortex is not very sensitive to errors of this kind. On the other hand, an error of a few pixels in the rendering of the masking of a virtual object by a real object is easily perceptible. The border between the real image and the virtual image is therefore situated along the silhouette of the real objects, and this silhouette is still quite difficult to identify as precisely as needed, whether this is with computer vision or depth sensors. Finally, we cannot forget that real objects are viewed without any additional special light, while virtual objects are most often perceived with the help of a screen or, at the least, a device that brings in a light source. They may naturally appear brighter than their real counterparts if compensation mechanisms are not used.

3.3. Complexity and scientific challenges of 3D interaction

3.3.1. *Introduction*

Over the last few years, we have seen the advent of a new generation of 3D interfaces for the general audience (e.g. Microsoft Kinect, Oculus Rift, Leap Motion, HTC Vive, see section 3.1), which remodels the scientific challenges related to 3D interaction with virtual or mixed worlds. VR-AR being accessible to the general public has extended the field of applications that use 3D interaction, while also adding new challenges to the fundamental research on man–machine interactions and interfaces. In this section, we will identify the principal scientific challenges faced today by research laboratories and also companies, when they work to introduce interaction with virtual worlds in programs they develop. We have chosen to present the different challenges by replacing them in the 3D interaction loop, which we will recapitulate in the next section.

3.3.2. *Complexity and challenges surrounding the 3D interaction loop*

In this chapter, we have chosen the *3D interaction loop* as the explanatory framework for the scientific challenges surrounding 3D interaction with virtual or mixed environments. This loop comes from the perception–action loop [FUC 05], which is very often used in the literature to explain the challenges in virtual reality and augmented reality. Figure 3.21 represents the 3D interaction loop with the three principal challenges identified. This loop illustrates the different components of a user's interaction with a virtual or mixed environment. Beyond just the purely visual rendering of a 3D environment, VR-AR aims to immerse the user in a virtual or mixed world.

The user can thus interact with the digital content and perceive the effects of their actions through different sensory feedback. Enabling the user to truly immerse themselves in increasingly complex virtual environments brings in some important challenges that research in VR-AR must confront: the user's gestures must be captured and then directly transmitted to the virtual world in order to modify it in real-time. Sensory feedback refers not only to visual feedback but must be combined with auditory and haptic feedback in a global, multimodal response.

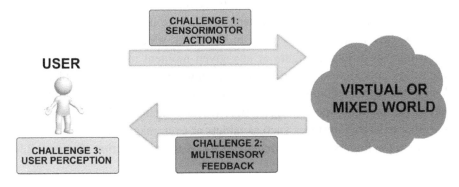

Figure 3.21. *A representation of the three main scientific challenges that arise within the 3D interaction loop*

In this context, we identify three significant challenges, which we will discuss in detail in the following sections, and which are diagrammatically depicted in Figure 3.21:

– challenge 1: "sensory-motor actions for interaction";

– challenge 2: "multisensory feedback";

– challenge 3: "user's perception".

3.3.3. *Challenge 1: sensory-motor actions for interaction*

3.3.3.1. *An explosion in capturing user data*

When it comes to interaction with virtual or mixed worlds, the first challenge is to transcribe user actions in the world with which the user wishes to interact. A few years ago, user actions were, for the most part, restricted to a rough capture of the user's movements. However, there has since been considerable progress in 3D interfaces and today it is possible to capture various kinds of data on the user. The most common data captured is data on movement. This information makes it possible to retrieve the different positions of the user and then transcribe this into the virtual or mixed world. As many capture solutions emerge on the market, especially for the general public, it is possible to record the positions of different parts of the user's body (their arms, their legs, their head) or the entire body. Nonetheless, very precisely capturing the members of a body remains a key challenge. Thus, capturing the user's hand, an indispensable tool for interaction with virtual or mixed worlds, is still not very precise. Moreover, we are still not always able to distinguish different fingers at any given moment in the interaction. An interesting approach to remedy this technological data capture problem is to design interaction techniques using existing interfaces. In the case of tracking hands, for example, the "Thing" [ACH 15] or Finexus [CHE 16] techniques use other existing interfaces such as tablets or even magnetic sensors in order to capture the fingers in a way that enables real-time interaction (Figure 3.22).

Figure 3.22. *Illustration of an interaction technique called the "Thing" that uses a tactile tablet in order to capture the movements of the hand and animate a virtual hand [ACH 15]*

Parallel to the challenge related to the spatial precision of data captured from the user, the temporal dimension is also a source of scientific challenges. Even today, real-time tracking of user movements is a significant challenge. The temporal dimension is particularly difficult to achieve in AR: the physical and virtual worlds must be precisely adjusted but the sensors available today are not precise enough. Thus, AR applications are still limited in numbers for cases where a precise overlaying of the real and virtual worlds is required. All the same, these applications have huge potential and offer many paths for prospective research in the years to come, whether for augmented medicine or civil engineering, to name just two of the possible fields.

3.3.3.2. *Choosing an interaction technique*

In parallel to capturing user data, there are several possible options to transcribe these data in the virtual or mixed worlds. *Perfect isomorphism* may be implemented in order to match all the degrees of freedom of the user in the real world with those in the virtual world, so as to reproduce the real world action as accurately as possible. Given the material limitations discussed above in capturing the movements of the user, this perfect isomorphism has often proven to be difficult to implement. The choice of *weak isomorphism* is thus generally preferred: the user will then have recourse to mechanisms that are generally called *interaction techniques* in order to carry out tasks in the virtual environment. These techniques of interaction can then allow themselves some deviations from actions in the real world, allowing the user to execute actions that would be impossible to carry out in everyday life. *Non-isomorphic* techniques generally make it possible to be more efficient with respect to isomorphic techniques, with notable improvements in the time taken to carry out a task or its degree of precision. They also make it possible to carry out tasks that cannot be executed in an isomorphic manner due to material constraints. Finally, the degree of isomorphism of a VR-AR application will depend on the application context: a high degree of isomorphism is often desired in scenarios where the objective is to reproduce real situations, while for other scenarios, which might be more removed from the real physical world, a deviation with respect to the real world may be more easily accepted by the user.

It is customary to choose an interaction technique based on the task to be carried out [LAV 17]: selecting an object, manipulating an object, navigating a virtual environment or controlling a system. One of the challenges that interaction techniques of the future will face is the ability to widen their genericness so as to be applicable in other contexts than the one they were designed for. This challenge is strongly linked to the present dependence of these techniques on both the proposed application and the material restrictions on available 3D interfaces. The unification of several data flows in an interaction metaphor is yet to be explored. The rise in the number of 3D interfaces, as well as their compatibility, will surely allow new categories of interaction techniques to emerge.

3.3.3.3. *The 3D interfaces of tomorrow*

Over and beyond motion capture, there are many other types of user data that can now be recorded, related to the diversity in the new 3D interfaces proposed over the last few years, both in laboratories and within companies. For instance, it is now possible to track the entire body of the user with the help of interfaces that use the user's equilibrioception [MAR 11] (Figure 3.23). On a smaller scale, the user's eyes can be tracked in real time thanks to increasingly high-performance systems. The user's abilities can also be enhanced, for example, with 360° vision [ARD 12]. Finally, it is now also possible to capture the user's physiological measurements, such as their muscle activity[8] or even more innovatively to measure brain activity using a brain–computer interface [LEC 13] (see section 6.2). The principal scientific challenge related to this multitude of data resides in the processing of the data: even today, there are many scientific problems to overcome in order to successfully synchronize the data and transcribe it, in all its richness, to interact with a virtual or mixed world.

Figure 3.23. *Illustration of a new category of interfaces where the whole body of the user is used to interact with virtual worlds. The interface, called "Joyman", uses human equilibrioception to establish the law of control that makes it possible to navigate virtual environments [MAR 11]*

In parallel to the increasing amount of data that can be captured from the user, the nature of the 3D interfaces used to interact with virtual worlds has also constantly been evolving over the last few years. Thus, heavy and expensive VR equipment is used less often these days, giving way to light interfaces that are more and more accessible to the general public. The scientific challenge related to the 3D interfaces of tomorrow will be the ability

---

8 http://www.myo.com

to offer *natural* interaction with the virtual or mixed world, by minimizing the material constraints. The solutions that can offer this interaction are those that capture data without markers, such as the Microsoft Kinect, or even interfaces that use the human body as the projection surface [HAR 11], and these are examples of the new generation of 3D interfaces that will develop over the coming years.

3.3.4. *Challenge 2: multisensory feedback*

The feedback that the user receives when they interact with a virtual or mixed world is fundamental to give meaning to the actions they just carried out in the real or virtual world. In order to improve interaction, different sensory modalities of the user are brought into play: not only sight, but also hearing and touch are fundamental sensory modalities. In this section, we will identify the scientific challenges related to these different sensory modalities.

3.3.4.1. *Visual feedback*

Sight is the sense that is most used in the majority of interactive systems, especially virtual reality or mixed systems, in order to offer feedback to the user.

Even though current LCD screens have attained a high degree of technological maturity, using them for stereoscopic 3D rendering remains a problem. Indeed, in recent years, we have seen an unprecedented growth in 3D movies and television, but the fact that we still have to wear glasses to visualize this 3D content is an obstacle to more widespread use and the quality of the rendering is not always up to the mark. A possible solution could be the use of HMDs (which are getting democratized); however, too many problems arise to enable the user to interact with the virtual environment. Cohabitation with the real environment is also problematic. These questions are the subject of many research projects [GUG 17]. An initial challenge is to improve 3D rendering techniques for non-immersive screens. In an immersive context, this consists of facilitating interaction with the displayed content and of allowing the user to continue interacting with the real world.

Different research projects, over the last few years, have proposed displays on non-planar surfaces. These may be skin [HAR 11] or even a set of objects in a room [JON 13, JON 14, PEJ 16]. The rendering is carried out by projectors that modify the projection in real time based on a 3D reconstruction of the physical environment in order to correctly project the scene. The challenge for these applications is the availability of miniature and powerful projection systems, such that they can be carried out by the user, for example. A second challenge is the integration of vision systems and 3D reconstruction systems in order to render them truly useful over a wide range of applications. Developing display surfaces that are dynamically deformable [NAK 16], dynamically reconfigurable [LEG 16] or integrated into the user's clothes [POU 16] are all avenues of research to be explored and which will see significant development in the coming years.

3.3.4.2. Force feedback

Comparative to other sensory modalities, the haptic modality, related to the sense of touch, is largely under-exploited even today. The main reason for this is based on the many material constraints that generally prevent adequate haptic feedback to the user when interacting with a virtual object. Unlike other sensory feedback, haptic feedback requires much higher refresh rates [COL 95] and therefore requires high-performance equipment that is often costly. In addition to this, receptors in the human body that make it possible to restitute the sense of touch are situated all over the body, multiplying the contact surfaces between the equipment and the user. Existing haptic devices today are principally focused on force feedback to the user's hands, in either a kinesthetic or a tactile manner. Very few devices, however, offer force feedback over several degrees of freedom or, if they do, the majority are reduced to a single point of contact. The main scientific challenges of the future are thus related to designing equipment that is adapted to provide high-quality force feedback. In parallel, the need for compact and reasonably priced devices is an additional, yet indispensable constraint for the democratization of these devices in interactions with virtual or mixed worlds. In addition to material constraints, much progress remains to be made to obtain high-performance haptic feedback algorithms. Indeed, in order to transcribe haptic sensations to the user, information related to the physical form of the virtual objects are essential so that they are as close as possible to the physical form of the real objects. In this context, research on physical simulation has been proposed, first of all for rigid objects [LIN 08], and then for deformable objects [DUR 06] and, finally, for fluids [CIR 11a] (Figure 3.24). There are still many more properties that can be used in order to transcribe the sensations of the real world as finely as possible, and there are very few efficient algorithms for these properties. The transmission of sensations to the user's hand is an example of a scientific challenge where current models are just beginning to simulate interactions with surfaces that can be deformed on contact [TAL 15].

Figure 3.24. *Photograph of new physical models that allow the modeling of virtual environments made up of solid, deformable and liquid objects. They also allow the user to interact with two haptic devices [CIR 11a]*

3.3.4.3. *Multimodal feedback*

A large challenge in the field of research today is combining the different sensory modalities. The challenges here are both material- and software-related. From a material point of view, there is a need for high-performance interfaces that allow different signals to be coupled while guaranteeing a certain quality of feedback to the user, especially in terms of bandwidth needed, which remains very high for haptic feedback. From a software point of view, we must be able to offer algorithms that make it possible to synchronize the different sensory modalities. Upstream this requires high-performance models of the virtual environments for which visual, auditory and haptic signals must all be generated. Such models are necessarily based on the laws of physics and their simulation in interactive time is, today, an important computing challenge. Initial solutions were proposed in recent years [CIR 13a], but they are still almost never used in real applications. This is especially due to the complexity of the virtual scenes to be simulated so as to obtain satisfactory feedback for a given application.

3.3.5. *Challenge 3: users and perception*

Interaction with virtual or mixed worlds necessarily implies taking into account the human dimension, unique to each user. This human dimension can be divided into two main areas: one that is centered on each user's individual perception, and the second that focuses on the interaction between many users.

3.3.5.1. *The challenge of better understanding a human being's abilities*

Knowledge and understanding of perceptive, motor and cognitive abilities of human beings are essential to the development of different VR-AR technologies in order to reduce some of the side-effects observed with these technologies – "cybersickness", for example.

Human factors associated with perceptive, motor and cognitive abilities in real environments have been studied for over a century by researchers in the fields of perception science, movement science and cognitive science. Interaction with man-made technologies brings in artifacts that do not exist in reality, such as the introduction of latency (which is a feature of any interactive system) the introduction of perception conflicts or the creation of unrealistic situations.

These questions, unique to virtual systems, have already been addressed by the scientific community through different studies [STA 98]. However, more work remains to be done here to systematically analyze the different perceptive, motor and cognitive factors related to virtual reality and mixed reality, which may affect user experience. Replication studies are also being carried out with the goal of extrapolating existing results to larger contexts and for a wider range of users. All these projects make it possible to create design guides, not only for material systems but also for operating systems and, above all, applications.

3.3.5.2. *How do you enable multi-user interaction?*

Going beyond the perception of a single user interacting with a virtual world, one of the significant scientific challenges today is the presence of multiple users interacting with a virtual environment. Designing collaborative environments where many users can work together presents two difficulties: (1) material design and software design for collaborative systems that incorporate many users who may be in the same place or even in different places, and (2) designing effective collaborative techniques of interaction in order to allow each user to be informed by the actions of other users and thus be able to carry out common interactions.

From a material point of view, collaborative environments require putting in place local or extended networks between several computing machines, which may have a significant impact on the consistency of the shared virtual environment. From a software point of view, collaborative environments face the same challenges as more classic environments. In addition to these, we have problems of interoperability between the rendering engines (for graphics, physics and behaviors). The presence of high-level collaboration systems that enable synchronization between the different software involved represents one of the alternatives that is being used more and more often, the other being the direct distribution of data [LEC 15].

From an interaction technique's point of view, multiple issues remain to be resolved in order to facilitate interaction between multiple users. The majority of techniques proposed at this point have been proposed in an applicative context, primarily for virtual prototyping or assembly operations or maintenance. While current collaborative systems allow the simultaneous manipulation of several objects by several users, an important challenge remains in enabling multiple users to manipulate the same object. Communication between users is also an area that needs improvement in order to transcribe the maximum amount of information between users and into the environment itself. Thus, the coming years will see a large amount of research devoted to the significant problem of integration, to enable the introduction of multimodal data, captured from each user, as well as from the environment itself.

3.3.6. *Conclusion*

We have introduced the main scientific challenges related to 3D interaction with virtual or mixed environments by reviewing the different stages of the 3D interaction cycle. There are many challenges, both from the technological and scientific points of view, and we do not claim to have offered an exhaustive list. Meeting each of these challenges will make it possible to popularize and diversify VR-AR technologies, both for the general public and for professionals.

3.4. Visual perception

The immersion and presence of one or more users in a virtual environment always comes at the cost of sensory compromises, or even conflicts. In effect, VR devices are based on technological sleight-of-hand that confuses the human system of perception in a more or less transparent way. This creates perceptual biases and therefore a cognitive load, which can sometime be a source of irritation or even physical discomfort. It is thus essential to study human perception, in interaction with these new technologies for a better adoption of these devices.

A user's perception of, and reaction to, a VR system are mainly studied using questionnaires, which are sometimes accompanied by objective experimental measures. The discomfort and uneasiness that are caused by the system are often clubbed under various terms such as *simulator sickness*, *motion sickness*, *cybersickness* and *visually induced motion sickness*.

As these technologies have opened up to the general public and in new fields of applications, such as multimedia, it is important to precisely define these terms to help different fields come together. We will first present a general glossary of terms related to the discomfort and sickness provoked by virtual reality interfaces, the indications for and symptoms of these problems, and then methods to evaluate them. We will then present the influence that certain technological factors of the visual immersive interfaces have on human perception and reactions.

3.4.1. *A glossary of terms related to unease, fatigue and physical discomfort*

3.4.1.1. *Virtual space sickness*

In VR, the reactions of unease, fatigue and physical discomfort experienced when using an immersive system are often measured using the Simulator Sickness Questionnaire (SSQ) [KEN 93]. This questionnaire classifies symptoms into three categories: nausea, denoted by SSQ-N, oculomotor (headaches, visual fatigue) denoted by SSQ-O and disorientation (vertigo, dizziness) denoted by SSQ-D. The severity of each problem is evaluated through different questions, on a scale of 0 to 3. The scores obtained in each category are then combined for an overall score. Depending on the objective of the study, the discomfort is evaluated using either this overall score or the score for each category. This questionnaire was designed in the 1990s, mainly for flight simulators, most often inducing both visual and movement stimuli. Today, the term *cybersickness* is increasingly being used for this discomfort; however, the evaluation method often remains the same. Other concepts are sometimes used, such as *motion sickness*, mainly with respect to simulators, and *visually induced motion sickness* (VIMS), mainly to evaluate the discomfort created by vection[9].

It is difficult to find consensus on the definition of each term and how to distinguish it from others. Nonetheless, we propose comparing these problems through different readings and past research. The main difference between *simulator sickness* and *cybersickness*, on the one hand, and *motion sickness* and VIMS, on the other, seems to reside in the types of symptoms. In VIMS and *motion sickness*, we will, in effect, focus more on the symptoms induced by a sensation of movements and linked to nausea. Thus, the Fast Motion Sickness questionnaire, which is sometimes used to measure these two concepts, has a higher correlation with the SSQ-N category than the SSQ-O and SSQ-D [KES 04] sections. From another point of view, the difference between *simulator sickness* and *motion sickness*, on the one hand, and *cybersickness* and VIMS, on the other, mainly resides in the types of stimuli and effects that provoke the discomfort. Thus, there will be a preponderance of visual effects in the causes for *cybersickness* and VIMS, while *motion* and *simulator sickness* are more likely to be caused by a combination of visual and movement effects. According to Stanney *et al.*, these differences in stimuli would explain why the disorientation was higher in *cybersickness* than in *simulator sickness* [STA 97]. Finally, *cybersickness* can be distinguished from VIMS by the fact that it is not related to virtual reality, while VIMS is the more widely used term in a VR context (VIMS can be used when there is discomfort that is provoked by a conflict between the visual system and the sensation of movement, regardless of the technology that is the source of this discomfort) [REB 16, KES 15].

Based on our analysis of the literature, the terms *simulator, motion, cyber* and *visually induced motion sickness* seem to be distinguished from one another based on the types of symptoms, types of induced stimuli and the

---

9 Vection is the sensation of movement induced by an optical flux.

types of technologies used. However, there are some intersections and the definitions may sometimes vary from one study to another. Table 3.1 illustrates our vision of this glossary.

We will also remind the reader that, despite these differences, these four concepts are most often evaluated using the same questionnaire (the SSQ), which divides the symptoms into three classes which are not independent of each other.

	Stimuli	Technologies	Symptoms
Simulator sickness	Visual stimuli and movements	All types of simulators	All types of symptoms
Motion sickness	Visual stimuli and movements	All types of simulators	Predominantly symptoms of nausea
Cybersickness	Chiefly visual stimuli[10]	Digital technologies	All types of symptoms
Visually Induced Motion Sickness	Visual	All types of technologies	Predominantly symptoms of nausea

Table 3.1. *Overview of an existing glossary of "simulator sickness"*

One of the challenges in carrying out research on "virtual space sickness" is how to take into account both intra-sensory and inter-sensory conflicts. More specifically, the conflicts between the visual and vestibular systems. As concerns the quality of experience with multimedia systems, which is focusing more and more on visual perception in the immersive HMDs, the concept of fatigue and visual discomfort have been introduced to support research on comfort and the quality of stereoscopic video systems. Although these concepts are limited to a single sensory dimension (sight) – they can contribute to a more general definition of a "virtual space sickness" glossary and generic methods to study and evaluate this problem.

3.4.1.2. *Quality of experience, comfort and stereoscopic video systems*

According to Urvoy *et al.*, the quality of experience when using stereoscopic video systems may be defined across three dimensions [URV 13a]:

– *visual quality*, which refers to image quality, independent of depth;

---

10 The user may carry out movements or move around; however, most often, no movements are directly from the system.

– *depth quality*, which refers to the quality of 3D effects, chiefly in terms of realism and presence;

– *visual comfort*, which refers to physiological and psychological demands resulting from the visualization of stereoscopic content.

The visual and depth qualities are sometimes clubbed together under the single concept: *naturalness* of images [LAM 11].

One of the objectives in the field of multimedia experience quality, is to offer objective models that are capable of predicting the quality that will be perceived. It is therefore essential to clearly define the different aspects that we wish to model and which may influence the quality that is experienced. In the context of stereoscopic systems, the concepts of visual discomfort and fatigue have therefore been particularly studied. Visual fatigue and visual discomfort can be distinguished on perceptual and temporal aspects [URV 13b]:

– *visual discomfort* is visual uneasiness that is immediately perceived by the observer through one or more negative sensations (e.g. ocular pain, irritation, double vision or blurred vision, convergence difficulties);

– *visual fatigue* is caused by repeated visual efforts (e.g. recurrent large changes in the convergence distance), which is most often associated with symptoms perceived through physiological signs. An observer who experiences fatigue needs an adequate period of rest to recover. There are many signs and symptoms of visual fatigue: the presence of tears on eyelashes, a change in blinking frequency, a feeling of dryness in the eyes, heterophory[11], accommodation and vergence problems, changes in fusion interval, headaches, etc.

These definitions, illustrated in Figure 3.25, differentiate between *signs* (objective cues that correspond to physiological measures obtained using a defined protocol) and *symptoms* (subjective cues expressed by the user to describe their perceived mental or physical state), provoked by exposure to stereoscopic stimuli; and the manner in which they reveal this discomfort or fatigue. This distinction makes it possible to clearly define evaluation

---

11 This is the pathological deviation of the eyeballs, which only appears when the vision in both eyes is dissociated. Heterophory is different from heterotropy or strabismus, as it is not a permanent deviation.

methods. As discomfort is an immediate perception, constructed and evaluated by the user, the best solution is to measure it and ask the user to evaluate it in real-time [YAN 02]. This technique, however, remains invasive and modifies the patient's real experience. As visual fatigue combines signs and systems, it is often evaluated using subjective questionnaires [YAN 02] complemented by ophthalmological measurements (accommodation, vergence and dilation of the pupils) [URV 13a].

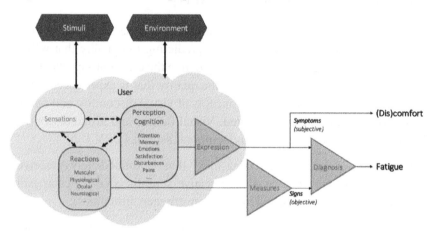

Figure 3.25. *Visual fatigue and discomfort: context and terminology, as given by [URV 13b]*

3.4.1.3. *Objective and physiological measures*

When using a questionnaire, the user is asked to give feedback on their own experience. They may also interpret questions and what they think are the expected answers, which could skew the results. To limit this bias, we have recently seen an increase in the use of physiological measurements (e.g. skin conductance, cardiac and respiratory rhythm, muscle tension, cerebral activity) to evaluate discomfort, fatigue and cybersickness [MOO 17, REB 16], implicitly and in real-time. These physiological measurements may also be accompanied by measurements of posture, which may reveal discomfort and uneasiness [REB 16].

These measurements have been facilitated by the recent development of portable, low-cost sensors. However, there are still challenges to be overcome in the analysis and interpretation of this data, which is rich but often noisy and not stable from one user to another. Thus, while the links between signs and symptoms seem to be well-defined for visual fatigue and discomfort, thereby facilitating the interpretation of physiological measurements, using these measurements to study cybersickness will require, here also, a clearer glossary of "virtual space sickness". At present, this glossary focuses more on symptoms than on signs.

3.4.2. *Display factors*

Several studies have tried to compare the impact of the display systems to the sensations of discomfort, fatigue and uneasiness. They often concluded that there was a greater sensation of uneasiness with HMDs. However, the variety of differences from one display system to the next prevented them from establishing solid conclusions. In this section, we will therefore discuss the influence of certain material characteristics of immersive rendering systems on perception and a sensation of discomfort, fatigue and cybersickness.

3.4.2.1. *Monoscopy, stereoscopy and bi-ocular*

In stereoscopic rendering devices, two slightly different images are presented to each eye to reproduce the vision of relief and depth. If the two images are displayed across the entirety of a screen and are separated by polarization or temporal frequency, we speak of a stereoscopic screen. In the case of HMDs, where two images are not superimposed, we speak of a bi-ocular display. As a result of this procedure, and if the disparity between the images respects the interocular distance, the user is able to visualize a scene with relief features, which often makes it appear natural and immersive. Nonetheless, restitution processes for stereoscopic vision bring in different ocular and cognitive constraints, sources of discomfort and visual fatigue.

The best-known constraint is undoubtedly the de-synchronization of demands on accommodation and vergence, illustrated in Figure 3.26. When watching videos or virtual 3D scenes in stereoscopy, the user must accommodate the screen while converging on the "real" position of the object. Several studies have shown signs of visual fatigue linked to this accommodation/vergence conflict, such as difficulty with convergence and oculomotor instability, increased fusion time or reduced stereoscopic acuity [URV 13a]. However, it appears that the variations in the conflict (related to rapid movements at great depths) are more important than the conflict itself, and they are the source of visual uneasiness [SPE 06, YAN 04, EMO 05].

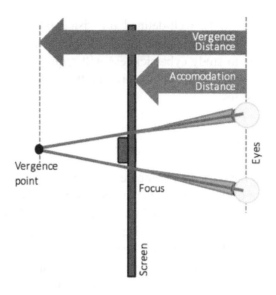

Figure 3.26. *Accommodation-vergence conflict*

Other cognitive constraints, mainly related to the limitations of binocular fusion and the integration of different depth cues, may lead to visual uneasiness in stereoscopic visualization. The zone over which the human visual system is able to fuse the images perceived by each eye is called "Panum's fusional area". Fusion is not possible outside this zone: only one of the two images is interpreted, either by suppressing the other, or by alternating between the two. Thus, for visualizing the 3D content in relief, the proposed stimuli must be situated within Panum's area. This area is, moreover, influenced by different characteristics of the virtual experience related to 3D content and also through the visualization system. In effect, Panum's area increases with the size and illumination of the stimulus, but is reduced when the spatial frequency and temporal depth modulations increase. The visualization of content that is dark, detailed, small in size and with frequent depth movements may thus provoke episodes of double vision and result in visual fatigue and discomfort [URV 13a]. Thus, Panum's area increases with the viewing angle, exposure time and exposure frequency (drag): long and repeated immersive visualizations are thus conducive to a better perception of large differences.

The first good practice when creating 3D content visualized in stereoscopy is to restrict the collection of foveal stimuli to a zone of comfort defined as the association of Panum's fusional area and the depth of the field[12] (see Figure 3.27). This comfort zone is located, depending on how it is specified, around ±0.2 diopters for the depth of field and ±1° of the angle of disparity with the screen (which corresponds to 1% and 2% of the screen size in terms of crossed and uncrossed disparities. [URV 13a]. Other solutions also make it possible to reduce the accommodation/vergence conflict. Foveal feedback consists of modifying the resolution or sharpness of the image depending on the position of fixations by the observer, maximizing the sharpness at the level of fixation and adding fuzziness in peripheral vision. The fuzzy effects modify the depth cues and size cues of the objects [HEL 10, WAN 11], and diminish the role of accommodation [OKA 06]. This reduces the accommodation–vergence conflict. The use of foveal feedback has been shown to be effective in reducing visual fatigue for both classic stereoscopic screens and HMDs [CAR 15a]. The challenge with this technique is to predict or precisely know the user's fixation positions, based on precise saccadic models or real-time eye-tracking. Other, and more complex, material solutions propose reducing the accommodation/vergence conflict in HMDs through multifocal or multi-lens display systems [KON 16, AKE 04, LIU 09, HU 14].

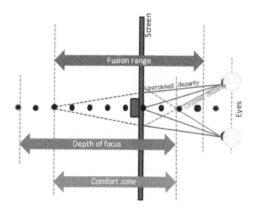

Figure 3.27. *Sensory and cognitive constraints in stereoscopic vision, according to [URV 13b]*

---

12 The depth of the field is the zone over which the human visual system is able to accommodate.

3.4.2.2. *Latency*

Latency corresponds to the time between a user action that leads to displacement in the virtual environment (a nod of the head, for example) and the feedback from the environment on the screen, corresponding to the new point of view. Latency arises due to the refresh frequency of different components of the systems as well as the data transport and processing times. Several studies have shown a link between the increase in latency and feelings of uneasiness [JEN 04, JEN 00, WIL 96, DRA 01]. However, this relationship seems more complex than a simple linear correlation, and these results cannot always be replicated in experiments where HMDs were used [NEL 00, MOS 11b, MOS 11a]. Thus, more than the average latency, cybersickness [ST 15] is likely to be caused by changes in latency during the experience. Furthermore, the HMDs produce variable latency, with the amplitude between 10 and 100 ms, chiefly due to the interaction between the acquisition and refreshing frequencies of motion sensors and screens [WU 13]. The advent of virtual experience *streaming* in HMDs may also influence the latency variance, directly related to the transmission speed of data and feedback.

3.4.2.3. *Field of vision*

One of the important aspects in visual interfaces in virtual reality is the size of the immersed visual field. This immersed visual field may greatly vary from one display system to another.

In an immersive room formed of several screens, the immersed visual field is almost total (the mounts of the stereoscopic glasses may occlude parts of the natural visual field) and the user continues to perceive their own body: loss of equilibrium and vestibulo-ocular conflicts are reduced. An immersive-screen-type system only immerses part of the natural visual field in the virtual world and the real world is left perceptible on the periphery, which can lead to sensory inconsistencies. Many studies have shown that, with this type of visual interface, there is an increase in cybersickness when the immersed visual field increases, especially for a horizontal angle between 60° and 140° [SEA 02, DUH 01, LIN 02]. As with immersive screens, the immersed visual field in HMDs is reduced (about 100° by 100° in the case of the Oculus Rift and HTC Vive headsets today). However, unlike immersive screens, the real world is hidden. The user therefore cannot see their own body, and this can create postural instability and uneasiness. Thus, Moss and Muth demonstrated that cybersickness was increased by the occlusion of the peripheral vision in an HMD with a visual field of 50° (horizontal) and 30° (vertical) [MOS 11b].

The increase in discomfort and uneasiness following an increase in the immersed visual field can be explained by the fact that peripheral vision is most sensitive to movement. Thus, vection, the sensation of movement from optic flow, will be more intense in the case of a greater visual immersion [BRA 73, WEB 03]. Moreover, it has been proved that this vection is the cause of VIMS and cybersickness [KES 15, PAL 17]. This question becomes all the more important today, given that we are seeing the development of headsets with greater and greater immersive capabilities, which are being more widely used to visualize multimedia and video content where the movements of the camera and movements of the head may be de-correlated. This can, thereby, create dynamic stimuli in the peripheral vision that are unpredictable and very uncomfortable (see, for example, [KIM 15, PAL 17] on the influence of passive navigation on cybersickness in an HMD). On adding blurriness to peripheral vision, foveal feedback may also be a solution to diminish the feeling of discomfort induced by moving visual stimuli.

Another aspect, potentially troubling and related to the field of vision, is the ratio between the immersed visual field (physical visual field) and the geometric visual field that is directly dependent on the focal length of the camera and its position in the scene (virtual for synthetic content, or real for photographs and 360° videos). Draper *et al.* [DRA 01] were the first to demonstrate that a ratio of 1 minimized cybersickness. However, many subsequent studies have shown the reverse; that is, different physical and geometric visual fields (or the external and internal visual fields) made it possible to reduce the feeling of discomfort and uneasiness [TOE 08, BOS 10, EMM 11]. Moss and Muth [MOS 11b] could not find that this ratio had any significant influence on cybersickness when using an HMD. These differences in results may be explained by the different display systems used: HMDs for [MOS 11b, DRA 01] and immersive screens for [TOE 08, BOS 10, EMM 11]. The value of the ratio could also have influenced these results. Indeed, if the two fields of vision, physical and geometric, are very different, then the visual stimuli cannot stimulate the vestibular system in a natural manner and the sensation of vection will therefore be reduced. This leads to a reduction in the realism, in presence and in cybersickness [TOE 08, EMM 11]. All of this research studies the use of virtual reality headsets for multimedia applications, where the zoom-in/zoom-out effects and camera placement may lead to a feeling of discomfort or uneasiness.

3.4.2.4. *Qualities of the screens*

The intrinsic qualities of a screen – image resolution, dynamic brightness range, range of color and refresh frequency – may also influence perception of the scene and induce visual discomfort.

The resolution of these immersive display systems remains a sizeable challenge when it comes to improving the image quality of virtual reality applications. Let us take the case of the HTC Vive headset. The resolution of this headset is about 14 pixels per degree (horizontal) and 8 pixels per degree (vertical), which is far from the acuity limit of human vision (which is 1 minute of an angle, which would correspond to a resolution of 60 pixels per degree). The user may thus see pixels on the screen and, especially in complex scenes which are highly detailed, the image may be difficult to read and the experience may produce discomfort or even visual fatigue.

The recent development of screens called the *High Dynamic Range* (HDR) and *Wide Color Gamut* (WCG), which are capable of reproducing a much greater range of light and color contrasts, are now entering the world of virtual reality headsets. For example, the Samsung Galaxy Note 7 supports HDR videos and may be used in the Samsung Gear VR headset. These new technologies raise several questions concerning HDR/WCG images that are processed by *tone* and *gamut mapping* operators[13]. In particular, the naturalness of the images may modify their realism and thus the presence of the user [BAR 10, KRA 14]. Thus, an increase in contrast in virtual reality headsets brings in the question of visual comfort.

Finally, the refresh frequency directly influences the latency of the system, which may lead to discomfort and uneasiness.

---

13 Operators that carry out tonal and gamut matching.

3.4.3. *Conclusion*

By striving towards greater immersion for the user, the visual rendering systems in VR create sensory and cognitive constraints, which are sometimes a source of discomfort, fatigue and uneasiness. The study of human perception, in relation to the factors that create these constraints, is essential to the development of comfortable display technologies and content. A stimulating and ambitious challenge for the study of "virtual space sickness" is integrating the effects of intra- and inter-sensory conflicts, which require a clear and transversal definition (across the senses, sensations and manipulated technologies) of the signs and symptoms of cybersickness. This would then make it possible to develop robust and precise evaluation methods and scales, both subjective and objective, which would help give greater scientific validity to the obtained results.

At present, we are mainly interested in the perceptual effects of technologies that enable the presence of the user to be increased with greater immersion, realism and interaction. However, new AR tools, where we superimpose digital information on reality, perceived through a non-opaque screen[14], also address new problems relative to the study of cybersickness, mainly related to the creation of real/virtual perceptual inconsistencies.

3.5. Evaluation

3.5.1. *Objectives and scope of this section*

This section is centered on the human aspects of evaluation. The chosen framework is the use, design and selection of VR-AR systems[15], as opposed to evaluation centered on the verification of technical reliability and respect of technical specifications. It can be complemented by additional readings, especially [BUR 06b, BUR 06a, LOU 14, HAL 15]. The challenges of mixed reality are presented in other reference works (e.g. [GAB 99, BUR 06b, BUR 06a, LIV 13, JUL 01, LOU 14]).

---

14 For example, the Microsoft HoloLens.

15 This research was partly carried out as part of the McCoy Critical (Models for Adaptive Feedback Enrichment and Orchestration-based Virtual Reality in Critical Situations) project no. ANR CE14-24 0021.

3.5.2. *Evaluation: a complex problem*

3.5.2.1. *Definition*

"Evaluation" refers to the "action of evaluating", that is, the action of measuring, estimating, determining or even judging a value. An evaluation may serve several purposes (e.g. designing, selecting, accompanying learning and development, monetization) and the subjects of evaluation may be of varying degrees of complexity: evaluating the utility of a medicine, the efficiency of an interaction metaphor, the performance of a learning software or even the societal impact of a public policy notion. The concept of evaluation is thus shared across many disciplines in the human sciences (e.g. economics, education science, psychology, ergonomics), life sciences (e.g. medicine, biology), and engineering and design sciences (e.g. computer sciences, virtual reality, mechanics).

3.5.2.2. *Summative and formative evaluations: quantitative and qualitative methods*

Depending on the objective of the evaluation, there are two approaches that can be distinguished: *summative evaluation* and *formative evaluation*. Summative evaluation aims to measure the quality of a system and/or quantify aspects of the performance of participants. This is most often the basis for a *quantitative* approach (e.g. in the form of a single score or multiple scores, for example cost and efficiency) in order to rank them with respect to either a standard reference, or by comparing them with the competing alternatives. *Quantitative methods* refer to the methods of collecting quantifiable data (e.g. workforce, frequency, numerical values) through diverse data-gathering tools such as the questionnaire, recording physiological data, observation of behavior (most often instrumental observation) and collecting traces. The appropriate statistical analysis method is used depending on the variables (nominal, ordinal, numerical) and the characteristics of the procedures used (especially sampling size and characteristics of the sample). These contain at least a descriptive analysis of each variable and the crosses between the variables. If needed, when justified by the questions and conditions, this is then followed by the appropriate inference tests. The objective of the summative evaluation is therefore to help make a decision. For example, choosing between several alternatives, between an existing system and a new system, and evaluating the cost or impact of this decision, or even verifying its real effectiveness, for example, when using an environment for learning purposes. It is also possible to predict or estimate the value of performances or dimensions of human behavior using situations in the simulation and freeing oneself from certain constraints in the real world.

Formative evaluations aims to produce data – most often *qualitative* or mixed (quantitative/qualitative) data on the observed activity and processes put in place by users in their interactions with a system, on the difficulties encountered and the most probable factors that would explain these difficulties, on the identification of unforeseen needs, or even on potential ideas for solutions to the problems and questions thus identified. *Qualitative methods*, in particular, focus on exploring, understanding and providing greater information on the relevant aspects of human activity studied in a given situation. For example, how interactions are conducted with the system. These methods generally make use of the analysis and elaboration of categories based on the material collected, for example verbal content gathered from a subject's speech, responses to open questions, or further questioning for more detailed information, analysis of the content of the traces produced by the subject when performing an activity, the types of observed behavior. Among these methods, we can mention the monograph study, individual exploratory interviews, collective interviews (i.e. focus groups), overt observation, documentary analyses, expert inspection of the interface, etc. In this context, it is possible to use statistics adapted to the analysis of nominal variables but not systematically. It depends on the objective and characteristics of the situation where information is gathered. The essential objective of formative evaluation beyond stimulating research by identifying factors that could explain validity, acceptability and the use of these new systems is to give the researcher or designer feedback, both on the system that is being evaluated and any future changes that would be desirable, and also on the development of research tools and procedures.

3.5.2.3. *Articulating formative and summative approaches: quantitative and qualitative methods*

The current trend consists of developing a formative evaluation at least as much as a summative evaluation is being developed, or even to combine the two in a complementary manner in the context of a study. Attributing a value or a score is not always sufficient inasmuch as it is a case of also (or especially) identifying factors to explain the obtained score, as well as the strongest keys to improvement. Additionally, in present-day research we are seeing a methodological change towards collecting data and indicators based on several approaches (triangulation methodology). Ingeniously articulating the advantages and drawbacks of these methods is consequently an important development, especially as evaluation concerns prototypes being developed, with a direct effect on the complexity of the evaluation and the types of approaches to put in place. The objectives and needs of evaluation, in terms of questions and samples, depend on whether a finalized, complete tool is being evaluated, or a prototype of interfaces focusing on usability of the devices and/or quality of immersion, or even a particularly innovative concept or idea for a system. (Table 3.2).

Nature and level of maturity of the object being evaluated	Possible objectives for summative evaluation	Possible objectives for formative evaluation
Usage in real/realistic context	– Deciding, choosing a tool – Measuring the effectiveness, usability, performance, behavior – Generalizing: testing hypotheses, testing theories, etc.	Informing design, explaining observed performances, supporting implantation, identifying determinants for use and acceptance, identifying emerging needs, preparing the next version, etc.
Interaction	– Deciding between different devices and/or metaphors and/or types of HMIs – Measuring the usability, relevance of design principles, impact of such and such factor on usage, the precision, speed, etc.	Informing design, explaining observed performances, supporting implantation, identifying factors that impact comprehension and interaction with the device
Concepts, ideas	– Decision: herarchization, selecting propositions – Measurement: originality, perceived utility, acceptability *a priori*	Carry out a detailed elaboration, identify new concepts and ideas, enlarge possible uses

Table 3.2. *Articulate objectives and approaches depending on the level of maturity and nature of the system being evaluated*

Specifically centered on the ergonomic evaluation of interfaces, a particular class of methods is characterized by the absence of the method that places the users in various situations. Generally focused on usability and the ergonomic quality of a mixed reality environment or tool, these methods are derived by adapting methods from the field of human–machine interaction: Norms, Styleguides and Recommendations adapted to mixed reality systems [BAC 04], the use of Nielsen Heuristics, adapted to the first virtual environments [STA 03] or even cognitive inspection to evaluate collaborative virtual environments [TRO 03]. In the last few years, few methods and tools seem to have been proposed for virtual environments. On the contrary, there are several recent proposals for mobile augmented reality, based on a usability questionnaire that was specific to these technologies (e.g. [KO 13, KOU 15]). This class of method has the advantage of being low cost, compared with the construction and conduction of experiments with participants. However, they do not seem to be efficient enough to be used exclusively for design. For example, [SCH 14] compared the efficiency of three techniques (expert inspection, documentary inspection and user tests) to identify problems with the usability of two virtual environments. They observed that the expert inspection identified a much lower number of problems when compared with the other two techniques (documentary inspection and user tests), while these two techniques appeared to be highly complementary (Figure 3.28).

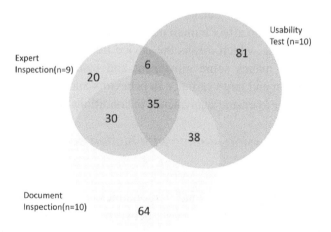

Figure 3.28. *The count and distribution of usability problems identified in two virtual environments based on the technique used to identify the problems: expert inspection, documentary inspection and user test; from [SCH 14]*

3.5.2.4. *Taking into account the features of mixed reality when evaluating*

Mixed reality has specific features in terms of difficulties and the types of abilities and skills required from the users. There is, first of all, a heightened importance in the physical and gesture-based dimension in activity associated with the usage of the device, the introduction of depth in the interaction space and mobility. This heightened physical dimension makes it much more difficult to use and interpret physiological data collected from user situations, as they are susceptible to being influenced by several physiological variables (e.g. cardiac frequency, skin conductance).

Another important characteristic is the intertwining (more or less transparent to the users) of information present in the real environment and the artificial information from the informatics system, or even the competition or interference between these sources and the information.

Finally, the particularity of using such a system in an open, outdoor environment brings in two additional difficulties: (1) variations in the parameters in the ambience, which may affect the reliability and efficiency of the technical devices (e.g. outside brightness in the day, strong contrasts, humidity) and may also affect human performance (e.g. external temperature, rain); (2) mobile use, which means the device functioning as the participant travels around or makes some movement and results in potentially large degrees of freedom and large variance in behaviors and data gathered, as well as making it harder to ensure equivalence in conditions between participants.

3.5.3. *Evaluation using studies with human subjects*

3.5.3.1. *Validity: a central concept*

Validity, in psychology and ergonomics, usually refers to the (multi-dimensional) relation that exists between a theory (or any theoretical element: model, hypothesis, concept, instrument, text, etc.), on the one hand, and the empirical reality it is supposed to represent, on the other. Indeed, there are multiple classifications of types and sub-types of validity, which differ, overlap or may even exclude each other, depending on how the evaluation is designed (e.g. exposure and discussion in [MAR 86]).

Theoretical validity is the relationship between the procedure and equipment put in place for the study, on the one hand, and the concepts and theoretical elaborations mobilized to instruct the question or problem, on the other hand. With respect to the target questions, this validity has a bearing on (1) the appropriate nature of the concepts and concepts for the measuring tools that were chosen or developed, (2) identifying variables and the more pertinent and representative relationships between them and (3) selecting indicators that are statistically correlated to usual and relevant external criteria in order to process the question.

Internal validity refers to the degree of certainty that we may have with respect to the fact that the experimental manipulations of the situation are indeed at the origin of the observed effects, rather than other external factors which were not controlled. These external factors are related to the characteristics of the participants (e.g. events that occurred simultaneously with data gathering, maturity effects, re-test effects, regression effects by selecting extreme scores, etc.) or at the same time as single or multiple interactions between these characteristics and the components of the experimental situations (see [CAM 63] for an in-depth discussion of the factors that could threaten internal validity and how the different forms of the experimental plan contribute to controlling these factors). *Internal* validity is based mainly on (1) the choice of an experimental plan that makes it possible to control external factors that may have an effect on the collected data, and (2) using the appropriate statistical test procedures to estimate the magnitude of an effect and conclude whether or not it exists.

External validity – often likened to *ecological* validity – characterizes the possible degree of generalization of the observed results beyond the experimental situation itself, to other groups of individuals and other types of situations and conditions than those involved in the study. [BRA 68] distinguishes two dimensions related to external validity: the *validity of the population* – which concerns the question of the generalization of a population that is larger than the sample actually studied, and *ecological* validity, which refers to the degree to which it is possible to generalize results and behaviors observed in a specific study (i.e. in a restricted set of situations and indicators that were unique to the study) to the range of target situations and problems in the "natural" milieu. *Ecological* validity thus assumes that the observed effect is not just the consequence of the artificial characteristics of the environment alone [BRA 68], but that the same effect would be observed in other environments, especially the "natural" environment.

The concept of *ecological* validity returns to the more general question of validity of studies carried out by observation in an artificial milieu, which is often simplified and modified to enable the control of experimental factors in the laboratory, contrary to the observation of human behavior in its "natural milieu". Indeed, the simplification and reduction of "variables" present in the experimental environment may lead to behavior and performance that is modified, or even created solely in that situation due to the absence of information or dimensions in the environment that are usually mobilized in activities and to generate behavior [SNO 74].

Thus, there is no unique and absolute methodological response today to guarantee the *ecological* validity of a study and its results. In effect, this results from the interaction between many factors that are internal to both the participants and the context, as well as the system and the scenario used.

3.5.3.2. *Evaluating validity, activity and ergonomics depending on the destination and maturity of the system?*

One of the consequences of evaluation is the need to define criteria (qualitative and quantitative) and indicators or dimensions for analysis. These depend most often on the chosen objectives for the system. From this point of view, using user satisfaction as the sole means of evaluating quality is becoming less and less acceptable; studies are increasingly looking beyond performance (precision, rapidity) and criteria for utility, to other dimensions of activity (e.g. cognitive costs, learning) and, more broadly, the user experience (e.g. presence, engagement, persistence in use, psychological comfort or discomfort, confidence) depending on the type of application. The proposed use of the system as well as its contexts of use initially define the uses and performances that will serve as the evaluation framework. There are four principal categories: tools to produce scientific data on behavior, learning tool, tools used to execute a task, and finally, tools for entertainment or cultural purposes. These categories are the same as the different central categories for evaluation: internal and external validity, for the first two, and utility, usability, user experience and other criteria related to the ergonomics of a system for the third and fourth. In the following section, we will discuss these and other associated criteria.

3.5.3.2.1. The controlled simulation of real environments to study human behavior

When this is the purpose of a mixed reality environment or tools, the main objective is to bring about a simulacrum of a situation with reference to the properties of a real environment and a real situation, which must then be recreated as accurately and authentically as possible; this is the case with driving simulators, for example, or any other use for the varied mixed reality devices used to study any facet of human activity. Two types of applications may co-exist in this category:

– *Research purposes*: data is gathered in a more controlled laboratory setting. The data gives information on some aspect of behavior in the "natural" milieu;

– *Used for studying for design purposes*: in this case, a future activity or use is represented such that users, who represent future users, are placed in this situation and studied.

A recurring problem in this context is that of internal and external validity, with the latter generally being considered the same as the concept of ecological validity.

3.5.3.2.2. The simulation of (real) environments for learning, training and behavioral modification

The purpose of a system of this kind is to create a simulacrum of a situation that facilitates learning or the modification of a behavior (e.g. when used in a therapeutic framework). The simulacrum usually makes reference to the properties of a real environment and a real situation, as in the above-mentioned case, but here we can also have modifications and an enrichment of functions depending on the learning objectives or the goals of the behavioral modification, or even in response to the trainers' or therapists' needs.

The concepts of internal and external validity can also be used in the context of these learning tools, however with a different meaning from what we just saw. In effect, this would be evaluating the effectiveness of learning or developing skills, as well as the deployment of these acquisitions in a real task and situation. Thus, for Hoareau [HOA 16], the concept of *internal validity* may be interpreted as the evaluation of learning that is consecutive to the use of, and interaction with, the virtual experience/augmented reality. The author proposes using learning performance measures during the exposure and during the execution of the task, to verify the learning curve across the attempts in the VE/AR. In this context, the existence of such a curve is a measure of the internal validity of the tool, as it enables learning and improvement of performance. However, other approaches are also possible.

All of them try and address the following question: does the environment enable the expected learning or behavioral modification? *External validity* is then measured by the performance of the real task in real conditions.

3.5.3.2.3. Support for an action that is finalized or for a precise usage, a population and different contexts of use

The objective here is to design a tool that will aid in an activity that has been finalized. The environment that results from this may be partly imagined, while also integrating elements from real situations, so as to respond to a range of needs associated with the target activity for future users. There are two types of applications foreseen in this category, and each requires specific evaluation elements:

– *Online virtual worlds*: these offer communication and socialization activities, for example, *Second Life*;

– *Tools for work*: the created environment aims to provide the appropriate functions and representations to support the activity being carried out by an individual or a group of individuals, with a view to achieving the objectives of the task it is aiding in.

Any evaluation in this context must be based on the results obtained earlier from a needs analysis, as well as fit into a broader framework for a user-centered approach. In effect, we must promote evaluations that are not based on unreliable or irrelevant criteria (e.g. realism, satisfaction) but those that take into account criteria associated with the utility-value of the object. That is, those that make it possible to identify and precisely measure the improvements or significant benefits brought about by the tool, relative to the user's objectives, relative to existing or habitually-used tools, relative to the environment of use and to interdependencies with its other activities [LOU 13].

3.5.3.2.4. Games and derivatives: artistic installations

The objective of these systems is to give users an experience that is entertaining, engaging, artistic or esthetic, through the interaction with an environment that is totally or partially imaginary. Contrary to applications that aim to support user activity in executing a task towards an external goal, these types of environments are characterized by the fact that the user-subject's goal is motivated by the challenge provided by the application itself [CAR 15b] and/or the emotionally-dominated experience.

3.5.3.2.5. Destination and evaluation: an overview of questions and criteria

The criteria that are prioritized, as well as the data-gathering measures for evaluation, may differ depending on the device's destination. An overview of the dimensions and questions related to the destination is given in Table 3.3. Depending on the case, this may have to do with verifying validity in the case when the environment, is mobilized as a reconstruction of an ecological environment or to confirm/disprove hypotheses on the use of VE/AR, for example in terms of utility, acceptability, etc. Let us note in passing that the proposed classification does not imply a mutual exclusiveness of systems as multiple dimensions may be combined. For example, we may use mechanisms of a game for a mixed-environment dedicated to learning. One of the consequences of this could be that the internal and external validity, as well as the dimensions of engagement, and the user's experience quality, all constitute relevant variables to be measured. The collaborative dimension is an additional dimension that may be involved for different destinations (see section 3.5.5.4).

3.5.3.3. *Experiment plans: minimizing or neutralizing the effect of factors that could affect internal validity*

The construction of an experiment plan aims to isolate the effect of factors that interest the researchers, while neutralizing or minimizing the effect of other external factors that could influence the result. A first method would be to introduce a *control condition*. This may be obtained by assigning a section of the participants to a group that is not exposed to the treatment or experimental factors being manipulated in the experience. This is called a *control group*, and a plan with independent samples. Establishing the effect of conditions or the experimental treatments requires taking measurements before, after and even during the experiment. When the control group is put in place, it must be ensured that the absence of the treatment is the only difference between this and the other groups. For example, the task must be the same as the instructions and any additional training provided and so on. The experiments should also examine whether the treatment given to the control group will itself have an effect (positive or negative) on the activity of the participants (and therefore on the data gathered). For example, introducing a rest-period instead of the experimental treatment(s). When evaluating the impact of a new tool, for example, one method may be to compare two groups, one using the new tool and the other the existing tool.

	Intended application	Criteria	Underlying question
Tool for controlled simulation of real environments for study and research	– Research – Design	– External validity – Internal validity	– Is the observed effect indeed caused by the variables manipulated in the construction and execution of the simulated situation? – Can we generalize the results to the target population, and to similar environments and type of activities? – Are the observed results identical to or compatible with those seen in real situations?
Tool for controlled simulation of real environments for learning and behavior modification	– Training, education, learning – Use in cognitive and behavioral therapy	– Internal validity – External validity – Impact on the learning process and on interactions	– Does the environment enable the desired learning of behavioral changes? – Is the learning transferred to real situations? – How does the introduction of the tool modify the nature of the activity and interactions of the users involved (e.g. learners, trainers, patients, therapists)
Games, artistic installations	– Games and derivatives – Artistic installation	– Playability, engagement, entertainment experience, flow, emotion, esthetics – Usability and accessibility – Danger – Satisfaction – Acceptability	– Does the user's experience match the design objectives? – Is the system usable for and accessible to users with special needs? – Will using the system have any dangerous consequences for the user or their environment? Has the risk of errors been minimized? – How do the users estimate their satisfaction? – What is the acceptability (*a priori*) or acceptance (*a posteriori*) of the system?

| Tool adapted to a specific use, population or pre-determined contexts of use | – Online virtual universe
– Work-related tool | – Utility
– Usability and accessibility
– Danger
– Satisfaction
– Acceptability
– Impact on processes and interactions | – Does the proposed tool offer any significant advantage or ease of use for the user relative to their objectives, relative to existing or habitually used tools, or relative to the environment where it will be used and to the dependencies on other activities?
– Is it usable, accessible for users with special needs
– Will using the system have any dangerous consequences for the user or their environment? Has the risk of errors been minimized?
– How do the users estimate their satisfaction?
– What is the acceptability (*a priori*) or acceptance (*a posteriori*) of the system?
– How does the introduction of the tool modify the nature of the activity and interactions of the users involved (e.g. learners, trainers, patients, therapists) |

Table 3.3. *Criteria and questions related to the evaluation based on the purpose of VE/AR being studied*

When the plan includes several experimental groups and conditions, we must ensure that all the groups are similar from the point of view of the characteristics of the participants of the sample (experience or any other factor that may impact performance and the gathered data). A good practice to follow is to use domain knowledge – especially the state of the art of the literature on the concerned activity – to characterize the sample using previously taken measures of the characteristics of the participants that are relevant to the task, so as to verify the equivalence of the two groups, or even to form the groups by matching them to characteristics measured beforehand. Similarly, criteria to evaluative performance must be applied in an equivalent manner for both groups. Performance cannot be measured using different tools, for example, depending on the condition compared. The risk here is that any difference that may be observed (beyond the different units and scales of measurements) will result from differences in the instruments and not from any difference in the variable being measured.

In certain cases, it is possible to use each subject as their own control, by comparing the measurements taken in the real situation before and after exposure. We then speak of a *single-subject* experiment. However, a difficult aspect with this plan is that the interpretation of any improvement may also be linked to a confounding factor: maturation time. That is, certain skills may see improved performance after a certain time, even without additional practice, especially if they are intensely practiced [ROL 82].

There exist other plans *without control groups* which are reserved for situations where it is not possible to form control groups. However, these *"non-experimental"* groups are considered to have low internal validity and require very good arguments for being chosen.

3.5.3.4. *Sample size and composition*

The composition of the sample poses three notable problems: (1) the definition of the population we wish to study – and to which we wish to generalize the results obtained, in cases where the objective is to generalize findings; (2) the required sample size to test the existence of any effect; and (3) recruiting and access to participants.

All too often there is no explicit and clear definition of the target population, instead there is only the description of the characteristics of the sample. Moreover, it is rarely that the aim is to generalize a population accessible to the study (e.g. psychology students), instead, generalization is envisaged to a much larger population. In addition, to appreciate the ability to generalize to this target population (external validity) it is necessary to have precise knowledge about the characteristics.

The increasing size of a sample is often associated with better representativity of results, which may translate to better external validity. However, in reality, things are more complex. Generally speaking, a rule of thumb is that the number of subjects required increases as the magnitude of the effect to prove diminishes, and/or the basic frequency of the event becomes smaller. The sample size must therefore be chosen based on the expected impact of the effect, which may be estimated based on reports in the literature, and/or based on a pilot study.

As much as possible, we avoid samples smaller than 20 subjects per condition.

3.5.4. *Drawbacks to overcome*

3.5.4.1. *Information that is often incomplete on the procedure and specific characteristics of the systems*

Comparing results between studies is often an arduous task today as a result of a crucial lack of detail. First of all, on the methodological front, the information on the procedure is often incomplete, the factors to be manipulated and the precise operationalization of the experimental conditions are often loosely defined or vague. As concerns the precise characteristics of the systems involved: they are often general and not very detailed. Moreover, there is no systematic and complete classification of the characteristics of the systems and the activities being studied that would enable us to describe them in such a way that they could be compared systematically and rigorously. If this were possible, it would open up the way to carry out meta-analyses of published research.

3.5.4.2. *Frequently seen biases in methodology*

Studies published at present often have a bias that limits their wider use. Among the most frequent are the absence of a control condition in the experimental plan, the small number of subjects per group, using subjective measures with no reference to behavior and performance, or even measuring a unique variable, etc. Other methodological biases are related to the data processing and analysis. For example, we can note that there is a trend to focus on "statistical significance" rather than the semantic and scientific importance of the effect relative to the field. The distinction between these two aspects is not anecdotal: the first relates to generalizing the existence of an effect (independent of its magnitude), while the second relates to the magnitude of the observed effect (see [COR 94] on the same). Usual inference tests (e.g. variance analysis, student tests, χ^2) are used to arrive at a conclusion on the possibility of generalizing the effect observed on a sample[16], but does not make it possible to conclude whether the observed

---

16 Let us recall here that a common error is to conclude that there is no effect if the result of the test is non-significant while it may just be that the researcher cannot arrive at a conclusion on the meaning of the statistical test.

effect is negligible or important. Moreover, studying the magnitude of the effects leads to the question of their importance for the question and the scientist. This involves defining before-hand, if possible, the values from which we may consider an effect to be important or negligible, which is the same as measuring the importance from the descriptive step. In the majority of cases, the importance of the effect is judged based on the knowledge on the field from which the problem is taken, especially on effects that are generally reported in literature. In the case where such a reference outside the study may not exist, several authors (in particular refer to the arguments and reference values in [COR 94]) suggest basing oneself on an internal reference from within the gathered data (Table 3.4). Furthermore, the magnitude of the effect is one of the elements required to allow other researchers to use published results to carry out meta-analyses.

Situations	Indicators	Benchmark values		
		Weak effect	Medium effect	Large effect
Comparison of an average to the norm	$ER = \frac{M - \mu_0}{S}$	0.20	0.50	1.00 (0.80)
Comparison of the means of two matching groups	$EC = \frac{D}{S_d}$	0.20	0.50	1.00 (0.80)
Comparison of the means of two independent groups	$EC = \frac{M_1 - M_2}{S_{intra}}$	0.20	0.50	1.00 (0.80)
Comparison of the means of k independent groups	$\eta^2 = \frac{S^2_{inter}}{S^2_{totale}}$	0.01	0.06	0.20 (0.14)
	$f^2 = \frac{S^2_{inter}}{S^2_{intra}}$	0.01	0.06	0.25 (0.16)
Linear correlation	$R = \frac{Cov(X,Y)}{S_x S_y}$	0.10	0.24 (0.30)	0.45 (0.50)
	$R^2 = \frac{Cov^2(X,Y)}{S^2_x S^2_y}$	0.01	0.06 (0.09)	0.25 (0.25)
Independent towards a contingency table	$R^2_c = \frac{\phi^2}{l}$	0.01	0.06 (0.09)	0.25 (0.25)

Table 3.4. *Benchmark values proposed by Rouanet and Corroyer [COR 94] for different situations of data-analysis. The values between parentheses are the values initially proposed by [COH 77]*

3.5.4.3. *The situations of the study are often simplified and not very ecological*

In many tests, especially those focused on usability, the tasks given to the subject are short and artificial, more an elementary interaction than finalized activity in situations that have the aim of saving a certain ecology. Additionally, even though they open up avenues to explore, a limited number of results is directly transposable to the design of a complete tool as, except in laboratories, the devices are never used in an isolated manner and in the absence of constraints and organizations that characterize the real context. Thus, carrying out an analysis of a complete system in context alone makes it possible to specify the overall importance of each element relative to the overall functioning [ANA 07].

3.5.4.4. *Adhering to theories and models of human activity that must be reinforced*

In many studies, the potentiality of the proposed prototypes are not built on a theoretical framework in a sufficiently detailed manner to allow for empirical investigation – for example, in terms of learning models or activity models, the link between action, comprehension and development of competencies. One of the explanations for this is probably the fact that the focus is only on the identified technological barriers, setting aside the human and organizational dimension or, at best, contenting oneself with a naive mode, which may be abstract and not precise enough for the end-user and their activities.

3.5.5. *Evolutions in measuring performance and behavior, characterizing participants*

Over the last several years, we have seen the development, or the increased use, of measuring instruments across diverse dimensions which may be of interest in the evaluation of mixed reality devices. Several types of measurements are commonly used for the subject's performance in the task, efficiency, satisfaction, user experience, workload or even the different dimensions of usability of the interaction devises (for examples of measurements across these different categories, see [BUR 06b]; see also Table 3.5). The rest of this section will focus on presenting some of these measurements that we find remarkable or interesting, whether they have to do with a certain rigor and standardization, or whether they are an interesting innovation in terms of the modes of measurements that were used earlier.

Dimensions	Quantitative measures (examples)	Qualitative and/or subjective measures (examples)
Performance relative to the goals associated with the task	– Number or percentage of tasks or attempts executed successfully – Deviations with respect to a reference solution/ performance – Spatial precision – Error rate – Just Noticeable Difference (JND), etc.	– Judgment by experts – Questionnaire – Likert scale – Semi-structured interview – Auto-confrontation, etc.
Efficiency, temporal	– Duration of tasks – Reaction time (RT) – Duration % of time for specific steps in the interaction, etc.	– Judgment by experts – Questionnaire – Likert scale – Semi-structured interview – Auto-confrontation, etc.
Efficiency in terms of actions on the interface	– Total number of required actions – Sub-optimal sequence of actions or patterns of interaction – Number or % of necessary actions executed, etc.	– Judgment by experts – Questionnaire – Likert Scale – Semi-structured interview – Auto-confrontation, etc.
Workload, stress	– Physiological measures (cognitive oculometry, skin resistance, EEG, cardiac frequency, etc.) – Double-task paradigm (mental load) – Variations in modes of operation and control	– Self-evaluation questionnaire – Judgment by experts
Intelligibility, memorization and learnability of the system or interaction	– Level of intelligibility of the system for the user – User's ability to predict the behavior of the system – Time required to learn to use the system easily – Number of functions memorized in a given time, etc.	– Judgment by experts – Questionnaire – Likert scale – Semi-structured interview – Auto-confrontation, etc.

Table 3.5. *Examples for measurements used in evaluations that mobilize mixed-reality systems*

3.5.5.1. *Measuring workload*

Many different measurements for workload – especially mental work – are used, among which the National Aeronautics and Space Administration Task Load Index questionnaire (NASA-TLX is probably one of the most frequently used. This is a multi-dimensional scale made up of five sub-categories (mental demand, physical demand, temporal demand, performance and frustration). It offers two advantages: it is a tool that has become a relatively standard measure, which facilitates comparisons, and it is relatively simple to use, both for the researcher as well as for the respondent. It does, nonetheless, have certain limitations, including the fact that it is a self-evaluation. It is used after the performance of the task (or requires interrupting the task) and consequently makes it difficult or even impossible to take into account dynamic fluctuations in workload over time, etc. Other methods make it possible to evaluate work load, such as the double task method, eventually adapted with the aim of measuring other constructions such as awareness of the situation (see, for example, SPAM – Situation Present Assessment Method; [DUR 04]). Physiological measurements may also be used in order to estimate the evolution of the workload such as measuring cardiac rhythm, electrodermal activity or variations in pupil size. However, these measurements are not generally sufficient, especially as they are very sensitive to physical activity by the subject, as well as to variations in the parameters of the subject's environment (e.g. variance in light, for pupil size).

3.5.5.2. *Measuring presence*

Used in a certain number of contexts, measuring presence uses various approaches, among which the most widely used, often chosen out of convenience, emerge from the self-evaluation questionnaire. There are many examples of these approaches, which are distinguished mainly on the basis of their theoretical fundamentals and the targeted dimensions (e.g. physical presence, co-presence, social presence). The QP presence questionnaire [WIT 98] is probably one of the most widely used approaches, along with the shorter Slater-Usoh-Steed questionnaire [SLA 94] and the group presence questionnaire [SCH 01]. Beyond the theoretical debates on the dimension of presence as a subjective experience, on factors that influence this, as well as on the relations that they have with the objectives for use, using a standardized measure for this dimension may also constitute a dimension that makes it possible to characterize the situations where subjects are studied and offer an additional indicator to compare different published studies. For certain authors, measuring presence may provide an estimation of the psychological validity of simulators and virtual reality environments.

3.5.5.3. *Measuring acceptability: the SUS questionnaire (System Usability Scale)*

The acceptability and perceived usability of mixed-reality prototypes are increasingly being evaluated with the help of a simple measuring tool: the SUS (System Usability Scale; [BRO 96]). This is a simple questionnaire made up of 10, Likert-scale type items, which are used to calculate the overall value for the subject evaluation that users assign following their first time using this device. This offers three advantages: it is simple and quick to use and does not pose any comprehension problems when going from one subject to another; it gives an overall score ranging from 0 to 100 that represents a composite measurement of usability; it is usable and used for a large variety of systems and interfaces. This makes it possible to compare several versions of the same system. A study carried out by Bangor *et al.* [BAN 08] on 2324 questionnaires resulting from 206 tests and covering a large range of systems and interfaces showed that it was reliable to evaluate the acceptability of a product/system. Moreover, an additional advantage is the fact that, unlike with other questionnaires on acceptability, the scores obtained may be associated with adjectives to facilitate the interpretation and comparison of scores (Table 3.6). We can find examples for this in different studies [BAR 13, BOR 16, LEE 16]. Recently, there has been a version dedicated specifically to hand-held augmented reality tools [SAN 14].

Range (SUS score)	Central value (SUS score)	Scale of adjectives of usability	Acceptability
00.00–44.00	25.00	Worst imaginable	Not acceptable
44.00–51.00	39.17	Poor	Not acceptable
51.00–55.00	52.01	Fair	Marginal low
55.00–75.00	72.75	Good	Marginal high (<70.00)
			Acceptable (>70.00)
75.00–87.50	85.58	Excellent	Acceptable
87.50–100.00	100.00	Best imaginable	Acceptable superior

Table 3.6. *Interpretation of the SUS score in terms of usability and acceptability (adapted from Bangor* et al. *(2009; 2008))*

3.5.5.4. *Towards a multi-dimensional measurement of inter-user collaboration*

With the rise in multi-user applications, the question of assistance and measuring the impact of the proposed systems on collaboration becomes an important one. In spite of this, however, few studies explore and analyze effective collaboration processes in real or ecological situations. The analyses carried out in current studies – whether experiments in laboratories or studies in the field – mobilize different techniques for gathering and analyzing data (e.g. logs, interactions between participants) centered essentially on the quantification of interactions between participants at a fine level. Hornbaek [HOR 06], for example, identifies measures of "communication effort" according to studies, the number of turns per speaker, the quantity of words produced, the number of interruptions, the proportions of questions for clarification, etc. These measures pose many problems, among which are the difficulty in applying them to a study that mobilizes a prototype (due to problems with technological maturity, for instance), and the large amount of time and effort involved for the researcher. On a more fundamental level, these indicators do not reflect the multiple dimensions of collaboration and have often proven to be *ad hoc* and non-univocal. For example, the number of speaking chances a person gets explicitly reflects only on the information-exchange dimension. Moreover, a higher-level number of turns to speak may indicate close collaboration between participants, or may even indicate a difficulty in collaboration, leading to a greater volume of verbal exchanges. A low number of exchanges may similarly signify that important information was not exchanged. To remedy this difficulty, other method that aim to cover the multiple dimensions off the collaboration have been proposed [MEI 07]. We have proposed an adaptation of this method in the context of using collaborative virtual environments for design [BUR 09]. This method makes it possible to rapidly extract video clips, inasmuch as it uses subjective indicators while guaranteeing high inter-coder fidelity. The quality of the collaboration is evaluated here along seven dimensions: (1) the fluidity of collaboration, (2) support for mutual understanding, (3) information exchange to resolve problems, (4) arguments and decision-making, (5) work processes and time-management, (6) balancing contribution and (7) individual orientation vis-à-vis collaboration. A self-evaluation questionnaire for participants also makes it possible to measure their experience along these different dimensions. The method was adapted and recently applied in the context of the analysis of the patient-therapist collaboration that made use of an augmented reality tool [WRZ 12] and for evaluating the quality of distance-collaboration supported by augmented reality in a task for gathering clues at a crime-scene [LUK 15].

3.5.6. *Conclusion and perspectives*

The evaluation of VR-AR environments and tools, as well as the evaluation *using* VR-AR environments and tools, are a non-trivial, multi-dimensional problem. The investigation and formalization of dimensions involved in the evaluation, depending on its purpose and objectives (e.g. research vs. design vs. learning) make up an important avenue for future research. Carrying out solid, controlled studies is also an important future prospect, especially with the objective of better understanding and improving the ecological validity of these new environments. A challenge that has already been highlighted is the development of a more systematic framework of descriptions of the systems and conditions under which the studies are carried out, in order to improve comparisons between studies and eventually in order to facilitate meta-analyses. From this point of view, it is also important to remember that studies must be replicated to support the generalization of the obtained results.

The development of new tools for evaluation is also an important future prospect. These may be propositions in a framework for evaluating VR-AR environments and taking into account new challenges, (e.g. brain–computer interfaces [LOU 14], acceptability of AR hand tools [SAN 14]). A trend that should be amplified is the execution of controlled tasks that aims to measure the efficiency and effective contribution of such and such an evaluation technique in improving the mixed reality environments that are thus designed.

As concerns mixed reality applications for learning, in particular, they have focused essentially on learning content, technical gestures and highly formalized procedures (e.g. [ANA 07]; for a recent review, see [MIK 11]). A new path of work is broadening the scope of this type of application to include high-level cognitive skills such as the cluster of "Non-Technical Skills" [FLI 08].

3.6. Bibliography

[ACH 15] ACHIBET M., CASIEZ G., LÉCUYER A. *et al.*, "THING: introducing a tablet-based interaction technique for controlling 3D hand models", *Proceedings of the 33rd Annual ACM Conference on Human Factors in Computing Systems*, CHI'15, New York, USA, ACM, pp. 317–326, 2015.

[AKE 04] AKELEY K., WATT S.J., BANKS M.S., "A stereo display prototype with multiple focal distances", *ACM Transactions on Graphics (Proc. of SIGGRAPH)*, vol. 23, no. 3, pp. 804–813, 2004.

[ALL 07] ALLARD J., COTIN S., FAURE F. *et al.*, "SOFA - an open source framework for medical simulation", in PRESS I. (ed.), *MMVR 15 - Medicine Meets Virtual Reality*, pp. 13–18, February 2007.

[AMB 99] AMBROSI G., BICCHI A., DE ROSSI D. *et al.*, "The role of contact area spread rate in haptic discrimination of softness", *Proceedings of the IEEE International Conference on Robotics and Automation*, pp. 305–310, 10–15 May, 1999.

[ANA 07] ANASTASSOVA M., BURKHARDT J.-M., MÉGARD G. *et al.*, "Ergonomics of augmented reality for learning: A review | L'ergonomie de la réalité augmentée pour l'apprentissage: Une revue", *Travail Humain*, vol. 70, no. 2, 2007.

[ARA 10] DE ARAUJO B., GUERREIRO T., FONSECA M.J. *et al.*, "An haptic-based immersive environment for shape analysis and modelling", *Journal of Real-Time Image Processing*, vol. 5, pp. 73–90, September 2010.

[ARD 12] ARDOUIN J., LÉCUYER A., MARCHAL M. *et al.*, "FlyVIZ: a novel display device to provide humans with 360° vision by coupling catadioptric camera with HMD", *Proceedings of the 18th ACM Symposium on Virtual Reality Software and Technology*, VRST'12, New York, USA, ACM, pp. 41–44, 2012.

[ARG 13] ARGELAGUET F., ANDUJAR C., "A survey of 3D object selection techniques for virtual environments", *Computers & Graphics*, vol. 37, no. 3, pp. 121–136, 2013.

[AVR 12] AVRIL Q., GOURANTON V., ARNALDI B., "Fast collision culling in large-scale environments using GPU mapping function", *Eurographics Symposium Proceedings*, pp. 71–80, 2012.

[BAC 04] BACH C., Elaboration et validation de Critères Ergonomiques pour les Interactions Homme-Environnements Virtuels, PhD thesis, University of Lorraine, 2004.

[BAD 14] BADLER N.I., KAPADIA M., ALLBECK J. *et al.*, "Simulating heterogeneous crowds with interactive behaviors", *EUROGRAPHICS 2014 Tutorials*, April 2014.

[BAK 15] BAKR M., MASSEY W., ALEXANDER H., "Can virtual simulators replace traditional preclinical teaching methods: a student's perspective?", *International Journal of Dentistry and Oral Health*, vol. 2.1, November 2015.

[BAN 08] BANGOR A., KORTUM P.T., MILLER J.T., "An empirical evaluation of the system usability scale", *International Journal of Human-Computer Interaction*, vol. 24, pp. 574–594, 2008.

[BAR 10] BARKOWSKY M., LE CALLET P., "On the perceptual similarity of realistic looking tone mapped high dynamic range images", *IEEE International Conference on Image Processing*, pp. 3245–3248, 2010.

[BAR 13] BAROT C., LOURDEAUX D., BURKHARDT J.-M. *et al.*, "V3S: a virtual environment for risk-management training based on human-activity models", *Presence*, vol. 22, no. 1, pp. 1–19, 2013.

[BEN 07] BENALI-KHOUDJA M., HAFEZ M., KHEDDAR A., "VITAL: an electromagnetic integrated tactile display", *Displays*, vol. 28, pp. 133–144, July 2007.

[BEN 14a] BENDER J., ERLEBEN K., TRINKLE J., "Interactive simulation of rigid body dynamics in computer graphics", *Computer Graphics Forum*, vol. 33, no. 1, pp. 246–270, The Eurographs Association & John Wiley & Sons, Ltd., February 2014.

[BEN 14b] BENKO H., WILSON A.D., ZANNIER F., "Dyadic projected spatial augmented reality", *Proceedings of the 27th Annual ACM Symposium on User Interface Software and Technology*, UIST'14, ACM, pp. 645–655, 2014.

[BEN 15] BENKO H., OFEK E., ZHENG F. *et al.*, "FoveAR: combining an optically see-through near-eye display with projector-based spatial augmented reality", *Proceedings of the 28th Annual ACM Symposium on User Interface Software & Technology*, UIST'15, ACM, pp. 129–135, 2015.

[BIM 06] BIMBER O., RASKAR R., "Modern approaches to augmented reality", *ACM SIGGRAPH 2006 Courses*, SIGGRAPH'06, ACM, 2006.

[BOR 16] BORSCI S., LAWSON G., SALANITRI D. *et al.*, "When simulated environments make the difference: the effectiveness of different types of training of car service procedures", *Virtual Reality*, vol. 20, no. 2, pp. 83–99, 2016.

[BOS 10] BOS J.E., DE VRIES S.C., VAN EMMERIK M.L. *et al.*, "The effect of internal and external fields of view on visually induced motion sickness", *Applied Ergonomics*, vol. 41, no. 4, pp. 516–521, 2010.

[BOS 13] BOSSE T., HOOGENDOORN M., KLEIN M. C.A. *et al.*, "Modelling collective decision making in groups and crowds: Integrating social contagion and interacting emotions, beliefs and intentions", *Autonomous Agents and Multi-Agent Systems*, vol. 27, no. 1, pp. 52–84, 2013.

[BOW 04] BOWMAN D.A., KRUIJFF E., LAVIOLA J.J. *et al.*, *3D User Interfaces: Theory and Practice*, Addison Wesley, 2004.

[BRA 68] BRACHT G.H., GLASS G.V., "The external validity of experiments", *American Educational Research Journal*, vol. 5, no. 4, pp. 437–474, 1968.

[BRA 73] BRANDT T., DICHGANS J., KOENIG E., "Differential effects of central versus peripheral vision on egocentric and exocentric motion perception", *Experimental Brain Research*, vol. 16, no. 5, pp. 476–491, 1973.

[BRI 08] BRIDSON R., *Fluid Simulation for Computer Graphics*, A K Peters/CRC Press, September 2008.

[BRO 96] BROOKE J., *"SUS-A quick and dirty usability scale." Usability evaluation in industry*, CRC Press, June 1996.

[BRU 15] BRUNEAU J., OLIVIER A.H., PETTRÉ J., "Going through, going around: a study on individual avoidance of groups", *IEEE Transactions on Visualization and Computer Graphics*, vol. 21, no. 4, pp. 520–528, April 2015.

[BRU 16] BRUDER G., ARGELAGUET F., OLIVIER A.-H. *et al.*, "CAVE size matters: effects of screen distance and parallax on distance estimation in large immersive display setups", *PRESENCE: Teleoperators and Virtual Environments*, vol. 25, no. 1, MIT Press, 2016.

[BUR 06a] BURKHARDT J.-M., "Ergonomie, facteurs humains et Réalité Virtuelle", in FUCHS P., MOREAUX G., BERTHOZ A. *et al.* (eds), *Le Traité de la Réalité Virtuelle Vol. 1*, pp. 117–150, Presses de l'école des mines de Paris, Paris, 2006.

[BUR 06b] BURKHARDT J.-M., PLÉNACOSTE P., PERRON L., "Concevoir et évaluer l'interaction Utilisateur-Environnement Virtuel", in FUCHS P., MOREAU G., BURKHARDT J.-M. *et al.* (eds), *Le Traité de la Réalité Virtuelle Vol. 2*, pp. 473–520, Presses de l'école des mines de Paris, Paris, 2006.

[BUR 09] BURKHARDT J.M., DÉTIENNE F., HÉBERT A.M. *et al.*, "An approach to assess the quality of collaboration in technology-mediated design situations", *European Conference on Cognitive Ergonomics: Designing beyond the Product—Understanding Activity and User Experience in Ubiquitous Environments*, Valtion Teknillinen Tutkimuskeskus Symposium, p. 30, 2009.

[CAM 63] CAMPBELL D.T., STANLEY J.C., "Experimental and quasi-experimental designs for research on teaching", in GAGE N.L. (ed.), *Handbook of research on teaching*, pp. 171–246, Rand McNally, Chicago, 1963.

[CAR 15a] CARNEGIE K., RHEE T., "Reducing visual discomfort with HMDs using dynamic depth of field", *IEEE Computer Graphics and Applications*, vol. 35, no. 5, pp. 34–41, 2015.

[CAR 15b] CAROUX L., ISBISTER K., LE BIGOT L. *et al.*, "Player-video game interaction: A systematic review of current concepts", *Computers in Human Behavior*, vol. 48, pp. 366–381, 2015.

[CAS 16] CASSOL V., OLIVEIRA J., MUSSE S.R. *et al.*, "Analyzing egress accuracy through the study of virtual and real crowds", *2016 IEEE Virtual Humans and Crowds for Immersive Environments (VHCIE)*, pp. 1–6, March 2016.

[CHE 16] CHEN K.-Y., PATEL S.N., KELLER S., "Finexus: tracking precise motions of multiple fingertips using magnetic sensing", *Proceedings of the 2016 CHI Conference on Human Factors in Computing Systems*, CHI'16, New York, USA, ACM, pp. 1504–1514, 2016.

[CHI 12] CHINELLO F., MALVEZZI M., PACCHIEROTTI C. *et al.*, "A three DoFs wearable tactile display for exploration and manipulation of virtual objects", *Proceedings of the Haptics Symposium*, 4–7 March 2012.

[CHU 14] CHU M.L., PARIGI P., LAW K. *et al.*, "Modeling social behaviors in an evacuation simulator", *Computer Animation and Virtual Worlds*, vol. 25, nos. 3–4, pp. 373–382, Wiley Online Library, 2014.

[CIN 05] CINI G., FRISOLI A., MARCHESCHI S. *et al.*, "A novel fingertip haptic device for display of local contact geometry", *Proceedings of the IEEE Worldhaptics Conference*, pp. 602–605, 18–20 March 2005.

[CIR 11a] CIRIO G., MARCHAL M., HILLAIRE S. *et al.*, "Six degrees-of-freedom haptic interaction with fluids", *IEEE Transactions on Visualization and Computer Graphics*, vol. 17, no. 11, pp. 1714–1727, November 2011.

[CIR 11b] CIRIO G., MARCHAL M., HILLAIRE S. *et al.*, "The virtual crepe factory: 6DoF haptic interaction with fluids", *SIGGRAPH Emerging Technologies*, Vancouver, Canada, p. 17, August 2011.

[CIR 13a] CIRIO G., MARCHAL M., LECUYER A. *et al.*, "Vibrotactile Rendering of Splashing Fluids", *EEE Transaction Haptics*, vol. 6, no. 1, pp. 117–122, January 2013.

[CIR 13b] CIRIO G., MARCHAL M., OTADUY M.A. *et al.*, "Six-DoF Haptic Interaction with Fluids, Solids, and their Transitions", *IEEE Worldhaptics Conference*, Daejeon, South Korea, April 2013.

[COH 77] COHEN J., *Statistical power analysis for the behavioral sciences*, Academic Press, New York, 2nd edition, 1977.

[COL 95] COLGATE J., STANLEY M., BROWN J., "Issues in the haptic display of tool use", *Proceedings of the IEEE/RSJ International Conference on Intelligent Robots and Systems*, 1995.

[CON 03] CONTI F., BARBAGLI F., BALANIUK R. *et al.*, "The CHAI libraries", *Proceedings of Eurohaptics 2003*, Dublin, Ireland, pp. 496–500, 2003.

[COR 94] CORROYER D., ROUANET H., "Sur l'importance des effets et ses indicateurs dans l'analyse statistique des données", *L'année psychologique*, vol. 94, pp. 607–623, 1994.

[CRU 92] CRUZ-NEIRA C., SANDIN D.J., DEFANTI T.A. *et al.*, "The CAVE: audio visual experience automatic virtual environment", *Communications of the ACM*, vol. 35, no. 6, pp. 64–72, ACM, June 1992.

[CUI 12] CUI X., SHI H., "An overview of pathfinding in navigation mesh", *IJCSNS*, vol. 12, no. 12, p. 48, 2012.

[CUR 16] CURTIS S., BEST A., MANOCHA D., "Menge: A modular framework for simulating crowd movement", *Collective Dynamics*, vol. 1, pp. 1–40, 2016.

[CUT 89] CUTKOSKY M., "On grasp choice, grasp models, and the design of hands for manufacturing tasks", *IEEE Transactions on Robotics and Automation*, vol. 5, no. 3, pp. 269–279, June 1989.

[DAA 94] DAAMS B.J., *Human Force Exertion in User-product Interaction: Backgrounds for Design*, Delft University Press, 1994.

[DON 09] DONIKIAN S., MAGNENAT-THALMANN N., PETTRÉ J. *et al.*, "Course: Modeling Individualities in Groups and Crowds", MUSETH K., WEISKOPF D. (eds), *Eurographics 2009 - Tutorials*, The Eurographics Association, 2009.

[DOS 05] DOSTMOHAMED H., HAYWARD V., "Trajectory of contact region on the fingerpad gives the illusion of haptic shape", *Experimental Brain Research*, vol. 164, pp. 387–394, 2005.

[DRA 01] DRAPER M.H., VIIRRE E.S., FURNESS T.A. *et al.*, "Effects of image scale and system time delay on simulator sickness within head-coupled virtual environments", *Human Factors: The Journal of the Human Factors and Ergonomics Society*, vol. 43, no. 1, pp. 129–146, 2001.

[DUH 01] DUH H.B.-L., LIN J.J.-W., KENYON R.V. *et al.*, "Effects of field of view on balance in an immersive environment", *IEEE Virtual Reality*, pp. 1–7, 2001.

[DUI 13] DUIVES D.C., DAAMEN W., HOOGENDOORN S.P., "State-of-the-art crowd motion simulation models", *Transportation Research Part C: Emerging Technologies*, Elsevier, vol. 37, pp. 193–209, 2013.

[DUR 04] DURSO F.T., DATTEL A.R., "SPAM: the real-time assessment of SA", in BANBURY S., TREMBLAY S. (eds), *A Cognitive approach to situation awareness: theory and application*, pp. 137–154, Ashgate, Hampshire, UK, 2004.

[DUR 06] DURIEZ C., DUBOIS F., KHEDDAR A. *et al.*, "Realistic haptic rendering of interacting deformable objects in virtual environments", *IEEE Transactions on Visualization and Computer Graphics*, vol. 12, no. 1, pp. 36–47, January 2006.

[DUR 15] DURUPINAR F., GUDUKBAY U., AMAN A. *et al.*, "Psychological parameters for crowd simulation: from audiences to mobs.", *IEEE Transactions on Visualization and Computer Graphics*, vol. 22, no. 9, pp. 2145–2159, 2015.

[EMM 11] VAN EMMERIK M.L., VRIES S. C.D., BOS J.E., "Internal and external fields of view affect cybersickness", *Displays*, Elsevier B.V., vol. 32, no. 4, pp. 169–174, 2011.

[EMO 05] EMOTO M., NIIDA T., OKANO F., "Repeated vergence adaptation causes the decline of visual functions in watching stereoscopic television", *Journal of Display Technology*, vol. 1, no. 2, pp. 328–340, 2005.

[FAN 09] FANG H., XIE Z., LIU H., "An exoskeleton master hand for controlling DLR/HIT hand", *Proceedings of the IEEE/RSJ International Conference on Intelligent Robots and Systems*, pp. 2153–0858, 10–15 October 2009.

[FEI 09] FEIX T., PAWLIK R., SCHMIEDMAYER H.B. *et al.*, "A comprehensive grasp taxonomy", *Proceedings of Robotics, Science and Systems Conference: Workshop on Understanding the Human Hand for Advancing Robotic Manipulation*, 2009.

[FLI 08] FLIN R., O'CONNOR P., CRICHTON M., *Safety at the sharp end: a guide to non-technical skills*, Ashgate Publishing, 2008.

[FRE 14] FREY J., GERVAIS R., FLECK S. *et al.*, "Teegi: tangible EEG interface", *Proceedings of the 27th Annual ACM Symposium on User Interface Software and Technology*, UIST'14, New York, USA, ACM, pp. 301–308, 2014.

[FUC 05] FUCHS P., MOREAU G. (eds), *Le Traité de la Réalité Virtuelle*, Les Presses de l'Ecole des Mines, Paris, 3rd edition, March 2005.

[FUC 09] FUCHS P., MOREAU G., DONIKIAN S., *Le traité de la réalité virtuelle Volume 5 - Les humains virtuels*, Les Presses de l'Ecole des Mines, 3rd edition, 2009.

[GAB 99] GABBARD J.L., HIX D., SWAN II J.E., "User-centered design and evaluation of virtual environments", *IEEE Computer Graphics and Applications*, vol. 19, pp. 51–59, 1999.

[GAN 16] GANDRUD J., INTERRANTE V., "Predicting destination using head orientation and gaze direction during locomotion in VR", *Proceedings of the ACM Symposium on Applied Perception*, SAP'16, New York, USA, ACM, pp. 31–38, 2016.

[GAO 03] GAO X.-S., HOU X.-R., TANG J. *et al.*, "Complete solution classification for the perspective-three-point problem", *IEEE Transactions on Pattern Analysis and Machine Intelligence*, vol. 25, no. 8, pp. 930–943, 2003.

[GAR 08] GARREC P., FRICONNEAU J., MÉASSON Y. *et al.*, "ABLE, an innovative transparent exoskeleton for the upper-limb", *Proceedings of the IEEE/RSJ International Conference on Intelligent Robots and Systems*, pp. 1483–1488, 22–26 September 2008.

[GIR 16] GIRARD A., MARCHAL M., GOSSELIN F. *et al.*, "HapTip: displaying haptic shear forces at the fingertips for multi-finger interaction in virtual environments", *Frontiers in ICT*, vol. 3, April 2016.

[GIU 10] GIUNTINI T., FERLAY F., BOUCHIGNY S. *et al.*, "Design of a new vibrating handle for a bone surgery multimodal training platform", *Proceedings of the 12th International Conference on New Actuators*, pp. 602–605, 14–16 June 2010.

[GLO 10] GLONDU L., MARCHAL M., DUMONT G., "Evaluation of physical simulation libraries for haptic rendering of contacts between rigid bodies", *Proceedings of the ASME 2010 World Conference on Innovative Virtual Reality (WINVR 2010)*, 12–14 May 2010.

[GLO 12] GLONDU L., SCHVARTZMAN S.C., MARCHAL M. *et al.*, "Efficient collision detection for brittle fracture", *Proceedings of the ACM SIGGRAPH/Eurographics Symposium on Computer Animation*, Eurographics Association, pp. 285–294, 2012.

[GON 15] GONZALEZ F., BACHTA W., GOSSELIN F., "Smooth transition-based control of encounter-type haptic devices", *Proceedings of IEEE International Conference on Robotics and Automation*, pp. 291–297, 26–30 May 2015.

[GOR 12] GORLEWICZ J., WEBSTER III R., "A formal assessment of the haptic paddle laboratories in teaching system dynamics", *Proceedings of the Annual Conference of the American Society of Engineering Education*, pp. 25.49.1–25.49.15, 10–13 June 2012.

[GOS 06] GOSSELIN F., ANDRIOT C., FUCHS P., "Les dispositifs matériels des interfaces à retour d'effort", pp. 141–202, Presses de l'Ecole des Mines, February 2006.

[GOS 12] GOSSELIN F., "Guidelines for the design of multi-finger haptic interfaces for the hand", *Proceedings of the 19th CISM-IFToMM RoManSy Symposium*, pp. 167–174, 12–15 June 2012.

[GOS 13] GOSSELIN F., BOUCHIGNY S., MÉGARD C. *et al.*, "Haptic systems for training sensorimotor skills: a use case in surgery", *Robotics and Autonomous Systems*, vol. 61, pp. 380–389, April 2013.

[GRO 07] GROSSMAN T., WIGDOR D., "Going Deeper: a Taxonomy of 3D on the Tabletop", *IEEE TABLETOP '07*, pp. 137–144, 2007.

[GUG 17] GUGENHEIMER J., STEMASOV E., FROMMEL J. *et al.*, "ShareVR: enabling co-located experiences for virtual reality between HMD and non-HMD users", *Proceedings of the 2017 CHI Conference on Human Factors in Computing Systems*, CHI'17, New York, USA, ACM, pp. 4021–4033, 2017.

[HAL 15] HALE K.S., STANNEY K.M., *Handbook of Virtual Environments: Design, Implementation, and Applications*, CRC Press, 2015.

[HAP 16] HAPPICH J., "Feeling virtual objects at your fingertips", *Electronic Engineering Times Europe*, pp. 24–25, 2016.

[HAR 11] HARRISON C., BENKO H., WILSON A.D., "OmniTouch: wearable multitouch interaction everywhere", *Proceedings of the 24th Annual ACM Symposium on User Interface Software and Technology*, UIST'11, New York, USA, ACM, pp. 441–450, 2011.

[HAW 15] HAWORTH B., USMAN M., BERSETH G. *et al.*, "Evaluating and optimizing level of service for crowd evacuations", *Proceedings of the 8th ACM SIGGRAPH Conference on Motion in Games*, MIG'15, New York, USA, ACM, pp. 91–96, 2015.

[HE 16] HE L., PAN J., NARANG S. *et al.*, "Dynamic group behaviors for interactive crowd simulation", *Proceedings of the ACM SIGGRAPH/Eurographics Symposium on Computer Animation*, SCA'16, Eurographics Association, Aire-la-Ville, Switzerland, pp. 139–147, 2016.

[HEL 10] HELD R.T., COOPER E.A., O'BRIEN J.F. *et al.*, "Using blur to affect perceived distance and size", *ACM Transactions on Graphics*, vol. 29, no. 2, 2010.

[HER 94] HERNDON K.P., VAN DAM A., GLEICHER M., "The challenges of 3D interaction: a CHI'94 workshop", *SIGCHI Bulletin*, ACM, vol. 26, no. 4, pp. 36–43, 1994.

[HIN 94] HINCKLEY K., PAUSCH R., GOBLE J.C. *et al.*, "A survey of design issues in spatial input", *UIST '94: Proceedings of the 7th ACM Symposium on User Interface Software and Technology*, pp. 213–222, 1994.

[HIR 92] HIRATA Y., SATO M., "3-dimensional interface device for virtual work space", *Proceedings of IEEE/RSJ International Conference on Intelligent Robots and Systems*, pp. 889–896, 7–10 July 1992.

[HOA 16] HOAREAU C., Elaboration et évaluation de recommandations ergonomiques pour le guidage de l'apprenant en EVAH : Application à l'apprentissage de procédure dans le domaine biomédical, PhD thesis, University of Western Brittany, 2016.

[HOR 06] HORNBÆK K., "Current practice in measuring usability: Challenges to usability studies and research", *International Journal of Human-Computer Studies*, vol. 64, no. 2, pp. 79–102, February 2006.

[HOS 94] HOSHINO H., HIRATA R., MAEDA T. *et al.*, "A construction method for virtual haptic space", *Proceedings of the International Conference on Artificial Reality and Tele-Existence*, pp. 131–138, 1994.

[HU 14] HU X., HUA H., "High-resolution optical see-through multi-focal- plane head-mounted display using freeform optics", *Optic Express*, vol. 22, no. 11, pp. 13896–13903, 2014.

[HUB 93] HUBBARD P.M., "Interactive collision detection", *Virtual Reality, 1993. Proceedings of the IEEE 1993 Symposium on Research Frontiers in*, IEEE, pp. 24–31, 1993.

[INA 00] INAMI M., KAWAKAMI N., SEKIGUCHI D. *et al.*, "Visuo-haptic display using head-mounted projector", *Proceedings - Virtual Reality Annual International Symposium*, IEEE, pp. 233–240, 2000.

[JAK 16] JAKLIN N., On weighted regions and social crowds: autonomous-agent navigation in virtual worlds, PhD thesis, Utrecht University, 2016.

[JEN 00] JENNINGS S., CRAIG G., REID L. *et al.*, "The effect of visual system time delay on helicopter control", *Proceedings of the Human Factors and Ergonomics Society Annual Meeting*, vol. 44, no. 13, pp. 69–72, 2000.

[JEN 04] JENNINGS S., REID L.D., CRAIG G. *et al.*, "Time delays in visually coupled systems during flight test and simulation", *Journal of Aircraft*, vol. 41, no. 6, pp. 1327–1335, American Institute of Aeronautics and Astronautics, November 2004.

[JOH 07] JOHANSSON R.S., FLANAGAN J.R., "Tactile sensory control of object manipulation in humans", in GARDNER E., KAAS J.H. (eds), *The Senses: a Comprehensive Reference*, vol. 6, Elsevier, December 2007.

[JON 06] JONES L.A., LEDERMAN S.J., *Human Hand Function*, Oxford University Press, 2006.

[JON 13] JONES B.R., BENKO H., OFEK E. *et al.*, "IllumiRoom: Peripheral Projected Illusions for Interactive Experiences", *Proceedings of the SIGCHI Conference on Human Factors in Computing Systems*, CHI '13, New York, USA, ACM, pp. 869–878, 2013.

[JON 14] JONES B., SODHI R., MURDOCK M. *et al.*, "RoomAlive: magical experiences enabled by scalable, adaptive projector-camera units", *Proceedings of the 27th Annual ACM Symposium on User Interface Software and Technology*, UIST '14, New York, USA, ACM, pp. 637–644, 2014.

[JOR 15a] JORDAO K., Interactive design and animation of crowds for large environments, PhD thesis, INSA Rennes, 2015.

[JOR 15b] JØRGENSEN C., Scheduling activities under spatial and temporal constraints to populate virtual urban environments, PhD thesis, University of Rennes 1, France, 2015.

[JUL 01] JULIER S., FEINER S., ROSENBLUM L., "Mobile Augmented Reality: a Complex Human-Centered System", in *Frontiers of Human-Centered Computing, Online Communities and Virtual Environment* pp. 67–79, Springer London, 2001.

[KAL 14] KALLMANN M., KAPADIA M., "Navigation meshes and real-time dynamic planning for virtual worlds", *ACM SIGGRAPH 2014 Courses*, ACM, p. 3, 2014.

[KAR 14] KARAMOUZAS I., SKINNER B., GUY S.J., "Universal Power Law Governing Pedestrian Interactions", *Physics Review Letter*, American Physical Society, vol. 113, p. 238701, December 2014.

[KEN 93] KENNEDY R.S., LANE N.E., BERBAUM K.S. *et al.*, "Simulator sickness questionnaire: an enhanced method for quantifying simulator sickness", *The International Journal of Aviation Psychology*, vol. 3, no. 3, pp. 203–220, 1993.

[KES 04] KESHAVARZ B., HECHT H., MAINZ J. G.-U., "Validating an efficient method to quantify motion sickness", *Human Factors*, vol. 53, no. 4, pp. 415–426, 2004.

[KES 15] KESHAVARZ B., RIECKE B.E., HETTINGER L.J. *et al.*, "Vection and visually induced motion sickness: How are they related?", *Frontiers in Psychology*, vol. 6, no. APR, pp. 1–11, 2015.

[KIJ 97] KIJIMA R., OJIKA T., "Transition between virtual environment and workstation environment with projective head mounted display", *Virtual Reality Annual International Symposium, IEEE 1997*, pp. 130–137, March 1997.

[KIM 15] KIM J., CHUNG C. Y.L., NAKAMURA S. *et al.*, "The Oculus Rift: A cost-effective tool for studying visual-vestibular interactions in self-motion perception", *Frontiers in Psychology*, vol. 6, no. MAR, pp. 1–7, 2015.

[KIN 10] KING H.H., DONLIN R., HANNAFORD B., "Perceptual thresholds for single vs. multi-finger haptic interaction", *Proceedings of the IEEE Haptics Symposium*, pp. 95–99, September 2010.

[KO 13] KO S.M., CHANG W.S., JI Y.G., "Usability principles for augmented reality applications in a smartphone environment", *International Journal of Human-Computer Interaction*, vol. 29, no. 8, pp. 501–515, August 2013.

[KOC 07] KOCKARA S., HALIC T., IQBAL K. *et al.*, "Collision detection: A survey", *ISIC. IEEE International Conference on Systems, Man and Cybernetics, 2007*, IEEE, pp. 4046–4051, 2007.

[KOK 16] KOK V.J., LIM M.K., CHAN C.S., "Crowd behavior analysis: A review where physics meets biology", *Neurocomputing*, Elsevier, vol. 177, pp. 342–362, 2016.

[KON 16] KONRAD R., COOPER E.A., WETZSTEIN G., "Novel optical configurations for virtual reality: evaluating user preference and performance with focus-tunable and monovision near-eye displays", *Proceedings of the 2016 CHI Conference on Human Factors in Computing Systems*, CHI'16, New York, USA, ACM, pp. 1211–1220, 2016.

[KOU 15] KOUROUTHANASSIS P.E., BOLETSIS C., LEKAKOS G., "Demystifying the design of mobile augmented reality applications", *Multimedia Tools and Applications*, vol. 74, no. 3, pp. 1045–1066, February 2015.

[KRA 14] KRASULA L., FLIEGEL K., LE CALLET P. *et al.*, "Objective evaluation of naturalness, contrast, and colorfulness of tone-mapped images", TESCHER A.G. (ed.), *Applications of Digital Image Processing XXXVII*, SPIE, vol. 9217, September 2014.

[KUL 09] KULIK A., "Building on realism and magic for designing 3D interaction techniques", *IEEE Computer Graphics and Applications*, vol. 29, no. 6, pp. 22–33, November 2009.

[LAM 11] LAMBOOIJ M., IJSSELSTEIJN W., BOUWHUIS D.G. *et al.*, "Evaluation of stereoscopic images: beyond 2D quality", *IEEE Transactions on Broadcasting*, vol. 57, no. 2, pp. 432–444, 2011.

[LAU 10] LAUTERBACH C., MO Q., MANOCHA D., "gProximity: hierarchical GPU-based operations for collision and distance queries", *Computer Graphics Forum*, vol. 29, no. 2, pp. 419–428, 2010.

[LAV 17] LAVIOLA J.J., KRUIJFF E., MCMAHAN R. *et al.*, *3D User Interfaces: Theory and Practice*, 2nd Edition, Addison Wesley, 2017.

[LEC 13] LECUYER A., GEORGE L., MARCHAL M., "Toward adaptive VR simulators combining visual, haptic, and brain-computer interfaces", *IEEE Computer Graphics and Applications*, vol. 33, no. 5, pp. 18–23, 2013.

[LEC 15] LE CHÉNÉCHAL M., CHALMÉ S., DUVAL T. *et al.*, "Toward an enhanced mutual awareness in asymmetric CVE", *Proceedings of the International Conference on Collaboration Technologies and Systems (CTS 2015)*, Atlanta, United States, 2015.

[LEE 16] LEE M.-M., SHIN D.-C., SONG C.-H., "Canoe game-based virtual reality training to improve trunk postural stability, balance, and upper limb motor function in subacute stroke patients: a randomized controlled pilot study", *Journal of Physical Therapy Science*, vol. 28, no. 7, pp. 2019–24, July 2016.

[LEG 07] LE GRAND S., "Broad-phase collision detection with CUDA", *GPU Gems*, vol. 3, pp. 697–721, 2007.

[LEG 16] LE GOC M., KIM L.H., PARSAEI A. *et al.*, "Zooids: building blocks for swarm user interfaces", *Proceedings of the 29th Annual Symposium on User Interface Software and Technology*, UIST '16, New York, USA, ACM, pp. 97–109, 2016.

[LEG 17] LE GOUIS B., LEHERICEY F., MARCHAL M. *et al.*, "Haptic rendering of FEM-based tearing simulation using clusterized collision detection", *IEEE Word Haptics Conference*, Munich, Germany, p. xx, June 2017.

[LEH 15] LEHERICEY F., GOURANTON V., ARNALDI B., "GPU Ray-Traced collision detection: fine pipeline reorganization", *Proceedings of the 10th International Conference on Computer Graphics Theory and Applications (GRAPP'15)*, 2015.

[LEH 16] LEHERICEY F., Ray-traced collision detection: Quest for performance, Thesis, INSA Rennes, September 2016.

[LIN 98] LIN M., GOTTSCHALK S., "Collision detection between geometric models: A survey", *Proceedings of the IMA Conference on Mathematics of Surfaces*, vol. 1, pp. 602–608, 1998.

[LIN 02] LIN J. J.-W., DUH H. B.L., ABI-RACHED H. *et al.*, "Effects of field of view on presence, enjoyment, memory, and simulator sickness in a virtual environment", *Proceedings of the IEEE Virtual Reality Conference 2002*, VR '02, Washington, DC, USA, IEEE Computer Society, p. 164, 2002.

[LIN 08] LIN M.C., OTADUY M., *Haptic Rendering: Foundations, Algorithms and Applications*, A K Peters, Massachusetts, 2008.

[LIU 09] LIU S., HUA H., "Time-multiplexed dual-focal plane head-mounted", *Optical Letters*, vol. 34, no. 11, pp. 1642–1644, 2009.

[LIU 10] LIU F., HARADA T., LEE Y. *et al.*, "Real-time collision culling of a million bodies on graphics processing units", *ACM Transactions on Graphics (TOG)*, vol. 29, no. 6, p. 154, 2010.

[LIV 13] LIVINGSTON M.A., *Human Factors in Augmented Reality Environments*, Springer, New York, 2013.

[LOU 13] LOUP-ESCANDE É., BURKHARDT J.-M., RICHIR S., "Anticiper et évaluer l'utilité dans la conception ergonomique des technologies émergentes: une revue", *Le travail humain*, vol. 76, no. 1, p. 27, 2013.

[LOU 14] LOUP-ESCANDE É., LECUYER A., Towards a user-centred methodological framework for the design and evaluation of applications combining brain-computer interfaces and virtual environments: contributions of ergonomics, Report , INRIA RR-8505, 2014.

[LUK 15] LUKOSCH S., LUKOSCH H., DATCU D. *et al.*, "Providing information on the spot: using augmented reality for situational awareness in the security domain", *Computer Supported Cooperative Work (CSCW)*, vol. 24, no. 6, pp. 613–664, December 2015.

[MAR 86] MARK M.M., "Validity typologies and the logic and practice of quasi-experimentation", *New Directions for Program Evaluation*, vol. 1986, no. 31, pp. 47–66, Wiley, 1986.

[MAR 11] MARCHAL M., PETTRÉ J., LÉCUYER A., "Joyman: A human-scale joystick for navigating in virtual worlds", *IEEE Symposium on 3D User Interfaces, 3DUI 2011, Singapore, 19-20 March, 2011*, pp. 19–26, 2011.

[MAR 14] MARCHAL M., 3D Multimodal Interaction with Physically-based Virtual Environments, University of Rennes 1, November 2014.

[MAR 16] MARTINEZ M., MORIMOTO T., TAYLOR A. *et al.*, "3-D printed haptic devices for educational applications", *Proceedings of the IEEE Haptics Symposium*, pp. 126–133, 8–11 April 2016.

[MEI 07] MEIER A., SPADA H., RUMMEL N., "A rating scheme for assessing the quality of computer-supported collaboration processes", *International Journal of Computer-Supported Collaborative Learning*, vol. 2, no. 1, pp. 63–86, 2007.

[MER 12] MERLHIOT X., LE GARREC J., SAUPIN G., "The XDE mechanical kernel: Efficient and robust simulation of multibody dynamics with intermittent nonsmooth contacts", *Second Joint International Conference on Multibody System Dynamics*, 2012.

[MIK 11] MIKROPOULOS T., NATSIS A., "Educational virtual environments: a ten year review of empirical research (1999–2009)", *Computers & Education*, vol. 56, pp. 769–780, 2011.

[MIL 94] MILGRAM P., KISHINO F., "A taxonomy of mixed reality visual displays", *IEICE Transaction Information Systems*, vol. E77-D, no. 12, pp. 1321–1329, December 1994.

[MIN 07] MINAMIZAWA K., FUKAMACHI S., KAJIMOTO H. *et al.*, "Gravity grabber: wearable haptic display to present virtual mass sensation", *Proceedings of ACM SIGGRAPH, Emerging Technologies*, 5–9 August 2007.

[MOO 17] MOON S.-E., LEE J.-S., "Implicit analysis of perceptual multimedia experience based on physiological response: a review", *IEEE Transactions on Multimedia*, vol. 19, no. 2, pp. 340–353, 2017.

[MOS 11a] MOSS J.D., AUSTIN J., SALLEY J. *et al.*, "The effects of display delay on simulator sickness", *Displays*, Elsevier B.V., vol. 32, no. 4, pp. 159–168, 2011.

[MOS 11b] MOSS J.D., MUTH E.R., "Characteristics of head mounted displays and their effects on simulator sickness", *Human Factors*, vol. 53, no. 3, pp. 308–319, 2011.

[MOU 10] MOUSSAÔD M., PEROZO N., GARNIER S. *et al.*, "The walking behaviour of pedestrian social groups and its impact on crowd dynamics", *PLoS ONE*, Public Library of Science,vol. 5, no. 4, pp. 1–7, 2010.

[NAK 05] NAKAGAWARA S., KAJIMOTO H., KAWAKAMI N. *et al.*, "An encounter-type multi-fingered master hand using circuitous joints", *Proceedings of the IEEE International Conference on Robotics and Automation*, pp. 2667–2672, 18–22 April 2005.

[NAK 16] NAKAGAKI K., VINK L., COUNTS J. *et al.*, "Materiable: rendering dynamic material properties in response to direct physical touch with shape changing interfaces", *Proceedings of the 2016 CHI Conference on Human Factors in Computing Systems*, CHI'16, New York, USA, ACM, pp. 2764–2772, 2016.

[NAV 14] NAVARRO C.A., HITSCHFELD N., "GPU maps for the space of computation in triangular domain problems", *2014 IEEE International Conference on High Performance Computing and Communications, 2014 IEEE 6th International Symposium on Cyberspace Safety and Security, 2014 IEEE 11th International Conference on Embedded Software and Systems (HPCC,CSS,ICESS)*, pp. 375–382, August 2014.

[NEA 06] NEALEN A., MÜLLER M., KEISER R. *et al.*, "Physically based deformable models in computer graphics", *Computer Graphics Forum*, vol. 25, no. 4, pp. 809–836, 2006.

[NEL 00] NELSON W.T., ROE M.M., BOLIA R.S. *et al.*, "Assessing simulator sickness in a see-through HMD: effects of time delay, time on task, and task complexity", *IMAGE 2000 Conference*, 2000.

[OKA 06] OKADA Y., UKAI K., WOLFFSOHN J.S. *et al.*, "Target spatial frequency determines the response to conflicting defocus- and convergence-driven accommodative stimuli", *Vision Research*, vol. 46, no. 4, pp. 475–484, 2006.

[OLI 13] OLIVIER A.-H., MARIN A., CRÉTUAL A. *et al.*, "Collision avoidance between two walkers: Role-dependent strategies", *Gait & Posture*, vol. 38, no. 4, pp. 751–756, 2013.

[OLI 14] OLIVIER A.-H., BRUNEAU J., CIRIO G. *et al.*, "A virtual reality platform to study crowd behaviors", *Transportation Research Procedia*, Elsevier, vol. 2, pp. 114–122, 2014.

[PAB 10] PABST S., KOCH A., STRASSER W., "Fast and scalable *cpu/gpu* collision detection for rigid and deformable surfaces", *Computer Graphics Forum*, vol. 29, no. 5, pp. 1605–1612, 2010.

[PAL 17] PALMISANO S., MURSIC R., KIM J., "Vection and cybersickness generated by head-and-display motion in the Oculus Rift", *Displays*, vol. 46, pp. 1–8, 2017.

[PAR 09] PARIS S., DONIKIAN S., "Activity-driven populace: a cognitive approach to crowd simulation", *IEEE Computer Graphic Apply*, IEEE Computer Society Press, vol. 29, no. 4, pp. 34–43, July 2009.

[PEJ 16] PEJSA T., KANTOR J., BENKO H. *et al.*, "Room2Room: enabling life-size telepresence in a projected augmented reality environment", *Proceedings of the 19th ACM Conference on Computer-Supported Cooperative Work & Social Computing*, CSCW '16, New York, USA, ACM, pp. 1716–1725, 2016.

[PEL 16] PELECHANO N., FUENTES C., "Hierarchical path-finding for Navigation Meshes (HNA*)", *Computers & Graphics*, vol. 59, pp. 68–78, 2016.

[PET 12] PETTRÉ J., WOLINSKI D., OLIVIER A.-H., "Velocity-based models for crowd simulation", *Conference on Pedestrian and Evacuation Dynamics*, 2012.

[POU 16] POUPYREV I., GONG N.-W., FUKUHARA S. *et al.*, "Project Jacquard: Interactive Digital Textiles at Scale", *Proceedings of the 2016 CHI Conference on Human Factors in Computing Systems*, CHI '16, New York, USA, ACM, pp. 4216–4227, 2016.

[RAS 98a] RASKAR R., WELCH G., FUCHS H., "Seamless projection overlaps using image warping and intensity blending", *Fourth International Conference on Virtual Systems and Multimedia*, 1998.

[RAS 98b] RASKAR R., WELCH G., FUCHS H., "Spatially augmented reality", *First IEEE Workshop on Augmented Reality (IWAR'98)*, pp. 11–20, 1998.

[REB 16] REBENITSCH L., OWEN C., "Review on cybersickness in applications and visual displays", *Virtual Reality*, vol. 20, no. 2, pp. 101–125, 2016.

[RIE 11] RIES B.T., Facilitating effective virtual reality for architectural design, PhD thesis, University of Minnesota, 2011.

[RIO 14] RIO K.W., RHEA C.K., WARREN W.H., "Follow the leader: Visual control of speed in pedestrian following", *Journal of vision*, vol. 14, no. 2, p. 4, 2014.

[ROL 82] ROLFE J., CARO P., "Determining the training effectiveness of flight simulators: Some basic issues and practical developments", *Applied Ergonomics*, vol. 13, no. 4, pp. 243–250, December 1982.

[ROL 95] ROLLAND J.P., HOLLOWAY R.L., FUCHS H., "Comparison of optical and video see-through, head-mounted displays", *Proceedings of SPIE*, vol. 2351, pp. 293–307, 1995.

[SAN 14] SANTOS M. E.C., TAKETOMI T., SANDOR C. *et al.*, "A usability scale for handheld augmented reality", *Proceedings of the 20th ACM Symposium on Virtual Reality Software and Technology - VRST '14*, New York, USA, ACM Press, pp. 167–176, 2014.

[SCH 01] SCHUBERT T., FRIEDMANN F., REGENBRECHT H., "The experience of presence: factor analytic insights", *Presence: Teleoperators and Virtual Environments*, vol. 10, no. 3, pp. 266–281, June 2001.

[SCH 14] SCHMETTOW M., BACH C., SCAPIN D., "Optimizing usability studies by complementary evaluation methods", *Proceedings of the 28th International BCS Human Computer Interaction Conference on HCI 2014 - Sand, Sea and Sky - Holiday HCI*, BCS-HCI '14, UK, BCS, pp. 110–119, 2014.

[SEA 02] SEAY A.F., KRUM D.M., HODGES L. *et al.*, "Simulator sickness and presence in a high field-of-view virtual environment", *CHI '02 Extended Abstracts on Human Factors in Computing Systems*, CHI EA'02, New York, USA, ACM, pp. 784–785, 2002.

[SKE 13] SKEDUNG L., ARVIDSSON M., CHUNG J.Y. *et al.*, "Feeling small: exploring the tactile perception limits", *Nature Scientific Reports*, vol. 3, September 2013.

[SLA 94] SLATER M., USOH M., STEED A., "Depth of presence in virtual environments", *Presence: Teleoperators and Virtual Environments*, vol. 3, no. 2, pp. 130–144, January 1994.

[SNO 74] SNOW R.E., "Representative and quasi-representative designs for research on teaching", *Review of Educational Research*, vol. 44, no. 3, pp. 265–291, 1974.

[SPE 06] SPERANZA F., TAM W.J., RENAUD R. *et al.*, "Effect of disparity and motion on visual comfort of stereoscopic images", *Proccedings of SPIE*, vol. 6055, 2006.

[ST 15] ST. PIERRE M.E., BANERJEE S., HOOVER A.W. *et al.*, "The effects of 0.2 Hz varying latency with 20-100 ms varying amplitude on simulator sickness in a helmet mounted display", *Displays*, vol. 36, pp. 1–8, 2015.

[STA 97] STANNEY K.M., KENNEDY R.S., DREXLER J.M., "Cybersickness is not simulator sickness", *Proceedings of the Human Factors and Ergonomics Society Annual Meeting*, vol. 41, no. 2, pp. 1138–1142, 1997.

[STA 98] STANNEY K.M., MOURANT R.R., KENNEDY R.S., "Human factors issues in virtual environments: A review of the literature", *Presence: Teleoperators and Virtual Environments*, vol. 7, no. 4, pp. 327–351, 1998.

[STA 03] STANNEY K.M., MOLLAGHASEMI M., REEVES L. *et al.*, "Usability engineering of virtual environments (VEs): identifying multiple criteria that drive effective VE system design", *International Journal of Human-Computer Studies*, vol. 58, no. 4, pp. 447–481, April 2003.

[TAL 15] TALVAS A., MARCHAL M., DURIEZ C. *et al.*, "Aggregate constraints for virtual manipulation with soft fingers", *IEEE Transactions on Visualization and Computer Graphics*, vol. 21, no. 4, pp. 452–461, 2015.

[TAN 94] TAN H.Z., SRINIVASAN M.A., EBERMAN B. *et al.*, "Human factors for the design of force-reflecting haptic interfaces", *Proceedings of the 3rd International Symposium on Haptic Interfaces for Virtual Environment and Teleoperator Systems*, pp. 353–359, 1994.

[TAN 11] TANG M., MANOCHA D., LIN J. *et al.*, "Collision-streams: fast GPU-based collision detection for deformable models", *Symposium on interactive 3D graphics and games*, ACM, pp. 63–70, 2011.

[TES 05] TESCHNER M., KIMMERLE S., HEIDELBERGER B. *et al.*, "Collision detection for deformable objects", *Computer Graphics Forum*, vol. 24, no. 1, pp. 61–81, 2005.

[TIN 14] TINWELL A., "The Uncanny Valley in Games and Animation", 2014.

[TOE 08] TOET A., VRIES S. C.D., EMMERIK M. L.V. *et al.*, "Cybersickness and Desktop Simulations: Field of View Effects and User Experience", *SPIE Enhanced and Synthetic Vision*, vol. 6957, 2008.

[TRE 14] TRESCAK T., SIMOFF S., BOGDANOVYCH A., "Populating virtual cities with diverse physiology driven crowds of intelligent agents", *Social Simulation Conference*, 2014.

[TRO 03] TROMP J.G., STEED A., WILSON J.R., "Systematic Usability Evaluation and Design Issues for Collaborative Virtual Environments", *Presence: Teleoperators and Virtual Environments*, vol. 12, no. 3, pp. 241–267, 2003.

[TSA 05] TSAGARAKIS N.G., HORNE T., CALDWELL D.G., "SLIP AESTHEASIS: A Portable 2D Slip/Skin Stretch Display for the Fingertip", *Proceedings of the IEEE World Haptics Conference*, pp. 214–219, 18–20 March 2005.

[TSE 14]   TSETSERUKOU D., HOSOKAWA S., TERASHIMA K., "LinkTouch: a wearable haptic device with five-bar linkage mechanism for presentation of two-DOF force feedback at the fingerpad", *Proceedings of the IEEE Haptics Symposium*, 23–26 February 2014.

[URV 13a]   URVOY M., BARKOWSKY M., LE P., "How visual fatigue and discomfort impact 3D-TV Quality of Experience: a comprehensive review of technological, psychophysical and psychological factors", *Annals of Telecommunications*, vol. 68, nos. 11–12, pp. 641–655, 2013.

[URV 13b]   URVOY M., BARKOWSKY M., LI J. *et al.*, "Confort et fatigue visuels de la restitution stéréoscopique", in LUCAS L., LOSCOS C., REMION Y. (eds), *Vidéo 3D: Capture, traitement et diffusion*, pp. 309–329, Lavoisier, 2013.

[VAN 15]   VAN TOLL W., GERAERTS R., "Dynamically pruned A* for re-planning in navigation meshes", *2015 IEEE/RSJ International Conference on Intelligent Robots and Systems (IROS)*, IEEE, pp. 2051–2057, 2015.

[WAN 10]   WANG Q., HAYWARD V., "Biomechanically optimized distributed tactile transducer based on lateral skin deformation", *The International Journal of Robotics Research*, vol. 29, pp. 323–335, April 2010.

[WAN 11]   WANG J., BARKOWSKY M., RICORDEL V. *et al.*, "Quantifying how the combination of blur and disparity affects the perceived depth", *SPIE Electronic Imaging*, 2011.

[WEB 03]   WEBB N.A., GRIFFIN M.J., "Eye movement, vection, and motion sickness with foveal and peripheral vision.", *Aviation Space and Environmental Medicine*, vol. 74, 2003.

[WEL 11]   WELLER R., ZACHMANN G., "*Inner sphere trees and their application to collision detection*", pp. 181–201, Springer Vienna, 2011.

[WIL 96]   WILDZUNAS R.M., BARRON T.L., WILEY R.W., "Visual display delay effects on pilot performance", *Aviation Space and Environmental Medicine*, vol. 67, no. 3, pp. 214–221, 1996.

[WIT 98]   WITMER B.G., SINGER M.J., "Measuring presence in virtual environments: a presence questionnaire", *Presence: Teleoperators and Virtual Environments*, vol. 7, no. 3, pp. 225–240, June 1998.

[WOL 16]   WOLINSKI D., Microscopic Crowd Simulation: Evaluation and Development of Algorithms, PhD thesis, University of Rennes 1, France, 2016.

[WRZ 12]   WRZESIEN M., BURKHARDT J.-M., BOTELLA C. *et al.*, "Evaluation of the quality of collaboration between the client and the therapist in phobia treatments", *Interacting with Computers*, vol. 24, no. 6, pp. 461–471, November 2012.

[YAN 02]   YANO S., IDE S., MITSUHASHI T. *et al.*, "A study of visual fatigue and visual comfort for 3D HDTV / HDTV images", *Displays*, vol. 23, no. 4, pp. 191–201, 2002.

[YAN 04]   YANO S., EMOTO M., MITSUHASHI T., "Two factors in visual fatigue caused by stereoscopic HDTV images", *Displays*, vol. 25, no. 4, pp. 141–150, 2004.

[YAO 10]   YAO H.-Y., HAYWARD V., "Design and analysis of a recoil-type vibrotactile transducer", *Journal of the Acoustical Society of America*, vol. 128, pp. 619–627, August 2010.

[YOK 05] YOKOKOHJI Y., MURAMORI N., SATO Y. *et al.*, "Designing an encountered-type haptic display for multiple fingertip contacts based on the observation of human grasping behaviors", *The International Journal of Robotics Research*, vol. 24, pp. 717–729, September 2005.

[YOS 99] YOSHIKAWA T., NAGURA A., "A three-dimensional touch/force display system for haptic interface", *Proceedings of the IEEE International Conference on Robotics and Automation*, pp. 2943–2951, 10–15 May 1999.

[ZHO 10] ZHOU S., CHEN D., CAI W. *et al.*, "Crowd modeling and simulation technologies", *ACM Transactions on Modeling and Computer Simulation (TOMACS)*, vol. 20, no. 4, p. 20, 2010.

4

Towards VE that are
More Closely Related
to the Real World

For some years now, it has been clear that one of the challenges related to the appropriation and success of virtual environments is related to their ability to exist not only in parallel to the real world, but also in relation to it. We first spoke of the realism of virtual environments, whether in graphical or even behavioral terms, and discussed questions related to the transfer of learning in the VE to the real world. It must be noted that the main emerging issue is that of integrating the real and virtual worlds: this is a problem not only in terms of modeling the real world for integration into VE, but also in terms of the form in which these two worlds are overlaid to give the appearance of a single world. This is one of the objectives of augmented reality. While this chapter gives an overview of the current state of augmented reality, let us note that most of the following sections can also be interpreted as techniques that may be used in another context to connect VEs with the real world.

This chapter first examines the questions of pose computation (which could be used to locate a user in an immersive room or to model the real world), interactions in augmented reality, and the concept of presence in environments that combine real and virtual elements. We then move on to the concept of 3D interaction with tactile surfaces which, while indeed applicable to AR, can also be generalized to other tactile surfaces such as tablets or smartphones.

Chapter written by Géry CASIEZ, Xavier GRANIER, Martin HACHET, Vincent LEPETIT, Guillaume MOREAU and Olivier NANNIPIERI

4.1. "Tough" scientific challenges for AR

4.1.1. *Choosing a display device*

Augmented reality has benefited from the advantages of the latest display technology: improved resolution, contrast and refresh rate. According to the taxonomy for augmented reality display devices that was proposed by Bimber and Raskar [BIM 06], the display may be *head-attached* (HMDs, for example) or *hand-held* (mobile phones, for example). The screens used may be semi-transparent, as is the case with Google Glass, the Microsoft HoloLens or HUDs (Head-Up Display). The screen may also be opaque, as with mobile phones or digital tablets.

When the screen is opaque, the real environment is filmed by a camera and then displayed on the screen; the augmentation is directly overlaid onto the image. Certain HMDs (Head-Mounted Display) [ROL 95] are equipped with an opaque screen and cameras to capture the real environment and to simulate transparency. The limitations of this type of a headset are the latency between the acquisition of the video and the restitution onto a screen, a limited field of vision as well as loss in spatial resolution and brightness.

When the screen is semi-transparent, the real environment is seen through transparency and the augmentation is displayed onto the screen. Thus, to compensate for the limitations of opaque HMDs, other HMDs are made up of a semi-reflective slide located just in front of the user's eyes. Thus, the user can simultaneously observe the real environment through transparency, and visualize the augmentations through the reflections on the slide. The limitations of these systems are an even more limited field of vision, low brightness of the augmentation and accommodation problems (the real and virtual objects are not located at the same depth). At the time this book goes to print, the most buzz has been generated around the Microsoft HoloLens, a semi-transparent HMD, as well as the Meta 2, which is not yet commercially available.

HMPDs (Head-Mounted Projective Displays) [INA 00] are projective headsets. They require the use of a projector located close to the user's head, as well as retroreflective equipment arranged in the environment. The augmentation is projected by the projector and reflected towards the user by these retroreflective materials. Unlike HMDs, the image here is formed directly in the real environment, which makes it possible to reduce the accommodation problems [BIM 06]. Thanks to the retroreflective material, the problems with brightness and field of vision are also reduced. PHMDs (Projective Head-Mounted Displays) [KIJ 97] use a redirection of the projected image using mirrors.

Figure 4.1. *The Microsoft HoloLens augmented reality headset (© WikiMedia)*

The viability of these systems is closely linked to the evolution of the in-built technologies (miniaturization of screens and projectors, for example). It must be noted that these systems are incapable of delivering a black image when used in a bright environment. In effect, a black image implies that only transparency is used. All too often, however, these systems involve each user possessing a personal display device (sometimes shared) that introduces an intermediary for interaction with the real/virtual environment.

Initially proposed by [RAS 98b], *spatial augmented reality* makes it possible to augment the real environment without the need for a screen, by using a video projector, for instance. The augmentation is directly projected onto the surface of real objects: it is thus naturally a multi-user system (unlike HMDPs and PHMDs). Indeed, several users may simultaneously observe the augmentation of the object as this is physically found in the real world. This makes it possible to conceive of collaborative experiences, for instance, in which the user interactions are naturally visible to all users. By extending the Reality–Virtuality continuum (see Figure 3.14), spatial augmented reality is closer to the real environment. However, at present, the augmentation that is visualized is the same for all users (unlike with HMPDs and PHMDs).

Augmented spatial reality is often used in sound and light shows. In this context, it is generally called *projection mapping*. The projection surfaces are often large surfaces, like buildings. Given the size and complexity involved, it is necessary to use several video projectors. The zones of overlap and differences between the projectors must then be compensated for using an optical device or numerically [RAS 98a] to avoid being able to distinguish the image from each projector.

In recent times, we have seen a craze for displays integrated onto surfaces in our everyday life (e.g. walls, windows, electronic good). However, the technology of these screens is currently limited (e.g. rigidity, thickness). In this context, spatial augmented reality is used as a substitute for traditional screens and enables the simulation of geometrically complex displays. Harrison *et al.* [HAR 11] present a mobile and personal approach for displaying personal information directly onto the user's body. Several approaches have been proposed for telepresence [PEJ 16] or to augment the region surrounding a screen [JON 13, BEN 15]. Using a depth information system (the Microsoft Kinect, for example) and one or more video projectors, it is also possible to use a variety of projection supports (boards, walls, the human body) to simulate a rendering that depends on the point of view [BEN 14, JON 14]. The visual environment is thus completely transformed, as shown in Figure 4.2, taken from the famous demonstration of the invisibility cloak Inami [INA 03]. This demonstration also offers more serious applications such as a transparent cockpit, which would improve visibility for a driver [TAC 14].

Figure 4.2. *Adaptation of the projection to the viewer's point of view: demonstration of optical camouflage by Tachi Lab in 2003 [INA 03]*

4.1.2. *Spatial localization*

As has already been discussed in section 3.2.2, image-based localization offers several advantages compared to other spatial localization technology, and it has been used in recent AR solutions such as Project Tango by Google, the Microsoft HoloLens and PTC's Vuforia.

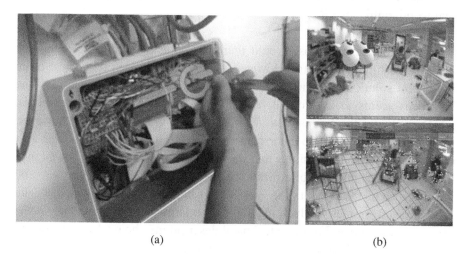

(a)   (b)

Figure 4.3. *Absolute and relative poses. (a) Absolute pose computation makes it possible to insert virtual segments, with respect to the real scene, but requires having at least the geometric reference data. (b) Relative pose computation is simpler to implement, as it directly estimates the geometry of the scene in the form of primitives (points in this case). However, this only allows the insertion of virtual elements in a marker that is dependent on the session and therefore different each time*

There are, in fact, two ways of considering the problem of spatial localization. One is using *absolute* pose, the other using *relative* pose. Both these approaches have problems, technical solutions and very different applications. To understand the difference between them, let us consider Figure 4.3. For the application on the left, we wish to help the user repair an object. The virtual elements here are defined in a marker associated with the box. To render these elements, we must know their position within the camera's frame. As we have already explained at the beginning of section 3.2.2, the solution is to calculate the pose of the camera using the same marker linked to the box. This is the absolute pose, as it calculates pose in a fixed frame, known beforehand, this being the box, here. It requires knowledge obtained beforehand about the object or scene, such as their 3D geometry and/or appearance.

Methods computing relative pose estimate the 3D geometry of the scene, rather than the pose itself. This is called SLAM (Simultaneous Localization and Mapping). As can be seen in Figure 4.3(b), this geometry can be found in the form of primitives, such as 3D points. Typically, in such an approach, the user must define where they wish to insert the virtual elements. This is useful for visualizing a 3D model in AR, for example, without losing contact with the real world, unlike in VR.

Calculating relative pose would therefore appear more complex, as we must also estimate geometry. However, this is the approach used most often by current solutions such as Project Tango and HoloLens, for example. The HoloLens seems to use four depth cameras in addition to color cameras, which facilitates the reconstruction of the geometry. Project Tango, however, can function with a single color camera. SLAM algorithms are indeed well controlled now. The difficulties that may still come about are the appearance of *drift* (an accumulation of errors in the estimation of the point of view and the geometry throughout the session), and the management of the reconstructed geometry, which may take up a large amount of memory if the session is a long one. For more technical descriptions, the reader may consult [NEW 11, ENG 14] and [MUR 15], among others.

If the SLAM algorithms work well, it is partly because they can make use of temporal coherence between images: during a session, the point of view changes in a continuous manner and the appearance of the scene changes very little or not at all. This makes it easier to match the images required for the pose computation, as shown in Figure 4.4.

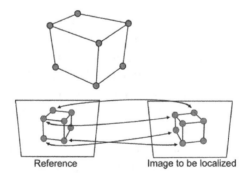

Figure 4.4. *The importance of matching for spatial localization. If we can match elements from an image with those of a reference image, and if the spatial position of these elements is known, we can then calculate the camera's pose for this image*

In the case where absolute pose is calculated, the matching problem is completely different: it applies to matching images of the session with the reference data, which may be very different. For example, we may need to match the image of the real scene with the images acquired and localized earlier or with a 3D model of a (real) object. Acquiring this reference data is restrictive and may take a lot of time and money. However, the major difficulty resides in the matching itself:

– in a case where reference data are images, these images have typically been acquired from different points of view for the user, at a different date. Thus, establishing correspondence between an image taken in summer and one taken in winter, for example, remains very difficult [VER 15];

– for a large-scale application, it is also essential that a very large number of reference images can be efficiently managed (see, for example, [ZEI 15]);

– the 3D model of an object mainly provides the geometry of the object, but not really its appearance. Hence, it is still difficult to use such a model as a reference for localization [WUE 07].

Research is still being carried out on these problems and, at present, there does not seem to be any turnkey solution.

Methods to compute absolute pose also generally require more computation time than methods to calculate relative pose. It is, however, possible to combine both types of pose computation. For example, [ART 15] proposes a localization method with absolute terrestrial coordinates and uses it as the initial pose for a much faster SLAM method, which can also find the pose for the rest of the session with the same absolute coordinates.

4.2. Topics in AR that are rarely or never approached

4.2.1. *Introduction*

Most of the work carried out in augmented reality has focused on problems related to computer vision or computer graphics. However, very little work has been carried out on aspects related to the problem of interaction between users and augmented environments, even though these are fundamental problems. Thus, the objective of this chapter is to describe the key trends in the field of interaction in augmented reality. We will mainly present techniques that were developed for systems where the augmentation is carried out on a screen (tablet or telephone) or through HMDs and systems where the augmentation is directly co-localized with the physical world (spatial augmented reality).

In any case, regardless of the technology used, the augmented reality systems are based on a credible match between the physical world and the virtual world. In the case of tablets or HMDs, the rendering of the virtual world is computed in real time based on the real scene, which is located behind the device. This is the first – and principal – level of interaction, where the user will change their point of view of the screen through natural movements of the head, or by moving the screen as though it were a window onto the virtual world. In the case of spatial augmented reality, this change in point of view is completely integrated; a user will see an augmented object as though he were looking at a real object. The possibility of changing one's point of view of a scene in a natural manner is a characteristic of augmented reality systems which distinguishes these from traditional contexts of applications. For example, on a desktop computer or a tablet, specific interaction mechanisms must be introduced to modify the point of view, for example, using a virtual trackball (see [JAN 15] for an overview of the state of the art of these techniques).

In augmented reality, interaction techniques principally focus on controlling the application (e.g. to indicate the augmentation to display) or selecting objects, especially to obtain information about these objects. Other, more advanced techniques, will enable the manipulation of virtual objects in the augmented scene.

4.2.2. *Hybridization through a screen or HMD*

4.2.2.1. *Interacting using a mobile device*

The majority of augmented reality applications use simple interactions, controlled through a tactile screen. This is mainly the case with the Diota Player[1] where the different display options are accessible through a graphic interface (Figure 4.5). Other applications may be based on simple tactile gestures, as is the case with the *Pokémon Go* application, where a virtual ball

1 Diota: http://www.diota.com

is thrown into the real world with a quick flick of a finger towards the top of the screen.

Figure 4.5. *Interaction using a graphic interface. Image: Diota (© Diota)*

Several authors have studied more advanced types of interaction, especially to position and orient virtual objects in the real scene. Marzo *et al.* [MAR 14b] are notable among these authors. They have recommended the combined use of movements of the mobile device to which the virtual object may be attached and tactile gestures on the surface of the screen, as shown in Figure 4.6.

Figure 4.6. *A combination of movements of the telephone and tactile gestures for the manipulation of 3D objects in mobile augmented reality (according to [MAR 14b]). For a color version of this figure, see www.iste.co.uk/arnaldi/virtual.zip*

4.2.2.2. Interactions in air

When using an HMD, the absence of a physical screen makes the interaction harder. Just selecting an option requires introducing specific interaction techniques. One approach that could be used is to associate a command with a specific gesture. Piumsomboon and colleagues propose a certain number of these fixed associations based on studies carried out with users [PIU 13]. These gestures, made in air, are also sometimes directly used to allow a pseudo-physical interaction with the virtual objects that constitute the augmented scene. This is mainly the case with the interactions carried out using HoloDesk [HIL 12], where the augmentation is carried out through a semi-transparent screen.

4.2.2.3. *Interaction with tangible objects*

Approaches where the interaction is directly carried out in air suffer from limitations such as user fatigue or imprecision. An interesting alternative approach consists of using elements of the real world in an opportunistic manner to allow users to interact with the help of physical objects [HEN 08]. Another approach consists of using tangible objects dedicated to the manipulation of virtual objects. This is mainly the case with the objects shown in Figure 4.7.

a) Tangible Volume; manipulation
of data using an augmented cube, ([ISS 16], (© Inria – AVIZ))

b) Hélios uses tangible objects to allow children to
manipulate astronomical bodies, ([FLE 15], (© Inria – Potioc))

Figure 4.7. *Examples of manipulation using tangible objects. For a color version of this figure, see www.iste.co.uk/arnaldi/virtual.zip*

4.3. Spatial augmented reality

4.3.1. *Hybridization of the real world and the virtual world*

If we wish to do away with HMDs or tablets, it may be useful to co-localize digital information directly with the physical world, using video projectors or small screens. For example, in MirageTable [BEN 12], the authors combine interaction with physical objects and virtual objects that are projected onto a curved screen. In OmniTouch [HAR 11], shown in Figure 4.8, the digital information is directly projected onto the user's hands and arms. Fingers that come into contact with this display are detected using a depth camera. PapARt[2], a development kit, helps make augmented objects interactive and is based on the same type of technology.

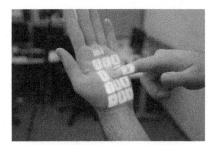

a) OmniTouch [HAR 11]: interaction with numerical
data projected onto the user's hand

b) Teegi [FRE 14]: interaction with a physical
representation of our brain activity

Figure 4.8. *Interactions in spatial augmented reality. For a color*
version of this figure, see www.iste.co.uk/arnaldi/virtual.zip

2 PapARt: https://project.inria.fr/papart

This type of approach, based on spatial augmented reality, makes it possible to bring the virtual and real closer together. Users interact directly with augmented objects without the intermediary of a screen. This may make group work easier and make interactions more engaging. For instance, Teegi (Figure 4.8) is a mediating device that was designed to allow a user, or a group of users, to understand the functioning of the brain. The user's movements are replicated by a physical model (Teegi) onto whose head the corresponding EEG activity is projected [FRE 14].

Other examples of interaction in spatial augmented reality are described in [MAR 14a].

4.3.2. *Current evolutions*

Going beyond the digital augmentation of objects, updating these objects is an area of development that could lead to some very interesting evolutions in interactive systems. For example, InForm [FOL 13], shown in Figure 4.9, is an augmented device whose shape may be modified in real time. This is the materialization of the *Radical Atoms* concepts, which was proposed by Hiroshi Ishii and his colleagues [ISH 12]. Another example of a reconfigurable augmented system is *BitDrones* where the pixels will be able to reconfigure themselves in space by means of small drones [RUB 15].

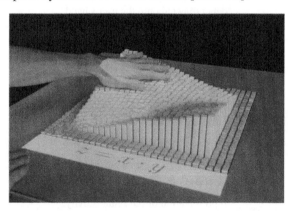

Figure 4.9. *InForm [FOL 13] – modification of the shape of an augmented object (© MIT). For a color version of this figure, see www.iste.co.uk/arnaldi/virtual.zip*

The different technological environments – desktop, virtual reality or augmented reality – have tended to evolve separately. Each of these offers advantages and is limited by certain drawbacks. One of the challenges today is to offer gateways or bridges between these different environments. Tangible Viewport [GER 16] is an early example of such a bridge: it combines desktop computers and spatial augmented reality within a unified environment.

4.4. Presence in augmented reality

The question of presence in augmented reality is not one that seems to arise spontaneously. And if this is the case, then there are several reasons for this, which must be examined, since, despite the arguments put forward, presence in augmented reality is an essential dimension of the experience brought about by the augmented reality interfaces.

4.4.1. *Is presence in reality the model for presence in virtual environments?*

The feeling of presence seems to be an essential dimension of experience only in two situations: either when the subject is in a real environment or when they are in a virtual environment. Thus, augmented reality would seem, at first glance, to be an environment where the feeling of presence was not involved. In theory, in a real environment, presence is evidence, or even tautology, at two levels: not only is the environment present (environmental presence), but, in addition, the subject is present within the environment (personal presence). This distinction between the dimensions of presence, shown by Heeter [HEE 92], is relevant not only in a real environment but also in a virtual environment. And if this distinction is valid for both types of environment, it is because presence in virtual reality, defined as the subject's feeling that they are in a place where, in reality, they are not, implicitly takes the model of presence in a real environment. In effect, it is presupposed in this definition that the feeling of presence in virtual reality must as much as possible approach the feeling that the subject experiences when in a real environment. Hence, presence is also defined as a type of experience of non-mediation [LOM 97], of transparency [MAR 03] or as a pseudo-natural immersion experience [FUC 05]. Furthermore, thinking of presence in virtual reality, as is the case here, using the model of "natural" presence in reality (i.e. exempt from mediation) implies an assumption that must be examined on both the theoretical and empirical levels. From a theoretical point of view, it is difficult to posit the objective existence of a reality *per se* which is not constructed subjectively [KAN 90] or socially [BER 66]. The idea of a natural reality and a completely natural relationship between the subject and this reality arises from the myth of nature – a pure and original environment shorn of every artifact. However, the distinction between the natural and artificial is more a result of dichotomies produced by categories of language than reality. "It is impossible to superimpose on man a lower layer of behavior which one chooses to call natural followed by a manufactured cultural or spiritual world. Everything is both manufactured and natural in man, as it were in the sense that there is not a word, not a form of behavior which does not owe something to purely biological being and which at the same time does not elude the simplicity of animal life and cause forms of vital behavior to deviate from their preordained direction through a sort of leakage and through a genius for ambiguity which might serve to define man" [MER 45]. Consequently, our relationship with the world is not natural or free of mediation – whether this mediation is in the form of language, art, a pair of glasses, a fork or an HMD. Thus, if presence is always more or less mediatized, even in that environment which we call "reality", then perhaps the model or ideal of presence cannot be found in our contact with natural reality. Now, it may be stated that even though we admit that relationship of the subject with reality is not natural, the relation of the subject to the virtual environment is quite strictly artificial in the sense that it is completely mediatized [TAN 04]. This argument, however, does not hold good for two reasons: first, even though we theoretically admit that the virtual environment is, from the sensory point of view, totally artificial in that all the subject's senses may be ideally connected to the interface, the relationship between this environment and the subject cannot, in itself, be totally artificial unless both parties (i.e. the environment and the subject) are artificial. Yet, from a psychological, biological or even ethical point of view, the subject cannot be reduced to a mere artifact. Second, it is technically impossible, at least at present, to empirically create a wholly artificial virtual environment. Indeed, even in a highly immersive environment, such as a cave, even though multiple sensory channels might be connected to the device, the subject's feet, for example, remain firmly planted on the (real) ground. In sum, complete presence is impossible within an absolutely natural real environment or an absolutely artificial environment. Moreover, while this conclusion may call into question the concept of presence shared by researchers and virtual reality practitioners, it has yet to be demonstrated that presence is a relevant dimension for a subject's experience in augmented reality.

4.4.2. Mixed reality: an end to the real versus virtual binary?

While the concept of mixed reality is best expressed in the real-virtual continuum [MIL 94] (which proposes a classification system for interfaces, going from reality to virtuality, via the intermediate states of augmented reality and augmented virtuality), it must be emphasized that the concept of reality has a very specific meaning for these authors. In effect, Milgram and Kishino see reality here not as "natural reality", but a mediatized representation of this reality: the perceived reality with which the subject interacts is an image of reality (e.g. film images on a screen, an HMD or in a CAVE), which may be augmented using virtual elements (i.e. synthetic events). The presupposition that the authors hold is that being captured through a camera neither augments nor diminishes reality but simply represents it in the form of an image (mainly visual and auditory) using an interface. This presupposition is not deliberately an epistemological one, it is the direct consequence of the purpose of the contribution that the authors wish to make (i.e. propose a taxonomy for mixed reality devices) without reflecting on the relevance of reducing reality to its mediatized representation in an image. This contribution falls within a technical and, in this case, taxonomic approach to the real-virtual continuum. And this approach is the reason that authors do not examine the question of presence, even though it may have implications for their model relative to the subject's experience. Thus, how can you confine the real environment and the virtual environment to two extremes of a continuum if the interfaces only differ in degrees? In other words, how can you not study the concept of presence if the binary (real vs. virtual) is actually more of a continuum? That is, there are only differences in degrees, but they are not completely contradictory concepts.

4.4.3. From mixed reality to mixed presence

If one is aware of the fact that presence is not an aspect of experience that is confined to the conditions of an absolutely real or absolutely virtual experience, then it is possible to think of presence as a dimension of experience that may be present all along the real-virtual continuum. This perspective opens the door to a concept of presence which, like mixed reality (e.g. augmented reality, diminished reality and augmented virtuality), is in itself mixed. The question then arises, how do we concretely establish the mixed character of presence? There are broadly two ways of measuring presence (which are not mutually exclusive). It is possible to infer presence based on qualitative or quantitative indicators, by focusing either on observable variables (e.g. the importing of patterns of behavior from the real environment to the virtual environment, cardiac rhythm and sweating) or using declarative methods (e.g. in-depth interviews and questionnaires). In the case of declarative methods, this involves asking the subject questions in order to know (at the minimum) whether they feel present in the environment (personal presence) and whether they consider the environment to be present (environmental presence). It has also been empirically, qualitatively [NAN 15b] and quantitatively [NAN 15a] shown that the subject may experience paradoxical feelings: a mixed presence which may, for example, be expressed through items such as "I was in both the real environment and the virtual environment" (mixed personal presence) or "the virtual environment existed, yet did not exist" (mixed environmental presence). Thus, even in a virtual environment (in this case, produced by a four-sided cave), there is a mixed presence. Parallel to this, a series of experiments were carried out on children playing an online game in augmented reality (the virtual version of the labyrinth Nestlé provides on certain cereal boxes). This made it possible to conclude that there existed a feeling of personal presence among almost all the subjects (who were questioned after one round of the game), even though the environment was augmented reality and not virtual reality [MUR 16]. These studies also tend to attest to the following facts: (1) virtual reality devices, meant to isolate the subject from the real environment by immersing them in a virtual environment, are subjectively experienced as mixed devices, producing mixed environments (both real and virtual); (2) augmented reality devices, which are not meant to be immersive, may theoretically cause a feeling of presence in the subject.

4.4.4. *Augmented reality: a total environment*

While the experience of an augmented reality environment falls within the framework of an immersive experience that may bring about a feeling of presence, this is because the subject perceives, and interacts with, an environment where the distinction between real and virtual elements is not relevant, in subjective terms. This argument is coherent with research that shows that presence and the perceived real nature of an environment in augmented reality are two different judgments [SCH 99, SCH 01]. Furthermore, on comparing presence in virtual reality and in augmented reality, it has been shown that the feeling of presence is higher in augmented reality [TAN 04]. This is probably because the synthetic elements are integrated into the real environment in which the subject, whatever they are doing, is already present. These contributions are finally and implicitly based on the idea that unlike a designer of augmented reality interfaces, who must technically distinguish real elements from virtual elements in order to overlay them, the subject who is experiencing an augmented reality environment is not experiencing two different environments. Both from the perception as well as the practical point of view, the subject interacts with only one environment – the mixed environment. As a result, even though this environment is hybrid (as it contains a mix of real and virtual elements), it is in this combined and total environment that the subject is present. If the subject has an immersive experience, it is because the augmented reality environment constitutes an alternative environment into which they are submerged. And while this does not do away with the real environment, it alters this environment and gives it new meaning, where elements from the real environment are augmented by other elements.

4.5. 3D interaction on tactile surfaces

This section aims to provide a (non-exhaustive) description of important innovations in the field of 3D interaction over the last decade. At the beginning of this book, we recalled that VR was based on two fundamental pillars: (1) immersion (e.g. visual, auditory and haptic) in a virtual environment, and (2) interaction between one or many users and this environment. Therefore, if we wish to offer an overview of this technology, it is not sufficient to describe new developments in equipment or software. While 3D interaction is less central to AR, its importance is rising nonetheless. From simple applications to visualize digital data that is superimposed on the natural view, RA systems today are offering users increasingly more refined interaction systems in order to enhance usage.

Moreover, even though this book is dedicated to VR-AR, the innovations described in the rest of this chapter go far beyond this context and have repercussions for many other fields, wherever the 3D manipulation of information is required.

4.5.1. *3D interaction*

The last decade has seen an unprecedented diversification of means of visualizing and interacting with 3D digital content. This has facilitated the emergence of new uses and the diversification of interaction styles, which defined the means available to a user to interact with a computer system [SHN 97].

Historically, the first interaction style was using a command language, which allowed expert users to enter commands (e.g. editing, manipulation) using specialized language. The second important generation proposed filling forms and using selection menus (often called "scrolling") in order to allow the input of commands and parameters by both expert users and novices. Finally, the third dominant interact style was based on directly manipulating the object of interest. These objects were represented in the form of interactive graphic objects that could be directly manipulated by the user through rapid, reversible and incremental actions. The WIMP (Windows, Icons, Menus, Pointer) interfaces used in desktops were based on direct interaction via the manipulation of the concerned object using a pointer (e.g. arrow, cursor) that was indirectly manipulated by a pointing device. In practice, depending on the task to be carried out, the manipulation is more or less direct. For example, it is very direct when modifying an image by moving its borders, or in moving an icon from one window to another to move a file from a folder. It is less direct when a user has to first select a portion of the text and then click on a button to convert the text to boldface text.

In 2007, Apple launched the iPhone and, doing so, launched the first smartphone that was based on multipoint tactile interaction (using several fingers) with capacitive technology, which was subsequently used by the majority of the smartphones that came out on the market. These interfaces were also based on a direct interaction style, but unlike the WIMP interfaces, the interaction was carried out in a co-localized manner (the manipulation and visualization spaces coincided) which made the interactions more direct. Tactile interfaces also allowed for a rise in gesture interaction, which is based on a vocabulary of gestures that enter commands, with parameters, if needed.

Thus, for example, the "swipe" is associated with the command to change between screens on a smartphone, or even using two fingers for translations, rotations and changes in the size allows the simultaneous manipulation of all the three commands and associated parameters. These interactions enable more direct manipulation of 2D objects. 3D interaction remains difficult using this kind of interface, even though many techniques have already been proposed to facilitate the associated tasks. In 2010, the iPad resulted in the democratization of the use of digital tablets, which were mainly distinguished by a larger tactile screen but generally had the same sensors as smartphones. Some models also enabled interaction using a digital stylus, which reduced occultation problems and offered greater precision than that offered by fingers. Interactions styles remained the same as those used with smartphones.

2010 was also the year that the Microsoft Kinect opened up new possibilities for interaction with 3D content. The predominant interaction style was gesture interaction, now in 3D instead of 2D. Today, there is no longer any need to hold and manipulate devices for interaction. The user can potentially interact using any part of their body, tracked by the Kinect's 3D camera, although hands remain the privileged means of interaction. This device was first used in video games, but has also been used in interactive applications for the general public. The use of this device, however, is limited by problems with gesture segmentation, capture precision and occultations. More precise 3D tracking of hands and fingers was then facilitated by the Leap Motion sensor (2012). While this was first restricted to desktop use, it can now be attached to an HMD to allow the user to interact using their hands in the virtual environment.

In 2013, Oculus Rift made it possible to widen the use of HMDs, which were, until then, restricted to experts. Interaction with a stereoscopic 3D environment is principally based on the direct interaction style, although other interaction styles are also used. 3D manipulation tasks may be carried out in a more direct manner, as it is possible to envisage controlling objects in a manner similar to reality, without breaking the task down into sub-tasks. Google Glass (2014) was based on the concept of a ubiquitous computer with the use of a small, remote screen. The predominant interaction style is vocal interaction combined with tactile interaction on one side of the glasses. This allows limited interaction with 3D environments or augmented reality environments. In 2016, the launch of the Microsoft HoloLens made it possible to envisage the democratization of augmented reality applications.

Unlike Google Glass, this device allowed the capture of the user's gestures, offering the possibility of direct as well as gesture interactions.

Generally speaking, in the current interfaces, we can observe a trend towards an integration of the interaction styles. An example of this is recent laptop computers that combine command language interactions, form filling, direct manipulation, 2D gesture and vocal interaction. This combination of interaction styles makes it possible to diversify the means available to the user to carry out a task, as some are better adapted to certain contexts than others. The new interfaces, based on HMDs and 3D gesture capture, allow more direct interaction with 3D environments.

4.5.2. *3D interaction on tactile surfaces*

4.5.2.1. *Introduction*

Popularized by the iPhone in 2007, interactive tactile surfaces, especially *multi-touch* screens with the ability to simultaneously detect several points of contact, have seen considerable growth in recent times. They allowed traditional digital applications based on mouse, keyboard and standard screens to evolve towards mobile applications (smartphones and tablets) and collective applications (tactile tables). With respect to more traditional desktop contexts, tactile surfaces facilitated direct interactions; the user directly "touches" what they see. Consequently, tactile interaction has been widely explored and used for 2D applications such as navigation using a map or visualizing photos. In effect, the execution of many bi-dimensional interaction tasks (opening, turning, zooming in on a map) is perfectly adapted to gesture interaction on tactile surfaces.

On the contrary, however, interaction with 3D content is less evident, as it requires an association of 2D gestures with actions that require greater control of a greater number of degrees of freedom (e.g. six degrees of freedom for 3D translations/rotations). Existing techniques that allow interaction with 3D content in the mouse/keyboard/screen context are not directly transferable to tactile as they were developed for a different interaction space. The objective of this section is to provide an overview of recent developments allowing users to easily and efficiently interact with 3D content displayed on tactile surfaces.

4.5.2.2. *3D manipulations*

A few authors have tried to stick as closely as possible to physical behavior to manipulate 3D objects. This is mainly the case with Reisman *et al.* [REI 09], who proposed extending the Rotate–Scale–Translate technique to 3D. This technique allows movement, turning and carrying out changes in scale on 2D objects. In their approach, they tried to resolve a system of constraints that ensured that 3D points located on the user's fingers would always be co-localized with the fingers. This resulted in an interaction that seemed intuitive, at first glance, but proved to be difficult to control when precise manipulations were required.

For more precise manipulation, other authors chose to separate the different degrees of freedom. This was mainly the method adopted by Hancock *et al.* and Martinet *et al.*, who proposed, respectively, the StickyTools [HAN 09] technique and the DS3 – Depth Separated Screen Space technique [MAR 10]. In these approaches, certain movements of the fingers are directly associated with movements of the object (e.g. to move the object in a plane parallel to the plane of the screen) while other movements are dissociated (e.g. translations in depth, for which using direct associations would be harder).

Finally, some authors tried to change desktop 3D manipulation techniques to adapt them to a tactile context. This was the case with the tBox [COH 11], which allowed a user to precisely manipulate translations, rotations and scale changes using a 3D transformation widget that was specially designed for tactile surfaces (see Figure 4.10). This is also the case with Eden [KIN 11], an interactive environment that allowed graphic designers to animate 3D scenes using 2D gestures.

4.5.2.3. *Controlling point of view*

A more traditional approach is used for controlling point of view, which consists of associating a language of gestures with camera movements. For example, two fingers coming closer or moving apart may be associated with the zoom operation, while congruent movements of the fingers may be associated with a Panning motion of the camera. The movements of a finger around a second, fixed, finger, may be associated with rotations of the camera around a pivot point, as can be done with tBox, for example. In order to refine the controls, Klein *et al.* [KLE 12] also propose using the border of the display window in the 3D data visualization frame (Figure 4.11).

Figure 4.10. *tBox 3D manipulation tool for tactile screens [COH 11] (© Inria – Potioc). For a color version of this figure, see www.iste.co.uk/arnaldi/virtual.zip*

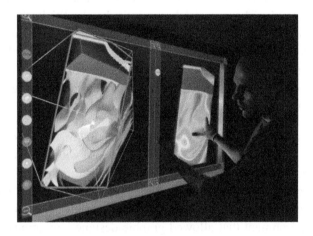

Figure 4.11. *Tactile interaction on a large screen for the visualization of scientific data [KLE 12] (© Inria – AVIZ). For a color version of this figure, see www.iste.co.uk/arnaldi/virtual.zip*

Dedicated widgets have also been proposed in parallel to the manipulation of objects. This is the case with Navidget [HAC 09], where the user moves around in the 3D scene by indicating the zone they wish to observe. Thus, the user may focus solely on the target, without having to think about the different movements they will have to carry out to arrive at the desired zone, as these will be controlled automatically by the camera. This makes it possible to make the interaction more fluid, avoiding changes in modes through menus or buttons, which is particularly significant in the case of tactile interaction.

4.5.2.4. *Multi surfaces and stereoscopic display*

In order to draw closer to the 3D nature of the observed data, while also retaining the advantages of an interaction based on tactile gestures, some authors have proposed new and original devices. We have, for example, Cubtile, from the company Immersion, where five faces of a cube may be used to execute multipoint gestures (see Figure 4.12, top). These gestures are then interpreted as 3D commands to manipulate objects or control the camera's point of view. This device is dedicated to indirect usage, where several participants can interact in front of a large screen.

Figure 4.12. *Cubtile (top) and Toucheo (bottom), two examples of devices that use tactile interaction for the manipulation of 3D objects (© Immersion – Inria Potioc). For a color version of this figure, see www.iste.co.uk/arnaldi/virtual.zip*

For Toucheo [HAC 11], the objective was to combine stereoscopic 3D display with 2D tactile interaction. In order to allow this, a stereoscopic screen was fixed, facing down, above a monoscopic, multipoint screen. A semi-transparent mirror was positioned between these two screens in order to reflect the stereoscopic images as well as to enable visualization of the bottom screen (see Figure 4.12, bottom). Thus, the user visualizes 3D stereoscopic objects that seem to float above the tactile surface and interacts with these objects through manipulation widgets that were specially designed for this device.

Other authors have tried to combine tactile interaction on a multipoint surface with 3D gesture interaction above the surface. This was mainly done with MockUp Builder [ARA 12], which allowed a user to prototype 3D objects by combing 2D and 3D gestures.

The research and development presented in these sections, among many other projects, have contributed to making interactions with 3D content displayed on tactile surfaces simpler, more efficient and richer. All the same, this type of interaction is still underexplored and there is scope for many new methods to be invented.

4.6. Bibliography

[ARA 12] ARAÚJO B.R.D., CASIEZ G., JORGE J.A., "Mockup builder: direct 3D modeling on and above the surface in a continuous interaction space", *Proceedings of Graphics Interface*, Toronto, Canada, May 28–30, 2012.

[ART 15] ARTH C., PIRCHHEIM C., VENTURA J. *et al.*, "Instant outdoor localization and SLAM initialization from 2.5D maps", *IEEE Transactions on Visualization and Computer Graphics*, vol. 21, no. 11, 2015.

[BEN 12] BENKO H., JOTA R., WILSON A., "MirageTable: freehand interaction on a projected augmented reality tabletop", *Proceedings of the SIGCHI Conference on Human Factors in Computing Systems*, CHI'12, New York, USA, pp. 199–208, 2012.

[BEN 14] BENKO H., WILSON A.D., ZANNIER F., "Dyadic projected spatial augmented reality", *Proceedings of the 27th Annual ACM Symposium on User Interface Software and Technology*, UIST'14, pp. 645–655, 2014.

[BEN 15] BENKO H., OFEK E., ZHENG F. *et al.*, "FoveAR: combining an optically see-through near-eye display with projector-based spatial augmented reality", *Proceedings of the 28th Annual ACM Symposium on User Interface Software & Technology*, UIST'15, pp. 129–135, 2015.

[BER 66] BERGER P., LUCKMANN T., *The social construction of reality: a treatise in the sociology of knowledge*, Anchor Books, New York, 1966.

[BIM 06] BIMBER O., RASKAR R., "Modern approaches to augmented reality", *ACM SIGGRAPH 2006 Courses*, SIGGRAPH'06, ACM, 2006.

[COH 11] COHÉ A., DÈCLE F., HACHET M., "tBox: A 3D transformation widget designed for touch-screens", *Proceedings of the SIGCHI Conference on Human Factors in Computing Systems*, CHI'11, New York, USA, pp. 3005–3008, 2011.

[CRU 92] CRUZ-NEIRA C., SANDIN D.J., DEFANTI T.A. *et al.*, "The CAVE: audio visual experience automatic virtual environment", *Communication ACM*, vol. 35, no. 6, pp. 64–72, 1992.

[ENG 14] ENGEL J., SCHÖPS T., CREMERS D., "LSD-SLAM: large-scale direct monocular SLAM", *European Conference on Computer Vision*, Zurich, Switzerland, 6–12 September 2014.

[FLE 15] FLECK S., HACHET M., BASTIEN J. M.C., "Marker-based augmented reality: instructional-design to improve children interactions with astronomical concepts", *Proceedings of the 14th International Conference on Interaction Design and Children*, IDC'15, New York, USA, pp. 21–28, 2015.

[FOL 13] FOLLMER S., LEITHINGER D., OLWAL A. *et al.*, "inFORM: dynamic physical affordances and constraints through shape and object actuation", *Proceedings of the 26th Annual ACM Symposium on User Interface Software and Technology*, UIST'13, New York, USA, pp. 417–426, 2013.

[FRE 14] FREY J., GERVAIS R., FLECK S. *et al.*, "Teegi: tangible EEG interface", *Proceedings of the 27th Annual ACM Symposium on User Interface Software and Technology*, UIST'14, New York, USA, pp. 301–308, 2014.

[FUC 05] FUCHS P., MOREAU G. (eds), *Le Traité de la Réalité Virtuelle*, Les Presses de l'Ecole des Mines, Paris, 2005.

[FUC 09] FUCHS P., MOREAU G., DONIKIAN S., *Le Traité de la Réalité Virtuelle Volume 5 - Les humains virtuels*, Les Presses de l'Ecole des Mines, Paris, 2009.

[GAO 03] GAO X.-S., HOU X.-R., TANG J. *et al.*, "Complete solution classification for the perspective-three-point problem", *IEEE Transactions on Pattern Analysis and Machine Intelligence*, vol. 25, no. 8, pp. 930–943, 2003.

[GER 16] GERVAIS R., ROO J.S., HACHET M., "Tangible viewports: getting out of flatland in desktop environments", *Proceedings of the TEI'16: Tenth International Conference on Tangible, Embedded, and Embodied Interaction*, TEI'16, New York, USA, pp. 176–184, 2016.

[HAC 09] HACHET M., DECLE F., KNDEL S. *et al.*, "Navidget for 3D interaction: camera positioning and further uses", *International Journal of Human-Computer Studies*, vol. 67, no. 3, pp. 225–236, 2009.

[HAC 11] HACHET M., BOSSAVIT B., COHÉ A. *et al.*, "Toucheo: multitouch and stereo combined in a seamless workspace", *Proceedings of the 24th Annual ACM Symposium on User Interface Software and Technology*, UIST'11, New York, USA, pp. 587–592, 2011.

[HAN 09] HANCOCK M., TEN CATE T., CARPENDALE S., "Sticky tools: full 6DOF force-based interaction for multi-touch tables", *Proceedings of the ACM International Conference on Interactive Tabletops and Surfaces*, ITS'09, New York, USA, pp. 133–140, 2009.

[HAR 11] HARRISON C., BENKO H., WILSON A.D., "OmniTouch: wearable multitouch interaction everywhere", *Proceedings of the 24th Annual ACM Symposium on User Interface Software and Technology*, UIST'11, New York, USA, pp. 441–450, 2011.

[HEE 92] HEETER C., "Being there: the subjective experience of presence", *Presence: Teleoperators and Virtual Environments*, vol. 1, no. 2, pp. 262–271, 1992.

[HEN 08] HENDERSON S.J., FEINER S., "Opportunistic controls: leveraging natural affordances as tangible user interfaces for augmented reality", *Proceedings of the 2008 ACM Symposium on Virtual Reality Software and Technology*, VRST'08, New York, USA, pp. 211–218, 2008.

[HIL 12] HILLIGES O., KIM D., IZADI S. *et al.*, "HoloDesk: direct 3D interactions with a situated see-through display", *Proceedings of the SIGCHI Conference on Human Factors in Computing Systems*, CHI'12, New York, USA, pp. 2421–2430, 2012.

[INA 00] INAMI M., KAWAKAMI N., SEKIGUCHI D. *et al.*, "Visuo-haptic display using head-mounted projector", *Proceedings of the IEEE Virtual Reality Annual International Symposium*, pp. 233–240, 2000.

[INA 03] INAMI M., KAWAKAMI N., TACHI S., "Optical camouflage using retro-reflective projection technology", *Proceedings of the 2003 IEEE / ACM International Symposium on Mixed and Augmented Reality (ISMAR)*, pp. 348–349, 2003.

[ISS 16] ISSARTEL P., BESANÇON L., ISENBERG T. *et al.* "A tangible volume for portable 3D interaction", *2016 IEEE International Symposium on Mixed and Augmented Reality*, Merida, Mexico, p. 5, September 2016.

[ISH 12] ISHII H., LAKATOS D., BONANNI L. *et al.*, "Radical atoms: beyond tangible bits, toward transformable materials", *Interactions*, vol. 19, no. 1, pp. 38–51, 2012.

[JAN 15] JANKOWSKI J., HACHET M., "Advances in interaction with 3D environments", *Computer Graphics Forum*, vol. 34, pp. 152–190, 2015.

[JON 13] JONES B., BENKO H., OFEK E. *et al.*, "IllumiRoom: peripheral projected illusions for interactive experiences", *Proceedings of the SIGCHI Conference on Human Factors in Computing Systems*, CHI'13, New York, USA, pp. 869–878, 2013.

[JON 14] JONES B., SODHI R., MURDOCK M. *et al.*, "RoomAlive: magical experiences enabled by scalable, adaptive projector-camera units", *Proceedings of the 27th Annual ACM Symposium on User Interface Software and Technology*, UIST'14, New York, USA, pp. 637–644, 2014.

[KAN 90] KANT E., *Critique de la raison pure*, Gallimard, Paris, 1990.

[KIJ 97] KIJIMA R., OJIKA T., "Transition between virtual environment and workstation environment with projective head mounted display", *Virtual Reality Annual International Symposium, IEEE 1997*, pp. 130–137, March 1997.

[KIN 11] KIN K., MILLER T., BOLLENSDORFF B. *et al.*, "Eden: a professional multitouch tool for constructing virtual organic environments", *Proceedings of the SIGCHI Conference on Human Factors in Computing Systems*, CHI '11, New York, USA, pp. 1343–1352, 2011.

[KLE 12] KLEIN T., GUÉNIAT F., PASTUR L. *et al.*, "A design study of direct-touch interaction for exploratory 3D scientific visualization", *Computer Graphics Forum*, vol. 31, no. 3, pp. 1225–1234, June 2012.

[LAV 17] LAVIOLA J.J., KRUIJFF E., MCMAHAN R. *et al.*, *3D User Interfaces: Theory and Practice, 2nd Edition*, Addison Wesley, Boston, 2017.

[LOM 97] LOMBARD M., DITTON T., "At the heart of it all: the concept of presence", *Journal of Computer-Mediated Communication*, vol. 3, no. 2, 1997.

[MAR 03] MARSH T., "Staying there: an activity-based approach to narrative design and evaluation as an antidote to virtual corpsing", in RIVA G., DAVIDE F., IJSSELSTEIJN W.A. (eds) *Being There: Concepts, Effects and Measurement of User Presence in Synthetic Environments* Ios Press, Amsterdam, 2003.

[MAR 10] MARTINET A., CASIEZ G., GRISONI L., "The effect of DOF separation in 3D manipulation tasks with multi-touch displays", *Proceedings of the 17th ACM Symposium on Virtual Reality Software and Technology*, VRST '10, New York, USA, pp. 111–118, 2010.

[MAR 14a] MARNER M.R., SMITH R.T., WALSH J.A. *et al.*, "Spatial user interfaces for large-scale projector-based augmented reality", *IEEE Computer Graphics and Applications*, vol. 34, no. 6, pp. 74–82, 2014.

[MAR 14b] MARZO A., BOSSAVIT B., HACHET M., "Combining multi-touch input and device movement for 3D manipulations in mobile augmented reality environments", *ACM Symposium on Spatial User Interaction*, Honolulu, United States, October 2014.

[MER 45] MERLEAU-PONTY M., *Phénoménologie de la perception*, Gallimard, Paris, 1945.

[MIL 94] MILGRAM P., KISHINO F., "A taxonomy of mixed reality visual displays", *IEICE Transactions Information Systems*, vol. E77-D, no. 12, pp. 1321–1329, 1994.

[MUR 15] MUR-ARTAL R., MONTIEL J.M.M., TARDÛS J.D., "ORB-SLAM: a versatile and accurate monocular SLAM system", *IEEE Transactions on Robotics*, vol. 31, no. 5, pp. 1147–1163, 2015.

[MUR 16] MURATORE I., NANNIPIERI O., "L'expérience immersive d'un jeu promotionnel en réalité augmentée destiné aux enfants", *Décisions Marketing*, vol. 81, pp. 27–40, 2016.

[NAN 15a] NANNIPIERI O., MURATORE I., DUMAS P. *et al.*, *Technologies, communication et société*, L'Harmattan, Paris, 2015.

[NAN 15b] NANNIPIERI O., MURATORE I., MESTRE D. *et al.*, *Frontières Numériques 2*, L'Harmattan, Paris, 2015.

[NEW 11] NEWCOMBE R., IZADI S., HILLIGES O. *et al.*, "KinectFusion: real-time dense surface mapping and tracking", *10th IEEE International Symposium on Mixed and Augmented Reality*, Basel, Switzerland, 26–29 October, 2011.

[PEJ 16] PEJSA T., KANTOR J., BENKO H. *et al.*, "Room2Room: enabling life-size telepresence in a projected augmented reality environment", *Proceedings of the 19th ACM Conference on Computer-Supported Cooperative Work & Social Computing*, CSCW'16, New York, USA, pp. 1716–1725, 2016.

[PIU 13] PIUMSOMBOON T., CLARK A.J., BILLINGHURST M. *et al.*, "User-defined gestures for augmented reality", *Human-Computer Interaction - INTERACT 2013 - 14th IFIP TC 13 International Conference*, Cape Town, South Africa, pp. 282–299, September 2–6, 2013.

[RAS 98a] RASKAR R., WELCH G., FUCHS H., "Seamless projection overlaps using image warping and intensity blending", *Fourth International Conference on Virtual Systems and Multimedia*, Gifu, Japan, 18–20 November, 1998.

[RAS 98b] RASKAR R., WELCH G., FUCHS H., "Spatially Augmented Reality", *First IEEE Workshop on Augmented Reality (IWAR'98)*, pp. 11–20, Seattle, USA, 1998.

[REI 09] REISMAN J.L., DAVIDSON P.L., HAN J.Y., "A screen-space formulation for 2D and 3D direct manipulation", *Proceedings of the 22Nd Annual ACM Symposium on User Interface Software and Technology*, UIST'09, New York, pp. 69–78, 2009.

[ROL 95] ROLLAND J.P., HOLLOWAY R.L., FUCHS H., "Comparison of optical and video see-through, head-mounted displays", *Proc. SPIE*, vol. 2351, pp. 293–307, 1995.

[RUB 15] RUBENS C., BRALEY S., GOMES A. *et al.*, "BitDrones: towards levitating programmable matter using interactive 3D quadcopter displays", *Adjunct Proceedings of the 28th Annual ACM Symposium on User Interface Software & Technology*, UIST'15 Adjunct, New York, USA, pp. 57–58, 2015.

[SCH 99] SCHUBERT T., FRIEDMANN F., REGENBRECHT H., *Embodied presence in virtual environments*, Springer, London, 1999.

[SCH 01] SCHUBERT T., FRIEDMANN F., REGENBRECHT H., "The experience of presence: factor analytic insights", *Presence: Teleoper. Virtual Environ.*, vol. 10, no. 3, pp. 266–281, 2001.

[SHN 97] SHNEIDERMAN B., MAES P., "Direct manipulation vs. interface agents", *interactions*, vol. 4, no. 6, pp. 42–61, 1997.

[TAC 14] TACHI S., INAMI M., UEMA Y., "The transparent cockpit", *IEEE Spectrum*, vol. 51, no. 11, pp. 52–56, 2014.

[TAN 04] TANG A., BIOCCA F., LIM L., "Comparing differences in presence during social interaction in augmented reality versus virtual reality environments: an exploratory study", RAYA M., SOLAZ B. (eds), *7th Annual International Workshop on Presence*, Valence, Spain, pp. 204–208, 2004.

[VER 15] VERDIE Y., YI K.M., FUA P. *et al.*, "TILDE: a temporally invariant learned DEtector", *IEEE Conference on Computer Vision and Pattern Recognition*, Boston, USA, 7–12 June, 2015.

[WUE 07] WUEST H., WIENTAPPER F., STRICKER D., "Adaptable model-based tracking using analysis-by-synthesis techniques", *12th Annual Conference on Computer Analysis of Images and Patterns*, Vienna, Austria, August 27–29, 2007.

[ZEI 15] ZEISL B., SATTLER T., POLLEFEYS M., "Camera pose voting for large-scale image-based localization", *IEEE International Conference on Computer Vision*, Santiago, Chile, 7–13 December 2015.

Scientific and Technical Prospects

After having explored the new families of applications (see Chapter 1), technological innovations related to VR-AR equipment and software (see Chapter 2), scientific problems and barriers arising from the complexity of this field (see Chapter 3) and the particular features of the real world-virtual world relationship (see Chapter 4), this chapter offers a view of future technical and scientific prospects, related to major evolutions in use. We will first take a prospective view of the impact of technological advances on applications in the entertainment field and, more generally, on the use of VR-AR by the general public (see section 5.1). We will then discuss the potential of brain-computer interactions (BCI; see section 5.2). Finally, in section 5.3, we analyze the possibilities opened up by alternative perception mechanisms for interactions in VR.

5.1. The promised revolution in the field of entertainment

5.1.1. *Introduction*

For several decades, many works of speculative fiction have depicted revolutions brought about by immersive technologies: communicating through holograms, immersion in a completely augmented, mixed world or even no longer being able to be certain whether the world around us is not an illusion. While anticipated applications had serious roles, such as increasing

Chapter written by Caroline BAILLARD, Philippe GUILLOTEL, Anatole LÉCUYER, Fabien LOTTE, Nicolas MOLLET, Jean-Marie NORMAND and Gaël SEYDOUX.

productivity, enhancing learning, assistance, design or exploration, they also offered a whole new world of escape, creation and entertainment. Thus, the attraction of these fantastic visions of a human completely overwhelmed by these alternative realities was that it would allow a person to escape from their world in a definitive manner and evolve in controlled environments, designed after their desires. New content creators will thus have every chance to bring these modern spectators to truly live their stories, outside books and movies, in a medium which is no longer a game, a film or an amusement park. This will generate a new medium for leisure and entertainment, where reality and virtuality blend into each other. In this section, we will look at how the development of immersive technologies over the last decade has made it possible to anticipate some of the profound changes we will see in entertainment in the future.

5.1.2. *Defining a new, polymorphic immersive medium*

Immersion is going to be at the heart of these new media. Here immersion is used in a broad sense, that is, from a point of view of immersion strictly by stimulation and substitution of the senses, as well as, from an interactive point of view, in a more or less active interaction the user has with his medium, or even from an augmented and social point of view. Moreover, it will not be intended for use solely within a narrative framework, like a film, but as a proper new medium. We can thus emphasize that immersive media will not be defined in any one way, but will be eminently *polymorphic*, which implies an unlimited nature: active or passive, strictly immersive or augmented/extended, with or without haptic feedback, free and game-like or totally contained and linear, for use in future immersion rooms, both multi-user and multi-site.

One segment of these new immersive media will therefore be completely *immersive*. Immersion is a global illusion, addressing all the perceptual senses of a human being. Thus, for this illusion to be perfect, it is essential to artificially recreate the exact set of stimuli in an environment that a human may perceive. However, even though realizable, this objective will require a considerable amount of time given how rich the human perceptual system is: beyond the five principal senses is a very complex system that must be considered, within which there are multiple interconnections to robustify perception of the self and the environment. Thus, perception of oneself in space is based on a continuous mix of information that comes chiefly – but not exclusively – from vision and hearing, the vestibular system, individual capacities of proprioception or even from the information received by internal organs. If the final goal is this perfect stimulation, the *illusion* that we mentioned earlier must work by combining the main senses and by distorting the feedback they provide. And so, taking this further: by deceiving the overall system we can even imagine that future innovative immersive experiences will give feedback that could not, in fact, be experienced in reality.

In the short-term, the industry will, in any case, focus on the main senses. Looking at the evolutions over the past decade, we can easily anticipate that different actuators will be available on the market, and the end-users can equip themselves as required. This may be for domestic use with light but limited devices, potentially integrated into an immersive consumer space in the home, or in the form of costlier and more comprehensive devices in immersive experience centers of the future. Taste and smell will therefore probably be rapidly processed in a primitive manner, using diffusion devices that offer limited but appropriate experiences to anchor the experience in the user's mind. One of the challenges facing developers will be the *wash-out* effect, that is, the ability of the systems to eliminate this feedback (taste, smell) and to return to a neutral state of perception. Vision, today, is quite logically the most explored sense in the virtual and augmented reality industry, especially using HMDs. Even though the field of vision and resolution are not yet at a level where they can be akin to human vision, immersive media can already start making use of this equipment. HMDs will also continue their progress, benefiting from revolutionary screens and technologies, in terms of quality and miniaturization. Other visual systems integrated into a user's living spaces will also be available, as we will see further down. Hearing is undoubtedly the feedback that is best rendered to the senses today thanks to spatial and binaural technologies. However, an essential sensory element is still missing – the sense of touch, which allows a subject to make physical sense of the virtual world in which they are immersed. Without a sense of touch, the experience cannot "exist". The sense of touch depends on receptors and corpuscles located under the skin, each of which responds to a particular task: heat, cold, pressure and/or pain. The nerve terminals in the skin are charged with transforming the information gathered by the sensory receptors into electrical nerve impulses, transmitted to the brain via the nerve fibers. A totally immersive medium must therefore stimulate these receptors for a true sensory experience. Even though haptic feedback is a field that was developed early on in virtual reality, the difficulty in stimulation, as well as the complexity and variability of equipment (e.g. exoskeletons or force feedback arms) have, for the moment, limited access to these technologies apart from dedicated experiments or simple vibrations in a general case. As we wait for new and accessible actuators, this equipment and their cost will undoubtedly allow the development of immersion rooms which will then become the site for the large-scale diffusion of immersive media, like the cinema hall became for films. Finally, all haptic peripheral devices must be associated with user experiences. Due to the heterogeneity of these peripheral devices, there will need to be standardization and higher-level abstraction layers in order to allow artists, for example, to create haptic channels, like we add soundtracks today, without knowing what the user uses or could use at home for the experience.

The concept of immersive media has, however, quite outstripped our current concept of media and of immersion in its strictest sense. It encompasses all the new media that allow the spectator to draw closer to the content, both emotionally and in sensory terms. Thus, interaction with content, personalization and interactions with the surrounding environment are all important components of the experience.

We can also anticipate that immersive media will enter the user's environment, adapting to the particular conditions of their habitat, to offer an experience augmented by a completely personalized mixed reality: the impact of emotionality is then decoupled, as it touches the personal space of the users (see Figure 5.1). Furthermore, the social component is also an essential characteristic of these new media, where individuals may come together for a shared experience, whether they are in the same place or at different sites. Far from isolating users, virtual reality may, on the contrary, bring them together and allow greater sharing, even though, paradoxically at first sight, it does seem to physically separate them. It is also interesting to note that adapting the media to the user's environment already indicates that it will not be limited to entertainment. In section 5.1.4, we will see that virtual reality has the potential to modify the inside of our living spaces and bring in new uses. For example, the quality that is expected from the immersive media could certainly interfere with current parallel developments in teleworking with tools for remote collaboration, thereby consolidating a sustainable virtual reality installation within the house and a potential associated office space.

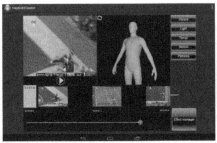

Figure 5.1. *Left: a haptic editor that makes it possible to associate a generic haptic channel with an immersive media. Right: immersive experiences are not only limited to totally immersive experiences, but can also take into account and occupy the user's personal space (© Technicolor). For a color version of this figure, see www.iste.co.uk/arnaldi/virtual.zip*

5.1.3. *Promised experiences*

The variability in immersive media makes it possible to use it for equally varied purposed in the world of leisure and entertainment. We will describe some experiences in different contexts, based on the setting (the house, cinemas or parks) or the content itself (sport, tourism, business).

As immersive media is rolled out, it will gradually enter our homes through gaming consoles, mobile telephones and other access points (e.g. Internet box, smart TVs), with the game becoming the primary vector of these supports. It is already possible to easily convert an empty space in the home into a total immersion space (peripheral devices are available to the general public on the market, which can be used for an area as large as a single room. These sensors allow the real-time tracking in space of a helmet and interaction devices such as controllers). These experiences will only grow richer and richer. While the initial wave of these experiences is spearheaded by games, we can see that content in the form of *films* is also becoming more easily available. This medium corresponds to another industry and although 360° videos are likely to be of limited interest in the long run, the evolution of this media in a convergent form, including technology that is unique to virtual reality (interaction, incarnation) or augmented reality (interaction of virtual content with the real world) makes it possible to produce new experiences where narration and emotion will be at the heart of the media. 360° videos will thus become true virtual reality experiences, being supplemented by the ability to involve the user in the film, thereby allowing interactions with the film itself and, finally, adding a social dimension by using videos of multiple points of view of one scene. This will allow users to see each other as part of the film they are watching (see Figure 5.2). These videos themselves will evolve and become volumetric, initially by covering the parallax in a limited displacement volume – that is, by being capable of moving with respect to objects to perceive their relative position in space (see Figure 5.3) – but in the long run, by completely free navigation. The means for consuming media at home will also evolve in this time, from the use of immersive headsets to more sophisticated and immersive TVs, in experiences that make use of multiple peripheral devices. Finally, virtuality will blend in with reality, offering more extensive experiences associated with TVs that are already in place, whether through augmented reality headsets or mobile devices (phones, tablets). These experiences (e.g. characters coming out of the TV frame and entering the user's living room, additional information, advertisements, extended means of interaction) will take into account the layout of the room, the furniture and the people present in the room, in order to dynamically adapt the content for perfect integration.

Figure 5.2. *A 360° video becomes a social virtual reality experience. On the left: the user is embodied by a character rendered in real life – hand lowered on the right – added to the video. The user's reflection can be seen in the astronaut's helmet – which is completely a part of the video. On the right: a multi-user experience, bringing together users from different points of view, in different forms within the film (Orbit2, © Technicolor)*

Theme parks are an example of successful attempts to immerse spectators within a "brand world". The trend is to make them actors in their own entertainment and, above all, to regularly change attractions. An attraction, such as the Harry Potter world in Disney World, Orlando, costs tens of millions of dollars to create. Thus, virtual reality offers a solution at more manageable costs to modify, enhance and widen these experiences. The first user trials for virtual reality were roller coasters (Six Flags) that combined the mechanical and the virtual. Physical sensations (the car gliding down the tracks) are associated with a virtual universe (which may be reworked any number of times for the same physical trace). This was a way of ensuring coherence between the inner ear sensation and the virtual simulation, thereby eliminating cognitive uneasiness. The economic model is certainly an interesting one, as it allows for great variety without the need to change everything. The bulk of the investment therefore goes into the mechanical part of these rides and their maintenance. What remains now is finding a solution to the problem of recharging the batteries of the (often wireless) peripheral devices or the rate of use (1200 people per hour, in a typical theme park attraction) that puts a great deal of pressure on the attraction and its reliability.

Figure 5.3. *Parallax, illustrated here by the relative movement of one object with respect to others, through a simple lateral translation of the camera. For a color version of this figure, see www.iste.co.uk/arnaldi/virtual.zip*

Furthermore, we are already seeing the rise of virtual reality experience centers – either small, independent structures that have taken the plunge at a reasonable cost (using HMDs and existing games or even using laser games); structures that are already significant in terms of investment, but are new and aim to be large-scale VR centers, such as The Void; or even notable and long-established actors, such as IMAX and its recently launched Imax VR Center. These centers will change and we will be able to enjoy these experiences as easily as we go to the cinema today. These centers promise a level of comfort and immersion that is hard to access at home, in terms of the cost and space required.

There are several immersive experiences that will stand to gain from these new immersive media, and one of the key beneficiaries is most certainly going to be the field of sports. Whether the subject enters the experience as a spectator or as an actor, VR will make it possible to participate in a sporting event "right up close" even while at home. That is, the spectator could be watching with their friends in the stadium, could hang out with the team in the locker room, or sit next to a racing car driver or a cyclist in a race. In the case of active experiences, we could see the emergence of new VR rooms that could transform the boring treadmill, stationary cycle, rowing machine and weight-training into an adventurous and sporting experience. VR can transport a player into another environment, while recounting the history of their field; we have recently seen the first steps taken towards this development. For example, a session of fixed cycling can transform itself into a cycling expedition through a mountain pass in the French Alps; a treadmill session can become a marathon in New York or Paris; bench presses or squats can become a flight over an island. These experiences will need to be sensory experiences, using new haptic equipment that will allow force and physical feedback from the world in which the sportsperson is immersed.

The advent of immersive media makes it possible to shrink the distance between the physical and temporal, thus offering new opportunities for traveling and discovering new cultures. For some years now, museums and tourist sites have offered visitors tablets through which they can visualize audio-visual information or 3D reconstructions of the historical site they are visiting, using augmented reality. This technology can also be used to guide the visitor, give them information on the go and offer recommendations and pre-visualizations of specific sites. It is also possible today to have an immersive experience in a distant site to prepare for a journey or simply discover new places while seated on your sofa. With a VR headset and videos from YouTube, you can walk into the middle of Times Square, swim past the Great Barrier Reef or take a cruise in Croatia. In the near future, we will be able to go even further, move around inside content that is physically distant, interact with this content, enter buildings, etc. Virtual reality will not only become a natural way of planning vacations, but can even become a tempting route to traveling without leaving your house. However, we must be careful: as the immersion is not likely to be total immersion, we can quite rightly ask ourselves if the wonder and happiness these virtual journeys may bring us can truly replace the experience of a real journey.

The line between leisure and consumerism becomes more blurred every day. A large part of our free time is spent searching for objects that we would like to own, whether acquiring them seems realistic or not. VR and AR can offer everyone a chance to project themselves into a world where acquisition and enjoying one's property can be immediate. We can easily replace old furniture by ultra-modern designer furniture, use a virtual mirror to change our clothes into perfectly tailored luxury outfits, or even have a brand new Ferrari constantly parked outside our house. Rather than escaping into a fictional world, we will be able to transform our appearance and our own world as we like. There is no doubt, however, that this new mode of virtual consumption will come at a price.

5.1.4. *Prospects*

The radio slowly became an integral part of most households, as did the television some years later. The technology that we will discuss here offers a much larger variety of interaction and consumption and thus has the potential to settle into and transform our residences through an integrated immersive space. This will make it simpler to communicate and share information with people in another location, to play, receive training or assistance and experience immersive media in its broadest sense. Current TVs offer images of a quality that make them veritable windows onto the content. Their evolution, however, remains limited by their very design. We can thus imagine the appearance of screens that are more immersive and integrated (at first, at least, very large TVs, curved, autostereoscopic, with integrated head-tracking, etc.) or even new means of projection that seek to reproduce holograms of collective imagination, or perfectly integrated devices (capture or tracking systems, for example) – all synchronized with the development of services and content that use these new properties. Just like network sockets (media) have become as standard as electric sockets, it is very possible that that standard house will evolve to integrate immersive systems.

Immersive media produced by private individuals themselves will also become more widespread. Today, we are seeing the early stages of the development of 3D photo booths, which will make it possible to obtain a veritable, static 3D scan of people. These quality services find their echo on simple smartphones with cameras, where the user can begin to digitize objects or their face. Depth sensors will gradually roll out for, and get integrated into, mobile phones, which will improve their ability to capture 3D models. Although, in the short term, all this will be more applicable to the field of entertainment, we can predict that these capturing mechanisms will become easy, of high quality and, above all, standardized. It will therefore be possible to reuse them just like digital photographs, especially the JPEG format. Taking this projection into the future a little further, we can imagine a family meal, where volumetric capture will be facilitated by devices integrated into the house or mobile devices. It would also be perfectly possible, in this context, to watch this scene, this immersive media, several times over from many different points of view so as to be able to re-experience it to the full.

Immersive or not, media creates an emotional link to its content. The creator's objective is to generate this emotion and that of the reporter is to transmit this emotion, whether it be fear, sorrow, joy, surprise, confidence, anger, disgust, etc. Nonetheless, what the user feels (arousal and valence) can differ depending on the individuals. It is thus essential that the emotional loop (action-reaction) be closed; that is, the experience must adapt itself to the spectator's emotional reaction. We must thus be able to measure this affective reaction. Recent progress made with physiological sensors (e.g. body temperature, cardiac rhythm, electrodermal response) and neurological sensors (electroencephalography) opens up the possibilities for technological solutions in this direction, that is, an immersive experience becoming an affective immersive experience.

One of the revolutions in immersive media is related to two emerging challenges: removing the boundaries between the real and virtual, and offering a social and shared experience. We are long past the stage of information and overlaying – we now enter that of augmentation and are guided by real-time technology, Artificial Intelligence, realistic rendering, perfect positioning in the world we are experiencing and perfect analysis of the real scene, towards a world where reality and virtuality become one. We will no longer "only see", we will *be* in this world. Being able to personify this experience at some point and, as described above, involving all our senses, will complete the feeling of perfect immersion. We will then no longer consider augmented reality as separate from virtual reality, but the distinction will be one of degrees – how closely allied are my real and virtual experiences and how deep in space and time? Clearly, these different levels can co-exist. There will certainly be some confusion, perception problems and new behaviors. However, the virtual reality experience will be more complete, truly virtual. Perhaps we will navigate through these experiences in either direction (from the real to the virtual or vice versa), and it may be possible to choose, with a cursor, the state we find most convenient.

Moreover, within this experience, the shared aspect will be of utmost importance. It already existed in the cinema inasmuch as sound and presence (the feeling of having someone in the next seat) allowed us to share the emotion that was experienced. People would scream together, cry together and all this in the same space. But this is still the façade. With immersive experiences, we will share, in the virtual sphere and, in time, in the mixed sphere, a period of entertainment and existence. This will involve a new manner of composing stories, taking into account interactions born out of the fact of sharing the same experience. We will see, we will feel the same thing and as our eyes meet, in that moment of complicity, we will feel all the more alive to the experience. In the middle of the scene unfolding around us, sharing occurs through interaction. Going further, thanks to artificial intelligence, we can imagine that the narrative scene will react and change how it unfolds. Here, we find ourselves in a theatrical space.

A last important prospect that must be mentioned here arises from the dangers of these media and, in particular, the *hacking* of a human. It is difficult to truly understand the impact of immersion today. For instance, virtual reality is used in therapy: for example, the treatment for pain associated with phantom limbs in the case of amputees. In this context, the positive impacts have been recognized as long-term impacts. In another context, when a movie is produced in the industry, it is verified that no properties (especially flashing lights) could trigger an epileptic attack. Conversely, however, many VR experiences today are accessible to anyone and have absolutely no quality control. Generally speaking, the user does not find the use of HMDs and experience consumption neutral by default. The kind of nausea triggered by motion sickness (temporary trouble in the vestibular system, generally related to a confusion over direction when we are moving in a vehicle) does not have the same impact as the nausea associated with seasickness (vestibular system affected, involving a persistent sensation of tilting and/or movement, generally brought about by an air or sea voyage), as the first passes rapidly, while the second can last for months. These negative impacts should not be neglected. However, going further, we can envisage very simply the deliberate use of these effects on a large scale, by persons with malicious intentions. It is thus incumbent on every industry to put in place systems to protect users. This may imply, among other things, the analysis and validation of content, and also monitoring the user's biofeedback. In addition to these security problems, it is also important to consider and study ethical problems (i.e. how far can we go?) and moral issues. These are questions that must be taken up by researchers in the Humanities.

5.2. Brain-computer interfaces

5.2.1. *Brain-computer interfaces: introduction and definitions*

A Brain-Computer interface or BCI can be defined as a system that translates a user's brain activities into commands or messages for an interactive application [CLE 16a, CLE 16b]. An example from the field of virtual reality: a typical BCI may allow a user to move an avatar or virtual object to the left or right, by imagining the movements of the left or right hands [LOT 13]. This is done by measuring the user's brain activity – generally using electroencephalography (EEG)[1], and then processing this by using the system in order to associate a command with a precise pattern of cerebral activity, for example the brain activity resulting from imagining moving the hand. BCI's thus enable a "hands-free" interaction with an application, in fact interaction free of any movement and muscular activity. They are quite quickly showing promise as tools to assist those with severe paralysis and have also recently become a new means of interaction with digital or virtual environments.

There are different types of BCIs: active, reactive or passive [ZAN 11]. With the "active" BCIs, the user must actively carry out a mental task (e.g. imagine moving a hand or carrying out a mental calculation), which will then be recognized from the brain signals and translated into a command to the application. "Reactive" BCIs use the subject's brain responses to a stimulus or

---

1 An EEG measures brain activity in the form of microcurrents present on the surface of the scalp and reflects the synchronized activity of millions of neurons in the cortex, the external layer of the brain.

event. For example, in the video game "MindShooter" [LEG 13] (see Figure 5.4), the wings and nose of a spaceship blink at different frequencies. When the user focuses on one of the wings or on the nose, their EEG signals in the brain areas will change in response to this visual stimulation (flashing) and, most importantly, will synchronize with the stimulation frequency. These signals are called *Steady-State Visual Evoked Potentials (SSVEP)*. They can thus be detected within EEG signals in order to identify which part of the spaceship the user is looking at and move the spaceship to the left, right or have it turn, depending on whether the user is looking at the left wing, the right wing or the nose. Finally, we have "passive" BCIs, which are not used to directly and deliberately control an application; instead, they estimate a user's mental state without the user deliberately sending commands to the application via the BCI. For example, a passive BCI will try to estimate the level of attention a user is paying to the application so as to then adapt the content or appearance of the application accordingly. For instance, if the user is not attentive enough, the application may try to "rouse" them with a specific sound or by varying its content to become more interesting.

Figure 5.4. *MindShooter, a video game inspired by the famous Japanese game "Space Invaders" and controlled here by a reactive BCI using SSVEP [LEG 13]*

5.2.2. *What BCIs cannot do*

In order to forestall fears or unjustified fantasies of BCIs (which happens only too often), it is as important to define what a BCI is *not*, as it is to define what it is, especially specifying what it cannot do! In particular – *BCIs cannot read a user's thoughts* [CLE 16a]! Even though a BCI is able to recognize from a person's EEG signals that they are imagining moving their hand, it is, for the time being, impossible to know what movement this may be. The BCI cannot tell the difference in EEG signals between a user imagining crooking a finger of their left hand at someone or snapping their fingers. In effect, the EEG measures the synchronized activity of millions of neurons and thus offers only a "blurred", noisy and imprecise version of what is really happening in the brain. We can essentially detect a mental state if it involves one (or several) large brain areas. Thus, current BCIs that use EEGs cannot detect what letter you are thinking of, nor the TV channel you would like to watch, nor whether or not you wish to switch on a light, the oven, or draw the blinds. Another important point with respect to BCIs based on the EEG is the influence of muscle contractions or eye movements. In effect, eye movements also generate electric currents (ElectroOculoGram – EOG), as does any muscle contraction (ElectroMyoGram – EMG), especially face and neck muscles, which can also be measured by the EEG sensors [FAT 07]. The EOG and EMG signals thus pollute EEG signals and can prevent the BCI from functioning properly. Unfortunately, these signals are also often a factor of confusion. For example, it is easy to believe that we can recognize from a user's EEG signals that they wanted to switch on a light, when all we have really recognized are movements of the head or eyes as they saw the light, from the EOG or EMG signals measured by the EEG. This is an important point to keep in mind as many commercial products called BCIs, and even some published scientific studies, claim to recognize many mental states from EEG signals, without having verified or proven beforehand that these are not muscular or ocular signals being recognized. At present, BCIs themselves, unfortunately, only allow the recognition of a limited number of mental states.

The rest of this chapter will now explain how BCIs function (section 5.2.3), then discuss the main applications of BCIs (section 5.2.4), and finally offer some future prospects in this field (section 5.2.5).

5.2.3. *Working principle of BCIs*

A BCI works as a closed interaction loop, starting with the measurement of the user's brain activity, followed by processing and classification of the brain signals measured in order to translate them into commands for the application, and ending with feedback sent to the user to indicate that the command has been recognized, so the user can gradually learn to use the BCI optimally. These steps are described below.

5.2.3.1. *Measuring brain activity*

There are many ways of measuring a user's brain activity in a BCI [WOL 06]. The EEG remains the most widely method used today, given its portability, moderate cost and the fact that it is non-invasive. EEG signals are, however, of low quality and chiefly reflect only activity in the cortex, the outside layer of the brain. MagnetoEncephaloGraphy (MEG), which measures brain activity in the form of magnetic currents, can potentially collect brain signals from deeper in the brain, that is, from the cortex and a little way below it. On the contrary, it is a very unwieldy and expensive apparatus and is therefore not used very much in practice. It is also possible to measure brain activity indirectly, by measuring oxygen consumption in the blood in different brain regions. In effect, the more active a brain area is, the greater the consumption of oxygen in order to function. Measuring oxygen concentration throughout the brain will thus enable us to see which regions are active. The oxygen concentration can be measured magnetically, using functional magnetic resonance imaging (fMRI – which also involves very unwieldy and very expensive apparatus, but makes it possible to measure activity throughout brain volume), or optically using near-infrared spectroscopy (NIRS). In effect, the properties of a light ray change depending on the oxygen concentration in the media (here, brain areas) through which it travels. Finally, it is also possible to measure brain activity using invasive sensors, that is, placing them within the skull through a surgical procedure [LEB 06]. These sensors can be placed directly inside the skull, on the surface of the cortex (ElectroCorticoGraphy (ECoG)) or even within the brain, to measure the activity of individual neurons, as mentioned earlier. The signal here is, of course, of a much higher quality, with much greater spatial resolution – however, this requires the user to undergo surgery. For Virtual Reality, EEG is still, by far, the most widely used technique. NIRS is being used more and more and could eventually be coupled with EEG. Finally, several research projects are also working on using fMRI techniques in VR.

5.2.3.2. *Processing and classifying brain signals*

Once brain activity is measured, the brain signals that have been collected must be processed and classified to identify the mental command that the user is sending (e.g. an imagined movement of the left or right hand) and then translate this command to the application. This is generally done by using the *machine learning* method (see [CLE 16a], Chapters 6, 7 and 9). The brain signals are first filtered (using both frequency filtration and spatial filtration) to identify the frequencies (EEG, MEG or ECoG are oscillating signals) and the relevant sensors (i.e. the corresponding brain region) to recognize the user's mental command. For example, to distinguish between an imagined movement of the left hand and an imagined movement of the right hand, we mainly use the frequencies μ (8–12 Hz) and β (16–24 Hz) of the EEG signals, as well as the frequency γ (>70 Hz) of ECoG signals and the sensors located above the motor areas (e.g. two electrodes situated on the left and on the right: C3 and C4 as per the standard international naming system used in EEG). The ideal frequencies and sensors may be identified starting with examples of data, using machine learning. The next step will typically be that of extracting what we call characteristics from the filtered brain signals. These describe the relevant content of the signal, for example the strength of the signal within the frequency bands of interest, or the amplitude of the signal at different time steps. Finally, these characteristics will be fed into an algorithm called a classifier, for example, a linear discriminant analysis (LDA) or a vast margin separator (VMS) that uses data to learn which values for these characteristics correspond to which class, that is, to which mental command. Once this class is identified, it can then be associated with a command, for example turning to the left when the class identified is an imagined movement of the left hand.

5.2.3.3. *Feedback and human learning*

Finally, another important factor for a BCI to function efficiently is the user themselves. In effect, the user must produce a specific pattern of brain activity which will then be recognized by the BCI. Consequently, if the user is unable to generate this pattern, the BCI cannot recognize it. Thus, learning to use a BCI, especially an active BCI using mental image tasks (e.g. imagining a movement, mental calculation) is something that is learnt and develops with training and practice, just like riding a bicycle (see [CLE 16a], Chapter 11). A key element in promoting this learning is the feedback provided to the user. This feedback is typically visual and indicates the mental command that the BCI has recognized so that the user can learn from this feedback and improve.

For example, this feedback may be in the form of a blue bar, which grows in the direction of the mental task that is recognized: to the left, if an imagined movement of the left hand has been recognized, or to the right, if an imagined movement of the right hand has been recognized. The larger the blue bar, the more confident the classifier is in the choice of task recognized. The user must therefore find the right strategy when imagining (e.g. should I imagine a slow movement? a fast one? using all fingers?) so that the bar becomes as large as possible in the right direction each time. This kind of learning technique is, however, still very rudimentary and imperfect, and does not respect basic principles in human learning theories or the psychology of education. Hence, this is an area in which more active research must be carried out [LOT 15].

5.2.4. *Current applications of BCIs*

Historically, BCIs were chiefly developed as tools to aid people with severe motor handicaps, to allow them to communicate, move or interact with their environment. This still remains the major field of application for BCIs, as described in section 5.2.4.1. There is, however, an increasing number of general applications using BCIs, such as the new Human-Machine Interaction (HMI) tool. Section 5.2.4.2 presents a few of the main BCI applications for HMI, chiefly for controlling video games or VR applications, to create HMIs or adaptive VR applications that can react to the user's mental state or, finally, to evaluate the ergonomics and human factors of HMI or VR applications.

5.2.4.1. *Assistive technologies and medical applications*

5.2.4.1.1. Communication

One of the very first applications of BCIs as an assistive tool was as a communication tool to allow severely paralyzed persons to select letters in order to be able to write a text [CEC 11]. The most famous example of a communication system that used BCIs (as well as the most widely used such system) is the "P300 speller". The idea behind the *P300 speller* is to display all the letters of the alphabet on a screen and have them flash up one after the other, or group by group. We then ask the user to count the number of times that the letter they want has lit up. Each time, we can observe a particular brain signal (which is therefore a reactive BCI) called the P300, which follows about 300 ms after a rare and pertinent event, here the fact that the letter the user wants to select has lit up. When the BCI detects this signal, it knows that the letter that just lit up is the letter the user wishes to choose, and it can thus select this letter.

5.2.4.1.2. Prosthetics, armchairs and domotic systems

With the same objective of providing aids to individuals with motor disabilities, BCIs that used EEGs were used to control simple prosthetics, for example opening or closing a prosthetic hand by imagining a movement of the hand [MIL 10]. Recent research on the use of invasive BCIs, using hundreds of electrodes implanted *in* the brain of a paralyzed user has shown that, after many weeks of training with the BCI, she was able to control a robotic arm over 10 degrees of freedom [WOD 14]. Non-invasive BCIs that use EEG have also been used to control wheelchairs: for example, going forwards, turning to the left or right by imagining movements of the feet, the left hand or the right hand, respectively [MIL 10]. Finally, BCIs may also be used for domotic applications. Thus, in [MIR 15], a reactive BCI, similar to the *P300 speller* described earlier, was used to control different domestic appliances such as the television, lights, air conditioner, etc. Different buttons (each button controlling the setting for a domestic appliance, for example to turn on or off the TV) were displayed on the screen and would flash, as with the letters in the *P300 speller*. The user could select them in the same way as earlier – by counting the number of times the desired button lit up, which would provide a P300 that the BCI could detect. This system was tested and validated on patients who were paralyzed.

5.2.4.1.3. Re-education

Finally and most recently, BCIs have shown themselves to be quite promising for post-stroke motor recovery [ANG 15]. In effect, a person who has suffered from a stroke may find themselves partially paralyzed as the stroke may have led to a lesion in the motor area of the brain. In classic re-education, to attenuate this damage, the patient is asked to move the paralyzed limb in order to activate the affected brain area and thus make use of brain plasticity to help in repairing the lesion. Unfortunately, immediately following a stroke, there may be complete paralysis of the limb and voluntary movements may therefore be impossible. This is where BCIs can come in as they can detect EEG signals in the patient if they do try to carry out a movement and if they activate the right motor-related area in the brain. Thus, the BCI may provide the patient with feedback that guides them in activating the brain area affected by the lesion. Clinical studies have shown that this approach did in fact improve the patient's recovery and thus reduced the paralysis [ANG 15].

5.2.4.2. *Human-machine interaction for all*

5.2.4.2.1. Video games and direct interaction in the virtual environment

From the 2000s onwards, and especially with the emergence of electrode helmets for the general public, it became possible to think of applying BCIs to video games and virtual reality [LÉC 08, NIJ 09, LOT 13]. Several proofs of concept trials were carried out in laboratories for video games or virtual environments that would be "steered by the brain" using a BCI [LÉC 08, NIJ 09]. BCIs were successfully used to carry out multiple 3D tasks, such as the selection of 3D targets or controlling virtual navigation [LÉC 08, LOT 13]. We can also take the example of the collaborative research project OpenViBE2 (2009–2013) which brought together French video game professionals and significant actors from academic fields in order to study the future of BCI-based video games (see [CLE 16b], Chapter 5). The main brain signals that can be used with the help of a BCI were tested in the context of a video game and/or direct interaction with a 3D virtual environment: P300, SSVEP (Figure 5.4), imagining movements (Figure 5.5) or even controlling one's concentration/relaxation level (Figure 5.6). During this project, game developers showed a keen interest in brain activity that seemed easier to explain to the user, and to learn, and seemed overall the most robust (the best recognition rates), such as SSVEP. Video games controlled by BCI are, in fact, reality now. Such games are already available for free using the OpenViBE software[REN 10], or for sale on the Internet on the sites of certain EEG-helmet manufacturers.

5.2.4.2.2. Adaptive or passive BCI-based interaction

Furthermore, the possibility of using BCI in a passive manner and thus detecting the user's mental state, not to explicitly control it and direct the application, but rather to adapt the content or the interaction, is an avenue for exploration that presents many advantages, especially for VR (we will speak here of adaptive interaction or implicit interaction) [LÉC 13, ZAN 11]. It was thus possible to propose a proof of concept that illustrated this approach in VR and allowed a virtual training environment through the user's cognitive load (measured directly through the EEG and in parallel to the user's 3D interaction) [LÉC 13]. This consisted of a simulator to train a surgeon in the right surgical gestures to perform a biopsy on a tumor in the liver (Figure 5.7). This simulator used a haptic interface that gave feedback on the insertion force of the needle, and the potential guiding forces activated when the cognitive load was judged to be "too high".

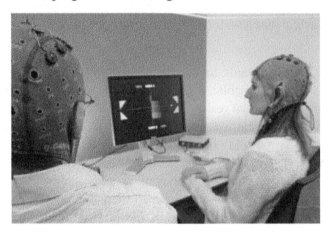

Figure 5.5. *The multi-player BCI game "BrainArena": both players are fitted with EEG helmets and can score goals to the left of right together, or can play against one another, by imagining movements of the left or right hand*

Figure 5.6. *The VR application "Virtual Dagoba": the user is fitted with a wireless EEG helmet and is immersed in an immersion room (Immersia, IRISA/Inria, Rennes) and a 3D scene inspired by the universe of the "Star Wars" films. The user can take the spacecraft up by concentrating (or bring it down by relaxing). For a color version of this figure, see www.iste.co.uk/arnaldi/virtual.zip*

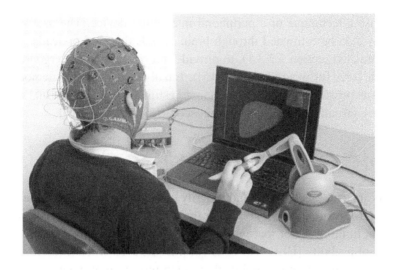

Figure 5.7. *Virtual reality simulator for haptic and BCI-based training: virtual aids (visual and haptic feedback) are activated based on the user's cognitive load and make it possible to guide the user in their task of inserting a needle to carry out a biopsy on a tumor in the liver*

This path considerably eases the constraints on performance in real time and the controllability of the BCI and makes it possible to envisage uses for gaming or VR, fully highlighting the contribution brain signals can make. This is at present a highly promising path for the BCI community in general [ZAN 11]. There are many applications: automatically adapting as a task is carried out, design and error correction, indexing content, entertainment and video games, etc. [GEO 10].

5.2.4.2.3. Neuroergonomics

Finally, without being used to directly interact with an HMI, BCI technology may be used to evaluate these HMIs and their ergonomic pros and cons, with or without VR. The study of the ergonomics of an HMI using neuronal signal analyses and knowledge of neuroscience is called *neuroergonomics* [PAR 08]. For example, by analyzing EEG groups, different groups (among which were our groups at Inria) demonstrated that it was possible to estimate the user's mental load on an ongoing basis during complex interactions, for instance, tasks involving navigation or the manipulation of 3D objects [FRE 17]. This allows us to evaluate how difficult it is to use a technique or a peripheral interaction device. The user's mental load may also be estimated through brain signals detected optically, through NIRS (see also section 5.2.3.1), to provide information on the ergonomics of a cockpit (see, for example, [GAT 15]). Finally, we have also demonstrated how it was possible to use EEG signals to estimate a person's visual comfort when they visualized objects in a stereoscopic display [FRE 17].

5.2.5. *The future of BCIs*

BCIs are a new technology and a highly promising new mode of interaction. However, BCIs often do not go further than the prototype stage in laboratories. The main limiting factor that prevents their practical use outside laboratories is a lack of usability [CLE 16a, CLE 16b]. BCIs, even when invasive, are still not effective enough at this point: they often misinterpret mental commands, not recognizing what the user wishes to communicate. They are also not very efficient, in that it takes time to install, calibrate and learn how to use them. Thus, at present, using BCIs as peripheral devices for direct interaction, to deliberately send commands to an application, is not very useful unless the subject is severely paralyzed. Indeed, other peripheral devices for interaction (e.g. gaze-tracking, controllers, mouse, gesture or speech recognition) will be more effective and efficient.

A major challenge in current research on BCI is therefore to enhance usability. For instance, we could improve the sensors that measure brain activity, the algorithms that process brain signals, or even the manner in which users learn how to control a BCI. There have already been many research projects on the processing of mental signals, but a far smaller number on human learning. We can thus expect greater progress on this front and hope to see BCIs become much more usable. Current methods to train humans, in particular, are the same for all users and in all contexts, and they do not explain to the users why their mental commands were (or were not) correctly recognized. Future training methods will thus be adapted to each user's profile and will also adapt themselves to their skills. They will also explain to the user how to improve their interaction with the system. This should allow users to rapidly acquire better control over many mental tasks and therefore much greater effectiveness and efficiency. Designing a new sensor system which will make it possible to measure brain activity in a non-invasive and portable manner, and with a much higher spatial resolution than with EEGs, will allow for huge progress, even though this is a revolution in itself.

In the coming years, we can expect significant developments of passive BCIs, which will not require as high usability as active BCIs for direct control. There are many potential applications of this kind of technology, especially in VR, to create interfaces, applications and adaptive systems, as well as to evaluate and characterize these systems. We can also foresee more and more applications using BCIs and VR together, as complementary tools. For example, both BCIs and VR are useful and efficient in post-stroke rehabilitation, and combining them seems a natural way of developing new methods for rehabilitation. Combining BCIs and VR also opens up the possibility of studying perception, motor gestures or even human behavior. In effect, VR will enable the creation of controlled and adaptive virtual environments, while the BCIs will be able to estimate the user's mental states (e.g. motor or cognitive) when confronted with these environments. These applications will be of benefit to everyone, not only individuals with severe paralysis, and thus they can potentially go beyond the laboratory and onto the market.

Finally, the availability of EEG sensors for the general public, as well as open-source and free software for designing real-time BCIs, such as OpenViBE [REN 10], facilitate growth, R&D and developments in BCIs, which are now in the hands of the general public (for an example of this, see NeuroTechX[2], an international network open to all). All of this promises significant scientific and technological progress in the field of BCIs, and thus we hope important social progress in the future, especially for virtual reality.

5.3. Alternative perceptions in virtual reality

5.3.1. *Introduction*

In this section, we will introduce how VR technologies may be used to alter users' perceptions. In effect, VR allows us to generate the sensory illusion of an alternative reality: not only can the user be transported to another place, another time, interact with objects or persons who are not physically present

---

2 http://neurotechx.com/

next to them, but using VR they can also feel things that are impossible or even alter their perception of their own body.

The sensory illusion from a VR experience corresponds to the most possible interpretation our brain offers, depending on the sensory stimuli it receives and our earlier knowledge and experience of the world. When the virtual situation *appears* to be the most plausible, then the feeling of *presence* may be generated and the user may react inside the virtual environment as they would in reality (for more details, see Slater [SLA 09]).

Notably, VR offers the possibility of creating sensory conflicts by creating contradictions in the Virtual Environment (VE) between the information reaching the user from several directions. These sensory conflicts may be problematic and certain conflicts must be avoided: for example, simulator sickness or *cybersickness*, both of which affect many users when the application introduces a conflict between the visual and vestibular (or proprioceptive, see section 5.3.4.1) information the user receives. Nonetheless, depending on the devices used to display the VE (e.g. screen, wall of images, HMDs such as the Oculus), it is possible to modify the user's perception (touch, perception of their own body and limbs, or even taste) by manipulating the information displayed and the stimulus felt by the user. We will talk about "pseudo-sensory" effect when a sensory mode strongly disrupts and influences the perception of a stimulus associated with another sensory mode to the extent that it produces a sensory illusion or alternative perception of the reality of the stimulation. Vision is often used to generate pseudo-sensory feedback, as it has been seen that sight very often dominates the other senses, especially when there is conflict between the senses (see, for example, [GIB 33, RAZ 01, BUR 05]).

The best known example of the "pseudo-sensory" effect is that of pseudo-haptic feedback, introduced by Lécuyer *et al.* [LÉC 00], where they wanted to restitute haptic information without using haptic interfaces (e.g. a force feedback arm) in virtual environments. The idea was to modify the visual stimulus perceived by the user in order to simulate haptic sensations.

This section aims to give an overview of how VR can be used to alter a user's perception. We will first look at how user perceptions can be altered in VR using pseudo-sensory feedback. We will then show that it is possible to generate illusions of movement for an immobile user by altering their movement in virtual reality, and thus overcoming the current limitations of VR technology related to movement in the VE. In the final section, we will introduce the concept of alternative perception of our body, and we will see that it is possible not only to modify the perception we have of our own body, thanks to VR technologies, but also to alter some of our behaviors.

5.3.2. *Pseudo-sensory feedback*

In this section, we discuss how the intentional creation of sensory conflicts in VR makes it possible to generate new modes of 3D interactions and new modes of "alternative" perception of the virtual environment in which the user is immersed. We will first present the concept of pseudo-haptic feedback and then extend this concept to other modalities (hearing, taste, etc.).

5.3.2.1. *Pseudo-haptic feedback*

The concept of pseudo-haptic feedback was introduced in 2000 in a pioneering paper by Lécuyer *et al.* [LÉC 00]. The idea was to make use of the properties of human perception and multi-sensory integration – that is, the way in which the human perceptual system integrates and interprets stimuli that come simultaneously from several sensory channels. More specifically, pseudo-haptic feedback was initially introduced by playing on visual feedback coupled with the user's actions. This approach then made it possible to simulate haptic sensations, not by using a dedicated haptic interface, but simple, passive input peripheral devices (e.g. mouse, joysticks, etc.) coupled with visual effects (or coming through any sensory channel other than touch). The pseudo-haptic feedback created a sort of "haptic illusion": the perception of a haptic property that could vary, while the user's real and physical environment remained constant. We will illustrate this approach and this notion of "pseudo-sensory" feedback in virtual reality through several examples, given below.

5.3.2.1.1. Pseudo-haptic sensation through visual feedback

A simple illustration of the concept of pseudo-haptic feedback is that of pseudo-haptic textures or images introduced by Lécuyer *et al.* [LÉC 04] and which consist of simulating tactile sensation of the texture or relief of 2D images as they are explored using a computer mouse.

Figure 5.8 presents the concept of pseudo-haptic texture, which consists of modifying the movement of the mouse cursor based on the information in the image. In effect, the movement of a mouse cursor usually depends directly on the movement of the mouse. To create an alternative sensation, for a pseudo-haptic texture, the speed and movement of the cursor are artificially modified, depending on the contents of the image[3].

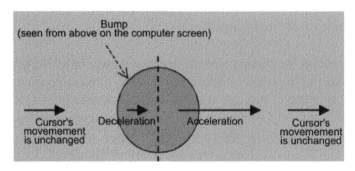

Figure 5.8. *Concept of pseudo-haptic texture: simulation of a bump over which the user moves the mouse cursor*

For example, to simulate a "bump" in an image, we must first reduce the displacement speed of the mouse cursor in order to simulate going up a slope, and then once half the "bump" is covered, accelerate displacement to give the perception of going down a slope. Similarly, we can also simulate a wall by abruptly stopping the movement of the mouse cursor, etc.

As we just saw, the concept of pseudo-haptic feedback consists of using visual feedback to give the user the illusion of a haptic sensation. This idea has primarily been used in the simulation of "basic" haptic properties such as:

– mass: in order to give users the illusion of objects being lighter or heavier than they truly are, Dominjon *et al.* [DOM 05] artificially modified the displacement speed of 3D objects manipulated on the screen by the user;

– friction: simulating resistance during displacement of an object over different surfaces. For example, the object will move more easily on a smooth surface (e.g. marble) than on a rough surface (e.g. sand) (see [LÉC 00]);

----

3 http://www.irisa.fr/tactiles/.

– rigidity: allows the simulation of the degree of hardness or elasticity of objects (see, for example, [LÉC 01]). The idea here is to deform the 3D object based on the force exerted by the user on an input peripheral device (see Figure 5.9);

– torque: in [PAL 04], Paljic *et al.* extended the notion of simulating rigidity to the concept of torque and torsional rigidity and compared the real and pseudo-haptic torsion of springs.

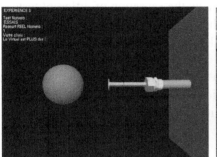 

Figure 5.9. *Simulation of the rigidity of an object through pseudo-haptic feedback [LÉC 00]*

5.3.2.1.2. Pseudo-haptic sensation through auditory feedback

The use of the auditory pathway to evoke pseudo-haptic sensations was proposed in a pilot study [MAG 08]. The results suggested that the sound of a harp or the fact of playing or not playing a sound during the use of a haptic peripheral device could evoke different sensations from those truly received by the user. However, this research remains relatively confidential and the results obtained, even though promising, will need much more investigation into the best way of evoking haptic sensations by playing sounds.

More recently, Serafin *et al.* [SER 10] tried to measure whether users were capable of feeling that they were walking over dips or bumps, just by making them listen to the sound of footsteps on different types of surfaces. In reality, we are able to tell unconsciously whether we are marching on a bump, in a dip or a flat surface, based on the temporal interval between two steps and also based on the time between the instant when our heel touches the ground and that when the tips of the toes touch the ground. Thus, by varying these parameters, researchers were able to impart to participants the sensation of marching on a bump or in a dip, just by making them listen to the sound of footsteps.

5.3.2.2. Pseudo-gustatory feedback and other senses

The concept of pseudo-sensory feedback has also been applied to the sense of taste. The idea was to give participants the sensation of different tastes by changing the visual aspect of what they were eating and using an olfactory feedback system that diffused artificial scents simulating real odors.

Narumi *et al.* [NAR 11] proposed a very innovative approach, which makes it possible to modify the taste of cookies for a user fitted with an HMD and an olfactory feedback system, as shown in Figure 5.10.

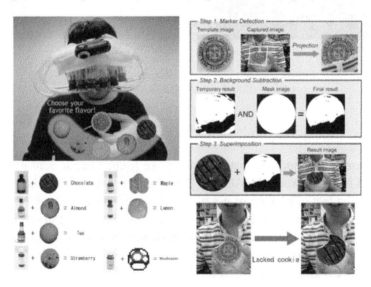

Figure 5.10. *The "Meta Cookie+" system proposed by [NAR 11]. For a color version of this figure, see www.iste.co.uk/arnaldi/virtual.zip*

The idea is to visually modify the appearance of a cookie presented to the user while also diffusing, with the artificial olfactory feedback system, odors that evoked the taste that we wish to simulate. The authors tested different experimental conditions, namely: (i) visual modification of the cookie's appearance alone (we display a chocolate cookie instead of a plain cookie); (ii) olfactory modification alone (we diffuse the smell of chocolate, for instance); (iii) a combination of visual and olfactory stimuli together (we display a chocolate cookie and diffuse an odor of chocolate). The results show that it is possible to modify the perceived taste of the cookie in this way and that the combination of the stimuli (experimental condition (iii)) yielded the best results.

5.3.3. *Alternative perception of movement*

In this section, we will examine how to give a user immersed in a VE the illusion of movement. Here again, the illusion of movement may be obtained by playing on visual stimuli presented to the users.

5.3.3.1. *Introduction*

One of the limitations of VR technologies corresponds to moving around within the VE. In a classic case, the user either physically moves around in the VE (by walking, for example) or they use peripheral devices that allow movement (e.g. controllers). Neither of these solutions is very satisfactory, although for different reasons. The use of the controllers allows the user to move simply and efficiently in large VEs, but they do not induce the sensation of movement in the user (who remains stationary). On the contrary, allowing the user to physically move around in the VR equipment very often limits the size of the VE.

In the rest of this section, we will explain how it is possible to influence the user's perception of their own movement through haptic feedback (see section 5.3.3.2) or even by influencing the movement of the camera in a virtual reality application (see section 5.3.3.3).

5.3.3.2. *Haptic Motion*

By nature, the sensation of mobility is multimodal, as it combines visual, tactile, proprioceptive, vestibular and even auditory information. It is possible to impart a sensation of mobility in VR to a stationary user, by having them visualize a scene in motion on a large screen or in a visioheadset. In effect, the stimulation of peripheral vision can make it possible to induce the illusion of "vection". You have almost certainly experienced this illusion of vection yourself: when in a train at a station and another train right next to yours started moving. In this case, you feel the sensation of moving in the opposite direction to the train that is moving, even though you are completely stationary.

Ouarti *et al.* [OUA 14] showed that it is possible to strongly reinforce the sensation of vection. Their approach, called *Haptic Motion* (see Figure 5.11), uses a force applied to the user's hand, this force being proportional to the acceleration presented in the visual displacement in the scene. By preventing the user from moving (the user's shoulders are held fixed), the authors showed that the reinforced sense of vection, both in terms of intensity as well as duration, was indeed due to haptic feedback and not any vestibular or proprioceptive sensations.

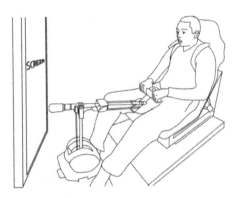

Figure 5.11. *"Haptic Motion": experimental device (taken from [OUA 14])*

With respect to the traditional devices used for movement simulation (mobile seats, for instance), the advantage of "haptic movement" is that it enables us to maintain the illusion of vection over a very long period and to do this in any direction or 3D orientation. This approach therefore offers a strong potential for application in the entertainment industry (theme parks, etc.) and also for VR.

5.3.3.3. *Movement of virtual cameras*

Another way to reinforce the sensation of locomotion in the virtual environment for a user who is stationary is to modify the movements of the virtual camera, for example, to simulate walking. These effects have been used for many years now in first-person video games and their use has also been studied in virtual environments.

The traditionally used approach [LÉC 06] to induce the sensation of walking, by only modifying the behavior of the virtual camera in a VE, is to apply an oscillatory movement to the virtual camera that films a first-person view in VE. This then makes it possible to give the user the sensation of walking by reproducing the characteristic visual flux a human experiences when walking. Using this idea, Terziman *et al.* [TER 13] extended this concept of the movement of a virtual camera in order to also reproduce the motion of running or sprinting. Their method also made it possible to take into account topological changes in the VE (e.g. in the case of a steep climb or descent), and it can be configured to represent different states of fatigue and recovery, based on the morphology of the avatar we wish to depict (e.g. the weight, age and physical condition).

Finally, we have a group of techniques with a slightly different objective. These techniques are collectively known by the generic name "redirected walking". Initially proposed by Razzaque *et al.* [RAZ 01], they also make use of the movements of virtual cameras to alter the user's perception of motion. In the virtual environment, the users can control displacement and the orientation of their point of view, in particular by moving around physically in the VR room. In general, the movements executed in the real world are directly applied to the virtual environment. Thus, the displacements in the VE are constrained by the real dimensions of the VR equipment. The idea behind the "redirected walking" techniques is to manipulate the virtual cameras by amplifying the movements carried out by the user such that the movements carried out in the VE are different from those in the real world. This then makes it possible for users to move around in large virtual environments, despite the fact that the VR equipment is in a much smaller physical space. Thus, Steinicke *et al.* [STE 10] studied the threshold values to apply when amplifying movements in the "redirected walking" techniques. The user ultimately has the impression that they are walking in a straight line over long distances, when in reality they are going around in circles within the physical space.

5.3.4. *Altered perception of one's body*

So far we have seen how VR can be used to modify the user's perceptions of what they perceive in the VE. Thus, VR makes it possible to alter perception in order to reproduce haptic sensation (touch) or even to induce the feeling of movement in a user who is stationary. In this section, we will go further and show how VR also makes it possible to alter the perception that the user may have of their own body and therefore succeed in modifying the user's behavior on completely different aspects, such as racial biases, for example.

5.3.4.1. *Body-ownership illusions*

In this section, we will examine how to influence or alter the perception (conscious or unconscious) that we have of our own bodies, for example, the position and movements of different parts of our bodies. This perception is generally known as proprioception, also referred to as kinesthesia.

VR makes it possible for the user to completely immerse themselves in a VE and to be completely insulated from the real world, including their own body, when HMDs are used. Despite the phenomenon of *body ownership*, which refers to the fact that the perception a person has of their own body is effective and that the bodily sensations they experience are unique (for more details, see [TSA 07, VIG 11]), VR makes it possible to create body-ownership illusions where the perception of our own body is altered. The use of HMDs has enabled a new type of pseudo-sensorial effect, which makes it possible to modify the perception that we have of our own body. We then speak of "body-ownership illusion", an alteration of "body perception", *embodiment* or *virtual body ownership*.

Classic examples of body-ownership illusion (not necessarily from VR) are shown in Figure 5.12. In the "Pinocchio illusion" (Figure 5.12(a)), the biceps of a blindfolded participant are stimulated by vibrations when they touch the tip of their nose. These vibrations, when applied at a particular frequency, induce the illusion of the participant's arm becoming longer, which creates the illusion that the nose and/or the fingers of the participants have also become longer. Figure 5.12(d) shows the famous "Rubber Hand Illusion" [BOT 98, ARM 03]. The participant sees a rubber hand placed before them, while their own hand is out of the visual field. The experimenter stimulates both hands in a synchronous manner and, after a certain time has lapsed (which can vary between participants), the participant experiences perceptual distortion and can no longer tell where his real hand is. They perceive their hand somewhere between the real hand and the rubber hand [BOT 98].

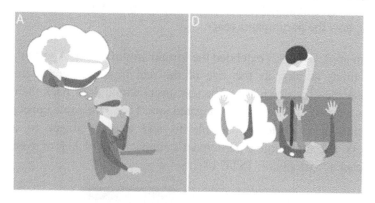

Figure 5.12. *Examples for body-ownership illusions (from [KIL 15]): Pinocchio Illusion (left) and Rubber Hand Illusion (right)*

5.3.4.2. *Altering body perception in VR*

Following the classic "body-ownership illusion" experiments, immersive VR has made it possible to develop new illusions by replacing the participant's body with 3D avatars, 3D models in human forms that may be animated in a coherent manner with the participant's movements using motion-tracking. For more information on the creation of avatars or interactive virtual humans, the reader is invited to refer to Chapter 5 of the *Virtual Reality Treatise*, which is dedicated to virtual humans [FUC 00].

In effect, the combination of motion-tracking and the use of HMDs makes it possible to offer the participant a replacement body, which we will generally call an *avatar*. The use of an avatar, instead of and in place of the real body of the user then makes it possible to create the body-ownership illusions during which it is possible to alter the perception of one's own body.

5.3.4.2.1. Altering a part of one's body in VR

Many laboratory experiments that use similar experimental protocol and installations (in terms of motion capture systems and visual interface) have shown that it is possible to alter the perception of a part of the user's body. Users thus unconsciously "accept" the fact that a modified part of their body is indeed a part of their body. The method used to ensure that this is indeed the case and that the users do not consider the new body or modified body part to be a tool or object that they control is to display, within the VE, a virtual threat and study how the participants react.

Kilteni *et al.* [KIL 12] extended the virtual arm of a user. A virtual limb up to three times as long as the size of the real limb was considered to be accepted as the user's own arm. The test: users would draw back their hand if there was a threat to the virtual, elongated arm. Using the same concept, other experiments have made it possible to add a sixth finger to a user's hand [HOY 16], to enlarge a participant's stomach [NOR 11], or even to give a participant a "virtual tail" [STE 13].

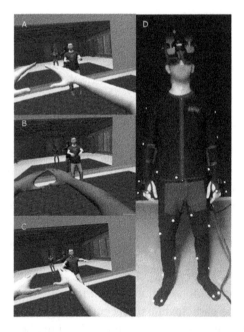

Figure 5.13. *Device used to influence the feeling of virtual incarnation of a participant using an HMD and a motion-tracking system (taken from [BAN 16])*

Similarly, it has also been possible to modify the integral perception that the user has of their body and not just one part. Figure 5.13 shows a VR experience that allows a participant to virtually embody or step into "the skin of another".

Thus, [BAN 13] showed that it was possible to have the adult participants in their experiment embody the virtual body of a 4-year-old child. The results of this experience also showed that once the child's body was accepted, the participants overestimated the size of objects, when compared to users who were not in a virtual body.

Other experiments have made it possible to highlight how powerful VR can be in modifying our perception of our bodies, which is due to our remarkable brain plasticity. It has thus been shown that it is possible to evoke a sense of ownership of a virtual arm with black skin in participants with white (Caucasian) skin [MAI 13] or even of an entire virtual body [PEC 13, KIL 13].

Certain experiments show that virtual incarnation has more profound impacts on the user's behavior. Indeed, Banakou and Slater [BAN 14] showed that when in a virtual avatar, it was possible to give participants the illusion that they had carried out an action that had actually been initiated by their avatar. A female or male avatar pronounced a word in the virtual environment in a higher pitch than the participant's voice. They showed that not only did the participants have the illusion of having pronounced this word, but when speaking they also unconsciously used a higher pitch than their "normal" voice.

5.3.4.2.2. Consequences of altered perception: modification of the participant's behavior beyond the VR experience?

Quite surprisingly, when VR enabled a user's perception to be altered, researchers showed that this modification of perception could have consequences for the user even beyond the VE and in the real world.

As we discussed earlier, it is possible to evoke the feeling of ownership of a virtual body or avatar whose skin color is different from the user's actual skin color. Studies have then showed that it was possible to reduce racial biases in participants by having them embody avatars with different skin colors. Thus, by having participants respond to a questionnaire that evaluated their racial biases a few weeks before and a few weeks after the experiment, [MAI 13, PEC 13] and [BAN 16] showed a significant reduction in this bias among those participants who had virtually taken on an avatar of a different skin color from their own.

Similarly, Yee and Bailenson [YEE 06] demonstrated that negative stereotypes of elderly persons were significantly reduced among participants who had taken on the avatars of elderly persons, as compared to those who took on the avatars of young people. The same authors, in [YEE 07], studied how virtually embodying another avatar can influence participants' interactions with other virtual characters, especially if these were tall or visually appealing.

Kilteni *et al.* [KIL 13] examined how an avatar's physical appearance could influence how the participants played a musical instrument. These researchers showed that participants with darker skin and dressed more casually played the djembe more "creatively" (the frequency and variations in the participants' movements were greater) than those whose avatar had lighter skin and was more formally dressed (in a suit).

Finally, the virtual incarnation of participants was also used to encourage the participants to engage in physical exercise [JAU 14], to reduce anxiety when speaking in public [PER 02, AYM 14] or even to sensitize participants to environmental problems by having them embody animals [AHN 16].

To conclude, it is possible to use VR to evoke a feeling of virtual incarnation, which makes it possible to give participants the illusion that a part of their body or their whole body is modified, and even to observe modification in their behavior that persists outside the virtual environment.

There are, however, a certain number of prerequisites for the function of body-ownership illusions. Petkova *et al.* [PET 11] first spoke of the importance of first-person view in the VE. This was confirmed by Maselli and Slater [MAS 13], who showed that this was a necessary condition for their functioning. In the same article, these authors have also highlighted that these illusions could take place even without using proprioception (i.e. without even asking the user to move) or synchronous visuo-tactile stimulations; that is, simply seeing an avatar in a posture corresponding to that of the user was sufficient to cause the illusion. Nonetheless, they also demonstrated that proprioception and synchronous visuo-tactile cues reinforce the illusion, as is also the case when the virtual avatar resembles the user's body, in terms of cloths and skin color.

5.3.5. *Conclusion*

We have seen varied examples of altered perceptions in VR and seen how it is possible to suggest movements in VR. We have shown how perception of all or a part of one's body can be altered and even that it is possible to observe changes in participants' behavior following VR experiences.

VR thus makes it possible not only to reproduce real and credible stimuli, but also to generate new, altered perceptions, and to study the impact this will have on what the user feels or their behavior. This is an extremely new and rich field of study, which offers very interesting research prospects on ways to alter user perceptions and also on the limits of brain plasticity: how far can we modify the perception we have of ourselves?

The pseudo-sensory effects presented here do not include all human senses and do not discuss all the possible combinations. A question that could then be posed is: do these "gaps" result from a lack of work in the field or are certain combinations impossible? Is it possible to stimulate all the senses in VR and can we simulate everything using only certain senses or should we, on the contrary, use all the senses for a complete simulation? What is or are the relation(s) between the senses? Is there symmetry or anti-symmetry?

As we have seen, it is still difficult, or even impossible, at present to evoke sensations related to certain senses either due to lack of work on the subject (e.g. smell) or due to technical/technological limitations. As we have illustrated all through this section, the concept of pseudo-sensory effect is close to the concept of sensory illusion. Have we arrived here? Can we truly consider pseudo-sensory effects to be an illusion? This question still triggers debates within the scientific community and thus opens the door to new research and experiments on ways to evoke sensations without directly stimulating our sensory receptors.

There are various applications for this technology. There is, of course, entertainment and, more specifically, video games. Furthermore, there is VR training for sports and training in specific sports moves, as well as for re-education and recovery for treating neuropathic pains, such as the phantom limb syndrome, where virtual reality has shown very promising results.

Impacts related to the behavior modification brought about by virtual incarnation (see section 5.3.4.2.2) also seem very promising ways of treating psychological or social problems. However, an important question related to these modifications is: will they persist over time? Current results do not tend to validate this hypothesis; however, is this only because of the relative simplicity of the virtual experiences that we can produce at this point? Current technological limitations will, of course, reduce and we can thus ask ourselves if these modifications will persist longer. In any case, the possibility of modifying behavior through VR raises an important ethical question: can we "manipulate" people's behavior in this way? Studying the ethical aspects of VR is a vast and relatively neglected field at present. We must, however, note the work done by Madary and Metzinger [MAD 16], who have proposed an ethical code governing the use of VR.

5.4. Bibliography

[AHN 16] AHN S.J., BOSTICK J., OGLE E. *et al.*, "Experiencing nature: Embodying animals in immersive virtual environments increases inclusion of nature in self and involvement with nature", *Journal of Computer-Mediated Communication*, vol. 21, no. 6, pp. 399–419, 2016.

[ANG 15] ANG K.K., GUAN C., "Brain–computer interface for neurorehabilitation of upper limb after stroke", *Proceedings of the IEEE*, vol. 103, no. 6, pp. 944–953, 2015.

[ARM 03] ARMEL K.C., RAMACHANDRAN V.S., "Projecting sensations to external objects: evidence from skin conductance response", *Proceedings of the Royal Society of London B: Biological Sciences*, vol. 270, no. 1523, pp. 1499–1506, 2003.

[AYM 14] AYMERICH-FRANCH L., KIZILCEC R.F., BAILENSON J.N., "The relationship between virtual self similarity and social anxiety", *Frontiers in Human Neuroscience*, vol. 8, p. 944, 2014.

[BAN 13] BANAKOU D., GROTEN R., SLATER M., "Illusory ownership of a virtual child body causes overestimation of object sizes and implicit attitude changes", *Proceedings of the National Academy of Sciences*, vol. 110, no. 31, pp. 12846–12851, 2013.

[BAN 14] BANAKOU D., SLATER M., "Body ownership causes illusory self-attribution of speaking and influences subsequent real speaking", *Proceedings of the National Academy of Sciences*, vol. 111, no. 49, pp. 17678–17683, 2014.

[BAN 16] BANAKOU D., HANUMANTHU P.D., SLATER M., "Virtual embodiment of white people in a black virtual body leads to a sustained reduction in their implicit racial bias", *Frontiers in Human Neuroscience*, vol. 10, p. 601, 2016.

[BOT 98] BOTVINICK M., COHEN J., "Rubber hands /'feel/' touch that eyes see", *Nature*, vol. 391, no. 6669, pp. 756–756, 1998.

[BUR 05] BURNS E., PANTER A.T., MCCALLUS M.R. *et al.*, "The hand is slower than the eye: a quantitative exploration of visual dominance over proprioception", *Proceedings of the 2005 IEEE Conference 2005 on Virtual Reality*, VR'05, Washington, DC, USA, pp. 3–10, 2005.

[CEC 11] CECOTTI H., "Spelling with non-invasive Brain-Computer Interfaces - Current and future trends", *Journal of Physiology-Paris*, vol. 105, no. 1, pp. 106–114, 2011.

[CLE 16a] CLERC M., BOUGRAIN L., LOTTE F., *Brain-Computer Interfaces 1: Foundations and Methods*, ISTE Ltd, London and John Wiley & Sons, New York, 2016.

[CLE 16b] CLERC M., BOUGRAIN L., LOTTE F., *Brain-Computer Interfaces 2: Technology and Applications*, ISTE Ltd, London and John Wiley & Sons, New York, 2016.

[DOM 05] DOMINJON L., LÉCUYER A., BURKHARDT J.M. *et al.*, "Influence of control/display ratio on the perception of mass of manipulated objects in virtual environments", *Proceedings of the 2005 IEEE Virtual Reality Conference*, VR 2005, pp. 19–25, March 2005.

[FAT 07] FATOURECHI M., BASHASHATI A., WARD R. *et al.*, "EMG and EOG artifacts in brain computer interface systems: A survey", *Clinical Neurophysiology*, vol. 118, no. 3, pp. 480–494, 2007.

[FRE 17] FREY J., HACHET, LOTTE F., "EEG-based neuroergonomics for 3D user interfaces: opportunities and challenges", *Le Travail Humain*, vol. 80, pp. 73–92, 2017.

[FUC 00] FUCHS P., MOREAU G., DONIKIAN S., *Le traité de la réalité virtuelle Volume 5 : les humains virtuels*, Presse des Mines, Paris, 2000.

[GAT 15] GATEAU T., DURANTIN G., LANCELOT F. *et al.*, "Real-time state estimation in a flight simulator using fNIRS", *PloS One*, vol. 10, no. 3, p. e0121279, 2015.

[GEO 10] GEORGE L., LÉCUYER A., "An overview of research on passive brain-computer interfaces for implicit human-computer interaction", *International Conference on Applied Bionics and Biomechanics*, Venice, Italy, October 2010.

[GIB 33] GIBSON J.J., "Adaptation, after-effect and contrast in the perception of curved lines", *Journal of Experimental Psychology*, vol. 16, no. 1, pp. 1–31, 1933.

[HOY 16] HOYET L., ARGELAGUET F., NICOLE C. *et al.*, ""Wow! I Have Six Fingers!": Would You Accept Structural Changes of Your Hand in VR?", *Frontiers in Robotics and AI*, vol. 3, p. 27, 2016.

[JAU 14] JAUREGUI D. A.G., ARGELAGUET F., OLIVIER A.-H. *et al.*, "Toward "Pseudo-Haptic Avatars": modifying the visual animation of self-avatar can simulate the perception of weight lifting", *IEEE Transactions on Visualization and Computer Graphics*, vol. 20, no. 4, pp. 654–661, 2014.

[KIL 12] KILTENI K., NORMAND J.-M., SANCHEZ-VIVES M.V. *et al.*, "Extending body space in immersive virtual reality: a very long arm illusion", *PLoS ONE*, vol. 7, no. 7, pp. 1–15, 2012.

[KIL 13] KILTENI K., BERGSTROM I., SLATER M., "Drumming in immersive virtual reality: the body shapes the way we play", *IEEE Transactions on Visualization and Computer Graphics*, vol. 19, no. 4, pp. 597–605, 2013.

[KIL 15] KILTENI K., MASELLI A., KORDING K.P. *et al.*, "Over my fake body: body ownership illusions for studying the multisensory basis of own-body perception", *Frontiers in Human Neuroscience*, vol. 9, p. 141, 2015.

[LEB 06] LEBEDEV M., NICOLELIS M., "Brain-machine interfaces: past, present and future", *Trends in Neurosciences*, vol. 29, no. 9, pp. 536–546, 2006.

[LÉC 00] LÉCUYER A., COQUILLART S., KHEDDAR A. *et al.*, "Pseudo-haptic feedback: can isometric input devices simulate force feedback?", *Proceedings of the 2000 IEEE Virtual Reality Conference*, pp. 83–90, 2000.

[LÉC 01] LÉCUYER A., BURKHARDT J.M., COQUILLART S. *et al.*, "Boundary of illusion: an experiment of sensory integration with a pseudo-haptic system", *Proceedings of the 2001 IEEE Virtual Reality Conference*, pp. 115–122, March 2001.

[LÉC 04] LÉCUYER A., BURKHARDT J.-M., ETIENNE L., "Feeling bumps and holes without a haptic interface: the perception of pseudo-haptic textures", *Proceedings of the SIGCHI Conference on Human Factors in Computing Systems*, CHI '04, New York, USA, pp. 239–246, 2004.

[LÉC 06] LÉCUYER A., BURKHARDT J.M., HENAFF J.M. *et al.*, "Camera motions improve the sensation of walking in virtual environments", *IEEE Virtual Reality Conference (VR 2006)*, pp. 11–18, March 2006.

[LÉC 08] LÉCUYER A., LOTTE F., REILLY R. *et al.*, "Brain-computer interfaces, virtual reality and videogames", *IEEE Computer*, vol. 41, no. 10, pp. 66–72, 2008.

[LÉC 13] LÉCUYER A., GEORGE L., MARCHAL M., "Toward adaptive VR simulators combining visual, haptic, and brain-computer interfaces", *Computer Graphics and Applications*, vol. 33, no. 5, pp. 18–23, 2013.

[LEG 13] LEGÉNY J., VICIANA ABAD R., LÉCUYER A., "Toward contextual SSVEP-based BCI controller: smart activation of stimuli and controls weighting", *IEEE Transactions on Computational Intelligence and AI in games*, vol. 5, no. 2, pp. 111–116, 2013.

[LOT 13] LOTTE F., FALLER J., GUGER C. *et al.*, "Combining BCI with virtual reality: towards new applications and improved BCI", in ALLISON B.Z., DUNNE S., LEEB R. *et al.* (eds), *Towards Practical Brain-Computer Interfaces*, Springer, Berlin-Heidelberg, 2013.

[LOT 15] LOTTE F., JEUNET C., "Towards improved BCI based on human learning principles", *3rd International Brain-Computer Interfaces Winter Conference*, Sabuk, South Korea, 12–14 January 2015.

[MAD 16] MADARY M., METZINGER T.K., "Real virtuality: a code of ethical conduct. Recommendations for good scientific practice and the consumers of VR-technology", *Frontiers in Robotics and AI*, vol. 3, p. 3, 2016.

[MAG 08] MAGNUSSON C., RASSMUS-GRÖHN K., "A pilot study on audio induced pseudo-haptics", *Proceedings of the International Haptic and Auditory Interaction Design Workshop*, pp. 6–7, 2008.

[MAI 13] MAISTER L., SEBANZ N., KNOBLICH G. *et al.*, "Experiencing ownership over a dark-skinned body reduces implicit racial bias", *Cognition*, vol. 128, no. 2, pp. 170–178, 2013.

[MAS 13] MASELLI A., SLATER M., "The building blocks of the full body ownership illusion", *Frontiers in Human Neuroscience*, vol. 7, p. 83, 2013.

[MIL 10] MILLÀN J. D.R., RUPP R., MÜLLER-PUTZ G. *et al.*, "Combining Brain-Computer Interfaces and Assistive Technologies: State-of-the-Art and Challenges", *Frontiers in Neuroprosthetics*, vol. 4, no. 161, 2010.

[MIR 15] MIRALLES F., VARGIU E., RAFAEL-PALOU X. *et al.*, "Brain–computer interfaces on track to home: results of the evaluation at disabled end-users' homes and lessons learnt", *Frontiers in ICT*, vol. 2, p. 25, 2015.

[NAR 11] NARUMI T., NISHIZAKA S., KAJINAMI T. *et al.*, "*Meta cookie+: an illusion-based gustatory display*", pp. 260–269, Springer, Berlin-Heidelberg, 2011.

[NIJ 09] NIJHOLT A., PLASS-OUDE BOS D., REUDERINK B., "Turning shortcomings into challenges: brain-computer interfaces for games", *Entertainment Computing*, vol. 1, no. 2, pp. 85–94, 2009.

[NOR 11] NORMAND J.-M., GIANNOPOULOS E., SPANLANG B. *et al.*, "Multisensory stimulation can induce an illusion of larger belly size in immersive virtual reality", *PLoS ONE*, vol. 6, no. 1, pp. 1–11, 2011.

[OUA 14] OUARTI N., LECUYER A., BERTHOZ A., "Haptic motion: Improving sensation of self-motion in virtual worlds with force feedback", *Haptics Symposium (HAPTICS)*, 2014.

[PAL 04] PALJIC A., BURKHARDT J.-M., COQUILLART S., "Evaluation of pseudo-haptic feedback for simulating torque: a comparison between isometric and elastic input devices", *Proceedings of the 12th International Conference on Haptic Interfaces for Virtual Environment and Teleoperator Systems*, HAPTICS'04, Washington, DC, USA, pp. 216–223, 2004.

[PAR 08] PARASURAMAN R., WILSON G., "Putting the brain to work: neuroergonomics past, present, and future", *Human Factors*, vol. 50, no. 3, pp. 468–474, 2008.

[PEC 13] PECK T.C., SEINFELD S., AGLIOTI S.M. *et al.*, "Putting yourself in the skin of a black avatar reduces implicit racial bias", *Consciousness and Cognition*, vol. 22, no. 3, pp. 779–787, 2013.

[PER 02] PERTAUB D.-P., SLATER M., BARKER C., "An experiment on public speaking anxiety in response to three different types of virtual audience", *Presence: Teleoperators and Virtual Environments*, vol. 11, no. 1, pp. 68–78, 2002.

[PET 11] PETKOVA V., KHOSHNEVIS M., EHRSSON H.H., "The perspective matters! multisensory integration in ego-centric reference frames determines full-body ownership", *Frontiers in Psychology*, vol. 2, p. 35, 2011.

[RAZ 01] RAZZAQUE S., KOHN Z., WHITTON M.C., "Redirected walking", *Eurographics 2001 - Short Presentations*, Eurographics Association, 2001.

[REN 10] RENARD Y., LOTTE F., GIBERT G. *et al.*, "OpenViBE: an ppen-source software platform to design, test and use brain-computer interfaces in real and virtual environments", *Presence: Teleoperators and Virtual Environments*, vol. 19, no. 1, pp. 35–53, 2010.

[SER 10] SERAFIN S., TURCHET L., NORDAHL R., "Do you hear a bump or a hole? An experiment on temporal aspects in footsteps recognition", *Proceedings of Digital Audio Effects Conference*, pp. 169–173, 2010.

[SLA 09] SLATER M., "Place illusion and plausibility can lead to realistic behaviour in immersive virtual environments", *Philosophical Transactions of the Royal Society of London B: Biological Sciences*, vol. 364, no. 1535, pp. 3549–3557, 2009.

[STE 10] STEINICKE F., BRUDER G., JERALD J. *et al.*, "Estimation of detection thresholds for redirected walking techniques", *IEEE Transactions on Visualization and Computer Graphics*, vol. 16, no. 1, pp. 17–27, 2010.

[STE 13] STEPTOE W., STEED A., SLATER M., "Human tails: ownership and control of extended humanoid avatars", *IEEE Transactions on Visualization and Computer Graphics*, vol. 19, no. 4, pp. 583–590, 2013.

[TER 13] TERZIMAN L., MARCHAL M., MULTON F. *et al.*, "Personified and multistate camera motions for first-person navigation in desktop virtual reality", *IEEE Transactions on Visualization and Computer Graphics*, vol. 19, no. 4, pp. 652–661, 2013.

[TSA 07] TSAKIRIS M., HESSE M.D., BOY C. *et al.*, "Neural signatures of body ownership: a sensory network for bodily self-consciousness", *Cerebral Cortex*, vol. 17, no. 10, p. 2235, 2007.

[VIG 11] DE VIGNEMONT F., "Embodiment, ownership and disownership", *Consciousness and Cognition*, vol. 20, no. 1, pp. 82–93, 2011.

[WOD 14] WODLINGER B., DOWNEY J., TYLER-KABARA E. *et al.*, "Ten-dimensional anthropomorphic arm control in a human brain- machine interface: difficulties, solutions, and limitations", *Journal of Neural Engineering*, vol. 12, no. 1, p. 016011, 2014.

[WOL 06] WOLPAW J., LOEB G., ALLISON B. *et al.*, "BCI meeting 2005–workshop on signals and recording methods", *IEEE Transaction on Neural Systems and Rehabilitation Engineering*, vol. 14, no. 2, pp. 138–141, 2006.

[YEE 06] YEE N., BAILENSON J., "Walk a mile in digital shoes: The impact of embodied perspective-taking on the reduction of negative stereotyping in immersive virtual environments", *Proceedings of PRESENCE 2006: The 9th Annual International Workshop on Presence*, August 2006.

[YEE 07] YEE N., BAILENSON J., "The proteus effect: the effect of transformed self-representation on behavior", *Human Communication Research*, vol. 33, no. 3, pp. 271–290, 2007.

[ZAN 11] ZANDER T., KOTHE C., "Towards passive brain-computer interfaces: applying brain-computer interface technology to human-machine systems in general", *Journal of Neural Engineering*, vol. 8, 2011.

6

The Challenges and Risks of Democratization of VR-AR

6.1. Introduction

After over 50 years of research and development of applications for primarily professional purposes, virtual reality is finally accessible to everyone. Recent changes in equipment, especially in the so-called "VR" headsets, have led to a change in meaning of the very expression "virtual reality". In effect, we often read that it is sufficient to use VR equipment to "make" virtual reality. In other words, it seems fair to ask ourselves whether using such equipment is necessary and sufficient to implement a VR application. The response is obviously a resounding *no*. Indeed, this type of equipment, which we will call "HMD" in the rest of this section, is first and foremost only a display device with which to see images.

To understand the impact that the use of HMDs has had, it is necessary for us to understand the user's sensorimotor functioning, especially that of vision. Indeed, this invasive visual interface applies to any user and their usage has consequences for the other senses and on the user's motor actions. In order to provide a basic understanding of sensorimotor functioning in humans, it is useful to go over some fundamental concepts. First, our senses allow us to perceive the world around us and also to perceive ourselves [FUC 16]. This reality has a strong influence on the understanding of problems and solutions for the optimal use of HMDs. Let us recall that even though human vision

Chapter written by Philippe FUCHS.

plays a fundamental role in VR, it is very important to take into account the other senses that must be studied, such as hearing, skin sensitivity and proprioception. Skin sensitivity is sensitivity to pressure, vibrations and temperature, while proprioception is the sensitivity to position in space, movements of the body and force exerted by muscles, and allows us to be conscious of our own movements. It is orchestrated by sensors situated on muscles, tendons and articulations, in the vestibular system, the inner ear and, last but not least, by vision.

For a more detailed study of the sensorimotor aspects of human beings, the reader can refer to Philippe Fuchs' book [FUC 16], as well as Volume 1 of *The Virtual Reality Treatise* [FUC 05].

In any VR application, the human is immersed in and interacts with a virtual environment (VE); they perceive, decide and act according to a classic process represented by the "perception, decision, action" (PDA) loop (see Figure 6.1). This loop must be implemented despite the technological, physiological and cognitive constraints we will examine further down.

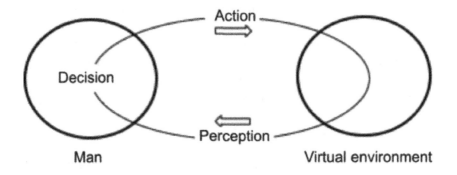

Figure 6.1. *The classic "perception, decision, action" loop*

The insertion of sensory, motor and/or sensorimotor interfaces disrupts the PDA loop, or rather PDA loops, as the working of each of the senses uses an independent PDA loop (see Figure 6.2). The app designer's talent thus lies in controlling these disruptions through a judicious choice of elementary interactions, appropriate devices and efficient software aids to facilitate the user's behavior in the VE.

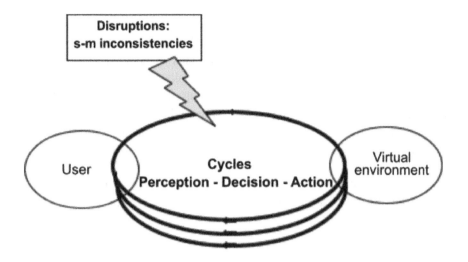

Figure 6.2. *Sensorimotor incoherences disrupt the level
of immersion and sensorimotor*

Three fundamental VR problems can be seen in the diagram in Figure 6.2. These must be addressed by the application designer:

– *The analysis and modeling of human activity in VE*: how does a user fitted with an HMD behave when confronted with sensorimotor inconsistencies in a virtual world?

– *Implementing immersion and interaction*: which are the interfaces and interaction techniques that generate these inconsistencies?

– *Modeling and realizing the VE*: what are the tools and algorithms that limit the nuisance of these artifacts?

This section aims to remind app designers and developers of the basic rules to respect in order to produce efficient applications that can, among other things, offer users a sufficiently high adaptability *vis-à-vis* artificial immersion. In effect, we must constantly keep in mind that these technologies, by their very nature, disrupt the user's physiological and sensorimotor functioning. For example, stereoscopic vision creates sensorimotor inconsistencies between the accommodation and vergence of the eyes. This incoherence has been widely known and documented over a very long time by specialists in the field; let us recall that this was discussed in section 3.4 of this very book. With the recent large-scale development of HMDs, there is still limited feedback received from the general public on the experience of using it. To guard against the lack of detailed studies, certain HMD manufacturers warn about the possible risks associated with the use of their products and do not recommend using them below a certain age. Nonetheless, the question of the level of adaptation of a human being faced with this visual immersion in a virtual world remains open. Certain users will be more sensitive than others and we do not really know why.

We will now discuss the problems that could result from the use of HMDs before we put forward a few solutions.

6.2. Health and comfort problems

6.2.1. *The different problems*

The use of HMDs, by nature, poses problems of comfort and health. These problems may be induced by applications, creating discomfort that is mainly due to:

– the user's psychological activity being disrupted in the VE: it is highly probable that in the future, the use of HMDs by general users will intensify, for leisure as well as gaming activities. In the context of use related to panoramic photographs or 360° videos, the device must be used for relatively short periods to minimize the risk of addiction. On the contrary, when used for video games, the player may use HMDs for several hours. In the latter case, psychological consequences may be seen following prolonged immersion. A fundamental question arising from this: is an HMD likely to increase addiction to video games? This question, which must be answered by psychologists and psychiatrists, has not yet been debated, as the practice is not yet widespread;

– a poor interfacing between the visual system and the HMD: when using an HMD, the user will observe a virtual scene via an optical device which has very few customizable settings to adapt to the user's morphology and is not perfectly adapted to their visual characteristics, which can provoke ophthalmological problems.

This becomes all the more important when we consider that a large section of the population already suffer from ophthalmological deficiencies: in China, for example, the incidence of myopia among adolescents is close to 90% today [DEL 15]. In addition, the few optical adjustments that are available, as well as the rare calibration protocols, such as [PLO 15], are very rarely checked for quality or, in any case, are very rarely used by professionals;

– another ophthalmological impact, perhaps the most constricting, concerns prolonged exposure to certain wavelengths, corresponding to blue light (from 515 to 555 nanometers) emitted by the screens of an HMD. These may cause long-term damage (risk of AMD – Age-related Macular Degeneration);

– unsafe technological devices: the main safety issue resides in the visual and, in some cases, acoustic isolation of the user wearing an HMD.

How do we remedy the absence of direct vision of the real environment, especially if it is dynamic during the running of the application? The user's physical safety will be particularly compromised if they are standing in a room rather than sitting in a fixed seat. In effect, the visual and acoustic isolation prevents them from being alert to what is happening in the real environment;

– sensorimotor incoherences: VR techniques induce incoherences almost systematically, whether for a single sense (such as the incoherence between accommodation and vergence of the eyes in stereoscopic vision, already mentioned in this chapter), or between several senses (e.g. locomotion on a treadmill resulting in perceptual incoherence between vision and the vestibular system), or between the senses and motor responses (e.g. manipulating virtual objects without force feedback). In the real world, the set of sensory stimuli received is used by an individual to construct a coherent representation of their environment. In the virtual world, the user seeks this same coherence and will interpret what he perceives with respect to what he experiences, despite the sensorimotor incoherences. The rest of this section focuses specifically on the study of sensorimotor incoherences.

6.2.2. *Sensorimotor incoherences*

Sensorimotor incoherences are of many different kinds. The type most frequently seen is latency (see section 3.4), which can cause the user discomfort in their activity in the VE by creating a lag between the visual feedback resulting from their own actions. This latency is caused by technological performance (insufficient computing power or communication power). In a multi-sensory context, there is the additional difficulty of having to synchronize latencies between senses in order to make them coherent.

In certain classic and well-documented cases, we know from experience that the user can adapt to certain incoherences, consciously or unconsciously, and some of these adaptations are almost naturally made. This is the case, for example, with virtual movement in front of a small computer screen or game console. In effect, this creates a visuo-vestibular incoherence where, despite a (virtual) movement in the VE, the user remains stable in the real environment, in perfect coherence with their peripheral vision (anchored in the real world) and their vestibular system, thereby creating an incoherence with their central vision.

It is rare to see users having difficulty in adapting to this case of a virtual movement in front of a screen that does not cover their peripheral vision. The use of an HMD represents a problem of quite different complexity, which we will describe further on.

Apart from the visuo-vestibular incoherences, there are a large number of sensorimotor incoherences that we will classify by type in order to structure our analysis. The objective is to propose recommendations to VR application designers in order to enhance user comfort. We have chosen to focus on disruptive incoherences (there are indeed some beneficial ones, whose study is beyond the scope of this section), which will be presented in three classic VR interaction paradigms: observation, navigation and manipulation.

6.2.2.1. *Observation*

– Temporal visuo-motor incoherence: a problem resulting from latency between the movement of a user's head and the display on the HMD screen from the point of view that would result from the movement. This incoherence is not very disturbing and can even be imperceptible if it is lower than one-twentieth of a millisecond, which is now the case in some recent HMDs. If this is not the case, the user perceives delayed movement, which may be out of sync by a few milliseconds with what the vestibular system detects, causing gaze instability [STA 02].

– Visuo-temporal incoherence: there is disruptive incoherence if the frequency of the displayed images (FPS: frames per second) is too low when compared to the visual system's requirements for perceiving images without flickering and with continuous movements of the objects in motion. This does not depend on retinal persistence, but on neurophysiological mechanisms such as the phi phenomenon and beta movement.

– Oculomotor incoherence: in stereoscopic vision, the "accommodation–vergence" incoherence becomes a problem if the retinal disparities that the user has to contend with, exceed a certain limit (of the order of 1.5°), which is a function of exposure time and the user's visual capacities, among other things. Some people are so sensitive to this incoherence that they are unable to even fuse together and view these kinds of images.

– Visuo-spatial incoherence: a disruptive incoherence is created if the HMD's field of vision is different from the field of vision of the camera filming the VE. Certain designers use this trick to artificially increase the user's field of vision: most HMDs offer a very small horizontal field of vision, of the order of 100°, as compared to the horizontal human field of vision, with eyes and head unmoving, of 180°.

– Visuo-motor incoherence in positioning: the movement of the head in the real environment is a command for a visual rotation in the VE which may be different as the sensor is imprecise with rotations because it does not measure translations. If this is the case, it cannot detect the small translations of the head which may exist even when the observer is standing or sitting relatively still.

– Spatial visuo-motor incoherence: the designer of a VR application may wish to program an unnatural visual observation:

- an amplification of the virtual rotation, with respect to the rotation of the head, to allow the user to see across a larger field of vision without turning their head too much;

- an amplification of virtual translation, with respect to the translation of the head, to allow the user to artificially see their movement;

- or, even more disruptive, the point of view displayed does not at all correspond to the point of view from the user's head, for example, for a "third-person view" of the VE (or objective view). The observer sees their avatar (the representation of their own self) in the VE. The observer may watch themselves or look elsewhere. The point of view may also be that of a virtual character, for example the person opposite the observer.

6.2.2.2. *Navigation*

– Visuo-vestibular (or visuo-proprioceptive) incoherence: this is the classic case of virtual displacement by vection, without the real displacement of the user. This incoherence is well known and constitutes one of the kinds of "simulator sickness" discussed in section 3.4. This affects the user when they exceed a certain kinematic limit of displacement. Regardless of the mode of navigation, including walking on a treadmill, and despite the proprioception of real walking being coherent with the virtual displacement, the fact remains that the vestibular system is wrongly stimulated as the user is stationary in the real environment.

– Visuo-postural incoherence: this is when the user remains standing and stationary in the real environment, although they are moving in the VE by vection. The user must control their vertical posture despite the perceptual incoherences. The vestibular system and proprioceptive stimuli indicate to the brain that the body is stationary.

6.2.2.3. *Manipulation*

– Visuo-manual incoherence: if there is a gap between the location of the user's real hand and the virtual hand represented in the HMD (due to technical reasons, for example), then there is a visuo-manual incoherence. In certain cases, the user may adapt to this, for instance, by interacting in an unnatural manner using "teleoperation" (i.e. the remote manipulation of a virtual object).

The first five disruptive incoherences for observation (visual), even though they are not all specific to HMDs, are all due to technical difficulties in making HMDs that are "perfect enough" (latency, image display frequency, stereoscopic screens without oculomotor incoherences, large fields of vision and precise head tracking). In cases where the visual observation is unnatural or unreal, the disturbances are experienced much more strongly by the user. The causes of sensorimotor disruptions are either due to technical problems or due to the unnatural, unreal interaction paradigms imposed by the app designers.

6.3. Solutions to avoid discomfort and unease

6.3.1. *Presentation of the process*

How do we remedy technical inadequacies in current HMDs? In our study, we analyzed each sensorimotor incoherence independently in order to simplify the task. However, in a general case, the coupling between the senses may interfere. For each disruptive, sensorimotor incoherence, it is possible to ask the following questions:

– How can we mitigate the impact of the sensorimotor incoherence has on the user's discomfort or uneasiness?

– Is it possible to remove the sensorimotor incoherence by modifying the working of the interaction paradigm?

– Can we remove the sensorimotor incoherence by modifying the functioning of the interface or by adding another interface?

– How can we adapt to the incoherence so as to do away with discomfort or uneasiness?

The first three questions are applicable to all cases of incoherence, while the question on adaptation must be globally studied as there is, at present, no specific research on adaptation to such-and-such a sensorimotor incoherence. Over 30 solutions have been presented in Philippe Fuchs' book [FUC 16], which is dedicated to HMDs. In this section, we have chosen just a few of them.

6.3.2. *Mitigation of the impact on visuo-vestibular incoherence*

Taking the classic case of virtual displacement by vection, without any real movement by the user, the incoherence disturbs the user when certain kinematic limits of movement are exceeded. We present a few solutions that may be complementary to each other:

– in order to limit the involvement of the vestibular system, we must minimize accelerations in translation and rotation, the tilting of the movements of the virtual camera (the point of view of the user in the virtual environment) and trajectories of the virtual camera which are too winding (relatively high bending radii);

– the perception of movement is most sensitive on the periphery of the visual field, detecting optical flux due to movements of vection and the movement of objects in the scene. We can envisage either reducing the observed field of vision by the occultation of images in peripheral vision, or attenuating the incoherence by injecting some spatial references from the real environment into images in peripheral vision, in order to stabilize the user (this solution, however, is detrimental to visual immersion), or even having objects in the VE that are immobile with respect to the real environment. In this last case, the classic example is that of a static driving simulator: the driver is well stabilized if the driving cabin is in their peripheral vision, as this is immobile in the real environment;

– in extending the above solution, it may be interesting to use an HMD with a visor that does not completely occlude vision: "video-glasses" that would allow the user to directly perceive the real environment in peripheral vision. In these conditions, the disruptive effects of visuo-vestibular incoherences are greatly attenuated, as if we were looking at a simple screen.

6.3.3. *Removing visuo-vestibular incoherence by modifying the functioning of the interaction paradigm*

Three different solutions may be used:

– if the real displacement of the person, who is standing in the real environment, is geometrically the same as the displacement in VE, then the trajectories and speeds in both environments are always the same. The constraint in this case is that both environments, real and virtual, must be of the same dimensions. The displacement in the VE must be identical and limited by the dimensions of the real room. This implies coherence between the visual stimuli, the stimuli for the vestibular systems and also other proprioceptive stimuli (neuromuscular spindles, the Golgi apparatus and articular receptors), the gestures in the VE being identical to the real environment;

– if the displacement in VE is carried out through the teleportation from one place to another, while the user remains stationary in the real world, then the continuous movements are removed and the vestibular system is no longer called into play as there is no longer any speed or acceleration. In this case, both senses are coherent thanks to the immobility of the person in the real and virtual environment. The user virtually goes from the starting point to the destination instantaneously. However, the visual transition from the point of view at the point of origin to that at the destination may be carried out in a fade-out to smoothen the effect of the teleportation;

– a radical solution is using augmented reality. This then requires that both real and virtual environments be geometrically identical, as they are overlapping. In this case, there is no longer incoherence! This technically requires using an AR headset. The user sees the real world, which stabilizes them even better thanks to their peripheral vision, which is based on the real environment, as it is technically impossible at present to display images in peripheral vision in AR headsets.

6.3.4. *Removing visuo-vestibular incoherence by modifying interfaces*

We have two different solutions in this category. Incoherence may be removed by materially recreating the right stimuli to the vestibular systems by using an interface with motion simulation (1D or 2D treadmill). The acceleration and incline stimuli to the user's body must, if possible, constantly match the visual movements (vection) of the user:

– with an interface with motion simulation, not only is the vestibular system involved, but so are the proprioceptive organs: muscles, tendons and joints (e.g. for effective walking), which must also be coherent. Following the desired virtual movements, we must determine a good interface with motion simulation, one which can create the right stimuli for the vestibular systems. Sometimes, there is no realistic solution, independent of the price of the interface;

– with an interface that involves walking on a 1D or 2D treadmill, the proprioceptive organs (muscles, tendons and joints) may be correctly stimulated to reduce incoherences, but the vestibular system is not (correctly) brought into play. The visuo-proprioceptive incoherences are reduced in this case (proprioception, globally), but visuo-vestibular incoherences are still present. We must take them into account and use a solution that makes it possible to attenuate visuo-vestibular incoherences.

6.3.5. *Levels of difficulty in adapting*

The question of the user adapting to immersion and interaction in a VE is much larger than only adapting to sensorimotor incoherences to avoid discomfort and uneasiness. In effect, the following four points must be considered:

– physiological adaptation to the visual interface, such as an HMD;

– cognitive adaptation to the interfacing;

– functional adaptation to the interaction paradigms;

– adaptation to sensorimotor incoherences.

6.4. Conclusion

In conclusion, an analysis of disruptive sensorimotor incoherences enabled us to propose, in specific contexts, solutions that would at least be able to attenuate the negative effects on the user's comfort and health. Some solutions depend on integrated technological progress in HMDs, while others have already been experimentally validated and some have yet to be explored. It is necessary to plan future experimentation in order to validate new solutions for the use of HMDs by the general public. Our analysis was based on the consideration of sensorimotor disturbances, with the aim of enhancing the user's comfort and health. This analysis is limited, however, as each incoherence was considered to be independent of the others and the postulated hypotheses must still be supported and validated.

Given the risks of a VR application's impact on a user's health and comfort, we can understand why HMD manufacturers put out recommendations restricting the use of their products. The main recommendations concern taking breaks when using the device, stopping in the case of uneasiness and not carrying out any physically complex tasks such as driving a car after a VR experience using an HMD. It is forbidden for children younger than 13 years of age to use an HMD. In the near future, it will be important to define precise rules for the use of HMDs and study any long-term effects they may have on all users, especially children, if the use of HMDs is going to become widespread. In France, the ANSES (The National Agency for Food, Environmental and Occupational Health & Safety – *Agence Nationale de la Sécurité Sanitaire de l'Alimentation, de l'environnement et du travail*) will study the potential impact of the use of virtual reality on health and will then issue recommendations. The content of VR applications must also be mastered and controlled, with warning messages if needed, as is already being done by several HMD manufacturers.

6.5. Bibliography

[CRU 92] CRUZ-NEIRA C., SANDIN D.J., DEFANTI T.A. *et al.*, "The CAVE: audio visual experience automatic virtual environment", *Communication ACM*, vol. 35, no. 6, pp. 64–72, ACM, June 1992.

[DEL 15] DELGIN E., "The myopia boom", *Nature*, no. 519, pp. 276–278, 2015.

[FRE 14] FREY J., GERVAIS R., FLECK S. *et al.*, "Teegi: tangible EEG interface", *Proceedings of the 27th Annual ACM Symposium on User Interface Software and Technology*, pp. 301–308, ACM, New York, USA, 2014.

[FUC 05] FUCHS P., MOREAU G. (eds), *Le Traité de la Réalité Virtuelle*, 3rd edition, Les Presses de l'Ecole des Mines, Paris, 2005.

[FUC 09] FUCHS P., MOREAU G., DONIKIAN S., *Le Traité de la Réalité Virtuelle Volume 5 – Les Humains Virtuels*, 3rd edition, Mathématique et informatique, Les Presses de l'Ecole des Mines, 2009.

[FUC 16] FUCHS P., *Les casques de réalité virtuelle et de jeux vidéo*, Mathématiques et informatique, Les Presses de l'Ecole des Mines, 2016.

[JON 13] JONES B.R., BENKO H., OFEK E. *et al.*, "IllumiRoom: peripheral projected illusions for interactive experiences", *Proceedings of the SIGCHI Conference on Human Factors in Computing Systems*, pp. 869–878, ACM, New York, USA, 2013.

[JON 14] JONES B., SODHI R., MURDOCK M. *et al.*, "RoomAlive: magical experiences enabled by scalable, adaptive projector-camera units", *Proceedings of the 27th Annual ACM Symposium on User Interface Software and Technology*, pp. 637–644, ACM, New York, USA, 2014.

[LAV 17] LAVIOLA J.J., KRUIJFF E., MCMAHAN R. *et al.*, *3D User Interfaces: Theory and Practice*, 2nd edition, Addison Wesley, 2017.

[PLO 15] PLOPSKI A., ITOH Y., NITSCHKE C. *et al.*, "Corneal-imaging calibration for optical see-through head-mounted displays", *IEEE Transactions on Visualization and Computer Graphics*, vol. 21, no. 4, pp. 481–490, 2015.

[STA 02] STANNEY K., KENNEDY R., KINGDON K., in STANNEY K.M. (ed.), *Handbook of Virtual Environments: Design, Implementation, and Applications*, IEA, Mahwah, 2002.

Conclusion

Where Will VR-AR be in 10 Years?

This book has two main objectives: one is to give an overview of the development in VR-AR in the last decade, while the other is an exercise in looking to the future by trying to imagine the main evolutions that will occur in the field. We have already listed a few, mainly scientific, prospects in Chapter 5 and, in this chapter, we will offer a broader view, based on an analysis of benefits, weaknesses, opportunities and risks accompanied by a list of the challenges that must be met[1].

Let us begin by briefly reviewing the main *benefits* that the use of VR-AR can bring in, described throughout this book (especially in the Introduction and Chapter 1):

– cost reduction: the design process (e.g. buildings, crowd management, automobiles);

– improved training and heightened safety: driving, monitoring industrial processes, etc.;

– allowing access to and studying complex data: big data, data that no longer exists or is no longer available, is inaccessible, imperceptible, etc.;

– executing precise gestures (education and training): surgical, industrial and sports;

Chapter written by Bruno ARNALDI, Pascal GUITTON and Guillaume MOREAU.
1 Certain components of this reflection emerged during a debate that was organized by the AFRV National Day in late 2016 in Brest.

– enhancing creativity: digital arts, storytelling, etc.;

– assisted driving: planes, cars and ships;

– assistance in carrying out industrial gestures (maintenance) or surgical procedures;

– offering augmented site visits: touristic and industrial.

Until quite recently, these benefits remained restricted to a few companies and research laboratories. So what were the main *weaknesses* that slowed down the development of VR-AR?

– first, there was the misinformation on these technologies and their potential power;

– second, there was the cost and complexity of implementing existing technology, which was limited, *de facto*, to large companies;

– third, there was the fact that their performance was still limited, notably in terms of field of vision (for HMDs) and the precision and reliability of position and localization sensors;

– finally (and this is in part a result of all the above points), there was a limited number of applications, which did not address all areas of interest of potential users.

As we have explained in this book, this situation has evolved over the last few years, and it is now relatively easy to highlight several explanatory factors that represent as many *opportunities* to amplify this development:

– technological innovations have made it possible to bring down costs significantly, thereby opening up these technologies to a wider audience: smaller companies first, and then the general public;

– these innovations were often developed by small companies, which were then bought by larger entities, resulting in these solutions being better funded and sustainable;

– many big actors in the digital world entered this field and their financial and industrial power should allow these technologies to further break down barriers and reach a larger public;

– last but not least, there is a highly dynamic international community composed of very active researchers who have already thought up innovations for the future.

Nonetheless, it is not possible to completely exclude the possibility of a commercial flip: there are many innovative technologies that have not succeeded as hoped, despite being high performing and receiving a great deal of industrial investment. For example, the mass-produced 3D TV suffered from a double complication: a lack of content (3D films and shows) at the time it was commercially released and a problem of acceptability by the user, especially given that it was necessary to wear stereoscopic glasses. We can thus list out several *risk* factors:

– currently, VR-AR applications only cover a relatively small number of domains. The lack of applications may thus lead to potential clients moving away from these technologies unless new solutions come up soon;

– not all users appreciate experiencing VR-AR: whether this is due to discomfort, social stigmatization[2] or simply because the interface is not adapted to meet their needs and their skills. The question of acceptability by the client therefore remains key to the adoption of a new product;

– a factor that amplifies the first two points is the large media buzz around these products that led to high hopes and expectations which, if disappointed, could lead to the media itself turning on these new products and attacking them. This is all the more true when this media buzz mainly addresses innovations in the equipment, neglecting its possible uses;

– finally (but, in our eyes, undoubtedly most importantly), we must not underestimate or ignore the possible harmful consequences of prolonged use of an HMD, especially by young users. As we have seen in Chapter 7, there are still many questions to be explored on this subject, and it is crucial to begin carrying out studies on the health of future users.

To add to this analysis and conclude this book, we offer you a list of prospective challenges, some of which are already being explored and others which are still emerging, to allow you to better understand, or even anticipate, the future of these fields:

– the problem of *acceptability* of the proposed solutions has now been clearly identified by VR-AR specialists. Researchers have put together multidisciplinary teams by bringing together specialists from the fields of

---

2 Many Google Glass users reported that they were embarrassed to wear the glasses in certain circumstances.

cognitive science, ergonomics and human–machine interfaces, and by carrying out user-centered studies; this problem is therefore being tackled head-on by the community and should diminish in the coming years;

– this effort is also being made by many large actors in the field of VR-AR application development, especially thanks to the growing importance of the concept of *User Experience* or *UX*, which, from being a marketing slogan, has become a key principle for developers (and not only in the field of VR-AR). Of course, diversity in use, as well as real – and durable – advantages of the services offered to the user are at the forefront of the qualities to develop;

– it must be hoped that the *education* of future application designers becomes more potent (in terms of both quantity and quality), so as to ensure that this industry has a pool of expert developers to draw on, which is crucial to its existence. Given this need, the pedagogic process must reach out to a wider population, from non-specialist actors to the general public, so that these evolutions can be better understood and better controlled;

– the entry of *large entities* (e.g. Google, Facebook, Apple, Microsoft, Samsung, Sony) should continue and contribute to making this domain sustainable (which requires considerable financial investment). This presence does not, however, signify the disappearance of small, innovative structures but must, on the contrary, help them grow thanks to the availability of equipment at low costs (because they are mass produced), and this should also lead to the emergence of industry standards that facilitate development;

– in terms of developments in use, one of the major goals is the ability to work and interact in groups in VR-AR. Whether this is within large companies, to contribute to collective processes, or whether this is for social networks to allow for exchanges between members of a community, these *collaborative* applications will explode as soon as several scientific and technological barriers are removed. Online games, at present, offer a reduced idea of the interest of these approaches and thus of the adhesion of the concerned public;

– we are convinced that the *performance of this equipment* (some of which is developed from technology that is still emerging) will develop in the coming years, starting with the quality of the visualization devices, especially in terms of the field of vision, which is too narrow at present. The use of light fields is a very promising avenue to improve the quality of the synthetic images used. VR, and especially AR, will benefit from the constant rise in communication speed, which will facilitate video streaming to ensure better resolution and refresh frequency. The arrival of small video projectors (pico projectors) displaying images in our immediate environment will allow the massive use of these AR services both for fixed use (in a building) and for mobile use. Finally, the ongoing development of contact lenses that display images will continue, especially to enhance the resolution of the displayed images, reduce their energy consumption (and thus, heat emission) and, above all, promote their acceptability to the user;

– we are delighted by the fact that, in 2017, ANSES (The French National French Agency for Food, Environmental and Occupational Health & Safety) began work on studying the potential impact of VR use on health and will then issue recommendations for users[3]. This now seems a crucial step to ensure the sustainable development of VR-AR.

---

3   https://www.anses.fr/fr/content/2017-faire-face-aux-expositions-du-quotidien-et-anticiper-les-risques-%C3%A9mergents

Postface

It would be interesting to adopt the style of speculative fiction and look into the future to imagine the possible uses VR-AR could bring about. As the main objective of this book was to give an overview of the scientific and technical developments over the last 10 years, let us try and maintain "temporal symmetry" by looking 10 years into the future...

It's 7 on a Monday morning, September 6, 2027. 21-year-old Marie has just woken up. The first thing she does is put in her contact lenses. Equipped with sensor systems (cameras, inertial unit, etc.) and a display system whose opacity can be adjusted, they can display information in 2D or 3D. Getting out of bed, Marie slips on her "tech" clothes, fitted with many sensors that capture information in real time to give to the microcomputer in her body. This is the size of a grain of rice and is implanted in her hand, in the skin between the thumb and index finger. These sensors measure a whole set of physiological data and all data on the wearer's movements.

As she does every morning, Marie prepares to go jogging. Her group of friends have decided to run along the edge of a cliff over a famous Norwegian fjord. She moves across the exercise zone in her house, equipped with a multi-directional treadmill, which, in these newer buildings, is built into the floor. With a verbal command, she starts the run and virtually joins up with the rest of the group. Her contact lenses block out the view of her apartment and display the view of a Norwegian fjord. Marie finds three friends who are

Chapter written by Bruno ARNALDI, Pascal GUITTON and Guillaume MOREAU.

ready to set off. Several very high-definition cameras are installed on the wall she is facing in the apartment. They continuously capture her face in order to reconstruct her expressions in real time and 3D so they can be transmitted correctly to her avatar, whose movements are guided by the positions captured by the sensors in her clothes. All the joggers are, of course, chatting away loudly and calling teasingly to each other. Microphones and speakers scattered around everyone's apartments also allow them to hear each other's breathing. Current technology allows them to run in a group across a geographical site chosen beforehand, providing an excellent restitution of the facial expressions of different participants and allowing them to gauge, for example, who is in form on that day or who is struggling with the pace the group has set. However, neither Marie nor her friends have acquired the latest top-of-the-line equipment that would allow them to reproduce slopes and rises. They can only run across flat ground, thereby limiting the sites they can choose to train on.

After wrapping up her morning run, Marie suddenly feels a mixture of apprehension and excitement. She's going back to school today! She's going to university where she will study psychology, majoring in "The Psychology of AI"[4]. This course studies two complementary aspects: first, psychology studied from a user's point of view using an AI system and, second, its converse, that is, the "psychology" of an AI system vis-à-vis its human user. She's keen to be on time and, given that this is a new location, she'd spent all of the past evening studying how to access the fleet of connected vehicles that the town made available to increase the safety of users and decrease traffic jams, the source of so much pollution. As she's not yet bought the systems upgrade that would allow her to use her contact lenses with this service, she'd hunted out an "old" HMD to explore the virtual city. As she slips it on, she smiles suddenly, thinking back to the first HMD her father had brought home, back when she was around 10 years old. Heavy, ugly and with a ridiculously small field of vision! She hadn't been able to understand how people used these for hours and hours for gaming! She reflected on the amount of hard work researchers and engineers must have put in this past decade to be able to propose the light and esthetically pleasing helmet she had on now, which wasn't constrained by the human field of vision. She had used this to visualize the route to take from the main entry to her classroom, in pedestrian mode.

---

1 AI: Artificial Intelligence.

She'd wound up the evening by wandering through virtual spaces made accessible on social networks by other students who were in her course.

Thanks to this preparation, she's now in class on time, settling in next to Pierre, whom she'd met the previous evening in his virtual space and with whom she'd had a fun conversation. As an introduction to their subject, the professor, who's taking their first lecture, has asked them to pull out the flexi screen stowed away in their armrests and to shape it into a semi-cylinder facing them so as to immerse themselves in the virtual environment that he would be using as a teaching support in this lecture. It is possible to make these screens translucent and the students can thus alternate between a direct, natural view of the teacher and other students and the immersion in the pedagogic VE to better understand certain complex concepts.

As the lecture ends, she and Pierre plan to lunch in the restaurant on campus. Like every young person who's had their final growth spurt, Marie loves sugar and red meat. Unfortunately, she's been diabetic since she was a child. Moreover, in the second quarter of the 21st Century, meat became quite rare as a result of the environmental costs of raising livestock. However, for a few years now, there have been systems with the coy name of "taste enhancers", which can modify the taste of any vegetable to mimic meat or even sugary cakes. These systems, entirely chemical, emerged in the early 2000s and became much more sophisticated over time as simulators that used heat appeared.

After their meal, they head to their first session of practical work where they will focus on the working of the human brain. Marie finds herself in a room with large white tables topped with a metal structure. This contains several apparatus, none of which she's familiar with. They remind her of machinery found in screening rooms, used for lighting and sound systems. When their teacher arrives, she asks the students to stand around these tables in groups of two and turn on the systems. Marie watches as a human head appears. She can see this perfectly thanks to the relief features, but she can also touch it. She realizes the metal structure is made up of projectors that display images as well as sensors that detect the positions of the users' hands. These then send the human's microcomputer tactile information to their fingers to simulate contact with the head. The teacher asks them to carry out a virtual dissection to reach the brain. To guide them, step-by-step, the table then displays a virtual animation that shows them precisely what gestures are to be used. The students can visualize this from any point of view, replay it as many times as needed, speed it up or slow it down, and so on. For Marie, this is a far cry from the MOOCs she discovered when in primary school, where all students would watch the same video. As the manipulations are complex, it is sometimes necessary to work with four hands and she uses Pierre's hands to interact using real instruments (she has been familiar with the idea of tangible interfaces since high school. They were introduced in their computer sciences classes and everyone used them) to work on the head they were studying. Their gestures, sometimes clumsy, lead to anatomical "damages" that are easy to correct by going back one step.

After several attempts, they manage to reveal the brain and then the second part of their practical work begins: they must observe which internal structures are brought into play during an exercise requiring short-term memory. Pierre gently chaffs Marie when she puts the headphone, equipped with miniature electrodes and meant for her to use to record her own brain electrical activity, around her ear. However, these are far less ridiculous than the first EEG helmets used by BCI pioneers about 20 years ago. After several fruitless attempts, Marie is able to visualize her own brain activity projected onto the brain on the table and, by penetrating it, she is able to see which internal structures are activated. The teacher congratulates both of them on their result and dismisses them.

Marie heads towards the sports department and decides to "revise" a highly technical tennis gesture which she has to work on, according to her trainer. Her service is not very powerful and she needs the training before her next match. The training technique her coach has recommended consists of passive galvanic stimulation. This technique uses a number of judiciously placed electrodes, spread out across the body. They make it possible to stimulate the command chain to muscles without really activating them. In practice, the data on the service action and speed of the current World No. 1 had been gathered and processed. They will now be used as a model to stimulate Marie's muscular command chain. She settles down on the training bench, having slipped into the suit containing the electrodes. Her personal computer sets up a dialogue with the computer in the suit in order to bring about the morphological adaptation required and the session can now commence. The principle behind this training, where the body does not move, is to reproduce gestures in order for the command chain to memorize the technical synchronization and chaining. In 2023, researchers had demonstrated that learning gestures in this way accelerated learning by up to four times. Marie goes through about 20 serves using this system. Her contact lenses display the images of her serve and the trajectory of the ball and, whenever it happens, its collision with the net. This enables total immersion in the training situation. Once this passive training is done, she must move on to actively implement this with a real racquet and ball so that she can happily note her progress.

Soon it's time to go home. After dinner, she immerses herself in her preferred series. There are no longer TV series since the viewer became active. Indeed, the screenplays no longer imagine a story, but a series of stories that anyone can choose from or mix as they wish. Moreover, there is no longer a single point of view, that of the person behind the camera; instead, each viewer can choose any point of view they choose. Marie has heard of a recent innovation, still way out of her budget, that makes it possible to truly become the actor in a certain segment of the series. She tells herself that even if she had it, she would be too tired this evening to fight off the bad guys.

She falls asleep thinking of Pierre.

Glossary

API – Application Programming Interface[1]: the collection of elements (functions, protocols, definitions etc.) that enable the development of software that interacts with existing systems.

CAVE: a parallelepipedic visualization system, where 3 or 6 faces are screens. Invented in 1992 by C. Cruz-Neira.

Cybersickness: a group of 'unpleasant' manifestations that may be experienced by a user in an immersive experience, ranging from passing uneasiness to more severe discomfort.

Degrees of freedom – DoF: see *Tracking*

GPU – Graphical Processing Unit: a material system that was initially designed to rapidly compute synthetic images. Thanks to the high-performing equipment and software used for these systems, today they are used for processing information that may not involve images but require a high computing power.

Head-Mounted Display – HMD: a visualization headset used in virtual reality. The concept was invented by I. Sutherland in 1968.

Head-Up Display – HUD: a visualization headset that enables natural, direct vision and which is used in augmented reality. Initially invented for use

---

1 Abbreviations are mentioned when they are frequently used.

in the military to allow airplane pilots to visualize synthetic information while preserving their vision of their real environment.

Middleware: software that provides communication between several software that must exchange information.

SDK – Software Development Kit: a set of software tools, generally provided by the manufacturer of the equipment to promote the development of applications that can run on that equipment.

Shader: a software programme used to compute the lighting effects on an object during a synthesis of images. There are several environments for the developer: OpenGL, DirectX, CG, etc.

Tracking: a mechanism to track the displacements of an entity (e.g. an object or a person) in space. This operation is fundamental as it then allows recalculation and the display of synthetic images, taking into account these displacements. Most often, tracking returns localization values (three coordinates) and orientations (three angles). We speak of Degrees of freedom (DoF).

List of Authors

Bruno ARNALDI
INSA Rennes
IRISA/Inria Rennes
Hybrid team
France

Ferran ARGELAGUET SANZ
Inria
IRISA/Inria Rennes
Hybrid team
France

Caroline BAILLARD
Technicolor Research & Innovation
Immersive Lab - Augmented Reality
Issy-les-Moulineaux
France

Jean-Marie BURKHARDT
IFSTTAR
Laboratoire de Psychologie des
Comportements et des mobilités
(LPC)
Versailles
France

Géry CASIEZ
University of Lille
CRIStAL/Inria Lille
Mjolnir team
France

Stéphane COTIN
Inria
MIMESIS
Strasbourg
France

Nadine COUTURE
ESTIA
LaBRI
Association Francophone Interaction
Homme Machine
France

Jean-Louis DAUTIN
CLARTE
Plateforme RV/RA
Changé
France

Stéphane DONIKIAN
Golaem
Rennes
France

Philippe FUCHS
Mines ParisTech
Centre de robotique
RV & RA team
Paris
France

Pascal GUITTON
University of Bordeaux
LaBRI - Inria Bordeaux
Potioc team
France

Florian GOSSELIN
CEA, LIST
Laboratoire de Robotique
Interactive Département
Intelligence Ambianteet
Systèmes Interactifs
CEA Saclay
Paris
France

Valérie GOURANTON
INSA Rennes
IRISA/Inria Rennes
Hybrid team
France

Xavier GRANIER
LaBRI – Inria
Manao team
Institut d'optique
Bordeaux
France

François GRUSON
ABFG4S
Rennes
France

Philippe GUILLOTEL
Technicolor Research & Innovation
Immersive Lab
Cesson-Sévigné
France

Martin HACHET
Inria
Potioc team
Talence
France

Richard KULPA
University of Rennes 2
Laboratoire M2S
Inria
Mimeticteam
ENS Rennes
Bruz
France

Sébastien KUNTZ
MiddleVR
Paris
France

Patrick Le CALLET
University of Nantes
LS2N UMR 6004
IPI team
Polytech Nantes
France

Anatole LÉCUYER
Inria
IRISA/Inria Rennes
Hybrid team
France

Vincent LEPETIT
LaBRI, Inria
Manao team
University of Bordeaux
France

Fabien LOTTE
Inria Bordeaux Sud-Ouest / LaBRI /
CNRS / University of Bordeaux
Potioc team
Talence
France

Domitile LOURDEAUX
Sorbonne Universities
University ofTechnology of
Compiègne
CNRS, Heudiasyc UMR 7253
ICI team
France

Maud MARCHAL
INSA Rennes
IRISA/Inria Rennes
Hybrid team
France

Nicolas MOLLET
Technicolor Research & Innovation
Immersive Lab - Virtual Reality
Issy-les-Moulineaux
France

Guillaume MOREAU
Ecole Centrale de Nantes
Ambiances, Architectures, Urbanités
IRISA/Inria
Hybrid team
Nantes
France

Olivier NANNIPIERI
I3M
University of Toulon
France

Jean-Marie NORMAND
École Centrale de Nantes
Ambiances, Architectures,Urbanités
IRISA/Inria
Hybrid team
Nantes
France

Jérôme PERRET
Haption GmbH
Germany

Jérôme ROYAN
IRT b-com
Cesson-Sévigné
France

Gaël SEYDOUX
Technicolor Research & Innovation
Immersive Lab
Issy-les-Moulineaux
France

Toinon VIGIER
University of Nantes
Laboratoire des Sciences du
Numérique de Nantes – UMR6004
Image PerceptionInteraction team
Polytech Nantes
France

Index

Other titles from

in

Computer Engineering

2018

ANDRO Mathieu
Digital Libraries and Crowdsourcing
(Digital Tools and Uses Set – Volume 5)

2017

BENMAMMAR Badr
Concurrent, Real-Time and Distributed Programming in Java

HÉLIODORE Frédéric, NAKIB Amir, ISMAIL Boussaad, OUCHRAA Salma,
SCHMITT Laurent
Metaheuristics for Intelligent Electrical Networks
(Metaheuristics Set – Volume 10)

MA Haiping, SIMON Dan
Evolutionary Computation with Biogeography-based Optimization
(Metaheuristics Set – Volume 8)

PÉTROWSKI Alain, BEN-HAMIDA Sana
Evolutionary Algorithms
(Metaheuristics Set – Volume 9)

PAI G A Vijayalakshmi
Metaheuristics for Portfolio Optimization
(Metaheuristics Set – Volume 11)

2016

BLUM Christian, FESTA Paola
Metaheuristics for String Problems in Bio-informatics
(Metaheuristics Set – Volume 6)

DEROUSSI Laurent
Metaheuristics for Logistics
(Metaheuristics Set – Volume 4)

DHAENENS Clarisse and JOURDAN Laetitia
Metaheuristics for Big Data
(Metaheuristics Set – Volume 5)

LABADIE Nacima, PRINS Christian, PRODHON Caroline
Metaheuristics for Vehicle Routing Problems
(Metaheuristics Set – Volume 3)

LEROY Laure
Eyestrain Reduction in Stereoscopy

LUTTON Evelyne, PERROT Nathalie, TONDA Albert
Evolutionary Algorithms for Food Science and Technology
(Metaheuristics Set – Volume 7)

MAGOULÈS Frédéric, ZHAO Hai-Xiang
Data Mining and Machine Learning in Building Energy Analysis

RIGO Michel
Advanced Graph Theory and Combinatorics

2015

BARBIER Franck, RECOUSSINE Jean-Luc
COBOL Software Modernization: From Principles to Implementation with the BLU AGE® Method

GHÉDIRA Khaled
Constraint Satisfaction Problems

ROCHANGE Christine, UHRIG Sascha, SAINRAT Pascal
Time-Predictable Architectures

WAHBI Mohamed
Algorithms and Ordering Heuristics for Distributed Constraint Satisfaction Problems

ZELM Martin *et al.*
Enterprise Interoperability

2012

ARBOLEDA Hugo, ROYER Jean-Claude
Model-Driven and Software Product Line Engineering

BLANCHET Gérard, DUPOUY Bertrand
Computer Architecture

BOULANGER Jean-Louis
Industrial Use of Formal Methods: Formal Verification

BOULANGER Jean-Louis
Formal Method: Industrial Use from Model to the Code

CALVARY Gaëlle, DELOT Thierry, SEDES Florence, TIGLI Jean-Yves
Computer Science and Ambient Intelligence

MAHOUT Vincent
Assembly Language Programming: ARM Cortex-M3 2.0: Organization, Innovation and Territory

MARLET Renaud
Program Specialization

SOTO Maria, SEVAUX Marc, ROSSI André, LAURENT Johann
Memory Allocation Problems in Embedded Systems: Optimization Methods

2011

BICHOT Charles-Edmond, SIARRY Patrick
Graph Partitioning

BOULANGER Jean-Louis
Static Analysis of Software: The Abstract Interpretation

CAFERRA Ricardo
Logic for Computer Science and Artificial Intelligence

HOMES Bernard
Fundamentals of Software Testing

KORDON Fabrice, HADDAD Serge, PAUTET Laurent, PETRUCCI Laure
Distributed Systems: Design and Algorithms

KORDON Fabrice, HADDAD Serge, PAUTET Laurent, PETRUCCI Laure
Models and Analysis in Distributed Systems

LORCA Xavier
Tree-based Graph Partitioning Constraint

TRUCHET Charlotte, ASSAYAG Gerard
Constraint Programming in Music

VICAT-BLANC PRIMET Pascale *et al.*
Computing Networks: From Cluster to Cloud Computing

2010

AUDIBERT Pierre
Mathematics for Informatics and Computer Science

BABAU Jean-Philippe *et al.*
*Model Driven Engineering for Distributed Real-Time Embedded Systems
2009*

BOULANGER Jean-Louis
Safety of Computer Architectures

MONMARCHE Nicolas *et al.*
Artificial Ants

2007

BENHAMOU Frédéric, JUSSIEN Narendra, O'SULLIVAN Barry
Trends in Constraint Programming

JUSSIEN Narendra
A to Z of Sudoku

2006

BABAU Jean-Philippe *et al.*
From MDD Concepts to Experiments and Illustrations – DRES 2006

HABRIAS Henri, FRAPPIER Marc
Software Specification Methods

MURAT Cecile, PASCHOS Vangelis Th
Probabilistic Combinatorial Optimization on Graphs

PANETTO Hervé, BOUDJLIDA Nacer
Interoperability for Enterprise Software and Applications 2006 / IFAC-IFIP I-ESA'2006

2005

GÉRARD Sébastien *et al.*
Model Driven Engineering for Distributed Real Time Embedded Systems

PANETTO Hervé
Interoperability of Enterprise Software and Applications 2005

Printed and bound by CPI Group (UK) Ltd, Croydon, CR0 4YY

27/10/2024

14580726-0005